Art: Context and Value

Art: Context and Value

Edited by Stuart Sim

The Open University

This reader is one part of an Open University integrated teaching system and the selection is therefore related to other material available to students. It is designed to evoke the critical understanding of students. Opinions expressed in it are not necessarily those of the course team or of the University.

The Open University
Walton Hall
Milton Keynes
MK7 6AA
First published 1992

Edited and designed by The Open University.
Typeset in 11 on 13 point Times New Roman by Speedlith Photo Litho Limited, Longford Trading Estate, Thomas Street, Stretford, Manchester M32 0JT.
Printed in Great Britain by MacKays of Chatham PLC, Badger Road, Lordswood, Chatham, Kent, ME5 8TD.
ISBN 0 7492 1106 7

1.1

Contents

Sources

Grateful acknowledgement is made to the following sources for permission to reproduce material in this book:
Plato, *The Republic*, trans. Lee, H.D.P., (1955), Penguin Classics, copyright © H.D.P. Lee, 1955; Zhdanov, A.A. (1934) *Soviet Writers' Congress*, 1934, reprinted by permission of Lawrence and Wishart Ltd from the *Soviets Writers' Congress 1934*, edited by Scott, H.G.; Lukács, G. 'Franz Kafka or Thomas Mann?' in Mander, J. and Mander, N. (trans) (1963) *The Meaning of Contemporary Realism*, The Merlin Press Ltd; Benjamin, W. (1973) 'What is epic theatre?' in Bostock, A. (trans) *Understanding Brecht*, Verso; Barthes, R. (1977) 'The death of the author' and 'Introduction to the structural analysis of narratives' in *Image – Music – Text*, HarperCollins; Williams, B. (1981) *Obscenity and Film Censorship*, HMSO; Taylor, R. (1978) *Art, An Enemy of the People*, Harvester Wheatsheaf, © Roger Taylor, 1978; Wolff, J. (1982) 'Aesthetic judgement and sociological analysis', *Aspects*, No. 21, 1982; Adorno, T. 'The philosophy of modern music' in Mitchell, A. and Bloomster, W. (trans) (1973) *Philosophy of Modern Music*, Sheed and Ward Ltd, London; Macherey, P. (1978) *A Theory of Literary Production*, Routledge; Eagleton, T. (1976) *Criticism and ideology*, Verso; Goodman, N. (1987) 'Art and authenticity' in *Philosophy Looks at The Arts*, Scolar Press; Koestler, A. (1964) *The Act of Creation*, Hutchinson. Permission granted by Peters, Fraser and Dunlop Ltd; Lessing, A. (1965) 'What is wrong with a forgery?', *Journal of Aesthetics and Art Criticism*, Vol. 23, No. 4, Summer 1965, pp. 461–71, The American Society for Aesthetics; Young, J.O. (1988) 'The concept of authentic performance'. Reprinted from the *British Journal of Aesthetics*, Vol. 28, pp. 228–38, by permission of Oxford University Press; Dickie, G. (1974) *Art and the Aesthetic: an institutional analysis.* Copyright © 1974 by Cornell University. Used by permission of the publisher, Cornell University Press; Tilghman, B.R. (1984) *But is it Art?*, Basil Blackwell Publishers; Binkley, T. (1976) 'Deciding about art' in Aagaard-Mogensen, L. (ed.) *Culture and Art,* Humanities Press, Atlantic Highlands, New Jersey; Hume, D. *Of The Standard of Taste and Other Essays*, edited by Lenz, J.W. (1965). Copyright © 1965 reprinted by permission

of Macmillan Publishing Company; Hampshire, S. (1967) 'Logic and appreciation' in Elton, W. (ed.) *Essays in Aesthetics and Language*, Basil Blackwell; Kennick, W.E. (1958) 'Does traditional aesthetics rest on a mistake'. Reprinted from *Mind*, Vol. LXVII, pp. 317–34, by permission of Oxford University Press; Beardsley, M.C. (1962) 'On the generality of critical reasons', *Journal of Philosophy*, Vol. LIX, No. 18, 30 August 1962, pp. 477–86, Columbia University; Wimsatt, W.K. and Beardsley, M.C. 'The Intentional Fallacy' in Wimsatt, W.K. (1970) *The Verbal Icon*, Methuen and Co; Beardsley, M.C. (1970) *The Possibility of Criticism*, Wayne State University Press; Beardsley, M.C. (1958) *Aesthetics*, Harcourt Brace Jovanovich, © Beardsley, M.C.; Hirsch, E.D. Jr (1969) 'The validity of interpretation' in *Validity in Interpretation*, Yale University Press, London; Saussure, F. de (1960) *Course in General Linguistics*, Peter Owen Publishers; Lévi-Strauss, C. (1970) *The Raw and the Cooked*, trans. Weightman, J. and D. Jonathan Cape; Derrida, J. (1978) 'Structure, sign and play in the discourse of the human sciences' in *Writing and Difference*, Routledge.

Introduction

A companion volume, edited by Robert Wilkinson, presented readings from the history of philosophical aesthetics on the subject of *Theories of Art and Beauty*. In this book we turn our attention to readings concerned with the context and value of art.

Art, it has been argued, is 'gratuitous'.[1] It is not a necessity of existence, and neither is the artist a necessary part of society. Yet some of our deepest experiences as individuals come from engagement with the arts and we ascribe considerable value to these experiences. It may be difficult to define precisely what that value is, but it is real enough to create debates about censorship and freedom of expression. Unless art has a social value there seems little point in arguing about whether *Lady Chatterley's Lover* should be published, *The Satanic Verses* brought out in paperback, or whether sex, violence, and anti-social behaviour should be portrayed on film and television screens. Individual opinions about art's value may differ, but society as a whole seems to be in no doubt that art matters and that it has an important stake in what artists do. State subsidy of the arts varies from society to society, and from government to government within a society, but its presence in any form concedes the point that art is taken to be a socially valuable activity (which is not to say that the *absence* of subsidy denies that value either). The fact that there are considerable ranks of reviewers, critics, and cultural commentators who go to make up the criticial industry offers further testimony to the idea that art, however gratuitous, is a highly significant part of social existence.

The role and value of art within society have been keenly debated issues among philosophers since the earliest days of Western philosophy. As he so often does, Plato establishes the grounds for the debate in *The Republic*. Plato takes art seriously enough to propose selectively applied censorship of dramatic poetry on the basis that the poet's appeal to the emotions may come to represent a threat to public order and morality in *The Republic's* ideal commonwealth. Thus he can recommend that:

> ...we shall treat him [the poet] with all the reverence due to a
> priest and giver of rare pleasure, but shall tell him that he and

his kind have no place in our city, being forbidden by our code, and send him elsewhere, after anointing him with myrrh and crowning him. For ourselves, we shall for our own good employ story tellers and poets who are severe rather than amusing, who follow the style of the good man and in all their works abide by the principles we laid down for them when we started out on this attempt to educate our military class.[2]

To put the case for poetry that appeals to our reason rather than to our emotions is already to suggest strong views concerning art's social role, and to defend censorship by the authorities (Plato's 'we' refers to the commonwealth's ruling class) is to acknowledge art's power to affect our behaviour. Art is seen to be a moral issue, a political issue, and an area of activity in which society at large has a considerable vested interest. Plato has set an agenda for the debate about the context and value of art which still shapes the discussions of late twentieth-century aesthetics.

Many theories have been put forward to explain the role and value of art and artistic activity, and this volume collects a wide range of readings, from Plato through to the late twentieth century, which address themselves to the philosophical issues concerning art's context and value. The material is grouped under three main headings: (Part One) Art, society and morality; (Part Two) Art and value; (Part Three) Criticism and interpretation. The readings have been selected on the basis of their ability to illustrate the major concerns in each area of debate. All are preceded by an editorial note designed to explain their particular importance to the debate, to draw attention to their main points of argument and, where appropriate, to cross-reference them with other readings in the volume. Taken collectively, the readings constitute a survey of the three stated themes and impart a sense of just what is at stake in each case. The readings are now discussed in turn.

In Reading 1 of Part One: Art, society and morality, Plato sets the agenda by putting forward some particularly trenchant views concerning the arts. The topics generated by his statements about art may be categorized as follows: the social role of art and the artist (does society need art? does the artist need society?); art and morality (can works of art be said to be moral or immoral?); censorship of art (is it ever justifiable? if so, on what grounds and according to what criteria?); the politics of art (should art be judged by political criteria?); art and pornography (how can society discriminate between erotic art and pornography? are either, or both, socially dangerous?).

Philosophical aesthetics offers the artist a wide range of social roles to adopt. The artist is variously portrayed in the literature as a threat to society, a law unto herself, an agent of the state, an agent of ideological subversion, and a potent symbol of freedom and the imagination. Plato's vision of the artist as a potential threat is present in much Marxist aesthetic theory. Thus in Readings 2 and 3 we find A. A. Zhdanov and Georg Lukăcs spelling out just what authors are and are not allowed to do in the name of political correctness. Plato, Zhdanov and Lukăcs all call for a didactic literature which can be used by the authorities to further their political aims. The assumption is that the artist has a duty to submit to political demands. The stress is accordingly on the artist's sense of social responsibility at the expense of her desire for personal expression. In each case, art is being judged by political criteria.

Personal expression is a notion essentially derived from romantic aesthetics, and there are various spirited defences of it as an ideal. The 'Art for art's sake' doctrine expounded by Walter Pater is one of the most uncompromising statements of the individualistic ethic in the arts, and represents the opposite end of the spectrum from Plato on the issue of the artist's social responsibility:

> To burn always with this hard, gemlike flame, to maintain his ecstasy, is success in life ... With the sense of the splendour of our experience and of its awful brevity, gathering all we are into one desperate effort to see and touch, we shall hardly have time to make theories about the things we see and touch ... Philosophical theories or ideas, as points of view, instruments of criticism, may help us to gather up what might otherwise pass unregarded by us ... The theory or idea or system which requires of us the sacrifice of any part of this experience, in consideration of some interest into which we cannot enter, or some abstract theory we have not identified with ourselves, or of what is only conventional, has no real claim upon us.[3]

One's responsibility, Pater argues, is primarily to oneself. It is not just abstract theory which has no claim on us but society as well.

Not all Marxists defend censorship or espouse the cause of didacticism, and there has been an influential 'modernist' strain in twentieth-century Marxism which has argued that art's role is to subvert traditional ideas and practices by means of experiment and formal innovation. The playwright Bertolt Brecht is one such exponent of modernist aesthetics, and in Reading 4 his associate, Walter Benjamin, outlines the Brechtian creed on theatre. A similar defence of art's subversive and liberating power comes from Roger Taylor (Reading 7), although it is in popular culture rather than high art where his main interest lies.

All the theories so far discussed envisage an important social role for the artist, but structuralist theory has challenged this assumption of importance. Structuralism sees art as expressing the deep structures of human thought rather than some highly personal vision on the part of the artist, and this has led to theories like Roland Barthes's 'the death of the author' (Reading 5) where, far from being a social threat, the creative artist is held to be a fairly marginal figure in art's social role.

Plato's assumption would seem to be that art can be defined as immoral if it fails unequivocally to reflect and uphold the moral standards of its society. Censorship only too easily follows on from such a view, and the criteria involved are explicitly political in nature. Even in a society more open in character than the one theorized by Plato, censorship of the arts can be a live issue. Obscenity and blasphemy are still grounds for banning works of art in Britain. Several of the twentieth century's major literary talents have suffered censorship for alleged obscenity, with James Joyce (*Ulysses*) and D. H. Lawrence (*Lady Chatterley's Lover*) being two notable examples. More recently blasphemy was a charge levelled by Muslim critics against Salman Rushdie's *The Satanic Verses*, although the fact that under British law blasphemy covers only Christianity vitiated the accusation. However, calls were made at the time for an extension of the blasphemy law to other religions. Although blasphemy is rarely successful as a basis for prosecution in Western societies nowadays, it is relatively easy to define. Obscenity poses more complex problems. Moral standards are not homogeneous through society, and they can change quite significantly from generation to generation, rendering agreement as to what would count as obscene at any one time extremely difficult to come by.

The Williams Committee on Obscenity and Film Censorship (Reading 6) tackled this problem in terms of the distinction between erotic art and pornography, concluding that there was little evidence that pornography could not also have artistic value. Since the Committee's report was published there has been a growing feminist campaign against pornography, and many feminist theorists would support censorship in this area on moral grounds. The vexed question of how to distinguish between eroticism and pornography remains, as does the problem of how to prove that works of erotic art or pornography have a direct effect on individual behaviour. In the absence of such a causal link it becomes difficult to defend censorship. Plato tends to assume such a causal connection (as do campaigners such as Mary Whitehouse), but provides no hard evidence that an audience uncritically absorbs all that it sees or reads and then proceeds to imitate the behaviour of fictional characters. Aristotle assumes the causal connection as well, but claims that it can lead to beneficial effects on the body politic. Tragedy, he holds, 'is the representation ... of incidents that awaken fear and pity'.[4] It has a cathartic effect by purging us of those emotions, thus enabling us to regain a sense of inward emotional balance.

Taking the opposite point of view, and arguing that art has *no* effect on human behaviour, is just as difficult to prove, and runs counter to our general perception of art as a valuable activity which can give us deep experiences on a personal level.

Even given general agreement as to art's value to society, explaining what the value is, and how it operates, has proved an extraordinarily complex problem in philosophical aesthetics, and continues to be one of the subject's central concerns. Part Two presents a series of readings on the relationship between art and value, starting with Janet Wolff's useful survey of the various types of theory of aesthetic value to be found in the literature (Reading 8). The readings are designed to illustrate the following issues and questions which arise from the problem of aesthetic value: theories of aesthetic value (what criteria go into the creation of an aesthetic theory of value?); value and politics (should aesthetic value be a political question, as Marxists claim?); value and authenticity (does value depend on the authenticity of the artwork? is it possible for forgeries to have aesthetic value?); the institutional context of art (can institutions confer aesthetic value on artworks? is such a practice justifiable?).

Aesthetic value has often been equated with moral value: that a work of art is good if a work of art is moral is a notion that Plato bequeathed to philosophical aesthetics. Renaissance neoclassicist aesthetic theorists (who took Plato and Aristotle as their main reference points) can often be found arguing this line. Thus the English literary theorist and poet Sir Philip Sidney claims that, 'no learning is so good, as that which teacheth and moveth to virtue; and ... none can both teach and move thereto so much as poetry; then is the conclusion manifest, that ink and paper cannot be to a more profitable purpose employed'.[5] To the neoclassical theorist the criteria for aesthetic value are effectively those for moral value.

Marxism substitutes political value for moral value, and has often seemed to be saying that a work of art is good if a work of art is politically correct. Political correctness in this context means being in favour of the class struggle, or showing sympathy for the oppressed in one's society and antipathy towards their oppressors. Unfortunately for the theory, works which do not display politically correct attitudes are often considered by the reading public to give aesthetic pleasure (and vice versa with those works which do), and the farther back one goes in history the more difficult it becomes to make works of art fit into preconceived political schemes. Janet Wolff has pointed out that Marxist theorists are prone to reduce aesthetic value to ideological value, and that a 'reductionist account does not enable us to understand the nature of aesthetic pleasure produced in the experience of the work' (Reading 8). Marx himself found it hard to explain the appeal of Greek art to a nineteenth-century audience, given its apparent remoteness from the contemporary concerns.[6] The problem Marxism has traditionally had with aesthetic value centres on the intrusive role played by politics. Leon Trotsky insisted that we ought to judge works of art by 'the law of art',[7] but detaching this from political considerations has been no easy matter, as we can see in the various Marxist theories of aesthetic value presented in Readings 10–12.

The extent to which value depends on authenticity has been much debated since the Van Meegeren affair, in which a Dutch artist admitted to forging several 'Vermeers'. A group of pieces (Readings 13–15) treats this affair and its implications for aesthetic theory, and conflicting views are expressed as to whether forgeries can have aesthetic value. One of the most important points at issue here is whether it is possible to contemplate a painting with an 'innocent eye'. This notion was put forward by the art critic Sir Herbert Read,[8] who suggested that we should approach the artwork in an unprejudiced way, as free of preconceived ideas as possible, in order to appreciate what it had to offer in its own terms. Whether it is possible, or even desirable, to suspend all knowledge of context prior to engaging with a work of art has been a subject of much controversy (Marxists in general would strongly disagree with Read, for example), and the positions adopted by theorists in the Van Meegeren case are largely dictated by the degree of belief demonstrated in the 'innocent eye'.

Many of those who dispute the 'innocent eye' notion tend to argue that experts have a key role to play in determining what can have aesthetic value. Experts are also to the fore in the 'institutional theory of art' and the 'authentic performance' argument in music. The institutional theorists claim that objects can be transformed into artworks, and acquire aesthetic value, when an expert from the 'artworld' (a term coined by the philosopher Arthur Danto) designates them as art. Readings 17–19 give a flavour of the debate created by this theory and its belief that aesthetic value can simply be conferred on objects by such representatives of the artworld as artists. The 'authentic performance' argument, which is considered in Reading 16, similarly accords power to experts – musicologists in this case – to say what conditions have to be met for proper musical value to be realized. The 'innocent ear' is no more acceptable to such theorists than the 'innocent eye'.

Value is a relative notion. Whatever the aesthetic theory of value, it allows for the possibility of degrees of value. That is where critics come in, applying their theories and methods to the task of evaluation of individual works of art. The Readings in Part Three are all concerned with the problem of evaluation. Major issues and questions that arise regarding evaluation are: aesthetic theory and criticism (what is the relationship between them? need criticism be grounded in philosophical theory?); interpretation and analysis of artworks (what are the criteria for critical value judgements? can such judgements be proved?); the nature of criticism (is it an objective or subjective activity?); continental aesthetics (how does modern French aesthetics differ from the Anglo-American tradition? what is the relationship between aesthetic theory and critical practice in structuralism and poststructuralism?).

Establishing general principles for critical interpretation has been a perpetual concern of philosophical aesthetics. In Plato's case, such principles are derived from the moral principles of his ideal commonwealth. A work is good or bad depending on how it reflects those moral principles. Neoclassical theorists would similarly discriminate on the basis of a work's ability to promote moral virtue. David Hume (Reading 20) argues that there are general principles of taste which can be discovered by observation of the judgements normally made in society by informed individuals. Many theorists have denied that general principles are at all necessary to criticism, and in Readings 21–22 Stuart Hampshire and W. E. Kennick, both of whom take the view that art is gratuitous, argue this line. M. C. Beardsley, on the other hand (Reading 23), takes specific issue with Kennick to insist that without a general criteria theory there can be no critical criteria at all. The various continental theorists of Readings 29–31 all see criticism as an applied form of philosophical theory, and the same would go for Marxist theorists and critics, as Readings 2–3 and 10–12 would suggest. The debate has many similarities to the 'innocent eye' controversy. Is there such a thing as pure, disinterested contemplation by an individual of an artwork, free from the constraints of theory? Or is theory *necessary* in order to make any sense of the work in front of us?

Another way of posing the questions above is to ask whether 'internal', or 'external' evidence is more relevant to interpretation and analysis of a work. External evidence – biography, history, theory – is called into question by W. K. Wimsatt and M. C. Beardsley, whose critical examination of the 'intentionalist fallacy' (that the role of the interpreter is to uncover the author's intention) has had such a dramatic impact on Anglo-American literary theory in recent decades. Readings 24–27 are all concerned with the problem of authorial intention, and the several appearances by Beardsley indicate his central importance to this debate. It is a debate which continues to have repercussions in the Anglo-American critical world.[9]

Continental aesthetics is much more explicitly grounded in theory than the Anglo-American tradition is in general. Structuralism and poststructuralism are both strongly theoretical methods of criticism, the former operating on the basis that there are deep structures in artworks (or 'texts', as structuralists usually call them) which express the deep underlying structures of human thought; the latter attacking the idea that the meaning of artworks can be pinned down with any sense of precision. Structural linguistics, with its stress on language as a self-contained system with its own self-regulating rules (see Reading 28), provided much of the motivation for the development of structuralism, and poststructuralist aesthetics is highly critical of this tradition and its founder Ferdinand de Saussure. Telescoping the debate between these movements very considerably, structuralism seeks to find underlying unity in texts while poststructuralism sees unity as an illusion, claiming that textual analysis simply reveals how indeterminate meaning really is. One side sees complex interlocking patterns in texts while the other denies that such patterns exist, except as an outside imposition on texts by critics.

The Anglo-American tradition in criticism has been very sceptical of such theorizing, particularly when it comes to poststructuralism, and has criticized the continentals as forcing texts to fit their theories – whether of deep structure or linguistic indeterminacy. A recent radical reworking of the 'intentionalist fallacy' argument, by Steven Knapp and Walter Benn Michaels, has summed up much of the distrust felt for continental aesthetics in the English-speaking world by claiming that, 'the whole enterprise of critical theory is misguided and should be abandoned'.[10] Such thinkers as Knapp and Michaels are taking the view that theory-led criticism ends up abusing texts by treating them as mere excuses for the demonstration and elaboration of abstruse philosophical theory. The continentals stand accused of breaching the implied contract between critic and reader, whereby the critic interprets the book for the reader (a process known as *explication de texte*) in order to help the reader better appreciate its value. The answer from the continental side would be that *explication de texte* gives far too much authority to the critic and author at the expense of the reader. Assumptions about value and the status of the artist in society lie behind the attitudes adopted on each side of the divide.

It will have become evident in the course of this introduction that there is a considerable linkage between the three parts of readings, and that questions of context and value are not easily separated. I would suggest that in the broadest sense of the term these are political issues: theories of the social role of art and the artist, of aesthetic value, and of criticism and interpretation, all assume a certain vision of society and how ideally it should operate. Authoritarian or totalitarian-minded thinkers are likely to argue for state control of the arts; equally, liberals are likely to defend freedom of expression in the arts with no less vigour than they do in other areas of life. Debates about aesthetic context and value are not, therefore, of importance to aestheticians alone, but raise some large-scale questions concerning the nature of social existence. Decisions about aesthetic matters are far from being gratuitous, politically speaking.

Acknowledgements

Many of my colleagues in The Open University on the *Philosophy of the Arts* course team have helped in the preparation of this volume, notably Drs Diané Collinson, Ossie Hanfling and Robert

Wilkinson. I should also like to thank Shirley Coulson for help with points of detail concerning production, and my secretary, Helen Sidlow, for preparaing the final manuscript from my many revisions.

Notes

1   See Readings 21 and 22.

2   Plato (1955) *The Republic*, trs. H. D. P. Lee, Penguin, p.137.

3   Pater, W. (1961) *The Renaissance*, Fontana, pp.222–3.

4   Aristotle (1965) 'On the Art of Poetry' in Aristotle, Horace and Longinus, *Classical Literary Criticism*, Penguin, p.248.

5   Sir Philip Sidney (1970) 'An Apology for Poetry' in *Selected Poetry and Prose*, ed. David Kalstone, New American Library, p.248.

6   See Karl Marx (1973) *Grundrisse*, Penguin, pp.110–11.

7   Leon Trotsky (1957) *Literature and Revolution*, University of Michigan Press.

8   See Herbert Read (1933) *The Innocent Eye*, Faber and Faber.

9   See, for example, the various papers in Mitchell, W. J. T. (ed.) (1985) *Against Theory: Literary Studies and the New Pragmatism*, University of Chicago Press.

10   Knapp, S. and Michaels, W. B. 'Against Theory', in ibid., pp.11–30.

PART ONE   ART, SOCIETY AND MORALITY

The Republic

Plato (427–347 BC)

Plato is one of the founders of Western philosophy, and his dialogues – the major source of our knowledge about his teacher, Socrates – have exercised a profound influence on Western thought. In what is generally regarded as his greatest work, The Republic, *he gives us a blueprint for the ideal state, which proves to be one organized on hierarchical lines with a governing class and a soldier class (the Guardians and the Auxiliaries) holding power over the mass of the population. A major concern of* The Republic *is the education of the Guardian class, and in the extract that follows the topic is treated in some depth, with particular emphasis being laid on the role of literature in the process. Plato has some very uncompromising views about literature and is notorious for being an advocate of both censorship and strict state control over the arts. Poets who refuse to conform to the state's requirement to produce didactic literature aimed at the education of the Guardian class will be banished from the Platonic commonwealth. The artist's social role under such a scheme is to be the mouthpiece of a state-sanctioned morality, and censorship is justified on the grounds of the need to maintain public order.*

Part Two [Book Two] Preliminaries

3 QUALITIES REQUIRED IN THE GUARDIANS

... Plato's main preoccupation is with the Guardian class (later to be subdivided into two); the producers, merchants, and others, who carry on the day-to-day economic life of society are hardly mentioned again. Plato is concerned with *government*, and his interest therefore is almost entirely confined to the *governing* class.

The Guardians are now compared to watchdogs, and shown to need physical strength, courage, and a philosophic temperament. Courage requires 'high spirits'. The Greek word which this phrase translates is used by Plato to cover a group of characteristics such as pugnacity, enterprise, ambition, indignation, which he will later regard as one of the three main elements of the mind or personality. In traditional English 'mettle' or 'spirit' (as e.g. in 'a man of mettle', 'a man of spirit') is a fair translation, and the slang term 'guts' and the politer 'vitality' have a somewhat similar meaning; compare also the distinction made in common parlance between qualities of the 'heart' and 'head'...

'There is,' said I, 'a certain similarity between the qualities needed in a good watchdog and those needed in our guardians. I mean that each must have keen perceptions and speed in pursuit, and also strength to fight if he catches his quarry.'

'Yes, he will need all these qualities.'

'And also courage, if he is to fight well.'

'Of course.'

'And no horse or dog or any other creature will have courage unless it has mettle and spirit. For have you not noticed what an irrepressible and unbeatable thing high spirits are, making their possessor quite fearless and indomitable in the face of danger?'

'I have indeed.'

'We know therefore what the physical qualities of our guardians must be, and that they must have high spirits as a quality of character.'

'Yes.'

'But if they have these qualities, Glaucon,' I said, 'won't they be aggressive in their behaviour to each other and to the rest of the community?'

'It won't be easy to prevent it.'

'And yet they ought to be gentle towards their fellow-citizens, and dangerous only to their enemies; otherwise they will destroy each other before others can destroy them.'

'True.'

'What are we to do, then?' I said. 'Where are we to find the gentle and generous disposition which will counteract their high spirits? If we deprive them of either quality, they won't make good guardians; yet we seem to be asking the impossible, and if so a good guardian is an impossibility.'

'I am afraid it is.'

I felt myself in a difficulty, but I thought over what we had just been saying, and then exclaimed: 'You know, we really deserve to be in a difficulty. For we have failed to press our analogy far enough.'

'In what way?'

'We have not noticed that there are natures which combine the qualities we thought incompatible.'

'And where are they to be found?'

'In different kinds of animal, but particularly in the watchdog which we have used as our analogy. For have you not observed that it is characteristic of a well-bred dog to behave with the utmost gentleness to those it is used to and knows, but to be savage to strangers?'

'Yes, I've noticed that.'

'The kind of guardian we were looking for is therefore quite a possibility and not at all unnatural.'

'So it appears.'

'Would you agree then that our prospective guardian needs in addition to his high spirits something of the disposition of a philosopher?'

'I don't understand what you mean,' he said.   376

'It is a remarkable characteristic which you will find in the dog. It is annoyed when it sees a stranger, even though he has done it no harm: but it welcomes anyone it knows, even though it has never had a kindness from him. Haven't you ever thought how remarkable this is?'

'I can't say I ever thought about it before,' he replied. 'But of course it's quite true.'

'And yet it is a trait that shows real discrimination and a truly philosophic nature,' I said, 'for the dog distinguishes the sight of friend and foe simply by knowing one and not knowing the other. And a creature that distinguishes between the familiar and the unfamiliar on the grounds of knowledge or ignorance must be gifted with a real love of knowledge.'

'There's no denying it,' he said.

'But is not philosophy the same thing as the love of knowledge?'

'It is.'

'And so for man too we may venture to lay it down that gentleness towards his own fellows and neighbours requires a philosophic disposition and a love of learning.'

'We may.'

'Then our perfect guardian must have the following character-istics: a philosophic disposition, high spirits, speed, and strength.'

'I entirely agree.'

Part Three [Book Two] Education : the first stage

In reading what follows it is important to have in mind one or two of the main features of Greek education. It was, normally, a matter for the private individual: and in making it the concern of the state, Plato was doing something that to the Athenian (though not to the Spartan; and Plato was to some extent influenced by Sparta) was an innovation. Education had three principal subdivisions. Reading and writing, physical education, and what we may call secondary or literary education. This last consisted mainly in a study of the works of the poets, which were learnt to be recited and, where necessary, sung to the lyre, so that it included a knowledge of music; it corresponded, broadly, to the 'secondary' stage of our own system, and was followed by two years military training which began at eighteen. It must also be remembered that the Greeks had no Bible, and what the Bible has been to us as a source of theology and morals, the poets were to the Greeks. And if Plato seems very preoccupied with the moral and theological aspect of the poets it is because it was from them that the ordinary Greek was expected to acquire his moral and theological notions.

1 SECONDARY OR LITERARY EDUCATION

Since the minds of the young are very impressionable we must, if we are to educate them properly, make sure that the poetry on which they are brought up is suitable for the purpose. Most existing poetry is unsuitable: (a) Theologically, because it misrepresents God. God is perfectly good, and therefore changeless and incapable of deceit, and must never be otherwise represented.

'We may assume then that our guardians need these qualities. But how are they to be brought up and educated? If we try to answer this question, I wonder whether it will help us at all in our main enquiry into the origin of justice and injustice? We do not want to leave out anything relevant, but we don't want to embark on a long digression.'

To which Adeimantus replied, 'I expect it will help us all right.'

'Then, my dear Adeimantus, we must certainly pursue the question,' I rejoined, 'even though it proves a long business. So let us set about educating our guardians as if we had as much time on our hands as the traditional story-teller.'

'Let us by all means.'

'What kind of education shall we give them then? We shall find it difficult to improve on the time-honoured distinction between the training we give to the body and the training we give to the mind and character.'

'True.'

'And we shall begin with the mind and character, shall we not?'

'Of course.'

'In this type of education you would include stories, would you not?'

'Yes.'

'These are of two kinds, true stories and fiction.[1] Our education 377 must use both, and start with fiction.'

'I don't understand you.'

'But you know that we begin by telling children stories. These are, in general, fiction, though they contain some truth. And we tell children stories before we start them on physical training.'

'That is so.'

'That is what I meant by saying that we start to train the mind before the body. And the first step, as you know, is always what matters most, particularly when we are dealing with those who are young and tender. That is the time when they are taking shape and when any impression we choose to make leaves a permanent mark.'

'That is certainly true.'

'Shall we therefore allow our children to listen to any stories written by anyone, and to form opinions the opposite of those we think they should have when they grow up?'

'We certainly shall not.'

'Then it seems that our first business is to supervise the production of stories, and choose only those we think suitable, and reject the rest. We shall persuade mothers and nurses to tell our chosen stories to their children and so mould their minds and characters rather than their bodies. The greater part of the stories current to-day we shall have to reject.'

'Which are you thinking of?'

'We can take some of the major legends as typical. For all are cast in the same mould and have the same effect. Do you agree?'

'Yes: but I'm not sure which you refer to as major.'

'The stories in Homer and Hesiod and the poets. For it is the poets who have always made up stories to tell to men.'

'Which stories do you mean and what fault do you find in them?'

'The worst fault possible,' I replied, 'especially if the story is an ugly one.'

'And what is that?'

'Misrepresenting gods and heroes, like a portrait painter who fails to catch a likeness.'

'That is a fault which certainly deserves censure. But give me more details.'

'Well, on the most important of subjects, there is first and foremost the foul story about Ouranos and the things Hesiod says he did, and the revenge Cronos took on him. While the story of 378 what Cronos did, and what he suffered at the hands of his son, is not fit to be repeated as it is to the young and innocent, even if it were true; it would be best to say nothing about it, or if it must be told, tell it to a select few under oath of secrecy, at a rite which required, to restrict it still further, the sacrifice not of a mere pig but of something large and expensive.'

'These certainly are awkward stories.'

'And they shall not be repeated in our state, Adeimantus,' I said. 'Nor shall any young audience be told that anyone who commits horrible crimes, or punishes his father unmercifully, is doing nothing out of the ordinary but merely what the first and greatest of the gods have done before.'

'I entirely agree,' said Adeimantus, 'that these stories are unsuitable.'

'Nor can we permit stories of wars and plots and battles among the gods; they are quite untrue, and if we want our prospective guardians to believe that quarrelsomeness is one of the worst evils, we must certainly not let them embroider robes with the story of the Battle of the Giants,[2] or tell them the tales about the many and various quarrels between gods and heroes and their friends and relations. On the contrary, if we are to persuade them that no citizen has ever quarrelled with any other, because it is sinful, our old men and women must tell children stories with this end in view from the first, and we must compel our poets to tell them similar stories when they grow up. But we can permit no stories about Hera being tied up by her son, or Hephaestus being flung out of Heaven by his father for trying to help his mother when she was getting a beating, or any of Homer's Battles of the Gods, whether their intention is allegorical or not. Children cannot distinguish between what is allegory and what isn't, and opinions formed at that age are usually difficult to eradicate or change; it is therefore of the utmost importance that the first stories they hear shall aim at producing the right moral effect.'

'Your case is a good one,' he agreed, 'but if someone wanted details, and asked what stories we were thinking of, what should we say?'

To which I replied, 'My dear Adeimantus, you and I are not writing stories but founding a state. And the founders of a state, though they must know the type of story the poet must produce, 379 and reject any that do not conform to that type, need not write them themselves.'

'True: but what are the lines on which our poets must work when they deal with the gods?'[3]

'Roughly as follows,' I said. 'God[4] must surely always be represented as he is, whether the poet is writing epic, lyric, or drama.'

'He must.'

'And the truth is that God is good, and he must be so described.'

'True.'

'But nothing good is harmful or can do harm. And what does no harm does no evil. Nor can a thing which does no evil be the cause of any evil.'

'That is true.'

'And what is good is of service and a cause of well-being.'

'Yes.'

'So the good cannot be the cause of everything. It can only account for the presence of good and not for evil.'

'Most certainly,' he agreed.

'Then God, being good, cannot be responsible for everything, as is commonly said, but only for a small part of human life, for the greater part of which he has no responsibility. For we have a far smaller share of good than of evil, and while we can attribute the good to God, we must find something else to account for the evil.'

'I think that's very true,' he said.

'So we cannot allow Homer or any other poet to make this stupid mistake about the gods, or say that "Zeus has two jars standing on the floor of his palace, full of fates, good in one and evil in the other", and that the man to whom Zeus allots a mixture of both has "varying fortunes sometimes good and sometimes bad", while the man to whom he allots unmixed evil is "chased by the gadfly of despair over the face of the earth".[5] Nor can we allow references to Zeus as "dispenser of good and evil". And we cannot approve if it is said that Athene and Zeus prompted the breach of solemn promises by Pandarus, or that the strife of the goddesses and the judgement of Paris was due to Themis and Zeus. Nor again 380 can we let our children hear from Aeschylus that "God implants guilt in man, when he wishes to destroy a house utterly." No: we must forbid anyone who writes a play about the sufferings of Niobe (the subject of the play from which these last lines are quoted), or the woes of the house of Pelops, or the Trojan war, or any similar topic, to say they are acts of God; or if he does he must give the sort of reason we are now demanding, and say that God's acts were good and just, and that the sufferers were benefited by being punished. What the poet must not be allowed to say is that those who were punished were made wretched through God's action. He may refer to the wicked as wretched because they needed punishment, provided he makes it clear that in punishing them God did them good. But if our state is to be run on the right lines, we must take every possible step to prevent anyone, young or old, either saying or being told, whether in poetry or prose, that God, being good, can cause harm or evil to any man. To say so would be sinful, inexpedient, and inconsistent.'

'I should approve of a law for this purpose and you have my vote for it,' he said.

'Then of our laws laying down the principles which those who write or speak about the gods must follow, one would be this: *God is the source of good only.*'

'I am quite content with that,' he said.

'And what about our second law? Do you think God is a kind of magician who can appear at will in different forms at different times, sometimes turning into them himself and appearing in many different shapes, at other times misleading us into the belief that he has done so? Or is he without deceit and least likely of all things to change his proper form?'

'I don't, at the moment, know what the answer to that is.'

'Well, if he does change his proper form, must not the change be due either to himself or to another?'

'It must.'

'And is not the best always least liable to change or alteration by an external cause? For instance, the healthiest and strongest animals are least liable to change owing to diet and exercise, or plants owing to sun and wind and the like.'   381

'That is so.'

'And characters which have most courage and sense are least liable to be upset and changed by external influences. And similarly any composite object, a piece of furniture or a house or a garment, is least subject to wear if it is well made and in good condition.'

'That is true.'

'So in general, whether a thing is natural or artificial or both, it is least subject to change from outside if its condition is good.'

'So it seems.'

'But the state of God and the Divine is perfect; and therefore God is least liable of all things to be changed into other forms.'

'That is so.'

'Then will God change or alter himself of his own will?'

'If he changes at all,' he replied, 'that must be how he does.'

'Will the change be for the better or for the worse?'

'Any change must be for the worse. For God's goodness is perfect.'

'You are absolutely right,' I said. 'And, that being so, do you think that any man or god would deliberately make himself worse in any respect? If you agree that this is impossible, then it must also be impossible for a god to wish to change himself. Every god is as perfect and as good as possible, and remains in his own form without variation for ever.'

'The conclusion is unavoidable.'

'So we cannot have any poet saying that the gods "disguise themselves as strangers from abroad, and wander round our towns in every kind of shape"[6], we cannot have stories about the transformations of Proteus and Thetis, or poets bringing Hera on the stage disguised as a priestess begging alms for "the lifegiving children of Inachus river of Argos". We must stop all stories of this kind, and stop mothers being misled by them and scaring their children by perversions of the myths, and telling tales about a host of fantastic spirits that prowl about at night; they are merely blaspheming the gods and making cowards of their children.'

'None of these things should be allowed.'

'Then if the gods are themselves unchangeable, will they use their power to deceive us into thinking that they appear in all sorts of disguises?'

'They might, I suppose.'

'Come,' said I, 'can God want to disguise himself and deceive 382 us, either in word or action?'

'I don't know,' he replied.

'But,' I asked, 'don't you know that gods and men all detest true falsehood, if I may so describe it?'

'I don't understand.'

'I mean that in things which touch most nearly the most important part of him no man really wants to be deceived, but is terrified of it.'

'I still don't understand.'

'Because you think I'm talking about something mysterious,' I answered. 'But all I mean is that no one wants to be deceived in his own mind about things and not to know the truth; that's where men are least ready to put up with falsehood and detest it most.'

'Yes, I agree with that.'

'But surely when a man is deceived in his own mind about something, we can fairly call his ignorance of the truth "true falsehood". For a false statement is merely some kind of representation of a state of mind, an expression consequent on it, and not the original unadulterated falsehood. Don't you agree?'

'Yes.'

'So real falsehood is detested by gods and men.'

'I agree.'

'But what about spoken falsehood? Is it not sometimes and on some occasions useful, and so not utterly detestable? We can use it, for example, as a kind of preventive medicine against our enemies, or when one of our own friends tries to do something wrong from madness or folly. And we can make use of it in the myths we are engaged in discussing; we don't know the truth about the past but we can invent a fiction as like it as may be.'

'That's perfectly true.'

'In which of these ways is falsehood of use to God? Does he need to make up fictions because he does not know the past?'

'That is absurd.'

'So God is not the author of poetic fictions?'

'No.'

'Does he tell lies because he is afraid of his enemies, then?'

'Certainly not.'

'Or because of the folly or madness of any of his friends?'

'God loves neither the foolish or the mad,' he replied.

'God has, then, no reason to tell lies; and we conclude that there is no falsehood at all in the realm of the spiritual and divine?'

'Most certainly.'

'God is therefore without deceit or falsehood in action or word, he does not change himself, nor deceive others, awake or dreaming, with visions or signs or words.'

'I agree entirely with what you say.'   383

'Do you agree then that the second principle to be followed in all that is said or written about the gods is that they shall not be represented as using magic disguises or fraud to deceive us in any way?'

'I agree.'

'And so among the many things we admire in Homer we shall not include the dream Zeus sent to Agamemnon. Nor shall we admire Aeschylus when he makes Thetis say that Apollo sang at her wedding in praise of her child

> Promising him long life, from sickness free,
> And every blessing: his triumphant praise
> Rejoiced my heart. Those lips, I thought, divine.
> Flowing with prophecy, must God's promise speak.
> Yet he the speaker, he our wedding guest,
> Phoebus Apollo, prophet, slew my son.

If a poet says this sort of thing about the gods we shall be angry and refuse to let him produce his play; nor shall we allow it to be used to educate our children – that is if our guardians are to grow up godfearing and holy, so far as that is humanly possible.'

'I agree entirely with your principles,' he said, 'and we can treat them as law.'

(b) Morally, most existing poetry is unsuitable because in its *representations* of gods and heroes it describes, and so encourages, various forms of moral weaknesses.

'As far as religion is concerned, then, we have now out-lined the sort of stories men ought and ought not to be brought up on, if they are to honour the gods and their parents, and know how important it is to love one another.' BK III

'And I think we are quite right,' he said.

'But what if they are to be brave? Must we not add something that will give them the least possible fear of death? Will anyone who fears death ever be brave?'

'Certainly not.'

'And will anyone who believes in terrors in the after-life be without fear of death, and prefer death in battle to defeat and slavery?'

'No.'

'It looks, then, as if we shall have to control those who write on this topic too. We must ask the poets to stop giving their present gloomy acount of the after-life, which is both untrue and unsuitable to produce a fighting spirit, and make them speak more favourably of it.'

'I agree,' he said.

'We must begin, then,' I said, 'by cutting out all passages such as the following –

> I would rather be a serf in the house of some landless man, with little enough for himself to live on, than king of all dead men that have done with life;[7]

or

> and expose to mortal and immortal eyes the hateful chambers of decay that fill the gods themselves with horror;[8]

or again

> Ah then, it is true that something of us does survive even in the Halls of Hades, but with no intellect at all, only the ghost and semblance of a man;[9]

and

> he alone has a mind to reason with: the rest are mere shadows
> flitting to and fro;[10]

and

> his disembodied soul took wing for the House of Hades, bewailing
> its lot and the youth and manhood that it left;[11]

and

> the spirit vanished like a wisp of smoke and went gibbering
> underground;[12]

and finally

> gibbering like bats that squeak and flutter in the depths of some
> mysterious cave when one of them has fallen from the rocky roof,
> losing his hold on his clustered friends, with shrill discord the
> company set out.[13]

We must ask Homer and the other poets to excuse us if we delete
all passages of this kind. It is not that they are bad poetry or are
not popular; indeed the better they are as poetry the more unsuitable
they are for the ears of children or grown-ups, if they are to prefer
death to slavery as free men should.'

'I absolutely agree.'

'We must get rid, too, of all those horrifying and frightening
names in the underworld – the Rivers of Wailing and Gloom, and
the ghosts and corpses, and all other things of this kind whose very
names are enough to scare everyone who hears them. They may
be useful for other purposes; but we are afraid they will scare our
guardians and make them jumpy and nervous.'

'And our anxiety is justified.'

'We must get rid of them, then, and require our poets to give
us an account on the opposite lines.'

'Clearly.'

'We must also, I suppose, cut out pitiful laments by famous
men.'

'We must,' he replied, 'if we are to be consistent.'

'Let us see if we shall be justified. We agree, surely, that one
good man does not think death holds any terror for another who
is a friend of his, and so would hardly mourn for him as if he had
suffered something terrible.'

'That is true.'

'And what is more, we reckon that the good man's life is the most complete in itself and least dependent on others. So the loss of son or brother, or of property or what not, will hold the least terrors for the good man, who, when some such catastrophe overtakes him, will mourn it less and bear it more calmly than others.'

'He will.'

'So we should be quite right to cut out from our poetry 388 lamentations by famous men. We can give them to the less reputable women characters or to the bad men, whom those we are bringing up as guardians of our state will be ashamed to imitate.'

'You are quite right.'

'We shall therefore again request Homer and the poets not to describe Achilles, the son of a goddess, as

sometimes lying on his side, sometimes on his back, and then again on his face,

and then standing up and

wandering aimlessly along the salt sea beach,[14]

or

picking up the dark dust in both hands and pouring it on his head;[15]

with all the weeping and wailing the poet describes. Nor can we allow a Priam, who was closely related to the gods, to

grovel in the dung and implore them all, calling on each man by his name.[16]

Still more emphatically shall we forbid the poets to represent the gods lamenting with words like

Ah misery me, the unhappy mother of the best of men.[17]

And least of all can we have them presuming to misrepresent the greatest of all gods by making him say

I have a warm place in my heart for this man who is being chased before my eyes round the walls of Troy.[18]

and

> Fate is unkind to me – Sarpedon whom I dearly love is destined
> to be killed by Patroclus son of Menoetius.[19]

For, my dear Adeimantus, if our young men take passages like these seriously and don't laugh at their absurdity, they are hardly likely to think this sort of thing unworthy of them as men, or to try to control the temptation to similar words and actions. They will feel no shame and show no endurance, but break into complaints and laments at the slightest provocation.'

'That is quite true.'

'But that is not the behaviour our argument has just required; and we must trust it till someone produces a better one.'

'Yes, we must.'

'And surely we don't want our guardians to be too fond of laughter either. A disposition to violent laughter commonly means 389 instability; and we must not therefore allow descriptions of reputable characters being overcome by laughter. And similar descriptions of gods are far less allowable.'

'Far less, I agree.'

'So we can't have Homer saying of the gods

> and a fit of helpless laughter seized the happy gods as they
> watched Hephaestus bustling up and down the hall.[20]

Your argument won't allow that.'

'Call it my argument if you like,' he replied; 'in any event we can't allow it.'

'And surely we must value truthfulness highly. For if we were right when we said just now that falsehood is no use to the gods and only useful to men as a kind of medicine, it's clearly a medicine that should be entrusted to doctors and not to laymen.'

'Yes.'

'It will be for the rulers of our city, then, if anyone, to deceive citizen or enemy for the good of the State; no one else must do so. And if any citizen lies to our rulers, we shall regard it as a still graver offence than it is for a patient to lie to his doctor, or for an athlete to lie to his trainer about his physical condition, or a sailor to his captain on any matter concerning the state of the ship or crew. And so if you find anyone else in our state telling lies, "whether he be craftsman, prophet, physician or shipwright,"[21] you will punish him for introducing a practice likely to capsize and wreck the ship of state.'

'We must punish him if we are to be as good as our word.'

'Then again we shall want our young men to be self-controlled; and for the mass of men does not self-control largely consist in obedience to their rulers, and controlling their own desire for the pleasures of eating, drinking, and sex?'

'I agree.'

'We shall approve therefore the sort of thing that Homer makes Diomede say,

Be quiet, man, and take your cue from me,[22]

and verses like those which follow it,

The Achaeans moved forward, breathing valour, in silent obedience to their officers.[23]'

'We shall indeed.'

'But what about

You drunken sot, with the eyes of a dog and the courage of a doe,[24]

and the lines that follow? Can we approve of them and other 390 impertinences of the rank and file against their commanders, in prose or verse?'

'We cannot.'

'For they are hardly likely to encourage the young to self-control, though we need not be surprised if they give pleasure in other ways. What do you think?'

'I agree.'

'Then is it likely to encourage self-restraint in the young, if the poets represent the wisest of men saying that he thinks the best moment of all is when

the tables are laden with bread and meat, and a steward carries round the wine he has drawn from the bowl and fills their cups?[25]

And what about lines like

death by starvation is the most miserable end that one can meet?[26]

And then there is the story of how Zeus stayed awake, when all the other gods and men were asleep, with some plan in mind, but forgot it easily enough when his desire was roused; he was indeed so struck by Hera's appearance that he wanted to make love to her on the spot, without going indoors, saying that he had never wanted her so much since the days when they first used to make love "without their parents' knowledge".[27] And there's the story of Hephaestus trapping Ares and Aphrodite in similar proceedings.'

'All these are most unsuitable,' he commented emphatically.

'But when a poet tells or a dramatist presents tales of heroic endurance against odds, then we must give him an audience. For instance, when Homer makes Odysseus strike himself on the chest, and "call his heart to order", saying,

Patience my heart! You have put up with fouler than this.[28]'

'We must certainly listen to him then.'

'But we must not let him make his characters mercenary or grasping. We cannot let a poet say,

The gods can be won with gifts, and so can the king's majesty.[29]

We cannot agree that Achilles' tutor Phoenix advised him properly when he told him not to stop being angry and help the Achaeans unless they brought him presents. Nor can we consent to regard Achilles as so grasping that he took Agamemnon's presents and refused to give up Hector's body unless he was paid a ransom.'[30]   391

'It would be quite wrong,' he said, 'to approve of things of this sort.'

'I say it with hesitation, because of Homer's authority,' I said, 'but it is really wicked to say these things about Achilles or believe them when we hear them said. There are other examples. Achilles says to Apollo,

You have made a fool of me, Archer-king, and are the most mischievous of gods: how much I should like to pay you out if I had the power.[31]

He refuses to trust the River Scamander, who is a god, and is ready to fight him, and he parts with the lock of his hair that he had dedicated to the River Spercheius and gives it to "the dead Lord Patroclus".[32] We can believe none of this, and we shall regard as untrue also the whole story of the dragging of the body of Hector round the tomb of Patroclus and the slaughter of prisoners at his pyre.[33] We cannot, in fact, have our citizens believe that Achilles, whose mother was a goddess, and whose father, Peleus, was a man of the utmost self-control and a grandson of Zeus, and who had in Chiron the wisest of schoolmasters, was so lacking in discipline that he combined in himself the two contrary and pestilential faults of grasping meanness about money and excessive arrogance to gods and men.'

'You are right,' he said.

'We must therefore neither believe nor allow the story of the dreadful ravages of Theseus, son of Poseidon, and Peirithous, son of Zeus, or any of the other lies now told about the terrible and wicked things done by other sons of gods and by heroes. We must compel our poets to say either that they never did these things or that they are not the sons of gods; we cannot allow them to assert both. And they must not try to persuade our young men that the gods are the source of evil, and that heroes are no better than ordinary mortals; that, as we have said, is a wicked lie, for we proved that no evil can originate with the gods.'

'Of course.'

'Moreover such lies are positively harmful. For those who hear them will be lenient towards their own shortcomings if they believe that this sort of thing is and was always done by the relations of the gods,

> kindred of Zeus, to whom belongs
> the ancestral altar high in heaven
> on Ida's mount,

and in whose veins

> still runs the blood of Gods.[34]

We must put a stop to stories of this kind before they breed vicious habits in our young men.'

392

'We certainly must.'

So far the argument has been confined to the poets' treatment of gods and heroes: similar rules cannot be laid down for the treatment of men until justice has been defined.

'We have now dealt with the kind of things that should and should not be said about gods and demi-gods, heroes and the life after death. If we ask what kind of literature still remains, the answer is, presumably, that which deals with human beings.'

'Clearly.'

'But we cannot deal with that topic at present.'

'Why not?'

'Because I am afraid that we shall find that poets and story-tellers have expressed the most erroneous opinions about it. They have said that unjust men are often happy, and just men wretched, that wrong-doing pays if you can avoid being found out, and that justice is what suits someone else but is to your own disadvantage. We must forbid them to say this sort of thing, and require their poems and stories to have quite the opposite moral. Do you agree?'

'I'm quite sure you're right,' he replied.

'But if you agree with me there, can I not already claim your agreement about the subject we are discussing?'

'Yes, that is a fair claim.'

'We must not agree, therefore, about the kind of thing that ought to be said about human life, until we have defined justice, and the advantages it brings to its possessor irrespective of appearances.'

'Quite true.'

(c) Formal requirements

Plato turns from content to form. He classes poetry according to the degree to which it employs what we should call 'direct speech' as opposed to indirect speech and narrative. Direct speech involves what he calls 'representation'; that is, it requires the poet or narrator to put himself in the position of the character speaking, think his thoughts and feel his feelings. Plato objects to this on the grounds that he does not want his Guardians to deviate from their own character by representing other characters, especially bad characters. If the discussion seems at times, to us, academic, we should remember that the Greek schoolboy, when reciting Homer, was 'expected to throw himself into the story and deliver the speeches with the tones and gestures of an actor', and that it is to such 'imaginative identification', and to any use of the drama in education that Plato, rightly or wrongly, objects.

'So much the for the subject-matter of literature. We must next deal with its presentation, and so cover both content and form.'

To this Adeimantus replied that he did not understand what I meant. 'Then I must explain,' I said; 'perhaps you will see if I put it this way. Any story or poem deals with things past, present, or future, does it not?'

'It must.'

'And for the purpose it employs either simple narrative or *representation*, or a mixture of both.'

'I'm still not quite clear what you mean.'

'I'm afraid you are laughing at my obscurity,' I said. 'So let me try to explain my meaning by confining myself to a particular example, like an incompetent lecturer. You know the beginning of

the *Iliad*, where the poet says that Chryses begs Agamemnon to release his daughter; and when Agamemnon gets angry and refuses, Chryses calls down the wrath of the gods on the Greeks?'   393
'Yes.'

'Well, up to the words

> He appealed to the whole Achaean army, and most of all to its two commanders, the sons of Atreus,[35]

the poet is speaking in his own person, and does not attempt to persuade us that the speaker is anyone but himself. But afterwards he speaks in the person of Chryses, and does his best to make us think that it is not Homer but an aged priest who is talking. This is the way in which he constructs his narrative right through the *Iliad* and *Odyssey*.'

'That is true enough,' he said.

'So his narrative includes both speeches and passages between speeches, does it not?'

'It does.'

'And when he speaks in the person of someone else, may we not say that he is imitating as near as he can the manner of speech of the character concerned?'

'And to imitate another person in speech or manner is to "*represent*" the person one is imitating?'

'It is.'

'This then is the way in which Homer and the other poets use representation in the course of their narrative.'

'Yes, I understand.'

'If, of course, the poet never pretended to be anyone but himself, his poetic narrative would be wholly devoid of representation. But to prevent any possibility of misunderstanding, I will explain how this could be done. Suppose that Homer, after telling how Chryses came with his daughter's ransom to beg her back from the Achaeans, or rather their kings, had gone on not as if it were Chryses speaking but Homer, there would have been no representation but only narrative. The passage would have run as follows (I'm not a poet, so I shall give it in prose) – The priest came and prayed that the gods would allow the Achaeans to capture Troy and return in safety, and begged the Achaeans to show their respect for the gods by releasing his daughter in exchange for the ransom. The others respected his request and agreed, but Agamemnon was angry and told him to go away now and never return; otherwise his sceptre and priestly garlands might afford him no protection. And he said that he would not release his daughter before she grew old with him in Argos, and that if he wanted to get home safely he had better go, and not annoy him any more. The old man was afraid when he heard what Agamemnon said, and departed without a word, but when he had left the camp he prayed earnestly to Apollo, calling on him by all his titles and reminding him of all the services he had rendered him in building temples and paying sacrifices; and he begged him in his prayer that, in return, he would avenge his tears on the Achaeans with his arrows. That,' I concluded, 'is how the passage would run in simple narrative without representation.'

'I see,' he replied.

'And so you will see,' I went on, 'that the opposite of this is when a poet omits the sections between the speeches and relies entirely on dialogue.'

'Yes, I understand,' he answered; 'that is what happens in tragedy, for example.'

'Exactly,' I said. 'And I think I have now made clear what I failed to explain before, that poetry and fiction fall into three classes. First, that which employs representation only, tragedy and comedy, as you say. Secondly, that in which the poet speaks in his own person; the best example is lyric poetry. Thirdly, that which employs both methods, epic and various other kinds of poetry. Is that clear?'

'Yes: I understand now what you were trying to say,' he said.

'And you will remember that just before that I said that we had settled the question of subject-matter and must now deal with that of form.'

'Yes, I remember.'

'What I meant, then,' I said, 'was that we must decide whether we should allow our poets to use representation in their narrative, and if so to what extent and for what purpose, or whether we should forbid it entirely.'

'I suspect,' he replied, 'that you are wondering whether we should allow tragedy and comedy in our state or not.'

'Maybe,' I replied, 'or maybe the question is more far-reaching. I don't know yet; we must follow the argument and see where it leads us.'

'Fair enough,' he said.

'Do you think, then, Adeimantus, that we want our guardians to be capable of playing many characters, or not? Does it not follow, from the principles we adopted earlier, that one man does one job well, and that if he tries to take on a number of jobs, the division of effort will mean that he will fail to make his mark at any of them?'

'The conclusion is unavoidable.'

'And it will also apply to representation; a man cannot play many characters as well as he can one.'

'He cannot.'

'He will therefore be unable to do anything worth while at all 395 well if he is to be a versatile character actor. For the same writers are incapable of equally good work even in two such closely allied forms of representation as comedy and tragedy. You did say they were forms of representation, did you not?'

'Yes; and it's true that a man can't write both.'

'Nor can the same people be reciters and actors, or actors in tragedy and comedy – all these being forms of representation.'

'True.'

'And we can subdivide human nature still further, and show that it is impossible to play many roles well, whether in real life or in representations of it on the stage.'

'That's very true.'

'But we argued originally that our guardians were to be freed from all forms of manual work; their life's work was to be the provision of perfect freedom for our state, a task to which they were to devote all their energies. That, therefore, is the only role they must play in life or literature; and with this end in view the only characters on which they must model themselves from their earliest years must be men of courage, self-control, independence, and religious principle. They must no more act a mean part than do a mean action or any other kind of wrong. For we soon reap the fruits of literature in life, and prolonged indulgence in any form of literature leaves its mark on the moral nature of a man, affecting not only the mind but physical poise and intonation.'[36]

'That is very true,' he replied.

'Since then we care for the moral welfare of our guardians,' I said, 'we will not allow them to take the parts of women, young or old (for they are men), nor to represent them abusing their husbands or presumptuously quarrelling with heaven, when they imagine themselves happy, or crying and complaining in misfortune. Far less can we permit representation of women in sickness or love or child-birth.'

'We must forbid this sort of thing entirely.'

'And the same is true of slaves – male or female – when they are behaving like slaves.'

'Agreed.'

'And of bad and cowardly characters whose behaviour is just the opposite of what we demand. They indulge in comic abuse and 396 back-chat, drunk or sober, and say and do things that are an offence against themselves and their neighbours. Nor do I suppose we shall tolerate representations of the actions or words of madmen. We must recognize that there are men and women who are mad and bad, but we cannot have them represented in poetry or drama.'

'You are quite right,' he said.

'Then can we tolerate representations of smiths or craftsmen at work, or men rowing triremes or in command of them?'

'No: because none of these are occupations to which our guardians should pay any attention.'

'And what about horses neighing and bulls bellowing, and rivers splashing and the sea roaring, and thunders rolling, and so on?'

'We have already forbidden madness and the representation of madness,' he replied.

'What you mean, I suppose, is that there is one style of narrative which the good man will employ when he has anything to say, and a different style in which the man of opposite character and upbringing will always choose to express him self.'

'Describe them,' he said.

'I think,' I replied, 'that the decent man, when he comes in the course of a narrative to a speech or action by a good man, will be willing to impersonate him and feel no shame at so doing. This will be especially true if he is representing the good man behaving with steadiness and determination, and only failing in a few respects and to a limited degree, owing to illness or love or drink or some other misfortune. But if he comes across an unworthy character, he will be ashamed to imitate it seriously, except perhaps for its short periods of good behaviour, because it falls below his standards. He has no practice in such representation, and will not consent to model himself on characters which his judgement despises as lower than his own, except perhaps for the purpose of amusement.'

'Very likely.'

'He will, in fact, make use of the form of narrative which we mentioned when we were talking of Homer's epics a few minutes ago, and will combine both representation and narrative, but the proportion of representation will be small. Or am I wrong?'

'No, that's just the kind of way in which he will express himself.'

'And other types of man will be all the readier to vary their 397 style the worse they are, and will think nothing beneath them. They will seriously try to represent in public all the things we were talking about. We shall have the noises of thunder and wind and hail, and of axles and wheels, the notes of trumpets, pipes, whistles, and every possible instrument, the barking of dogs, the baaing of sheep, and twittering of birds. All these will be represented with voice and gesture, and narrative will play but a small part.'

'That follows too.'

'These then are the two styles of expression to which I referred,' I said.

'Yes, I see,' he replied.

'And of these two styles, one is pretty uniform, needing merely music of appropriate mode and rhythm to accompany it. In fact if one handles it rightly one and the same mode can be employed throughout, because of the uniformity of the style, and the same is true of rhythm.'

'That is certainly true,' he said.

'The other style, on the other hand, will have the opposite requirements. It will need every kind of mode, and every kind of rhythm, if it is to find suitable expression. For its variety is unlimited.'

'That is true too.'

'But must not all poets and writers go in for one or other of these two styles or some combination of them?'

'They must.'

'Then what are we to do?' I asked. 'Are we to admit both styles and their combination into our city, or pick on one of them?'

'My own vote,' he replied, 'would go to the style which represents the good man.'

'And yet, Adeimantus,' I reminded him, 'the combination of the two styles is very pleasant, and the opposite style to the one you have chosen gives most pleasure of all to children and nurses and the general public.'

'Yes, if pleasure's what they're after.'

'But perhaps you will say that it is unsuitable for our state, because there one man does one job and does not play a multiplicity of roles.'

'It certainly is unsuitable.'

'And so ours is the only state in which we shall find (for example) the shoemaker sticking to his shoemaking and not turning pilot as well, the farmer sticking to his farming and not taking on court work into the bargain, and the soldier sticking to his soldiering and not running a business on the side?'

'Yes.'

'So if we are visited in our state by someone who has the skill 398 to transform himself into all sorts of characters and represent all sorts of things, and he wants to show off himself and his poems to us, we shall treat him with all the reverence due to a priest and giver of rare pleasure, but shall tell him that he and his kind have no place in our city, being forbidden by our code, and send him elsewhere, after anointing him with myrrh and crowning him. For ourselves, we shall for our own good employ story tellers and poets who are severe rather than amusing, who follow the style of the good man and in all their works abide by the principles we laid down for them when we started out on this attempt to educate our military class.'[37]

'That undoubtedly is what we should do,' he said, 'if we had the choice.'

'And I think,' said I, 'that that probably completes our survey of the literature to be employed in our education. Because we have dealt both with subject-matter and with form.'

'I agree,' he replied.

(d) Musical requirements

Music is dealt with on a similar basis. Greek music was employed largely as an accompaniment to song, and what this section is concerned to say is that, having laid down rules governing the content and form of poetry, we must now require their musical accompaniment to be appropriate. As appears from the text, the Greeks were more inclined than we are to associate certain types of music with certain types of feeling and sentiment. But the technicalities of Greek music are still not fully understood.

'Then we are left with the varieties of music and song to discuss,' I went on; 'and I suppose that it's pretty obvious to everyone what requirements we shall have to make about them, if we are to be consistent.'

Glaucon laughed, 'I'm afraid I'm not included in your "every-one",' he said; 'for at the moment I can't really suggest what we ought to say – though I'm not without my suspicions.'

'Well at any rate you can agree easily enough that song consists of three elements, words, mode, and rhythm.'

'Yes, I agree to that.'

'As far as the words are concerned, then, the same rules will apply as those we laid down for words not set to music, both for their content and form.'

'True.'

'And surely the mode and rhythm should suit the words.'

'Certainly.'

'But we agreed to ban dirges and laments, did we not?'

'We did.'

'Tell me then – you are a musician – which are the modes suitable for dirges?'

'The Mixed Lydian and the Extreme Lydian.'

'Then we can reject them,' I said: 'even women, if they are respectable, have no use for them, let alone men.'

'Quite right.'

'But drunkenness, softness, or idleness are also qualities most unsuitable in a Guardian?'

'Of course.'

'What, then, are the relaxing modes and the ones we use for drinking songs?'

'The Ionian and certain Lydian modes, commonly described as "languid".'

'Will they then,' I asked, 'be of any use for training soldiers?' 399

'None at all,' he replied. 'You seem to be left with the Dorian and Phrygian.'

'I'm no expert on modes,' said I; 'but I want one that will represent appropriately the voice and accent of a brave man on military service or any dangerous undertaking, who faces injury, defeat, or death, or any other misfortune with the same steadfast endurance. And I want another mode to represent him in the ordinary voluntary occupations of peace-time: for instance, persuading someone to grant a request, praying to God or instructing or admonishing his neighbour, or again submitting himself to the requests or instruction or persuasion of others, and in all showing no conceit, but moderation and common sense and willingness to accept the outcome. Give me these two modes, one stern, one pleasant, to express courage and moderation in good fortune or in bad.'

'The two modes you are asking for,' he rejoined, 'are the two I have just mentioned.'

'And so,' I went on, 'we shan't need for our music and song instruments of many strings with a wide harmonic range. We shan't keep craftsmen to make instruments of this kind, such as harps and harpsichords.'

'I suppose not.'

'Then shall we allow flutes and flute-makers in our city? Has not the flute the widest range of all, being in fact the original which other instruments of wide range imitate?'

'That's plain enough,' he said.

'We are left, then, with the lyre and the cithara for use in our city. Though the shepherds in the country might have some sort of pipe.'

'That seems to be the conclusion of our argument.'

'We aren't really doing anything revolutionary, you know,' I said, 'in preferring Apollo and his instruments to Marsyas and his.'

'No, I quite agree,' he replied.

'And what is more,' I pointed out, 'we are insensibly getting rid of the luxury from which we said our state suffered.'

'Quite right too,' he replied.

'Well, let us continue the process,' said I. 'After mode we should presumably deal next with rhythm. We shan't want very elaborate or varied combinations, but merely need to find which rhythms suit a life of courage and discipline. We shall then adapt the metre 400 and tune to the appropriate words, and not the words to the metre and tune. But it's your business to say what these rhythms are, as you did with the modes.'

'I'm afraid I really can't do that,' he replied. 'There are three basic types of rhythm, from which the various combinations are built up, just as there are four elements which go to build up the modes. So much I know and can tell you. But which are suited to represent which kind of life, I cannot say.'

'Well, we'll consult Damon[38] about it,' I said, 'and ask him what combinations are suitable to express meanness, insolence, madness, and other evil characteristics, and which rhythms we must keep to express their opposites. I seem to remember hearing him talking about "march rhythms" and "composite rhythms", "dactyls", and "heroics", arranging them in various ways and marking the stresses; he talked also, I think, about "iambics and trochees", and assigned them longs and shorts. And I believe that he praised or blamed the composition of the foot as well as the rhythm as a whole, or perhaps it was the combination of the two: I really can't remember. In any case, as I said, we can refer to Damon. For it would need a lot of argument to settle the details, don't you think?'

'It would indeed.'

Summary

Plato proceeds to sum up the general purpose of this stage of education – to train both character and moral and aesthetic judgement, these last two being closely allied. The influence of environment on growing minds is again emphasized: it is because of this that so rigid a censorship of the music and poetry to be used in education is required. If we miss a reference to any kind of scientific training, it should be remembered that mathematical and (so far as it then existed) scientific training is reserved for a later stage of the Guardians' education...

'But there is one thing we can decide at once, that beauty and ugliness result from good rhythm and bad.'

'That is undeniable.'

'And good rhythm is the consequence of music that suits good poetry, bad rhythm of the opposite; and the same is true of mode and tune, if, as we said a moment ago, both the rhythm and mode should be suited to the words and not vice versa.'

'The words must of course determine the music,' he said.

'But what about the style and content of the poetry themselves?' I asked. 'Don't they depend on character, just as the other things depend on them?'

'They must.'

'Good literature, therefore, and good music and beauty of form generally all depend on goodness of character; I don't mean that lack of awareness of the world which we politely call "goodness", but a character of real judgement and principle.'

'I quite agree.'

'And are not these things which our young men must try to acquire, if they are to perform their function in life properly?'

'They must.'

'And they are to be seen in painting and similar arts, in weaving 401 and embroidery, in architecture and furniture, and in living things, animals and plants. For in all of these we find beauty and ugliness. And ugliness of form and disharmony are akin to bad art and bad character, and their opposites are akin to and represent good character and discipline.'

'That is perfectly true.'

'It is not only to the poets therefore that we must issue orders requiring them to represent good character in their poems or not to write to all; we must issue similar orders to all artists and prevent them portraying bad character, ill-discipline, meanness, or ugliness in painting, sculpture, architecture, or any work of art, and if they are unable to comply they must be forbidden to practise their art. We shall thus prevent our guardians being brought up among representations of what is evil, and so day by day and little by little, by feeding as it were in an unhealthy pasture, insensibly doing themselves grave psychological damage. Our artists and craftsmen must be capable of perceiving the real nature of what is beautiful, and then our young men, living as it were in a good climate, will benefit because all the works of art they see and hear influence them for good, like the breezes from some healthy country, insensibly moulding them into sympathy and conformity with what is rational and right.'

'That would indeed be the best way to bring them up.'

'And that, my dear Glaucon,' I said, 'is why this stage of education is crucial. For rhythm and harmony penetrate deeply into the mind and have a most powerful effect on it, and if education is good, bring balance and fairness, if it is bad, the reverse. And moreover the proper training we propose to give will make a man quick to perceive the shortcomings of works of art or nature, whose ugliness he will rightly dislike; anything beautiful he will welcome, and will accept and assimilate it for his own good, anything ugly 402 he will rightly condemn and dislike, even when he is still young and cannot understand the reason for so doing, while when reason comes he will recognize and welcome her as a familiar friend because of his education.'

'In my view,' he said, 'that is the purpose of this stage of education.'

'Well then,' I went on, 'when we were learning to read we were not satisfied until we could recognize the letters of the alphabet wherever they occurred; we did not think them beneath our notice in large words or small, but tried to recognize them everywhere on the grounds that we should not have learned to read till we could.'

'That is true.'

'And we can't recognize reflections of the letters in water or in a mirror till we know the letters themselves. The same process of learning gives us skill to recognize both.'

'Yes, it does.'

'Then I must surely be right in saying that we shall not be properly educated ourselves, nor will the guardians whom we are training, until we can recognize the qualities of discipline, courage, generosity, greatness of mind, and others akin to them, as well as their opposites, in all their many manifestations. We must be able to perceive both the qualities themselves and representations of them wherever they occur, and must not despise instances great or small, but reckon that the same process of learning gives us skill to recognize both.'[39]

'You are most certainly right,' he agreed.

'And is not the fairest sight of all,' I asked, 'for him who has eyes to see it, the combination in the same person of good character and good looks to match them, each bearing the same stamp?'

'It is indeed.'

'And such a combination will also be most attractive, will it not?'

'Certainly.'

'It is, then, with people of this sort that the educated man will fall in love; where the combination is imperfect he will not be attracted.'

'Not if the defect is one of character,' he replied; 'if it's a physical defect, he will not let it be a bar to his affection.'

'I know,' I said; 'you've got, or once had, a boy friend like that. And I agree with you. But tell me: does excessive pleasure go with self-control and moderation?'

'Certainly not; excessive pleasure breaks down one's control just as much as excessive pain.'

'Does it go with other kinds of goodness?'

'No.'

'Then does it go with excess and indiscipline?' 403

'Certainly.'

'And is there any greater or keener pleasure than that of sex?'

'No: not any more frenzied.'

'But to love rightly is to love what is beautiful and good with discipline and intelligence.'

'I entirely agree.'

'Then can true love have any contact with frenzy or excess of any kind?'

'It can have none.'

'It can therefore have no contact with this sexual pleasure, and lovers whose love is true must neither of them indulge in it.'

'They certainly must not, Socrates,' he replied emphatically.

'And so I suppose that you will lay down laws in the state we are founding which will allow a lover to associate with his boyfriend and kiss him and touch him, if he permits it, as a father does his son, if his motives are good; but require that his association with anyone he's fond of must never give rise to the least suspicion of anything beyond this, otherwise he will be thought a man of no taste or education.'

'That is how I should legislate.'

'And that, I think,' said I, 'concludes what we have to say about this stage of education, and a very appropriate conclusion too – for the object of education is to teach us to love beauty.'

'I agree.'

Notes

1   The Greek word PSEUDOS and its corresponding verb meant not only 'fiction' – stories, tales – but also 'lies' – fraud and deceit: and this ambiguity should be borne in mind.

2   Such a robe was woven by Athenian maidens for presentation to Athene.

3   Plato uses gods (plural) or god (singular) indifferently: when he uses god we must not interpret him in terms of monotheism.

4   See note 3.

5   *Iliad*, XXIV, 527. Quotations from Homer are made, with his permission, from the translations by Dr Rieu in the *Penguin* series. In this particular passage the version quoted by Plato differs slightly from the accepted text.

6	*Odyssey*, XVII, 485.	21	*Odyssey*, XVII, 383.
7	*Odyssey*, XI, 489.	22	*Iliad*, IV, 412.
8	*Iliad*, XX, 64.	23	*Iliad*, III, 8; and IV, 431.
9	*Iliad*, XXIII, 103.	24	*Iliad*, I, 225.
10	*Odyssey*, X, 495.	25	*Odyssey*, IX, 8.
11	*Iliad*, XVI, 856.	26	*Odyssey*, XII, 342.
12	*Iliad*, XXIII, 100.	27	*Iliad*, XIV, 294 ff.
13	*Odyssey*, XXIV, 6.	28	*Odyssey*, XX, 17.
14	*Iliad*, XXIV, 10.	29	Proverbial.
15	*Iliad*, XVIII, 23.	30	*Iliad*, IX, 515; XIX, 278.
16	*Iliad*, XXII, 414.	31	*Iliad*, XXII, 15, 20.
17	*Iliad*, XVIII, 54.	32	*Iliad*, XXI, 130; XXIII, 140.
18	*Iliad*, XXII, 168.	33	*Iliad*, XXIV, 14; XXIII, 175.
19	*Iliad*, XVI, 433.	34	Aeschylus *Niobe*.
20	*Iliad*, I, 599.	35	*Iliad*, I, 15.

36   Plato is thinking of the dramatic recitation – 'representation' – which was, as we have seen, an essential part of Greek education, and it is with this that the Greek of the passage is in its literal sense concerned. I have diverged a little more than usual from the literal sense in order to bring out the meaning of the passage in modern terms. For it must be remembered that Plato thought these effects were also produced by merely *watching* drama...

37   The Guardians – their military function is still to the fore. The paragraph makes it clear that, though he is dealing primarily with education, Plato would have excluded from his state all poetry of the type to which he objects.

38   A well-known fifth-century musician.

39   There may be a reference here to Plato's 'Theory of Ideas'.

Soviet Writers' Congress, 1934

A.A. Zhdanov (1896–1948)

A.A. Zhdanov was Stalin's cultural commissar and one of the major champions of the aesthetic theory known as socialist realism. His address to the Soviet Writers' Congress in 1934 represents one of the clearest statements of the doctrine, with its insistence that authors tailor their material to fit the demands of state propaganda, becoming in the process what Zhdanov calls 'engineers of human souls'. Under such a scheme the arts become subservient to political considerations (in this case Soviet-style Marxism) and the social role of the artist is to promote the interests of the state by producing politically 'correct' works of art. The call for strict state control of the arts and for literature of a didactic character echoes Platonic aesthetic theory (see Readings 1 and 9), and implies a similar threat of censorship.

The key to the success of Soviet literature is to be sought for in the success of socialist construction. Its growth is an expression of the successes and achievments of our socialist system. Our literature is the youngest of all literatures of all peoples and countries. And at the same time it is the richest in ideas, the most advanced and the most revolutionary literature. Never before has there been a literature which has organized the toilers and oppressed for the struggle to abolish once and for all every kind of exploitation and the yoke of wage slavery. Never before has there been a literature which has based the subject matter of its works on the life of the working class and peasantry and their fight for socialism. Nowhere, in no country in the world, has there been a literature which has defended and upheld the principle of equal rights for the toilers of all nations, the principle of equal rights for women. There is not, there cannot be in bourgeois countries a literature which consistently smashes every kind of obscurantism, every kind of mysticism, priesthood and superstition, as our literature is doing.

Only Soviet literature, which is of one flesh and blood with socialist construction, could become, and has indeed become, such a literature – so rich in ideas, so advanced and revolutionary.

Soviet authors have already created not a few outstanding works, which correctly and truthfully depict the life of our Soviet country. Already there are several names of which we can be justly proud. Under the leadership of the Party, with the thoughtful and daily guidance of the Central Committee and the untiring support and help of Comrade Stalin, a whole army of Soviet writers has rallied around the Soviet power and the Party. And in the light of our Soviet literature's successes, we see standing out in yet sharper relief the full contrast between our system – the system of victorious socialism – and the system of dying, mouldering capitalism.

Of what can the bourgeois author write, of what can he dream, what source of inspiration can he find, whence can he borrow this inspiration, if the worker in capitalist countries is uncertain of the morrow, if he does not know whether he will have work the next day, if the peasant does not know whether he will work on his plot of ground tomorrow or whether his life will be ruined by the capitalist crisis, if the brain worker has no work today and does not know whether he will receive any tomorrow?

What can the bourgeois author write about, what source of inspiration can there be for him, when the world is being precipitated once more – if not today, then tomorrow – into the abyss of a new imperialist war?

The present state of bourgeois literature is such that it is no longer able to create great works of art. The decadence and disintegration of bourgeois literature, resulting from the collapse and decay of the capitalist system, represent a characteristic trait, a characteristic peculiarity of the state of bourgeois culture and bourgeois literature at the present time. Gone never to return are the times when bourgeois literature, reflecting the victory of the bourgeois system over feudalism, was able to create great works of the period when capitalism was flourishing. Everything now is growing stunted – themes, talents, authors, heroes...

Characteristic of the decadence and decay of bourgeois culture are the orgies of mysticism and superstition, the passion for pornography. The 'illustrious persons' of bourgeois literature – of that bourgeois literature which has sold its pen to capital – are now thieves, police sleuths, prostitutes, hooligans.

All this is characteristic of that section of literature which is trying to conceal the decay of the bourgeois system, which is vainly trying to prove that nothing has happened, that all is well in the 'state of Denmark,' that there is nothing rotten as yet in the system of capitalism. Those representatives of bourgeois literature who feel the state of things more acutely are absorbed in pessimism, doubt in the morrow, eulogy of darkness, extolment of pessimism as the theory and practice of art. And only a small section – the most honest and far-sighted writers – are trying to find a way out along other paths, in other directions, to link their destiny with the proletariat and its revolutionary struggle.

The proletariat of capitalist countries is already forging the army of its writers, of its artists – the revolutionary writers whose representatives we are glad to welcome here today at the first Congress of Soviet Writers. The detachment of revolutionary writers in capitalist countries is not large as yet, but it is growing and will continue to grow every day, as the class struggle becomes more intense, as the forces of the world proletarian revolution grow stronger.

We firmly believe that these few dozens of foreign comrades who are here today represent the nucleus, the core of a mighty army of proletarian writers which will be created by the world proletarian revolution in capitalist countries.

That is how matters stand in capitalist countries. Not so with us. Our Soviet writer derives the material for his works of art, his subject matter, images, artistic language and speech, from the life and experience of the men and women of Dnieprostroy, of Magnitostroy. Our writer draws his material from the heroic epic of the Chelyuskin expedition, from the experience of our collective farms, from the creative action that is seething in all corners of our country.

In our country the main heroes of works of literature are the active builders of a new life – working men and women, men and women collective farmers, Party members, business managers, engineers, members of the Young Communist League, Pioneers. Such are the chief types and the chief heroes of our Soviet literature. Our literature is impregnated with enthusiasm and the spirit of heroic deeds. It is optimistic, but not optimistic in accordance with any 'inward,' animal instinct. It is optimistic in essence, because it is the literature of the rising class of the proletariat, the only progressive and advanced class. Our Soviet literature is strong by virtue of the fact that it is serving a new cause – the cause of socialist construction.

Comrade Stalin has called our writers engineers of human souls. What does this mean? What duties does the title confer upon you?

In the first place, it means knowing life so as to be able to depict it truthfully in works of art, not to depict it in a dead, scholastic way, not simply as 'objective reality,' but to depict reality in its revolutionary development.

In addition to this, the truthfulness and historical concreteness of the artistic portrayal should be combined with the ideological remoulding and education of the toiling people in the spirit of socialism. This method in *belles lettres* and literary criticism is what we call the method of socialist realism.

Our Soviet literature is not afraid of the charge of being 'tendencious.' Yes, Soviet literature is tendencious, for in an epoch of class struggle there is not and cannot be a literature which is not class literature, not tendencious, allegedly non-political.

And I think that every one of our Soviet writers can say to any dull-witted bourgeois, to any philistine, to any bourgeois writer who may talk about our literature being tendencious: 'Yes, our Soviet literature is tendencious, and we are proud of this fact, because the aim of our tendency is to liberate the toilers, to free all mankind from the yoke of capitalist slavery.'

To be an engineer of human souls means standing with both feet firmly planted on the basis of real life. And this in its turn denotes a rupture with romanticism of the old type, which depicted a non-existent life and non-existent heroes, leading the reader away from the antagonisms and oppression of real life into a world of the impossible, into a world of utopian dreams. Our literature, which stands with both feet firmly planted on a materialist basis, cannot be hostile to romanticism, but it must be a romanticism of a new type, revolutionary romanticism. We say that socialist realism is the basic method of Soviet *belles lettres* and literary criticism, and this presupposes that revolutionary romanticism should enter into literary creation as a component part, for the whole life of our Party, the whole life of the working class and its struggle consist in a combination of the most stern and sober practical work with a supreme spirit of heroic deeds and magnificent future prospects. Our Party has always been strong by virtue of the fact that it has united and continues to unite a thoroughly business-like and practical spirit with broad vision, with a constant urge forward, with a struggle for the building of communist society. Soviet literature should be able to portray our heroes; it should be able to glimpse our tomorrow. This will be no utopian dream, for our tomorrow is already being prepared for today by dint of conscious planned work.

One cannot be an engineer of human souls without knowing the technique of literary work, and it must be noted that the technique of the writer's work possesses a large number of specific peculiarities.

You have many different types of weapons. Soviet literature has every opportunity of employing these types of weapons (genres, styles, forms and methods of literary creation) in their diversity and fullness, selecting all the best that has been created in this sphere by all previous epochs. From this point of view, the mastery of the technique of writing, the critical assimilation of the literary heritage of all epochs, represents a task which you must fulfil without fail, if you wish to become engineers of human souls.

Comrades, the proletariat, just as in other provinces of material and spiritual culture, is the sole heir of all that is best in the treasury of world literature. The bourgeoisie has squandered its literary heritage; it is our duty to gather it up carefully, to study it and, having critically assimilated it, to advance further.

To be engineers of human souls means to fight actively for the culture of language, for quality of production. Our literature does not as yet come up to the requirements of our era. The weaknesses of our literature are a reflection of the fact that people's consciousness lags behind economic life – a defect from which even our writers are not, of course, free. That is why untiring work directed towards self-education and towards improving their ideological equipment in the spirit of socialism represents an indispensable condition without which Soviet writers cannot remould the mentality of their readers and thereby become engineers of human souls...

And so our Soviet writers have all the conditions necessary for them to produce works which will be, as we say, consonant with our era, from which the people of our times can learn and which will be the pride of future generations.

Franz Kafka or Thomas Mann?

Georg Lukács (1885–1971)

Georg Lukács, philosopher, literary theorist and literary critic, is generally regarded as one of the major figures in twentieth-century Marxist thought. The author of some major works of Marxist theory, such as The History of Class Consciousness *(1922), Lukács also wrote extensively on literature, most notably in* The Theory of the Novel *(1920),* The Historical Novel *(1937), and* The Meaning of Contemporary Realism *(1957). In the following extract from the latter text Lukács argues the case for a literature that draws our attention to the social forces that shape us as individuals. Lukács calls his doctrine 'critical realism' and opposes it to a modernist tradition which claims that alienation is man's natural state ('the human condition' argument). For Lukács, the debate polarizes into a choice between the critical realism of Thomas Mann and the modernism of Franz Kafka. Critical realism can be regarded as Lukács' response to socialist realism, the orthodox Marxist aesthetic theory of the time (see Reading 2) which maintained a dogmatic insistence on political correctness. Lukács could be very critical of socialist realism, although he broadly accepted its doctrines.*

Franz Kafka is the classic example of the modern writer at the mercy of a blind and panic-stricken *angst*. His unique position he owes to the fact that he found a direct, uncomplex way of communicating this basic experience; he did so without having recourse to formalistic experimentation. Content is here the immediate determinant of aesthetic form – that is why Kafka belongs with the great realistic writers. Indeed, he is one of the greatest of all, if we consider how few writers have ever equalled his skill in the imaginative evocation of the concrete novelty of the world. Never was the quality of Kafka's achievement more striking or more needed than at the present day, when so many writers fall for slick experimentation. The impact of Kafka's work derives not only from his passionate sincerity – rare enough in our age – but also from the corresponding simplicity of the world he constructs. That is Kafka's most original achievement. Kierkegaard said, 'The greater a man's originality, the more he is at the mercy of *angst*.' Kafka, original in the Kierkegaardian sense, describes this *angst* and the fragmented world which – it is incorrectly assumed – is both its complement and its cause. His originality lies not in discovering any new means of expression but in the utterly convincing, and yet continually startling, presentation of his invented world, and of his characters' reaction to it. 'What shocks is not the monstrosity of it,' writes Theodor W. Adorno, 'but its matter-of-factness.'

The diabolical character of the world of capitalism, and man's impotence in the face of it, is the real subject-matter of Kafka's writings. His simplicity and sincerity are, of course, the product of complex and contradictory forces. Let us consider only one aspect. Kafka wrote at a time when capitalist society, the object of his *angst*, was still far from the high mark of its historical development. What he described and 'demonized' was not the truly demonic world of Fascism, but the world of the Hapsburg Monarchy. *Angst*, haunting and indefinable, is perfectly reflected in this vague, ahistorical, timeless world, steeped in the atmosphere of Prague. Kafka profited from his historical position in two ways. On the one hand, his narrative detail gains from being rooted in the Austrian society of that period. On the other hand, the essential unreality of human existence, which it is his aim to convey, can be related to a corresponding sense of unreality and foreboding in the society he knew. The identification with the *condition humaine* is far more convincing than in later visions of a diabolical, *angst*-inspiring world, where so much has to be eliminated or obscured by formal experimentation to achieve the desired ahistorical, timeless image of the human condition. But this, though the reason for the astonishing impact and lasting power of Kafka's work, cannot disguise its basically allegorical character. The wonderfully suggestive descriptive detail points to a transcendent reality, to the anticipated reality – stylized into timelessness – of fully developed imperialism. Kafka's details are not, as in realism, the nodal points of individual or social life; they are cryptic symbols of an unfathomable transcendence. The stronger their evocative power, the deeper is the abyss, the more evident the allegorical gap between meaning and existence.

The counterpart to this fascinating, though ill-starred, development in modern bourgeois literature is the work of Thomas

Mann...The world of Thomas Mann is free from transcendental reference: place, time and detail are rooted firmly in a particular social and historical situation. Mann envisages the perspective of socialism without abandoning the position of a bourgeois, and without attempting to portray the newly emergent socialist societies or even the forces working towards their establishment...

This apparently limited perspective is nevertheless of central importance in Thomas Mann's work: it is the main reason for the harmony of its proportions. Each section of a portrayed totality is placed in a concrete social context; the significance of each detail, its meaning for the evolution of society, is clearly defined. It is our world that Thomas Mann describes, the world in whose shaping we play a part, and which in turn shapes us. The deeper Thomas Mann probes into the complexity of present-day reality, the more clearly we come to understand our position in the complex evolution of mankind. Thus Thomas Mann, despite his loving attention to detail, never lapses into naturalism. For all his fascination with the dark regions of modern existence, Thomas Mann always shows up distortion for what it is, tracing its roots and its concrete origins in society...

Thomas Mann is concerned to investigate the demonic, the underworld of the human mind, within the context of present-day society. Early in his career he realized that the artist himself is one of the main mediators of this experience. It is therefore natural that he should have followed up this early insight with increasingly rigorous studies of the problem in its social context. The examination begun with *Tonio Kröger* ended with *Dr Faustus*. With Adrian Leverkühn, Mann's Faustus, the enquiry is concentrated on the present time, though it is a present seen in the perspective of history. The devil has to confess that, with Goethe, his assistance was strictly unnecessary, but that the social conditions of Leverkühn's time compelled the composer to seek guidance from the underworld. Yet Leverkühn's final monologue reveals the perspective of a new society, of socialism, under which the artist will be freed from his former enslavement. Indeed, the mere struggle for the social reformation of mankind may of itself suffice to break the power of the underworld...

Between these methods, between Franz Kafka and Thomas Mann, the contemporary bourgeois writer will have to choose. There is no necessity for a writer to break with his bourgeois pattern of life in making this choice between social sanity and morbidity, in choosing the great and progressive literary traditions of realism in preference to formalistic experimentation. (Of course, there are many writers who will choose socialism as a way of solving their personal dilemma. I only want to emphasize that this is not the only possible choice for the contemporary writer.) What counts is the personal decision... And today that is determined by the question: acceptance or rejection of *angst*? Ought *angst* to be taken as an absolute, or ought it to be overcome? Should it be considered one reaction among others, or should it become the determinant of the *condition humaine*? These are not primarily, of course, literary questions; they relate to a man's behaviour and experience of life. The crucial question is whether a man escapes from the life of his time into a realm of abstraction – it is then that *angst* is engendered in human consciousness – or confronts modern life determined to fight its evils and support what is good in it. The first decision leads then to another: is man the helpless victim of transcendental and inexplicable forces, or is he a member of a human community in which he can play a part, however small, towards its modification or reform?

These problems could well be expanded and generalized; but it is not necessary to do so here. The implications of our basic question – acceptance of *angst* or rejection – are clear enough. We see here, ideologically and artistically, the root of our modern dilemma. However passionately, however sophistically, the histor- ical origins of *angst* may be obscured, no work of art based on it can avoid – objectively speaking – guilt by association with Hitlerism and the preparations for atomic war. It is, indeed, of the nature of literature's social significance that it reflects the move- ments of its age even when it is – subjectively – aiming to express something very different (this opposition between subjective intention and objective compulsion is at the root of the modernist dilemma: modernism is in revolt against the anti-aestheticism of capitalism, and yet in the process revolts against art itself)...

The more *angst* predominates, the greater will be the levelling effect. We have seen this in the case of abstract and concrete potentiality. But the loss of any concern for ethical complexity, for the problems of society, is part of the same process. The question of the 'authenticity' of human behaviour is no longer important. Particularly in modernist writing, the differing reactions of human beings come to seem insignificant in the face of 'metaphysical' *angst* (and of the increasing pressures of conformity). The fact that in the midst of this 'permanent revolution', this endless 'revaluation of all values', there were writers of major talent who clung to the standards of nineteenth-century realism is, therefore, of ethical as much as of artistic significance. These writers' attitudes sprang from the ethical conviction that though changes in society modify human nature, they do not abolish it...

It is a difficult and complex task, yet it is perfectly possible, for a writer to change his attitude to himself, to his fellow human beings, and the world at large. The forces employed against him, admittedly, are enormously powerful. Nihilism and cynicism, despair and *angst*, suspicion and self-disgust are the spontaneous product of the capitalist society in which intellectuals have to live. Many factors, in education and elsewhere, are arrayed against him. Take, for instance, the view that pessimism is aristocratic, a worthier philosophy for an intellectual élite than faith in human progress. Or the belief that the individual – precisely as a member of an élite – must be a helpless victim of historical forces. Or the idea that the rise of mass society is an unmitigated evil. The majority of the press, highbrow and lowbrow, tends to minister to prejudices of this kind (it is their role in the campaign for the continuation of the Cold War). It is as if it were unworthy of the intellectual to hold other than dogmatic modernist views on life, art, and philosophy. To support realism in art, to examine the possibilities of peaceful coexistence among nations, to strive for an impartial evaluation of communism (which does not involve allegiance to it), all this may make a writer an outcast in the eyes of his colleagues and in the eyes of those on whom he depends for a livelihood. Since a writer of Sartre's standing has had to endure attacks of this kind, how much more dangerous is the situation likely to be for younger, less prominent writers.

These, and much more, are hard facts. But we must not forget that strong counter-forces are at work, particularly today; and that they are growing in strength. The writer who considers his own basic interests, those of his nation and of mankind as a whole, and who decides to work against the forces prevailing in the capitalist world, is now no longer alone. The further his explorations take him, the firmer his choice will be, and the less isolated will he feel, for he will be identifying himself with those forces in the world of his time which will one day prevail.

The period during which Fascism rose to power, like the period of Fascist ascendancy and the subsequent Cold War period, were hardly favourable to the growth of critical realism. Nevertheless, excellent work was done; neither physical terror nor intellectual pressure succeeded in preventing it. There were always critical realist writers who opposed war – in both its cold and hot manifestations – and the destruction of art and culture. Not a few works of high artistic merit emerged from the struggle. Today, the imminent defeat of Cold War policies, the new perspective of peaceful coexistence among the nations, should allow wider scope for a critical and realistic bourgeois literature. The real dilemma of our age is not the opposition between capitalism and socialism, but the opposition between peace and war. The first duty of the bourgeois intellectual has become the rejection of an all-pervading fatalistic *angst*, implying a rescue operation for humanity rather than any breakthrough to Socialism. Because it is these perspectives that confront him, the bourgeois writer today is in a better position to solve his own dilemma than he was in the past. It is the dilemma of the choice between an aesthetically appealing, but decadent modernism, and a fruitful critical realism. It is the choice between Franz Kafka and Thomas Mann.

What is epic theatre?

Walter Benjamin (1892–1940)

Walter Benjamin was a leading German Marxist critic and cultural theorist in the 1920s and 1930s. He was closely associated with the playwright Bertolt Brecht, on whose work he wrote extensively. Understanding Brecht *(1977) contains a range of essays by Benjamin on Brecht, including two versions of 'What is epic theatre?', the first of which is reprinted here. Benjamin outlines the principles of Brecht's doctrine of epic theatre, with its commitment to destroying the illusion of realism on stage by making visible the machinery of theatrical production, frequently interrupting the narrative action by song and dance, and encouraging non-realistic styles of acting, all in the name of the so-called 'alienation effect'. By means of the 'alienation effect' the audience is prevented from identifying with the characters and stage action as if they were real. The role of the artist under this theory is to challenge or shock the audience for political effect (both Brecht and Benjamin had Marxist sympathies). Epic theatre is designed to have a didactic function.*

Epic theatre is gestural. The extent to which it can also be literary in the traditional sense is a separate issue. The gesture is its raw material and its task is the rational utilization of this material. The gesture has two advantages over the highly deceptive statements and assertions normally made by people and their many-layered and opaque actions. First, the gesture is falsifiable only up to a point; in fact, the more inconspicuous and habitual it is, the more difficult it is to falsify. Second, unlike people's actions and endeavours, it has a definable beginning and a definable end. Indeed, this strict, frame-like, enclosed nature of each moment of an attitude which, after all, is as a whole in a state of living flux, is one of the basic dialectical characteristics of the gesture. This leads to an important conclusion: the more frequently we interrupt someone engaged in an action, the more gestures we obtain. Hence, the interrupting of action is one of the principal concerns of epic theatre. Therein lies the formal achievement of Brecht's songs with their crude, heart-rending refrains. Without anticipating the difficult study, yet to be made, of the function of the text in epic theatre, we can at least say that often its main function is not to illustrate or advance the action but, on the contrary, to interrupt it: not only the action of others, but also the action of one's own. It is the retarding quality of these interruptions and the episodic quality of this framing of action which allows gestural theatre to become epic theatre.

The job of epic theatre, it has been explained, is not so much to develop actions as to represent conditions. Most of the slogans of the dramaturgy of epic theatre have been ignored but this one has, at least, created a misunderstanding. Reason enough to take it up. Those 'conditions' which had to be represented were thought to be the equivalent of the 'milieu', or social setting, of earlier theoreticians. Thus understood, the demand meant no more than a plea for a return to naturalistic drama. Yet no one can be naive enough to champion such a return. The naturalistic stage is in no sense a public platform; it is entirely illusionistic. Its own awareness that it is theatre cannot fertilize it; like every theatre of unfolding action, it must repress this awareness so as to pursue undistracted its aim of portraying the real. Epic theatre, by contrast, incessantly derives a lively and productive consciousness from the fact that it is theatre. This consciousness enables it to treat elements of reality as though it were setting up an experiment, with the 'conditions' at the end of the experiment, not at the beginning. Thus they are not brought closer to the spectator but distanced from him. When he recognizes them as real conditions it is not, as in naturalistic theatre, with complacency, but with astonishment. This astonishment is the means whereby epic theatre, in a hard, pure way, revives a Socratic praxis. In one who is astonished, interest is born: interest in its primordial form. Nothing is more characteristic of Brecht's way of thinking than the attempt which epic theatres makes to transform this primordial interest directly into a technical, expert one. Epic theatre addresses itself to interested persons 'who do not think unless they have a reason to'. But that is an attitude absolutely shared by the masses. Brecht's dialectical materialism asserts itself unmistakably in his endeavour to interest the masses in theatre as technical experts, but not at all by way of 'culture'. 'In this way we could very soon have a theatre full of experts, as we have sports stadiums full of experts.'

Epic theatre, then, does not reproduce conditions but, rather, reveals them. This uncovering of conditions is brought about through processes being interrupted. A very crude example: a family row. The mother is just about to pick up a pillow to hurl at the daughter, the father is opening a window to call a policeman. At this moment a stranger appears at the door. 'Tableau', as they used to say around 1900. In other words: the stranger is suddenly confronted with certain conditions: rumpled bedclothes, open window, a devastated interior. But there exists a view in which even the more usual scenes of bourgeois life appear rather like this. The more far-reaching the devastations of our social order (the more these devastations undermine ourselves and our capacity to remain aware of them), the more marked must be the distance between the stranger and the events portrayed. We know such a stranger from Brecht's *Versuche*: a Swabian 'Utis', a counterpart of Ulysses, the Greek 'Nobody' who visits one-eyed Polyphemus in his cave. Similarly Keuner – that is the stranger's name – penetrates into the cave of the one-eyed monster whose name is 'class society'. Like Ulysses he is full of guile, accustomed to suffering, much-travelled; both men are wise. A practical resignation which has always shunned utopian idealism makes Ulysses think only of returning home; Keuner never leaves the threshold of his house at all. He likes the trees which he sees in the yard when he comes out of his fourth-floor tenement flat. 'Why don't you ever go into the woods,' ask his friends, 'if you like trees so much?' 'Did I not tell you,' replies Herr Keuner, 'that I like the trees in my yard?' To move this thinking man, Herr Keuner (who, Brecht once suggested, should be carried on stage lying down, so little is he drawn thither), to move him to existence upon the stage – that is the aim of this new theatre. It will be noticed, not without surprise, that its origins reach back a very long time. For the fact is that ever since the Greeks, the search for the untragic hero on the European stage has never ceased. Despite all the classical revivals, the great dramatists have always kept as far away as possible from the authentic Greek figure of tragedy. This is not the place to trace the path which winds through the Middle Ages, in Hroswitha and the mystery plays, or later, in Gryphius, Lenz and Grabbe, or to show how Goethe crossed it in the second *Faust*. But we may say that this path was a specially German one. If, that is, one can speak of a path at all, rather than an overgrown stalking-track along which the legacy of medieval and baroque drama has crept down to us over the sublime but barren massif of classicism. This track reappears today, rough and untended as it may be, in the plays of Brecht. The untragic hero is part of this German tradition. That his paradoxical stage existence has to be redeemed by our own actual one was recognized at an early date; not, of course, by the critics, but by the best contemporary thinkers such as Georg Lukăcs and Franz Rosenzweig. Plato, Lukăcs wrote twenty years ago, already recognized the undramatic nature of the highest form of man, the sage. And yet in his dialogues he brought him to the threshold of the stage. One may regard epic theatre as more dramatic than the dialogue (it is not always): but epic theatre need not, for that reason, be any the less philosophical.

The forms of epic theatre correspond to the new technical forms – cinema and radio. Epic theatre corresponds to the modern level of technology. In film, the theory has become more and more accepted that the audience should be able to 'come in' at any point, that complicated plot developments should be avoided and that each part, besides the value it has for the whole, should also possess its own episodic value. For radio, with its public which can freely switch on or off at any moment, this becomes a strict necessity. Epic theatre introduces the same practice on the stage. For epic theatre, as a matter of principle, there is no such thing as a latecomer. The implications of this suggest that epic theatre's challenge to the theatre as a social institution is far more serious than any damage it may inflict on the theatre as entertainment industry. Whereas, in cabaret, the bourgeoisie mingle with bohemia and, in variety, the gap between petty and big bourgeoisie is bridged for the space of an evening, the habitués of Brecht's theatre, where cigarette smoke is caught in the projector beam, are proletarians. For them there is nothing strange about Brecht's instruction to an actor to play the choosing of a wooden leg by the beggar in *The Threepenny Opera* in such a way that 'just for the sake of seeing this particular turn people will plan to revisit the show at the precise moment it occurs'. Neher's back-projections for such 'turns' are far more like posters than stage decorations. The poster is a constituent element of 'literarized' theatre. 'Literarizing entails punctuating "representation" with "formulation"; gives the theatre the possibility of making contact with other institutions for intellectual activities.' These institutions (media) even include books. 'Footnotes, and the habit of turning back in order to check a point, need to be introduced into playwriting too.'

But what is it that Neher's posters advertise? Brecht writes that they 'adopt an attitude towards events in such a way that the real glutton in Mahagonny sits in front of the depicted glutton'. Very well. Who can say that the acted glutton is more real than the depicted one? We can make the acted one sit in front of the more real one, i.e. we can let the depicted one at the back be more real than the acted one. Perhaps it is only now that we obtain a clue to the powerful and curious effect of scenes staged in this way. Some of the players appear as mandatories of the larger forces which, remaining in the background, are like Plato's Ideas in that they constitute the ideal model of things. Neher's back-projections, however, are materialist ideas; they relate to genuine 'conditions'; even when they approximate to actual events, the tremulousness of their contours still suggests the far greater and more intimate proximity from which they have been wrenched in order to become visible.

The literarization of theatre by means of verbal formulas, posters, captions, is intended to, and will, 'make what is shown on the stage unsensational'. (Brecht is fully aware of the connections between these methods and certain practices of Chinese theatre, a connection which we will examine at some future date.) Brecht goes still further in the same direction by asking himself whether the events portrayed by the epic actor ought not to be known in advance. 'In that case historical events would, on the face of it, be the most suitable.' One must, however, expect the dramatist to take a certain amount of licence in that he will tend to emphasize not the great decisions which lie along the main line of history but the incommensurable and the singular. 'It can happen this way, but it can also happen quite a different way' – that is the fundamental attitude of one who writes for epic theatre. His relation to his story is like that of a ballet teacher to his pupil. His first aim is to loosen her joints to the very limits of the possible...

Brecht lets the conditions speak for themselves, so that they confront each other dialectically. Their various elements are played off logically against one another. The docker Galy Gay in Brecht's *A Man's a Man* is like an empty stage on which the contradictions of our society are acted out. Following Brecht's line of thought one might arrive at the proposition that it is the wise man who is the perfect stage for such a dialectic. In any case Galy Gay is a wise man. He introduces himself as a docker 'who doesn't drink, smokes very little and hasn't any passions to speak of'. He is not tempted by the offer of sex with the widow whose basket he has carried. 'To be frank, I'd really like to buy some fish.' Yet he is introduced as a man 'who can't say no'. And this too is wise, for he lets the contradictions of existence enter into the only place where they can, in the last analysis, be resolved: the life of a man. Only the 'consenting' man has any chance of changing the world.

And so it happens that the wise proletarian Galy Gay, the man who keeps himself to himself, agrees to join the berserk ranks of the British colonial army, thereby consenting to the denial of his own wisdom. A moment ago he went out of his front door, sent by his wife on an errand to buy some fish. Now he meets three soldiers of the Anglo-Indian army who have lost a fourth while looting a pagoda. The three of them have their own reasons for finding a replacement for the missing man as soon as possible. Galy Gay is the man who can't say no. He follows the three soldiers without knowing what is in store for him. One by one he adopts thoughts, attitudes, habits such as a soldier in war must possess; when he is completely re-equipped, he won't even recognize his own wife when she eventually succeeds in tracking him down. Finally he becomes the much-feared conqueror of the Tibetan mountain stronghold of So al Dohowr. A man's a man, so a docker is a mercenary. He will treat his self-condition as mercenary no differently from the way he treated his dockerhood. A man's a man: this is not fidelity to any single essence of one's own, but a continual readiness to admit a new essence.

> Never give your exact name, what's the point?
> When you name yourself you always name another.
> Don't be so loud in stating your opinion. Forget it.
> What was it again, the opinion you held?
> Do not remember things for longer than they last.

Epic theatre casts doubt upon the notion that theatre is entertainment. It shakes the social validity of theatre-as-entertainment by robbing it of its function within the capitalist system. It also threatens the privileges of the critics. These privileges are based on the technical expertise which enables the critic to make certain observations about productions and performances. The criteria he applies in making his observations are only very rarely within his own control; he seldom worries about this, but relies upon 'theatre aesthetics' in the details of which nobody is particularly interested. If, however, the aesthetic of the theatre ceases to remain in the background, if its forum is the audience and its criterion is no longer the effect registered by the nervous systems of single individuals but the degree to which the mass of spectators becomes a coherent whole, then the critic as he is constituted today is no longer ahead of that mass but actually finds himself far behind it. The moment when the mass begins to differentiate itself in discussion and responsible decisions, or in attempts to discover well-founded attitudes of its own, the moment the false and deceptive totality called 'audience' begins to distintegrate and there is new space for the formation of separate parties within it – separate parties corresponding to conditions as they really are – at that moment the critic suffers the double misfortune of seeing his nature as agent revealed and, at the same time, devalued. Simply by the fact of appealing to an 'audience' – which continues to exist in its old, opaque form only for the theatre, but characteristically, no longer for film – the critic becomes, whether he means to or not, the advocate of what the ancients used to call 'theatrocratia': the use of theatre to dominate the masses by manipulating their reflexes and sensations – the exact opposite of responsible collectives freely choosing their positions. The 'innovations' which such audiences will demand are exclusively concened with what is realizable within existing society, and are thus the opposite of 'renovations'. Epic theatre attacks the basic view that art may do no more than lightly touch upon experience – the view which grants only to kitsch the right to encompass the whole range of experience, and then only for the lower classes of society. This attack upon the basis is at the same time an assault upon the critics' privileges. And this the critics have sensed; in the debate over epic theatre they must be considered an interested party...

The author, when discussing what distinguishes the epic theatre from the ordinary theatre of entertainment as a more serious art form, is right to point out: 'When we call the other theatre, the one that is hostile to us, merely culinary we create the impression that in our theatre we are against all fun, as though we could not imagine learning or being taught other than as an intensely unpleasurable process. One is often obliged to weaken one's own position in order to fight an opponent, and to rob one's cause of its breadth and validity for the sake of immediate advantage. Thus reduced purely to fighting form, the cause may win, but it cannot replace what it has defeated. Yet the act of recognizing of which we speak is itself a pleasurable act. The simple fact that man can be recognized in a certain way creates a sense of triumph, and the fact, too, that he can never be recognized completely, never once and for all, that he is not so easily exhaustible, that he holds and conceals so many possibilities within himself (hence his capacity for development), is a pleasurable recognition. That man can be changed by his surroundings and can himself change the surrounding world, i.e. can treat it with consequence, all this produces feelings of pleasure. Not, of course, if man is viewed as something mechanical, something that can be put into a slot, something lacking resistance, as happens today under the weight of certain social conditions. Astonishment, which must here be inserted into the Aristotelian formula for the effects of tragedy, should be considered entirely as a capacity. It can be learned.'

The death of the author

Roland Barthes (1915–80)

Roland Barthes is arguably the most influential of structuralist critics and he made many striking contributions to structuralist method. In Barthes we find a fully worked-out grammar of the narrative (see Reading 30, 'Introduction to the structural analysis of narratives'), a comprehensive theory of how literary codes operate within narrative (S/Z, published in 1973), as well as a key distinction he made between 'writerly' and 'readerly' texts (also S/Z). Readerly texts are held to impose the author's intended meaning on the reader, whose role in the process is thus an essentially passive one, whereas writerly texts are seen to be more open-ended and to allow greater scope for the reader to make up her own mind as to their meaning. Nineteenth-century realism would generally be describable as readerly, and formally experimental texts as writerly, although the distinction is by no means an obvious one to make. Barthes lays great stress on the active role of the reader, doing so at the expense of the authority traditionally associated with the author, whose social importance is accordingly downgraded. In the next extract Barthes puts forward the controversial doctrine of 'the death of the author', arguing that the author can no longer be regarded as an authority-figure or source of moral guidance. Texts take on a life of their own under these circumstances, with the author's social role being marginalized.

In his story *Sarrasine* Balzac, describing a castrato disguised as a woman, writes the following sentence: '*This was woman herself, with her sudden fears, her irrational whims, her instinctive worries, her impetuous boldness, her fussings, and her delicious sensibility.*' Who is speaking thus? Is it the hero of the story bent on remaining ignorant of the castrato hidden beneath the woman? Is it Balzac the individual, furnished by his personal experience with a philosophy of Woman? Is it Balzac the author professing 'literary' ideas on femininity? Is it universal wisdom? Romantic psychology? We shall never know, for the good reason that writing is the destruction of every voice, of every point of origin. Writing is that neutral, composite, oblique space where our subject slips away, the negative where all identity is lost, starting with the very identity of the body writing.

No doubt it has always been that way. As soon as a fact is *narrated* no longer with a view to acting directly on reality but intransitively, that is to say, finally outside of any function other than that of the very practice of the symbol itself, this disconnection occurs, the voice loses its origin, the author enters into his own death, writing begins. The sense of this phenomenon, however, has varied; in ethnographic societies the responsibility for a narrative is never assumed by a person but by a mediator, shaman or relator whose 'performance' – the mastery of the narrative code – may possibly be admired but never his 'genius'. The author is a modern figure, a product of our society insofar as, emerging from the Middle Ages with English empiricism, French rationalism and the personal faith of the Reformation, it discovered the prestige of the individual, of, as it is more nobly put, the 'human person'. It is thus logical that in literature it should be this positivism, the epitome and culmination of capitalist ideology, which has attached the greatest importance to the 'person' of the author. The *author* still reigns in histories of literature, biographies of writers, interviews, magazines, as in the very consciousness of men of letters anxious to unite their person and their work through diaries and memoirs. The image of literature to be found in ordinary culture is tyrannically centred on the author, his person, his life, his tastes, his passions, while criticism still consists for the most part in saying that Baudelaire's work is the failure of Baudelaire the man, Van Gogh's his madness, Tchaikovsky's his vice. The *explanation* of a work is always sought in the man or woman who produced it, as if it were always in the end, through the more or less transparent allegory of the fiction, the voice of a single person, the *author* 'confiding' in us.

Though the sway of the Author remains powerful (the new criticism has often done no more than consolidate it), it goes without saying that certain writers have long since attempted to loosen it. In France, Mallarmé was doubtless the first to see and to foresee in its full extent the necessity to substitute language itself for the person who until then had been supposed to be its owner. For him, for us too, it is language which speaks, not the author; to write is, through a prerequisite impersonality (not at all to be confused with the castrating objectivity of the realist novelist), to reach that point where only language acts, 'performs', and not 'me'. Mallarmé's entire poetics consists in suppressing the author in the interests of writing (which is, as will be seen, to restore the place of the reader). Valéry, encumbered by a psychology of the Ego, considerably diluted Mallarmé's theory but, his taste for classicism leading him to turn to the lessons of rhetoric, he never stopped calling into question and deriding the Author; he stressed the linguistic and, as it were, 'hazardous' nature of his activity, and throughout his prose works he militated in favour of the essentially verbal condition of literature, in the face of which all recourse to the writer's interiority seemed to him pure superstition. Proust himself, despite the apparently psychological character of what are called his *analyses*, was visibly concerned with the task of inexorably blurring, by an extreme subtilization, the relation between the writer and his characters; by making of the narrator not he who has seen and felt nor even he who is writing, but he who is *going to write* (the young man in the novel – but, in fact, how old is he and who is he? – wants to write but cannot; the novel ends when writing at last becomes possible), Proust gave modern writing its epic. By a radical reversal, instead of putting his life into his novel, as is so often maintained, he made of his very life a work for which his own book was the model; so that it is clear to us that Charlus does not imitate Montesquiou but that Montesquiou – in his anecdotal, historical reality – is no more than a secondary fragment, derived from Charlus. Lastly, to go no further than this prehistory of modernity, Surrealism, though unable to accord language a supreme place (language being system and the aim of the movement being, romantically, a direct subversion of codes – itself moreover illusory: a code cannot be destroyed, only 'played off'), contributed to the desacrilization of the image of the Author by ceaselessly recommending the abrupt disappointment of expectations of meaning (the famous surrealist 'jolt'), by entrusting the hand with the task of writing as quickly as possible what the head itself is unaware of (automatic writing), by accepting the principle and the experience of several people writing together. Leaving aside literature itself (such distinctions really becoming invalid), linguistics has recently provided the destruction of the Author with a valuable analytical tool by showing that the whole of the enunciation is an empty process, functioning perfectly without there being any need for it to be filled with the person of the interlocutors. Linguistically, the author is never more than the instance writing, just as *I* is nothing other than the instance saying *I*: language knows a 'subject', not a 'person', and this subject, empty outside of the very enunciation which defines it, suffices to make language 'hold together', suffices, that is to say, to exhaust it.

The removal of the Author (one could talk here with Brecht of a veritable 'distancing', the Author diminishing like a figurine at the far end of the literary stage) is not merely an historical fact or an act of writing; it utterly transforms the modern text (or – which is the same thing – the text is henceforth made and read in such a way that at all its levels the author is absent). The temporality is different. The Author, when believed in, is always conceived of as the past of his own book: book and author stand automatically on a single line divided into a *before* and an *after*. The Author is thought to *nourish* the book, which is to say that he exists before it, thinks, suffers, lives for it, is in the same relation of antecedence to his work as a father to his child. In complete contrast, the modern scriptor is born simultaneously with the text, is in no way equipped with a being preceding or exceeding the writing, is not the subject with the book as predicate; there is no other time than that of the enunciation and every text is eternally written *here and now*. The fact is (or, it follows) that *writing* can no longer designate an operation of recording, notation, representation, 'depiction' (as the Classics would say); rather, it designates exactly what linguists, referring to Oxford philosophy, call a performative, a rare verbal form (exclusively given in the first person and in the present tense) in which the enunciation has no other content (contains no other proposition) than the act by which it is uttered – something like the *I declare* of kings or the *I sing* of very ancient poets. Having buried the Author, the modern scriptor can thus no longer believe, as according to the pathetic view of his predecessors, that this hand is too slow for his thought or passion and that consequently, making a law of necessity, he must emphasize this delay and indefinitely 'polish' his form. For him, on the contrary, the hand, cut off from any voice, borne by a pure gesture of inscription (and not of expression), traces a field without origin – or which, at least, has no other origin than language itself, language which ceaselessly calls into question all origins.

We know now that a text is not a line of words releasing a single 'theological' meaning (the 'message' of the Author-God) but a multi-dimensional space in which a variety of writings, none of them original, blend and clash. The text is a tissue of quotations drawn from the innumerable centres of culture...

Once the Author is removed, the claim to decipher a text becomes quite futile. To give a text an Author is to impose a limit on that text, to furnish it with a final signified, to close the writing. Such a conception suits criticism very well, the latter then allotting itself the important task of discovering the Author (or its hypostases: society, history, psyché, liberty) beneath the work: when the Author has been found, the text is 'explained' – victory to the critic. Hence there is no surprise in the fact that, historically, the reign of the Author has also been that of the Critic, nor again in the fact that criticism (be it new) is today undermined along with the Author. In the multiplicity of writing, everything is to be *disentangled*, nothing *deciphered*; the structure can be followed, 'run' (like the thread of a stocking) at every point and at every level, but there is nothing beneath: the space of writing is to be ranged over, not pierced; writing ceaselessly posits meaning ceaselessly to evaporate it, carrying out a systematic exemption of meaning. In precisely this way literature (it would be better from now on to say *writing*), by refusing to assign a 'secret', an ultimate meaning, to the text (and to the world as text), liberates what may be called an anti-theological activity, an activity that is truly revolutionary since to refuse to fix meaning is, in the end, to refuse God and his hypostases – reason, science, law...

Thus is revealed the total existence of writing: a text is made of multiple writings, drawn from many cultures and entering into mutual relations of dialogue, parody, contestation, but there is one place where this multiplicity is focused and that place is the reader, not, as was hitherto said, the author. The reader is the space on which all the quotations that make up a writing are inscribed without any of them being lost; a text's unity lies not in its origin but in its destination. Yet this destination cannot any longer be personal: the reader is without history, biography, psychology; he is simply that *someone* who holds together in a single field all the traces by which the written text is constituted. Which is why it is derisory to condemn the new writing in the name of a humanism hypocritically turned champion of the reader's rights. Classic criticism has never paid any attention to the reader; for it, the writer is the only person in literature. We are now beginning to let ourselves be fooled no longer by the arrogant antiphrastical recriminations of good society in favour of the very thing it sets aside, ignores, smothers, or destroys; we know that to give writing its future, it is necessary to overthrow the myth: the birth of the reader must be at the cost of the death of the Author.

Obscenity and film censorship

Bernard Williams (b. 1929)

Plato and some Marxist theorists have argued for censorship of the arts on political grounds, but many arguments have also been put forward for censorship in defence of public morality. The prosecution of D. H. Lawrence's novel Lady Chatterley's Lover *under the Obscene Publications Act in 1960 is a famous test case in this regard. The relation of pornography and obscenity to art was considered in detail by the Committee on Obscenity and Film Censorship, chaired by the philosopher Bernard Williams, whose report was published in 1979. We reprint here a chapter from Bernard Williams's abridgement of the Report, which poses such questions as whether a work of art can be pornographic or obscene. The Committee's conclusion, as reported by Williams, is that there is no intrinsic reason why pornographic or obscene works should not also be capable of having artistic merit, but the difficulties of defending this position from any prosecution on the basis of the Obscene Publications Act are outlined. There are important issues regarding freedom of expression here: should the artist consider herself beyond questions of morality? Or does society have the right to demand that the artist not offend public decency? The feminist campaign against pornography in recent years has given this debate a new sense of urgency, although there is by no means general agreement yet as to what constitutes pornography or how its effect on behaviour can be determined.*

Chapter Eight   Pornography, obscenity and art

8.1   In the course of Chapter 7 [not reprinted here], we have referred almost all our discussion to *pornography*, rather than to *obscenity*. This emphasis was deliberate. 'Obscene', we shall suggest in this chapter, is a term which itself expresses the kinds of reactions we were discussing in Chapter 7, rather than telling one what kind of thing actually arouses those reactions. 'Pornography', on the other hand, we take to be a rather more objective expression referring to a certain kind of writing, picture etc. We have suggested that pornography does tend by its nature to be found offensive; and most of the publications and pictures which people find offensive are indeed pornographic. But we shall need to consider a little more precisely what pornography and obscenity are, in order to discuss an important question, the relations of pornography and obscenity to art. There is more than one reason why we thought that we should discuss this question. It has repeatedly surfaced in the history of this subject; it has constantly recurred, not surprisingly, in our own discussions; and it has been raised in various forms by many witnesses, some of whom were as certain that there could not possibly be an obscene work of art as others were that there could. The issues here are, moreover, deeply involved in both the theory and the practical use of the 'public good defence' under section 4 of the Obscene Publications Act 1959. The discussion in this chapter directly bears on our recommendations and has, we believe, important consequences for legislation on these subjects. We have not been convinced that it is impossible for any porno-graphic or obscene work to have artistic merit, and we shall try to explain why we have not. At the same time, we are convinced, for reasons that we shall give, that a public good defence with respect to artistic merit is inevitably unworkable. Any proposals for legislation must, we believe, accommodate both these conclusions.

PORNOGRAPHY

8.2 The term 'pornography' always refers to a book, verse, painting, photograph, film, or some such thing – what in general may be called a *representation*. Even if it is associated with sex or cruelty, an object which is not a representation – exotic underwear, for example – cannot sensibly be said to be pornographic (though it could possibly be said to be obscene). We take it that, as almost everyone understands the term, a pornographic representation is one that combines two features: it has a certain function or intention, to arouse its audience sexually, and also a certain content, explicit representations of sexual material (organs, postures, activity, etc.). A work has to have both this function and this content to be a piece of pornography.

8.3   It is useful to distinguish works that extend over time (novels, films) from those that do not (paintings, photographs: series of pictures are obviously an intermediate case). The former offer the possibility that they may have some sections that are pornographic and others that are not, leaving room for borderline questions about whether the work as a whole is pornographic. Some such questions are unanswerable. However, it has proved to be the case up to now that there has been a demand for works which maximise pornographic content, so there is, in both the novel and the film, a definite *genre* of the pornographic work, which consists almost exclusively of pornographic representations of sexual activity, often complex. There is virtually no plot, no characters, no motivation except relating to sexual activity, and only a shadowy background, which may involve a standard apparatus of a remote and luxurious *château*, numerous silent servants, and so forth. This is the 'ideal type' of a pornographic work evoked by Steven Marcus[1].

'OBSCENE' AND 'EROTIC'

8.4   We suspect that the word 'obscene' may now be worn out, and past any useful employment at all. It is certainly too exhausted to do any more work in the courts. However, leaving aside the peculiar legal *deprave and corrupt* definition we have considered in earlier chapters, it seems to us that, insofar as it is not just used as a term of abuse, it principally expresses an intense or extreme version of what we have called 'offensiveness'. It may be that it particularly emphasises the most strongly aversive element in that notion, the idea of an object's being repulsive or disgusting: that certainly seems to be the point when a person or animal is said to be, for instance, 'obscenely' ugly or fat.

8.5   The term 'erotic' sometimes seems to be used just as an alternative to 'pornographic', being milder with regard to both the content and the intention: the content is by this interpretation more allusive and less explicit, and what is intended is not strong sexual arousal but some lighter degree of sexual interest. There is another interpretation[2] of the term, however, perhaps more accurate and certainly more interesting, under which the erotic is what *expresses* sexual excitement, rather than causes it – in the same way as a painting or a piece of music may express sadness without necessarily making its audience sad. Theorists have not found the notion of expression at all easy to explain, but a work which expresses a given feeling can at least be said to 'fit' the feeling or to 'match' it, and, in virtue of doing that, to put one in mind of the feeling. In this sense an erotic work will suggest or bring to mind feelings of sexual attraction or excitement. It may cause some such feelings as well, and put the audience actually into that state, but if so that is a further effect. This difference comes out rather clearly in the case of romantic love. Many erotic works – and of course many works that are not erotic – express the feelings of romantic love, and invoke images of them in their audience, but the state they bring about in their audience is very rarely that of being in love. On this kind of account of the erotic, it will follow that what is represented in an erotic work of art need not be a mild version of the pornographic at all. There are countless erotic works of art, many of which have no explicit sexual content of any kind.

8.6   As we understand these various notions, pornography, obscenity and eroticism will be related in the following ways. Pornography will have some tendency to be obscene, but will not necessarily be so. We claimed in Chapter 7 that a tendency to be offensive is built into it, but it is not universally even offensive – it may have some other merit which cancels that effect. Still less must it inevitably be very strongly offensive or obscene. On the other hand, there will be obscene things which are not pornographic (e.g. it would be obscene to exhibit deformed people at a funfair, but that would not be a pornographic exhibition). Some pornography is erotic, but it is not altogether easy for it to be so: the explicit content and the intention of arousal tend to work against the expressive effect of eroticism rather than with it. Many things, certainly, will be erotic without being pornographic. The most unlikely combination, on the present account, is that of the erotic and the obscene. Since the erotic is intended to attract and hold the attention by being, in the sexual dimension, pleasant or delightful, it is hard to see how this could be combined with the object being found at the same time disgusting and repulsive. The idea is so difficult, that this combination might be said to be impossible, except that human reactions in these areas are so complex that we hesitate to say that anything is impossible.

8.7   Some people may find it paradoxical to say that it is hard, if not impossible, for something to be both erotic and obscene. Several of our witnesses have certainly found it natural to say of many publications or films that they were both. We do not deny that these words, and the word 'pornography', are often used with meanings which are more general and overlapping than those that we have just proposed. We claim only that there are significant and useful distinctions to be made here, and these words can helpfully be used, in the ways we suggest, to mark those distinctions. One body which submitted evidence to us, the Board for Social Responsibility of the Church of England, made some careful suggestions for distinguishing between these terms, and we found these helpful, even though the account we have given of the matter is not exactly the same as theirs.

ART

8.8   We have already assumed that there can be an *erotic* work of art, and we take it that few would disagree with this. The questions now are: Can there be a work of art which is pornographic? Can there be one which is obscene? As we have already explained, these are for us two different questions. We take first the question about pornography.

8.9   As we said in an earlier chapter, it is incontestable that almost all the pornography sold across (or under) the counter, or seen in the cinema, is from any artistic point of view totally worthless. However, there is more than one possible explanation of that fact. The interesting question, which we shall be concerned with, is whether it just follows from the nature of pornography that it is bound to be worthless. If it does not just follow, then other and more circumstantial explanations may be considered (though we shall not consider them here): as that it is simply not worth anyone's while, at least in the modern world, to make pornography more artistically interesting than it is.

8.10   Several arguments have been put to us, or have been implicit in evidence we have received, to the effect that pornography cannot possibly have any artistic value. The most general argument to this effect is probably that which has been expressed by Steven Marcus in saying 'literature possesses a multitude of intentions, but pornography possesses only one.'[3] A related consideration is that the 'one intention' of pornography – sexual arousal – is achieved through a blankly explicit, unmediated content. Marcus' point is made with respect to literature, but if it is valid it can be applied just as well to the visual arts. It will be claimed that pornography is by its nature purely instrumental, a crude device for achieving a particular effect, and has nothing to do with the complex concerns and intentions which properly belong to a work of art.

8.11   However, it is not clear why it should be impossible to combine other aims with the 'one intention' of pornography. In the case of the visual arts, there do exist some works which are indisputably pornographic in content and intention, but which are thought to succeed in realising other, artistic, concerns. There are many pornographic Japanese prints of the 18th century, works of the admired master Utamaro and others, which are regarded by critics as brilliant achievements. It can be reasonably claimed, moreover, that they are not merely of artistic interest despite being pornographic, but that their sexual intention is integrally bound up with their merits as expressive designs. Many great Western artists have of course produced pornographic works 'on the side', to make money or for diversion, and some of these works no doubt have merit; the peculiarity of the Japanese case is that there was a tradition of very considerable artists applying their talents to this *genre*. Of course – to repeat ourselves – there is no suggestion that the existence of these exotic works somehow sheds artistic respectability on the vast range of current pornographic material. What they do prove, however, if their merits are agreed, is that it is not the simple fact that it is pornographic that makes all that material artistically worthless.

8.12   In the case of works which are extended in time, such as the novel and the film, more specific arguments are advanced to suggest that if they are pornographic, they must be no good. Their participants are not characters, but mere locations of sexual possibilities; there is no plot, no development, no beginning, middle or end (a point made by the critic Adorno). Moreover, since there are no characters or genuine human presence, the whole effect is dehumanizing – destructive of any sense of personal individuality or life. These descriptions are obviously correct. It is perhaps worth adding that we do not entirely agree with those who in evidence to us or elsewhere have expressed this sort of idea by saying that the effect of pornography is to reduce everything to the *physical*. Among the various kinds of human presence which are lacking from literary pornography is, usually, any real sense of the human body. Because pornography ministers to fantasies of boundless sexual satisfaction, everything is weightless, untiring, effortlessly restored. The attempt to accommodate the same fantasies with photographs of actual people with actual bodies is partly what makes so many pornographic photographs and films grotesque.

8.13   These descriptions apply more strongly, of course, the closer the fiction in question gets to the schema of the unrelievedly pornographic work. But obviously they would not apply unqualifiedly to a work which had only some pornographic sections along with other matter, even if those sections were integral to the work. Moreover, even works which are totally pornographic can occasionally break away from the 'ideal type', and one or two writers have experimented with introducing psychological elements into the *genre*. Claims have been made by serious critics for the artistic merits of certain pornographic literary works (we have heard of none, as yet, with respect to thoroughly pornographic films). The arguments from the character of pornography do seem to suggest that concentratedly pornographic novels are going to be interesting pieces of literature only in rare cases, and then on a minor scale; but it does not seem to be impossible, even in the extreme case, and it would certainly be rash to claim on general grounds that any use of pornographic elements even in the context of other material must make a work worthless.

8.14 The arguments of the last four paragraphs have been concerned with questions of the intention and the structure of pornographic works. What has not yet been mentioned in this connection is their tendency to be offensive or obscene – in our present sense, that is to say, intensely or repellently offensive. This tendency raises a question about artistic value: can a work have any artistic interest and in that way command the attention of a reader or spectator, if it is at the same time found offensive? The question gets more pressing, the more insistent the offensiveness of the work. There may indeed be some pornographic works of artistic merit which do not even raise the question; these will be works in which the sexual content should not reasonably be regarded as offensive at all, and the merits of the work themselves contribute to cancelling the aspects of intrusion or violation that make other pornographic works offensive. The Japanese works already mentioned, and some Indian erotic sculptures, might be examples. Artistic merit can itself, in a case of this kind, contribute to the judgement whether a work is even offensive. There is another kind of work which may be experienced as offensive, and also be experienced as having aesthetic interest, but in the case of which these two experiences do not occur at the same time. These will be works which are found offensive at first, or by a spectator who remains distanced from them, but which lose that character for someone involved in them. The question of how one can combine at the same time aesthetic interest in the work and a sense that it is offensive will not then arise, though these works will still be 'offensive works', in the sense of works which could prove offensive to a casual viewer or to someone who came across them and was unwilling or unable to involve himself in them.

8.15 Thus there can be pornographic works of merit which are not reasonably regarded as offensive; and there can be initially offensive works which can, once the offensiveness is past, display their merits. But it would be unwise to deny that, beyond all this, there could be works which were, and remained, offensive, indeed intensely offensive or obscene, and yet possessed real merits. Experience of those merits, in such a case, would surely have to involve the fact of their obscenity, and not just co-exist with it; the repulsiveness would have to be an integral part of what was being displayed by the artist. Where the work is itself pornographic, the repulsiveness will not just be forgotten in sexual arousal, but will be part of it. Some critics have claimed that certain pieces of French literary pornography, notably by Georges Bataille, are significant works of this extreme kind.

8.16   An extraordinary work which illustrates, in a unique way, some of the complexities involved here is Pasolini's last film *Salò*. This film came repeatedly into our discussions, both because of its nature, and also because it was, during our enquiries, the subject of legal action. Having been refused a certificate by the British Board of Film Censors, it was shown in a London club but was quickly seized by the police, and those who had shown it indicted. While they were awaiting trial, the Criminal Law Act 1977 came into force, which changed the law applying to the cinema from the test of indecency to the *deprave and corrupt* test. Because of this, the Director of Public Prosecutions withdrew the proceedings, but took the unusual step of announcing that anyone who subsequently showed the film would be prosecuted. It has however recently been shown, though in a cut version. It has appeared in most other European countries.

8.17   The film displays scenes of extraordinary cruelty and repulsiveness, supposedly happening under the short-lived Fascist republic set up at Salò in 1944. It has the ritual form of a pornographic work – indeed, it is specifically modelled on Sade's *120 Days of Sodom*. All of us agreed that it is obscene, in the sense that it is ruthlessly and almost unwatchably repellent. On its other qualities, and its merits, we found ourselves in great disagreement. Most of us felt that it was manifestly not designed to produce sexual excitement, and that it took great care not to do so, even incidentally; on this view of it, the work, though obscene, is not pornographic, despite its form. Some of us, however, were more suspicious of its intentions. Those who were most impressed by it thought that it presented an extraordinary metaphor of political power and was a remarkable work, perhaps a masterpiece. For anyone with that opinion of it, it is a work that combines artistic control and seriousness with a deep and sustained obscenity.

8.18   Our conclusion is that there is no intrinsic reason why pornography or even obscene works should not be capable of having artistic merit, though there are undoubtedly reasons in the nature of such works, and even more in the general conditions of their production, to make that an unlikely and marginal occurrence, and the works, even when successful, generally of minor stature.

THE PUBLIC GOOD DEFENCE

8.19 The conclusion that a work can be pornographic or even obscene and still be of artistic merit is one that of course agrees verbally with the assumptions of the Obscene Publications Acts which, as we have explained in Chapter 2, allow for the possibility that a work might be obscene and yet it be for the public good that it be published on account of its literary or artistic merit. But the agreement is only verbal, since the Obscene Publications Acts of course adopt the definition of obscenity in terms of the tendency to deprave and corrupt, rather than a notion of extreme offensiveness. Moreover, the merits of the work which would allow it to be acquitted of an offence, even though obscene, are themselves implicitly expressed in causal terms, to match the causal nature of the *deprave and corrupt* test. The work's tendency, as obscene, to produce bad effects has to be weighed against its tendency, as having artistic merit, to produce good effects, and the jury is expected to weigh one of these causal properties against the other. But if there is a difficulty, on the side of 'obscenity', in ascribing harmful effects to a specific book (we shall take for the present discussion just the case of books), there is at least as much difficulty in ascribing good effects with respect to literary merit, and the task of showing why it was 'for the public good' that some particular book, with its particular literary merits, should be published, is one that might understandably have baffled the expert witnesses who were called under this section.

8.20 We emphatically reject a view which a few witnesses put to us, that books have no good or bad effects at all. Quite certainly books have all sorts of effects, and in particular it is a reasonable assumption of much education that good books – for instance, masterpieces of imaginative literature – tend to have a certain kind of good effect, such as deepening a reader's understanding of human life: though one should not suppose that they are the only effects those books can have, nor that their merit is just to be calculated in terms of such effects. It has been said to us as an argument for the suppression of pornography: 'If good books have good effects, then bad books must have bad effects'. First, it must be said, this does not even follow: if good books have good effects it may be that all that bad books do is fail to have good effects. This is not a purely formal or verbal point. In the sense in which great works can draw the reader to new possibilities, and extend his grasp, bad works may merely do nothing – they are inert, acquiescent, leave the reader as he was. Apart from this point, however, and indeed granting that bad books can have bad effects, the relevant contrast with good books does not of course lie in 'bad books' in the sense of pornographic or obscene books – it lies rather in books which are 'bad' because they fail to be works of creative literature, for instance because they are unoriginal and shallow and possibly, one may add, complacent or evasive as well, projecting some delusive image of life. There is room for much disagreement about the kinds of harms that might be ascribed to different kinds of bad literature, but if harm is done by bad fiction, there is certainly no reason to think that it is peculiarly done by obscene fiction, rather than by books that are bad because they are deceitfully sentimental, or even (some purist critics would suggest) just because they are badly written.

8.21 Critics, writers and other expert witnesses called by the defence under section 4 have been required to speak of the merits of the work in question in terms of these causal concepts, supposedly relating some good effect specifically to the work, of such a kind as to outweigh any tendency to deprave or corrupt which the work might also possess. The supposed causal character of these considerations, and the supposed weighing of them, constitute the first intractable feature of the public good defence. Moreover – and this point would apply to any such provision, even in less directly causal terms – the exercise has to be conducted in a court of law, the witnesses faced by cross-examination – circumstances which cannot make for the most sensible discussions of literary merit. It is not surprising that many absurd things have been said in the course of such proceedings, as by several expert witnesses for *Lady Chatterley's Lover*, or by the distinguished authority who was trapped into trying to think of otherwise unknown facts about 18th century London which one might learn from *Fanny Hill*. We have considerable sympathy for those who have gallantly gone to bat for works of art under these rules, but we can only regard the rules as absurd, as many of them must also have done.

8.22 Besides the causal nature of the concepts of section 4, and besides the drastic limitations of any court procedure, there is quite another reason of principle against any such exercise. The procedure involves weighing merit, but the merit will be possessed only by works which are, to some appropriate degree, *successful* works of art. The defence therefore has to take the form of claiming that the work in question is a good work; but this cannot be an appropriate requirement. If the law on obscenity is to protect artistic activity, it has to protect experimentation and the rights of new writers in particular, to try something out. It follows that it must protect the right to try and fail, and the experiment which issues in a bad book. The public good defence in terms of actual merit cannot do this, and it is entirely to be expected that its most famous victory was in defence of a work by a writer, D. H. Lawrence, who was absolutely outstanding, long dead, and already highly respectable. By contrast, the defence, using section 4, of *Last Exit to Brooklyn*, an indifferent book by an unknown writer, failed before a jury, though an appeal later was successful; in that case, the expert witnesses tended to exaggerate the book's merits, and they could scarcely have done anything else, granted the underlying idea of section 4.

8.23 Not only the requirement of merit, but the mere idea of the evidence being given by experts, tends in this same direction. It is as though informed persons, literary and artistic experts, are supposed to appear from the world of culture and inform the jury of how things stand there with the work under trial. Granted this, and the other features of the Act, it is not surprising that it has been criticised as elitist in conception, and as saying in effect that corrupting books are to be permitted so long as they are admired by professors. This criticism is largely unjust, but it hits at a basic fault in the Act, its absurd model of the role of expert opinion with regard to artistic or literary merit. The model is not so much elitist, as scholastic: it implies an informed consensus about merit which, for each work, already exists. In the real work, new works have to find their own way, and see whether they elicit any appreciation or not. No one may know, for some time, what to think about them. It is not just a matter of the *avant-garde*: works in some despised medium or style may subsequently turn out to have had more meaning than most experts would have originally supposed. (The recent history of critical taste with respect to Hollywood movies of the thirties and forties, compared to 'art' films of that period, is an object lesson in this.) The critical reputation of a work can continue to vary. Expert consensus, if it comes at all, and if it stays the same, must come after the event, and to assume that expert opinion is available at the event, that is to say at the time of publication, is merely to make the deathly assumption that all forms of artistic significance have already been recognised.

8.24 For all these reasons, we conclude that the idea of a public good defence, relating to artistic or literary merit, is basically misconceived, not merely in the form presented in section 4 of the Obscene Publications Act, but quite generally. We have argued in this chapter that it is not to be excluded in advance that pornographic or even obscene works can, to some degree, possess serious artistic interest. If our argument is correct, the law will have to accommodate that possibility, but without resting on the illusory hope of calling in experts to tell it when the possibility has come about.

Notes

1 'Pornotopia': *Encounter* 1966. The concept of an 'ideal type' is applied to Marcus's account by Morse Peckham: *Art and Pornography* (New York 1969).

2 Suggested in a paper by Antonia Phillips, commissioned by us, to which the present chapter is indebted.

3 'Pornotopia': *Encounter* 1966. A similar point is made by Norman St. John-Stevas, *Obscenity and the Law* (London 1957), page 137.

PART TWO ART AND VALUE

Art, an enemy of the people

Roger Taylor (b.1940)

In Art, an Enemy of the People *(1978) Roger Taylor argues provocatively that 'high' art can have a debilitating effect on popular culture. Taylor champions popular culture for political reasons; he has a Marxist outlook which leads him to identify high art with the cause of the bourgeoisie and popular culture with the cause of the proletariat. Accordingly, he claims that 'Art is a value the masses should resist'. The chapter title to the extract that follows, 'A warning of the corrupting influence of art on popular culture', clearly signals the politically influenced line that will be taken on the chapter's subject – jazz – which is seen to be an essentially proletarian form of expression, the liberating and subversive potential of which is lost when it is brought into the high art canon. Art's social role is very much a political one in Taylor's reading, with high art being treated as a repressive influence on mass culture and thus as serving the interests of bourgeois ideology.*

A warning of the corrupting influence of art on popular culture

If art is an historically localised set of social processes and not a basic human orientation then the status of jazz as art will depend upon its being located within these social processes. Less generally, if art is a form of life sustained and lived out by various societies that either were part of or grew out of the general seventeenth century European situation, and if throughout the proliferation of and changes in this form of life stratas at the top of the social hierarchies involved (all the societies involved being hierarchical) were and are responsible for the sustaining and living out of the form of life, then the status of jazz as art will concern locatable social processes within these stratas. As jazz is the creation of coloured people in the Southern States during the early part of this century and the latter quarter of the last, it did not begin its life within the higher social stratas, or where there were connections they were remote from these higher stratas' concern with the art continuum. If, therefore, jazz has subsequently been established as a recognised art form, or if, as seems more in keeping with the facts, inconclusive attempts have been made to establish jazz as such, then there should be locatable social traces of the attempted process of integration within the appropriate social strata. At a superficial level (the level of critical activity) these traces are easily uncovered. A consciousness of jazz as a possible art form emerges in the 1930s and is generated by the critical activities of some European intelligentsia, localised mainly in France, Britain and Scandinavia. There is at this time a similar though distinguishable process at work in the States, i.e. orchestral jazz. Gradually this consciousness spreads to encompass American critics, jazz men and a jazz public (the latter category is by the time of this spread a non-proletarian, intellectual, ambiguously bourgeois, anti-bourgeois group – though there are fluctuations in this, e.g. Bop audiences in the States and Trad audiences in Europe during the 50s).

It would not be difficult, therefore, to make plausible the argument that acceptance in the appropriate social area was a sufficient condition for jazz being a legitimate art form. In constructing this argument one could set up amusing contrasts between those committed to jazz as an art form, and, therefore, to the importance of discrimination (paradigm case being the intellectual, jazz critic and musicologist) and many of those within jazz, particularly jazz musicians, who, because not obsessed by the spectre of the art category, appal, or, at least, surprise, the jazz critic with their lack of discrimination. For example, Charlie Parker very much enjoyed the piece of music *Slow Boat to China*.

To detail this case, however, is not my primary intention. My interest is more in the fact that jazz writing (the major area where notions of jazz are made articulate) is a misinterpretation of jazz, because it seeks to relate jazz to an illusory concept of art as universal. In other words, jazz is misinterpreted because it is seen through the ideological function of the art concept, whereas jazz has entered within the boundaries of art because this seeing of it through the ideological function has been socially realised.

To begin with let me briefly indicate the way in which jazz is related to the art category as far as the most musicological or intellectual jazz critics are concerned. To this end I would like to draw attention to the writing of Hodier (A. Hodier, *Jazz Its Evolution and Essence*), Newton (F. Newton, *The Jazz Life*) and Marothy (J. Marothy, *Music and the Bourgeois. Music and the*

Proletarian). Hodier is a French intellectual and musicologist, Newton, who is apparently E. Hobsbawn in disguise, disclaims any proficiency as a musicologist, but brings to jazz writing an informed sociological sense, and Marothy is an Hungarian orthodox Marxist and musicologist.

There are real differences between these writers concerning the particular forms of jazz they wish to most highly recommend or prescribe. Hodier believes the history of jazz has produced a classical period of jazz (for Hodier the period between 1935–45) and that jazz before and since has been inferior. Newton, on the other hand, is prepared to accept the whole of what passes in contemporary jazz circles for *real* jazz, whereas, Marothy is committed to *real* jazz (i.e. non-commercial jazz) which affirms collective experience over against bourgeois ego-centredness. In Western jazz terms (passé terms really) this position leaves Marothy a 'trad fan'; one who is very much opposed to modern developments in jazz. Despite these differences there is something which links these three writers. None of them believes that the achievements of jazz measure up to what they would consider to be the great achievements of compositional art-music. They all have great enthusiasm for jazz, and find in it values far above, as they would consider them, the values of popular, commercial music, for which they all express a disdainful loathing. Newton, for instance, saw 50s rock n' roll as music for moronic masses. In fact, compared with 'high-culture' music both Newton and Marothy find in jazz refreshing qualities. For Newton, jazz has been a democratic, anti-snobbish activity, and for Marothy jazz has been the healthy voice of the revolutionary proletariat, as opposed to the decadent voice of a moribund bourgeoisie.

Despite these concessions to the value of jazz, when it comes to the point of supposing that absolute judgements are possible all three critics see the jazz tradition as having produced nothing equal to what they regard as the great achievements of art music. Marothy believes that the kind of jazz, of which he approves, is a proletarian folk music, which might subsequently be utilised by some great post-revolutionary composer for the ends of 'true' art. Newton, also, finds it meaningful to classify jazz by means of the folk category. For Newton, jazz is an urban folk music, which, surprisingly, has been able to maintain itself despite the commercialization of most forms of life within the capitalist society. For all three critics (two of whom, Hodier and Newton, are highly esteemed in jazz circles) jazz has failed, or simply has not produced great works of art, but in a scale of value which has 'high' art-music at the top, and commercial, pop-music at the bottom (all three are committed to this scale) jazz is very high up the scale.

The positioning of jazz, in the most intellectual of critical writing, corresponds closely to the general position of jazz within the culture. Within jazz itself, from the 1940s onwards, practitioners of jazz, writers on jazz, who deal with the subject in a more anecdotal way than Hodier etc. (e.g. Nat Hentoff) and many jazz fans have been convinced that jazz *is* a new art form, created in America, mainly, though not exclusively, by negroes, and that jazzmen have an identity as artists. (Hodier etc., allow that most jazz musicians have greater technical dexterity than high-brow musicians, apart possibly from keyboard players.) However, this internal conviction does not quite equal the general institutional position of jazz. A few examples illustrate this. For instance, the bulk of BBC's jazz programmes occur on Radio 2 late at night, indicating both that they are not programmes for the mass of Radio 1 and 2's audience, and that they are not for the Radio 3 audience. Radio 3 does put out a few jazz programmes, Jazz in Britain and Jazz Record Requests but they are very much squeezed into minority slots. This is no conspiracy against jazz on the part of the BBC, but reflects their Audience Research Department's findings on the jazz public. Thus, the main bulk of people interested in 'serious music' are not very interested in jazz, and the same is true of the audience for 'light music' and pop. The jazz audience has some respect for 'serious music', and on the whole is disdainful about commercial, pop music.

The complex of attitudes surrounding jazz then, places it on the borders of art music. A situation like this is, of course, fluid, but for the last fifteen years the jazz situation has remained rather static as major social changes have gone on apace without them taking up the jazz experience. In the 50s things were different, because a young, middle-class student audience developed a short-lived 'purist' interest in jazz. At that point, jazz was entering the art category at some speed, as is evidenced by the number of serious books published about jazz at that time. However, when the student bourgeoisie of the 60s turned away from jazz to developments within pop music, jazz ceased to develop in any major social sense, though this does not reflect on changes within jazz styles during this time. Jazz is today dealt with occasionally in a serious, intellectual way by the more serious, intellectual papers, but when this happens it happens as part of a column devoted normally to progressive, pop music. In other words, it is not a standard, regular feature of the art world, but it *is* on the borders of it. The depiction of jazz as a folk music by intellectual critics is a positive indication of its position. By saying 'folk music' the critic is saying 'this is a music I stand outside of, it is not the music of my social group, but it is a music that grows authentically out of real, social experience and is, therefore, valuable'. Of course, the critic qualifies the notion of 'folk' by words like 'urban' or 'proletarian'.

My interest, as it was stated earlier, can now be presented more accurately. It is an interest in the misinterpretations of jazz which have resulted from the actual bringing of it into the fringes of art by means of various perceptions of it through the ideological function of the concept of art (i.e. art as a universal activity). One of my main complaints will be that the application of art, as a universal category, to jazz has blunted a perception of jazz as particularity.

In order to explore this theme I shall begin by concentrating on the origins of jazz. Jazz, as Newton is eager to point out, is not a definable entity; it is an organic entity which has different, though related, significances at different times. A concrete point of departure on the beginnings of jazz is *A Pictorial History of Jazz* by Keepnews and Grauer Jr. On looking through the early photographs one notices changes taking place in the style of the photography. The very earliest photographs fulfil the minimal function of the photograph. The members of the bands are assembled so that they can all be seen. They carry their instruments. In many cases they wear uniform; the uniform of the band. The individuals are all assembled on the basis of them being members of a band. The individual band members look as though they have been made uncomfortable by being photographed; clearly, the photograph is not being used by them (individual by individual) for exhibitionist, self-advertisement. The photographs could almost be photographs of convicts, i.e. photographs of those who would prefer not to be photographed. Despite this, the photographs probably originate from the musicians' desire to be photographed. Photography is itself new and its application to coloured people rare. Even in 1939 photographic services for coloured people in the South were poor as is evidenced in the well-known letters from Bunk Johnson to Frederic Ramsey Jr, on his inability to send Ramsey photographs of himself – 'I'm pretty sure that you all know just how everything is down South with the poor colored man. The service here is really poor for colored people.'

However, a band as a whole is a larger economic possibility than an individual, and New Orleans, in the last century, afforded coloured people greater freedom than most other areas in the South. To be photographed itself conferred status. Slavery is only 30 years behind the recording of these assemblies. The band gives the negro status in his own eyes. The band is to be identified with the liberation of the negro, although this value is double-edged. The band's dress style is military and bands and music were an important part of the liberating armies. The musicians' instruments are in all probability instruments left over from disbanded military bands. They have, then, a symbolic significance, as well as conferring status as pieces of property possessed, and as signs of personal skill or expertise. These photographs conceal a shyness, a lack of social confidence in the photographic situation, but also a preparedness to stand and be photographed because of what the band and being a member of it signified.

As jazz spreads, so as to take in wider audiences, so the style of the photographs in the Keepnews and Grauer pictorial history change. The main bulk of the examples, in the changed style, occur in the early 20s, but the style can be found several years either side of this period. This second batch of photographs testify to the musicians as socially acceptable performers of some accomplishment. The air of social acceptability is induced by a conscious photographic style. The bands are posed. It is no longer sufficient to have everyone present and so make sure that they can be seen. The content of the photograph is now carefully arranged. The whole effect is one of neatness, precision plus shades of dignity. The ensemble is chic. The fashionable style of the 20s, involving a preference for whole shapes bounded by clear contours, all slightly exaggerated by a penchant for the slender invades the photographic presentation. The performers, then, are presented within the framework of what is fashionable, of what is of the moment. For this reason, they are presented as acceptable and desirable. They are part of *the scene*. Where the photographs are of coloured musicians they are presented as members of the chic ensemble, this is to say that the clean, conceptual contour of *bands* bounds the presentation of the performers. In these photographic sessions we are not treated to off-duty poses, the performers remain part of a fashionable decor. They are surrounded by a galaxy of gleaming instruments; they are the players of these instruments. The kind of playing which results is suggested by a distinction within the photographs in this style.

Many are of the performers sitting in their places on the bandstand; they come across as smooth and well-behaved. In other words they know their place. They are not slaves from Congo Square in New Orleans.

However, just as many of the photographs are posed shots of the band in action. The action is simulated. The overriding compositional structure owes nothing to realism. The emotional content of these photographs is one of rakishness and excitement. The smooth, well-behaved, coloured musicians indicate, in these photographs, the kind of music they play, or, and perhaps better, the kind of music they don't play. The more formal pose is undermined by the more anarchic one, though the anarchic pose is not genuinely anarchic; the orgiastic impulse is still well-repressed, but, now, it is showing. The musicians don't play stiff, formal music, they play music which is of 'now', which is fashionable, which repudiates the past.

The bands advertise themselves as being *Creole*, which strictly interpreted means, or meant, of Latin origins, though born in the Caribbean, and therefore, not of African origins. However, the concept of Creole in employment was a connived duplicity feeding off its literary meaning. Today the ordinary understanding of *Creole*, if not its dictionary approved meaning, is that of being light-coloured and of the Caribbean (lacking thereby a clear racial meaning). This movement in the concept came about as the result of people of various racial origins passing themselves off as Creole. The ordinary understanding of the concept gives up authoritarian literalness and yields to transparent social fact. When the Grauer/ Keepnews' photographs were taken, the literal interpretation of *Creole* was not totally debased by social abuse, and it could still signify social acceptability. This is not to say that anyone really believed that the members of Kid Ory's Creole Jazz Band were Creole, it was just more acceptable when everyone engaged in the transparent fantasy that they were. In terms of fashionable acceptability it was also imperative that they should not be Creole; the important fact was that *they should appear to be but yet be known not to be.* Here, we have an idea emerging that I shall make a lot of, namely that one enormously important life-project for the negro in the USA has been *living in order to dissemble.*

Creole band was part, therefore, of an acceptable image. In addition, the bands in the photographs appear in evening dress (there is even a band that calls itself the Tuxedo Jazz Band). We are, then, in a different world from the marching bands in their uniforms. Yet it is the same world, for it is known that many musicians appeared in both contexts. These photographs from the past present a concrete record of a lived ambiguity. On the one hand the negro stands self-conscious but obdurate, affirming the fact of his existence, on the other hand he negates himself in dissembling European-ness. However, what really is socially accept-able and integrates is the ambiguity...

The red-light district of New Orleans is, of course, an obligatory subject in describing the formation of jazz. However, the specific content of the New Orleans brothel is not really attended to. The normal thing is to allude to the seamy origins of jazz so as to strengthen the claim that jazz is an authentic music, springing from real life situations. The New Orleans brothel is, however, an interesting phenomenon. It is not generally uniform, but there is a uniform conception emanating from the top which pervades most set-ups to a greater or lesser degree. The top is Basin Street, which is not to be confused with some seedy street in Soho. The most famous establishment on Basin Street was Mahogany Hall, run by a chubby negro woman called Madame Lulu White. Here, in its most obvious form, we have the contrast and intermingling of black and white, African and European; the contrast declaring itself in the debasement of what is European. Thus, the house, which has four stories, five grand parlours on the ground floor, 15 bedrooms on the upper floors all with private baths, is called Mahogany Hall (i.e. a fine European house but a black house). Its owner is addressed as though French, she is Madame White, but though called White she is coloured (as a matter of fact she passed herself off as Creole). She is referred to in a guide of the period (Souvenir Booklet) as follows,

> As an entertainment Miss Lulu stands foremost, having made a life-long study of music and literature. She's well-read and one that can interest anybody and make a visit to her place a continued round of pleasure.

Here, then, we see her set up as an attraction within the context of European culture. However, the magnificence of the house (in fact a rather brassy and gaudy magnificence, gross copies of so-called finest European taste), the pseudo-culture of its hosts, is all in aid of the various satisfactions of prostitution. Mahogany Hall was not a lone exception. All the top establishments were structured by these values. Thus, the Arlington is referred to in the famous Blue

Book (nothing to do with Wittgenstein),

> The wonderful originality of everything that goes to fit out a mansion makes it the most attractive ever seen in this or *the old country*. Within the great walls of this mansion will be found the work of great artists from Europe and America.

Other establishments were run by Emma Johnson, known as the Parisian Queen of America (to rape the Queen of Paris) and the Countess *Willie* Piazza, where *Jelly Roll* Morton played piano (*Willie* and *Jelly Roll* both being expressions referring to the penis).

The significance of these establishments is neatly summarised by Clarence Williams talking in Hentoff's *Hear Me Talkin' to Ya*,

> And the girls would come down dressed in the finest evening gowns, *just like they were going to the opera*. Places like that were for rich people, mostly white.

These brothels for the rich were not exclusively inhabited by coloured prostitutes. Many white females were also employed. This would have had a different significance from the coloured girl parading in European finery, but it obviously fitted into the overall project. It is revealing to emphasise how different was the general sexual, fantasy life of the period, as served by these establishments, compared with contemporary sexual fantasy. Sex in New Orleans, during this period, was far removed from the allure of kinky boots, Spider Woman and PVC. Even at the lower end of the New Orleans sex industry the style of sexual fantasy drew on the same sources. Thus, Louis Armstrong describes the girls standing outside their 'cribs' dressed in 'fine and beautiful negligées', in other words apparelled in erotica which worked through the associations of Europe and high class.

The top brothels were not the nests in which jazz was hatched. The music for these establishments was provided by piano players. They were known as *professors* of the piano, thus, underlining the connection with European culture. Bands were not part of the setting because they were too obviously noisy and disruptive. There was no loud playing. The piano because of its bulk was property within property. It did not belong to the streets or the marching bands, and consequently, in the history of jazz, it had, at the beginning, a separate involvement. It is for this reason that early black playing of the piano expresses itself in compositional music, like rag-time, whereas in jazz proper we have to wait until Ellington for this to come about. The early, coloured piano-players were much closer to legitimate music than the instrumentalists in the street marching bands and dance bands, although this division was not absolute, as is evidenced by the different status of various instruments in the bands (e.g. the violin and clarinet were more closely associated with legitimate music than the other instruments). The piano comes into jazz, as jazz leaves the streets and enters the interiors. This movement is not simply the jazz band becoming sedentary, it is the influence of the jazz idiom and integral and attendant social attitudes upon the piano-players. One of the clearest expressions of this intersection is in the development of boogie woogie, where the left hand takes up the function of the guitar's rhythmic chording while the right hand fulfils the piano tradition of filling in so as to provide a total event.

In Countess Willie Piazza's place Jelly Roll Morton performs as professor of the piano, but the echoes of jazz pervade the sweet volume-level of the music. The black/white contrast is written into not only the name of Mahogany Hall, but into the musical atmosphere as well. This contrast is the meaning of the social experience that it was. An isolated, but important event which emphasises this meaning was the closure by the federal governments of the 'Storyville' district during World War I. This came about when four sailors were killed in the district. At the point of America showing solidarity with a particular European cause, it became necessary for the authorities to excise that which was anathema to it.

The contrast I have been examining is not confined to the sordid fringes of New Orleans society, although, in New Orleans, prostitution was in fact more than a fringe activity. The contrast is ubiquitous throughout New Orleans as a good-time town.

Until the 1850s New Orleans was the musical capital of America (H.A. Krun 'The Music of New Orleans' in Hodding Carter's (ed) *The Past as Prelude*), but this is misleading unless we concentrate on dancing and ballrooms. It is this which is the vastly popular activity. New Orleans did have an opera house, but it was not always popular, and probably would not have survived apart from the support of the ballrooms, in the form of their providing alternative sources of income for musicians. However, it was important that there was an opera house, for compared with the ballrooms, it allowed social consciousness to live out the contrasts

I have been arguing for. It was more important though, that there were the ballrooms.

The importance of the ballroom reveals itself when we know the kind of social experience it permitted and encouraged. Masked balls, in which social divisions of birth and colour were played down, were very popular. Prior to 1805 there was mixed dancing where white men (fathers and sons) would come together to revel and dance with free-coloureds and slaves, both men and women. From 1805 the Quadroon Ball was introduced by an Auguste Tersier, whereby, on Wednesdays and Saturdays, dances were held exclusively for white men and free-coloured women only (the category of free-coloured women being easily enlargeable by any coloured women a white man fancied setting up as such). The real significance of this move was the removal of the coloured male from the context in which the white male exhibited, through the mask of social conventions, his sexual desires. The Quadroon Ball proved an instant success. As a Louis Tastio wrote at the time,

> Every clerk and scrivener who can make up a few dollars, hurries to these unhallowed sanctuaries, and launches unreservedly into every species of sensual indulgence...Nor is it unusual to see members of the legislature mingling freely with these motley groups. (Quoted in Krun article.)

It is in these settings, and similar ones, that towards the end of the century the original jazz bands performed, alternating between this role and that of marching bands. The idea that jazz as dance music was an early twentieth-century invention of Tin Pan Alley, which is Francis Newton's claim, seems to me quite wrong. It was at the beginning a dance music, and more than this a dance music within a commercial setting. The ballrooms were in competition with each other and emerging out of this commercial rivalry we get the tradition of the 'cuttin'' contest, which was still apparent, though transformed greatly, at Mintons, when Monk, Parker and Gillespie set about inventing a jazz that no one else will be able to live with.

I have now said something about the social context in which a certain social project was lived out. A set of simplifying contrasts help to clarify my meaning. Being white, as encapsulated in New Orleans social experience, was *bringing blackness into whiteness*, and thereby obtaining some release from being white, but at the same time *not being black* and remaining white. The project was contradictory, it was to be white, but not be white and to be black but not be black (all of this from the standpoint of those who were white), it was to *bring blackness into whiteness as a whiteness* but at the same time *that which entered as a whiteness had to be a blackness.* We might say all of this constitutes the *American setting* or, at least the white American setting. The European grip on America is not strong but for a while a rather garbled version of European style is an inspiration, especially with certain powerful social classes. The American experience is the way in which this grip is gradually dismantled. Europe is the fantasy, and in the fantasy Europe is 'debased' and this is central to being American. This can be represented in economic terms for American capitalism is the powerhouse, which is the ultimately effective destroyer of the pervasiveness of European culture. But all of this is, at present, from the standpoint of white Americans. What is needed is an account of this complex from the other side. To approach this I shall return to an adjunct of my main enterprise, that adjunct being the formation of jazz.

In schematic form to be black is to be committed to a double dissembling. First there is *the being black*, but the having *to appear as white* though revealing blackness through the white pose. This is the demand white society makes on blacks. The demand, however, is twofold. It is the demand that what *is* black *makes itself white* through dutiful behaviour (dutiful, white labouring-classes) but that it remains black, i.e. slave, third-class citizen, non-equal. This demand is the exploitation of the blacks' productive capacity. Secondly, there is the more seductive demand (seductive to those demanding) that the excitement and release of blackness be offered through a disguise of whiteness. The black then *dissembles whiteness to have his blackness exploited*, but this is the external demand, and what we need to specify is how meeting the demand is interiorised. It is interiorised *by dissembling the dissembling.* This is to say the negro makes bland naivety at imitation indistinguishable, at an interpersonal level, from cynical mockery. If there is an awareness of this duplicity there is a tendency for whites to connive at it, because the desired object *blackness* is not simply shades of Africa and savagery, but the send up of uptight whiteness (this it seems to me is a contagious cultural influence)...

In the work songs and early blues we are dealing with material which, as all experts accept, was designed to be ambiguous. There is the meaning of the song which is acceptable to the European overseer, and there is the sardonic, send-up meaning (sometimes clandestine message) which delights the singers. An attitude is being bred here. It is that of not meaning what you say, and *living to say what you don't mean*, while at the same time implying what you mean and *living to imply meaning...* The Blues makes light of suffering so as to underline it. In the early jazz the perfectly acceptable European melody appears to be present, and to be holding the piece together, but something else is intertwined within it, which is something saying something else. Here, we are dealing with what is now called 'improvisation', but in the early days of jazz it was known to everybody as *'faking'*. (Perhaps we have run full circle when we get to Coleman Hawkins wondering whether or not Ornette Coleman might be faking and thus might not be for real.)

At one level the European hears ingenuous attempts at imitation, but as an explanation this is inadequate; there had been many earlier, negro bands (many of them military) who could play the music straight. Improvisation is a feature of West African music, but we would be woodenly empiricist if we left it at that, i.e. one element that went into some mysterious brew, brain-computer scramble etc. Improvisation is, in terms of the background, a congealed possibility, but in the New World context it is a chosen possibility, as a way, in the first instance, of dealing with the problematical contingencies of the work gang, e.g. the passing of the message. The improvisatory problem, in the context, is one of working some new provocative element into a settled, acceptable format without disturbing the format's acceptability. The skill is one of *working it in*. This is clearly brought out by a J.M. Mckin writing in 1862 and quoted in Marshal Sterns' *The Story of Jazz*:

> I asked one of these blacks – one of the most intelligent of them... where they got these songs. 'Day make 'em, sah!' 'How do they make them?' After a pause, evidently casting about for an explanation, he said, 'I'll tell you, it's dis way. My master call me up, and order me a short peck of corn and a hundred lash. My friends see it, and is sorry for me. When dey come to de praise-meeting dat night dey sing about it. Some's very good singers and know how; and dey *work it in...* work it in, you know, till dey get it right; and dat's de way.

In the early jazz the improvisation feeds off the melody and its harmony. In this way the acceptable statement is transformed. European standards of strict tempo are evaded, with the accents coming off the beat and the stressing of weak beats. This produces a music which is shifty and evasive rather than open and straightforward. I often feel that musicians brought up on classical music who, when trying to play jazz, meet insuperable difficulties do so because their training has been one of always trying, honestly and openly, to be in the right place at the right time. In a lot of jazz you have got to let things slip a bit only to redeem yourself at the last moment, like the clown on the tightrope. The important thing is, according to European standards, to be in the wrong place, but to know how to get back in line (note how Charlie Parker is revered for his extraordinary capacity for doing just that). Here is the source of the sense of release that the early jazz offers; i.e. a release from an on-the-go, goal-orientated, rule-bound, repressive consciousness. In this connection the attractions of primitive Africa and African rhythm seem more a cultural image surrounding the music than a feature of its intentional content. We have, in the music, the standards and the slipping from them, and for the musician, I am suggesting, the important thing is the living out of the ambiguity.

This is how the blacks come into the American experience, from the other end, so to speak... The image of the negro passively accepting Southern paternalism is an obvious historical fallacy (see *Negro in American History*, Director of Schools, New York City). Plantation owners and their families were often the prey of their slaves. The history of the negro in America is full of minor rebellions, which are inevitably followed by savage repression. But more than this, the negro is constantly working a fast one. He runs away, he appears to work but only does so at half pace, he feigns illness when he is healthy. We might note that all of these dodges are commonplaces in the contemporary life of cynical sections of the Western proletariat. The object of the black life is to 'two time' the white, boss race, or, it is one of the objects, and it is an object which transforms the way in which all other objects are sought and the way the seeking of them is lived. This two-faced quality is apparent just where the negro is often thought to be at his most straightforward and sincere, i.e. in religious devotions. Religious activity when permitted was for the negro the acceptable context in which to be unacceptable: the context in which to symbolically throw off social and ideological tyranny. Religious activity in America provided similar opportunities for migrating European proletarians (Shakers, etc.). The possibility of sincere, ingenuous response created the hesitation in white consciousness, which allowed black religious devotions to grow unimpeded. This possibility is more than hinted at by the European traveller Fredrika Bremer, when she visited a Methodist church attended by slaves (Blassingame).

> The *children* of Africa may yet give us a form of divine worship in which invocation, supplication, and songs of praise may respond to the inner life of the fervent soul!

Moreover, the mocking, deadpan tone of the negro is evident in his religious activities. The mode of expression is not just the song of deliverance. Compare the pomposity of the following European lyric, with the sharp send-up of the negro version which follows it.

> Praise to the living God
> All praised be his name
> Who was, and is, and is to be
> For aye thro' the same
> The one Eternal God.
> Ere aught that now appears
> The first, the last beyond all thoughts
> His timeless years.
>
> God is a God
> God don't never change
> God is a God
> And he always will be God.

Of course, blacks could not enter into these white practices without cost. Just as black was affecting white, so white was affecting black. Whites were becoming black and blacks were becoming white. Christianity as a repressive ideology takes its toll. Baldwin's novel *Go Tell it on the Mountain* is a graphic illustration of this. Despite this, religious practice was for the negro a further opportunity for saying one thing but meaning another.

Just as the serious intention behind the whites' religion is evaded and sent up, so is the serious intent behind the white man's band. This is underlined by the military associations which the band had for the negro. The negro gains, in American history, a concept of freedom through military experience. In the colonial war some measure of prestige accrued to the negro as a result of those instances where it became necessary to employ him for military ends. In the civil war, a successful outcome for the Northern armies promises the abolition of slavery. This prospect is concretely responded to by an estimated number of 186,000 negroes joining the Northern forces, many of them defectors from the South. About a sixth of this number failed to survive the conflict. The North and the policy of abolition come together as the war becomes protracted and difficult. It is realised that the economic strength of the South is heavily dependent on unwilling slave labour. Therefore, an alliance with the emancipationist cause, on the part of the North, is a tactic which undermines the security of the Southern economy. The invitation from the North to the Southern slave is to defect in return for which the North promises emancipation (i.e. wage labour). The promise of emancipation is carried into the South by the victorious Northern army, much of which is composed of negroes. The victory is paraded and celebrated by means of the exhibitionism of the military band. However, the promise is a false one, for though slavery is abolished the material circumstances of the negroes' life remain much as before. The concept of the band is thus adopted by the negro as a way of saying what you don't mean. New Orleans had a history of white marching bands; the black marching bands therefore develop their parody of the white band...

I estimate I have said enough to indicate what I take to be the meaning of the formation and early proliferation of jazz in and around New Orleans. What I have tried to do is to sketch in the *lived making* and early spreading of this process. As a methodology this is a departure from the standard empiricist enquiry, which breaks down the *fait accompli* into easily managed elements (e.g. polyphony, polyrhythm, blue notes, improvisation etc.) and then seeks to find something comparable in the pre-jazz background (e.g. African pentatonic scales, Anglo-Saxon hymns, etc.). The empiricist enquiry gives fusion (i.e. natural process) pre-eminence over human project. At the same time as recommending a certain methodology, one which insists on rendering the activity intelligible as something intentional, it is necessary to point out that the activity rendered is not simply transparent intentionality. The activity, because it is real, contains all sorts of possibilities for new departures which were undreamt of in its original formation. What new departures there are though, have still to be rendered as lived activity.

I am now in a position to declare my main point with more obvious intelligibility. To begin an exploration of jazz with the presupposition that it is art, or is a music of 'high aesthetic value' (the latter claim is typical of books on jazz, reflecting, I suspect, the actual borderline status of jazz) where one is committed to these values, prevents one from feeling jazz as hostile to oneself and a rejection of oneself, but, at the same time, feeling it as an undermining of oneself by being a release from oneself. Prevented from finding this interaction of objectives one fails to locate the white presence in early jazz. Early jazz is as much made out of white, commercial demands of black musicianship as it is made out of black musicianship itself. Jazz is a commercial music from the beginnings. It is not as though the commercialisation of jazz only gets under way with the Original Dixieland Jazz Band and beyond. It is true that as the record and radio industries develop so certain concepts of jazz are spread by the abstract hand of capitalism, and that prior to this commercialisation is under more concrete control. This isn't the difference between folk and commercial music, any more than the difference between the New Orlean's underworld and Capone's Chicago is the difference between folk culture and muscular capitalism. Being a musician in New Orleans was to have a trade, like cigar making or carpentry. If not full-time, it was a supplement to one's income. Even the playing at funerals, for the various lodges and secret societies, was on a commercial basis, and the music only became 'hot' (as they used to say of early jazz) after the band had been paid and they were on their way back to town.

To think of jazz as art is to think of it as an ally. From this standpoint one abstracts from the particularity of the lived process those elements which are compatible with the standpoint. Jazz as a lived process, having a predominant meaning thereby slips from view. As this happens a fantasy jazz emerges firmly within the grip of the aesthetics of Romanticism. Jazz is thereby seen as a clear, unambiguous, authentic expression of black feeling. Sometimes the straightforward expression of an African vitality and at other times the expression of suffering and the making of bitter ironic comment. There are the feelings, there is the vehicle and jazz is the communication of these feelings by means of the vehicle. In this way the jazzman is highlighted as the artist. This is to say that as long as his problem can be conceived simply as making the vehicle communicate his feelings, then his status as an artist is assured, even if it is a status as a lesser artist (folk artist). As soon as outside, commercial pressures are thought to intrude, i.e. when jazz is seen as being marketed and when whites are seen as playing a version of it because it is marketable (this is the conception of the ensuing process that the theory gives us) then the status of jazz as art becomes a complex problem: the problem of discrimination. While lost in the problem of discrimination the meaning of the ensuing process is not explored. The ideology sets up the meaning *a priori*. Thus, the meaning becomes, who was and who was not able to maintain themselves as authentic expressing artists against the tide of commercialism. The history is read for this interpretation and nothing more. Once this is done all that is left is to detail what has been accepted. Detailing involves the gathering of anecdotes and the analysis of the evolving musical techniques. Typically, also we get the lament that the great jazz artists have not been rewarded for their genius, although if in the money the jazzman is normally thought of as being of questionable status, e.g. Benny Goodman and Miles Davies (a similar process is to be found in pop-rock as a letter to the *Sunday Times* 12 Oct 1975 pointed out of that newspaper's colour supplement pop-rock feature).

A better understanding of the spreading of the jazz experience (especially concerning 20s and early 30s) comes from those who living with its spread took up a position of hostility towards it. Neil Leonard's book *Jazz and the White Americans* catalogues some of the opposition. In 1901 the American Federation of Musicians condemned ragtime, and recommended that its members refrain from playing it. In 1911 people found doing the Turkey Trot were taken to court and subsequently lost their jobs. By 1922 there was a play on Broadway by Hartly Manners called *National Anthem*, whose theme was the moral debasement and degeneracy brought about by jazz. The New York Times of the period was against it – 'With music of the old style even the most moving, the listener was seldom upset from his dignified posture.'

J.P. Sousa objected on the grounds that jazz employed primitive rhythms which excited the basic human instincts. This attitude was expressed in greater detail by a Dr Eliot Rawlings, quoted by Leonard.

> Jazz music causes drunkenness by sending a continuous whirl of impressionable stimulations to the brain, producing thoughts and imaginations which overpower the will. Reason and reflection are lost and the action of the persons are directed by the stronger animal passions.

The Catholic Telegraph of Cincinnati continues the theme,

...the music is sensuous, the embracing of partners is absolutely indecent, and the motions...they are such that as may not be described in a family newspaper. Suffice it to say that there are certain houses appropriate for such dances but those houses have been closed by law.

A Miss Alice Burrows publishing an article entitled 'Our Jazz Spotted Middle West' in the *Ladies Home Journal* for 1927 writes,

The nature of the music and the crowd psychology working together bring to many individuals an unwholesome excitement. Boy and girl couples leave the hall in a state of dangerous disturbance. Any worker who has gone into the night to gather the facts of activities outside the dance hall is appalled, first of all perhaps, by the blatant disregard of even the elementary rules of civilization. We must expect a few casualties in social intercourse, but the modern dance is producing little short of holocaust. The statistics of illegitimacy in this country show a great increase in recent years.

According to the Rev. Phillip Yarrow the Illinois Vigilance Association had discovered that for the year 1921–2 jazz had caused the 'downfall' of 1,000 girls in Chicago alone. The anti-movement was not without its sense of humour, as is evidenced by articles bearing titles like 'Does Jazz put the Sin in Syncopation?'.

Milton Mezzrow, the jazz clarinettist, recalls the official establishment attitude towards jazz in the 20s: 'Our music was called "nigger music" and "whore house music" and "nice" people turned up their noses at it.'

Religious dignitaries saw the wider implications. A.W. Bevan, a minister in Rochester, New York is quoted as saying, 'It has gotten beyond the dance and the music and is now an attitude toward life in general. We are afflicted with a moral and spiritual anemia.'

Dr J.R. Streton, a baptist clergyman in New York said,

I have no patience with this modern jazz-tendency, whether it be in music, science, social life or religion. It is part of the lawless spirit which is being manifested in many departments of life, endangering our civilization in its general revolt against authority and established order.

These outbursts against jazz were not confined to angry letters written to newspapers, but had practical implications as well. It needs to be remembered that these attitudes were linked to the attitudes behind 'prohibition'. In 1921 the General Federation of Women's Clubs with a membership of 2,000,000 voted to 'annihilate' the new music. At the time of prohibition there was legislation against jazz. The New York legislature passed the Cotillo Bill which empowered the Commissioner of Licences of New York City to regulate jazz and dancing. He banned both on Broadway after midnight. By 1929, 60 communities including Cleveland, Detroit, Kansas City, Omaha and Philadelphia had regulations prohibiting jazz in public dance halls.

The opposition to jazz has to be measured against the spread of jazz, but by itself it underlines the social meaning of jazz. Adherents of jazz, who view it as participating in eternal aesthetic verities, dismiss this opposition as reactionary and blinkered, not seeing that this opposition is a particular response to jazz as something concrete. In contrast, the adherents' response is abstract. The opposition expresses itself naively, but many of its positions have been presented with more sophistication (if this is thought a virtue) as does, for instance, Adorno (T. Adorno, *Prisms*, 'Perennial Fashion'). I am very much against Adorno's condemnation of jazz but I am in agreement with much of his analysis. It is a strange experience to agree with so much that is said but to be so fundamentally opposed to the whole. Consider, therefore, how Adorno's views present a more sophisticated opposition to jazz, whilst paralleling many features of my own analysis,

> However little doubt there can be regarding the African elements in Jazz, it is no less certain that everything unruly in it was from the very beginning integrated into a strict scheme, that its rebellious gestures are accompanied by the tendency to blind obeisance, much like the sado-masochistic type described by analytic psychology, the person who chafes against the father-figure while secretly admiring him, who seeks to emulate him and in turn derives enjoyment from the subordination he overtly detests...It is not as though scurrilous businessmen have corrupted the voice of nature by attacking it from without; jazz takes care of this all by itself.

He goes on,

> Among the symptoms of the disintegration of culture and educ-
> ation, not least is the fact that the distinction between autonomous
> 'high' and commercial 'light' art, however questionable it may be,
> is neither critically reflected nor even noticed anymore. And now
> that certain culturally defeatist intellectuals have pitted the latter
> against the former, the philistine champions of the culture industry
> can even take pride in the conviction that they are marching in
> the vanguard of the Zeitgeist... The legitimate discontent with
> culture provides a pretext but not the slightest justification for
> the glorification of a highly rationalized section of mass pro-
> duction, one which debases and betrays culture without at all
> transcending it, as the dawn of a new world sensibility, or for
> confusing it with Cubism, Eliot's poetry and Joyce's prose... An-
> yone who allows the growing respectability of mass culture to
> seduce him into equating a popular song with modern art because
> of a few false notes squeaked by a clarinet, anyone who mistakes
> a triad studded with 'dirty notes' for atonality, has already
> capitulated into barbarism.

Here, European Marxism declares itself as the defender of the old culture. This is an attitude we find in Marx and an attitude deeply entrenched in the Soviet Union. There is a clinging to the 'higher' life of the bourgeoisie as it evolved during the period of settled bourgeois dominance. This 'higher' life is in opposition to the real material life of the bourgeoisie. The real material life produces the possibility of proletarian life-styles which are antagonistic to, and unassimilable into the 'higher' life. Significantly Marxism seeks the disappearance of the proletariat, and where Marxism comes to terms with jazz it does so by denying the Adorno charge of barbarism; it sees jazz, rather, as art. This kind of identification is one Tom Wolfe goes in for. Wolfe is a heightened exaggeration of the Adorno opponent, and one I doubt Adorno imagined possible when writing 'Perennial Fashion'.

> ...Nobody will even take a look at our incredible new national
> pastimes, things like stock car racing, drag racing, demolition
> derbies, sports that attract five to ten million more spectators
> than football, baseball and basket ball each year. Part of it is an
> inbuilt class bias. The educated classes in this country, as in every
> country, the people who grow to control visual and printed
> communication media, are all plugged into what is, when one

gets down to it, an ancient, aristocratic aesthetic. Stock car racing, custom cars, and, for that matter, the jerk, the money, rock music...still seem beneath serious consideration, still the preserve of ratty people with ratty hair and dermatitis and corroded thoracic boxes and so forth. Yet all these rancid people are creating new styles all the time and changing the life of the whole country in ways that nobody ever seems to bother to record much less analyse. (T. Wolfe, *Kandy Koloured Tangerine Flake Streamline Baby*, Introduction)

Continuing his attack Adorno equates the specialist jazz fan with logical positivism,

There is a striking similarity between this type of jazz enthusiast and any of the young disciples of logical positivism, who throw off philosophical culture with the same zeal as jazz fans dispense with the tradition of serious music.

It would be interesting to know how many logical positivists were specialist jazz fans. I suspect quite a few.

Trying to account for the mass basis of jazz, Adorno puts forward an image that coincides with one I offered earlier, namely the stumbling clown.

Jazz must possess a 'mass basis', the technique must link up with a moment in the subject – one which, of course, in him points back to the social structure and to typical conflicts between ego and society. What first comes to mind, in quest for that moment, is the eccentric clown or parallels with the early film comics. Individual weakness is proclaimed and revoked in the same breath, stumbling is confirmed as a higher kind of skill. In the process of integrating the asocial jazz converges with the equally standardised schemas of the detective novel and its offshoots, which regularly distort or unmask the world so that asociality and crime become the everyday norm, but which at the same time charm away the seductive and ominous challenge through the inevitable triumph of order.

With the rise of the Nazi movement in Europe, Adorno took refuge in America. Judging from 'Perennial Fashion' Adorno appears to have integrated badly into American society. He writes,

...To comprehend the mass basis of jazz one must take full account of the taboo on artistic expression in America, a taboo which continues unabated despite the official art industry, and which even affects the expressive impulses of children;... Although the artist is partially tolerated, partially integrated into the sphere of consumption as an 'entertainer', a functionary – like the better-paid waiter subject to the demands of 'service' – the stereotype of the artist remains the introvert, the egocentric idiot, frequently the homosexual... A child who prefers to listen to serious music or practise the piano rather than watch a baseball game or television will have to suffer as a 'sissy' in his class or in other groups to which he belongs and which embody more authority than parents or teacher.

Here we have Adorno faced with the American experience one aspect of the making of which I have been trying to detail. His final verdict on jazz is that its subject expresses, 'I am nothing, I am filth, no matter what they do to me it serves me right', and that, 'Jazz is the false liquidation of art.'

These different forms of opposition bring out very clearly the view that jazz as a mass phenomenon was not an adjunct of art and 'high-culture', but a repudiation of it. This view I agree with. The opposition was in response to the spread of jazz, it was a response to the real threat posed by the jazz experience. This threat kept re-emerging in jazz, or in close offshoots of jazz, up until the closure of the bop/trad era. The different forms of threat were accompanied by different forms of opposition. From the end of the bop/trad era similar repudiations and threats emerged from cultural forms which sprang from the same roots as jazz but which constituted a distinct and separate branch e.g. Rock n' Roll. These developments carried with them their own forms of opposition, which have been depressingly similar to the forms of opposition I have just been exploring. On this evidence alone Adorno's concept of static revolution seems appropriate.

The recurring fact of jazz as threat, as repudiation, in the history of jazz, has to be set alongside the fact of jazz falling within the confines of art. The perception of jazz as art is not something separate from the history of jazz; it is a very important part of its history. In other words, the misinterpretations of jazz history have been part of jazz history and they have entered deeply into jazz in its entirety. To explore this theme it is necessary to explain the history of jazz as it follows on from the early period. Clearly, this is a vaster problem than that posed by the early history of jazz. In response to this larger problem I shall offer no more than a detailed sketch, which will try to account for the phenomenon of 'jazz as art', i.e. account for it as a distinct social phenomenon.

The spread of jazz is connected with the expressed, but repressed need which White America had for things of that kind (things which had the same social significance as jazz had developed during its formation). Jazz was not sought out as an area of knowledge, nor as an area in which to display expertise. For the mass of Americans it was a very abstract sign, to be in the proximity of which was to signify one's own free, unrepressed, undisciplined individuality. Jazz enabled a mass of people to signify this because as a sign, at a very obvious level, it challenged an accepted sense of authority and discipline. However, those caught up in the spread of jazz do not make real contact with an already evolved form of life. Those musicians who leave New Orleans to play in Chicago and New York lead a very self-enclosed, hermetically sealed-off existence. They do not in themselves spread the New Orleans life-style. Jazz entered the White American world as a fashionable, rude word (the word 'jazz', at this time had, clear, but repressed associations with 'fucking', just like 'rock n' roll' does at a later time) and as a pretext for and inducement to (syncopation itself was sufficient to induce) what the *New York Times* would have seen as undignified posture and movement in dancing. In other words, for the consumers, the jazz experience has the same significance as it had for Europeans in New Orleans, only it has this significance in diluted form. Just as the New Orleans' consumer could not assimilate what he took to be an orgiastic meaning without disguising the fact from himself, so even more so is this true of the Americans of the 'jazz age' and beyond. To be in a context bearing the label 'jazz' was really sufficient, it was not necessary to encounter jazz New Orleans style; in fact to do so was, often, to take on more than was bargained for. For instance, Louis Armstrong's first appearance in Britain at the London Palladium was a sell-out, but the packed audience, when confronted by Armstrong the perspiring negro constantly mopping his brow with a handkerchief, left in droves. They had come because the event bore the label 'jazz', they left because it went too far; it was more than they were ready for.

The jazz life widens through a manipulation of the label; the label often accompanying music thinly related to the initial stirrings of jazz. Jazz music, itself, was spread mainly by white imitators, black jazzmen being employed more in areas where the tendencies in society were at their most extreme. For example, two of the most important influences in spreading jazz were the all-white bands, The Original Dixieland Jazz Band (this band visited England in 1919) and the New Orleans Rhythm Kings, whereas black jazzmen operated in underworld haunts where America's uppercrust came to soil itself. Milton Mezzrow testifies to this latter point in Leonard's book,

> It struck me funny how the top and bottom crusts in society were always getting together during the prohibition era. In this swanky club, which was run by members of the notorious Purple Gang, Detroit's blue bloods used to congregate – the Grosse Pointe mob on the slumming kick, rubbing elbows with Louis the Wop's mob. That Purple Gang was a hard lot of guys... and Detroit's snooty set used to feel it was really living to talk to them hoodlums.

Mezzrow's notion of 'really living' is important; it underlines what the identification with the jazz experience was about. However, the 'really living' was ever transformed by moderating influences. This occurred in many ways.

A huge, advanced, capitalist industry was able to grow around a marketable concept of 'really living'. By 1921, 100,000,000 records were manufactured in America and (with fluctuations surrounding the Depression) by 1942 record sales reached 127,000,000. (*ibid.*) Throughout this period the sales of popular music far outstrip the market for classical music. By 1939 the sales proportions are 9:1 in favour of popular music. (*ibid.*) Throughout the period radio and cinema are expanding at the same explosive rate. For instance, by 1927 four-fifths of the American population attended the cinema at least once a week. (*ibid.*) These contexts, plus the similarly expanding dance hall business were the contexts in which popular music expanded and was expanded. The notion of popular music at this time cannot be separated from a general sense of jazz. The music the public required had to be 'jazzy', or 'syncopated' or 'swing' music. Jazz musicians themselves (now full professionals compared with their forbears in New Orleans), whether black or white, earned their living out of playing this kind of music. For instance, the revered Coleman Hawkins was to be found during the depression playing for the, at the time famous, now forgotten, Jack Hylton dance band. The profiteering which motivated the distribution of the concept of 'really living', became a monopolistic enterprise. The radio stations bought up the phonograph companies, and the film companies the music publishing businesses. Against the background of commercial monopoly there was strong pressure to sell music that both excited (stimulated the demand) and did not offend; the object was to sell to the greatest possible number. The music, therefore, had to be new, fashionable, 'really living', but at the same time refined.

Various musical forms answer to this demand, ranging through White Dixieland, Symphonic Jazz and certain types of Swing. White Dixieland, for instance, traded off the symbols of the South, the negro, the authentic savage, but presented them as the parts of a tropical island idyll. A typical example of this is the 1928 recordings by the Frankie Trumbauer orchestra with Bix Beiderbecke on cornet. Here, a young Bing Crosby sings about natives in Borneo, and 'darkies' who can make music simply by beating their feet on the 'Mississippi mud'. The music's style is jazzy, but distinguishable from Black New Orleans jazz. In comparison the music is not raucous, loud or orgiastic but it retains an expressive element of liberation. The pieces of music do not propagandise enrollment in any social organisation; their overall expressive content is one of expressing freedom from the sublimation of self in some larger social destiny. The positive side of this is the celebration of individualism, but the individualism celebrated is of a particular kind. It concerns individual sexual fulfilment, presenting itself in the disguised form of carnal romance, and a personal goodtime, a kind of happy individualism (what Beiderbecke, himself, stood for as a social symbol). As for the rest of experience, it is ignored. The jazz style reinforces the sense of liberation. In itself it is an active rejection of older forms of musical organisation. Moreover, it has clustered around it a set of recently acquired social associations, which vaguely gesture towards the wilder life of a primitive idyll. Features of the earlier music, which do not seem to be present, and which point to the transformations which have taken place, are a contagious, rebellious hysteria, a sense of send-up or mockery and an exhibitionist eroticism. The modifications in Trumbauer's music are individualism, fun and romance. The Trumbauer music is not negative, it positively constructs private dreams, which are presented as realisable dreams for all of America, certainly for all of White America; but this American dream has to be realised atomistically or separately. The music suggests that a happy, individualised, fun-existence is possible for all, and that this possibility is a challenge to all that is stuffy and restrained. It is this image which is commercially exploited and, therefore, in terms of the American public exploitable. Jazz was a convenient, pre-existing form for the expression of this image. 'Really living', in this commercial setting, is not at the point of interconnection between slaves and masters, or hoodlums and blue bloods, but its attractions can be related to what was sought in these other conjunctions.

The modification of the *'really living' experience* was not just a commercial stratagem relating itself to the threshold of social consciousness. It also sprang from the intentions of some of those who made the music. For instance, Paul Whiteman (set up as the King of Jazz by the media at the time) accepted jazz as a release from repressive mechanisms.

> In America, jazz is at once a revolt and a release. Through it we get back to a simple, to a savage, if you like, joy in being alive. While we are dancing or singing or even listening to jazz, all the artificial restraints are gone. We are rhythmic, we are emotional, we are natural. (*ibid.*)

At the same time this release is accepted, by Whiteman, in a repressed form. As he wrote of his Aeolian Hall concert in 1923,

> My idea for the concert was to show skeptical people the advance which had been made in popular music from the days of the discordant early jazz to the melodious form of the present. I believe that most of them had grown so accustomed to condemning the 'Livery Stable Blues' sort of thing, that they went on flaying modern jazz without realizing that it was different from the crude early attempts... My task was to reveal the change and try to show that jazz had come to stay and deserved recognition. (*ibid.*)

Whiteman's notion of modern jazz in this quotation has to be understood in terms of pieces like Gershwin's 'Rhapsody in Blue'. In fact George Gershwin's attitude was very similar to Whiteman's. He is quoted in Leonard's book as having said of jazz,

> Certain types of it are in bad taste, but I do think it has certain elements which can be developed. I do not know whether it will be jazz when it is finished.

This attitude was quite general and represents the first conceptual coupling of jazz and art as made by individuals having some social prestige. The critic Osgood wrote in the *Musical Courier* of his experience on first hearing 'symphonic jazz',

> Before the first sixteen bars were over the revelation of new jazz had descended upon me. By the end of the tune I was a happy convert... These gentlemen made music; languishing, crooning music, rude neither in sound nor tempo, music that soothed and yet, with insinuating rhythms, ear-tickling melody and ingenious decorations, stirred me within... While I had been going about, with my nose in the air, with patronising ignorance, somebody had put music into jazz.

By this time the *New York Times* was prepared to concede as much.

> ...arranged and played by experts [symphonic jazz] has much about it of interest and even of value, and all unite in condemning the inexpert and over enthusiastic disturbers of the peace.

An important factor in determining the modifying influence and the form it took sprang from the American college and high school audience making jazz something of its own. Jazz as a 'flash', new, social sign born of a concealed debasement of the European was converted, saved by means of a marriage with the latest, allegedly revolutionary flowerings of European culture, as they appeared, transplanted in teenage American higher education. The names of Debussy, Ravel and Milhaud represented avant-garde 'serious music' for many jazzmen of the period. They attended concerts of 'serious music', they received musical instruction from famous teachers in the classical tradition, and some of them openly experimented with the possibilities of symphonic jazz. The 'serious music' influence did not penetrate very deeply into the music, but it was there, through a commitment to the melodic, and a very conscious concentration on harmonies which take a long time to resolve themselves or remain unresolved. Music showing this influence is full of 'highs' and 'lows'. The music of Beiderbecke and Hoagy Carmichael is of this kind. The titles of their compositions reflect the mood, for example, 'In a Mist' and 'Stardust'. In these pieces we are at some distance from Louis Armstrong singing,

> 'Now I ain't rough and I don't bite,
> But the woman that gets me got to treat me right.'

Many negro band leaders of the period were graduates or came from prosperous middle-class backgrounds, for example, Lunceford, Henderson and Ellington. Many of Ellington's compositions exhibit the harmonic preoccupations I have just been mentioning. 'Highs' and 'lows' are very evident in pieces like 'In a Sentimental Mood' and 'Sophisticated Lady', and a conscious concern with wandering harmonies is ever present: a strong example of this occurs in bars 23 and 24 of 'Sophisticated Lady' where Ellington goes through the chord changes G, D dim, Cm, E♭7, D7 whilst the melody line plunges from B above MC to MC and then ascends to E, one octave up, before plunging again, this time to F sharp.

Where, then, the jazz experience in society involves taking up jazz music, the process involved is not only one of watering down in accordance with commercial dictates; it is, also, a positive conception of transformation. The excitement of the depraved is entered into by containing it. The containment is achieved not by abolitionist tendencies, nor by imposing on it a traditional sense of order, but by allying it with a specific sense of the bohemian and avant-garde. There was reverence for the art experience amongst many jazzmen. The clarinettist, Pee Wee Russell, provides a telling illustration of this, when describing, in Hentoff's book, how he felt when, at a Carnegie Hall concert, in a box paid for by Paul Whiteman, one of his fellow musicians kept falling off his seat in a drunken stupor. 'You see, we were ashamed and were conscious of the other people at the concert.'

It may be doubted whether New Orleans' Buddy Bolden would, in similar circumstances, have been as shame-faced. We are dealing with a social group which is a 'cut above' the 'proletarian rabble' and often there is a tradition of classical music in the background. For instance, Paul Whiteman played violin in both the Denver and San Francisco Symphony Orchestras and Beidebecke's parents had ambitions for him as a concert pianist (an early influence he never quite lost despite his prowess on the cornet). The milieu for the music was very much high school and campus gigs. The Austin High School Gang first heard its jazz not at The Deuces (Chicago low dive) but the Spoon and Straw (ice-cream parlour), listening to records by the New Orleans Rhythm Kings. Goodman, though not from a wealthy background himself, plays, as a teenager, for students at Chicago University and North Western University. (In fact, the whole Goodman success story has to be measured against the growth in American higher education and its production of, to a degree, a new autonomous social group. The growth of Goodman,

Artie Shaw etc. and Swing relates to jitterbugging American teenagers and, more influentially, teenage rioting.)

We have located, then, a certain cohesive group, within the history of jazz, involved in playing jazz, which is composed of white, middle-class youngsters who have some respect for 'high culture' and some knowledge of the tradition of classical music and contemporary European serious music. However, the social milieu is only a third of the story, for it has to be related both to the commercial growth of jazz and the excitement of American low life. It is in the latter setting that the coloured jazzmen often find their environment, scratching out a living between these engagements (often very temporary in character) and the making of the special category of 'race records' (records exclusively bought by coloured purchasers). This is not to say that jazz by the coloured jazzman is all of a piece. There is a real distinction between the coloured player meeting commercial demands and the coloured player playing on a more private basis. This contrast constitutes the reality of the black jazzman, and it relates to earlier ambiguities within jazz experience; it relates to them as a fragmentation of them. But more of this a little later, for what is being explored, now, is how the white American, middle, lower middle-class jazz setting relates to this other setting for jazz. What is clear is that the two settings are separate. This is testified to by two facts. Firstly, it is testified to by the resentment felt by black musicians for what they considered to be white imitators; the white jazzmen were commercially more fortunate in having wider commercial outlets. Secondly, it is testified to by the difficulties which beset mixed jazz groups on the road. For instance, the difficulties experienced by Billie Holiday on the road with white bands, or the difficulties often experienced by Benny Goodman in taking Hampton and Wilson with him. For the white jazzmen then, jazz was concretely present within the total American environment as a feature of low life (or life 'really lived'). To be involved with jazz was to be on the fringes of what passed for excitement in American Society. In this way jazz was not only something to be saved and brought within the confines of 'good music' (by coating it with a thin veneer of 'exciting' musical modernism; thus not negating it as something signifying excitement) but it was also, in its turn, sought as exciting salvation or as giving the feeling of this. Jimmy McPartland of the Austin High School Gang makes this clear in Hentoff's *Hear me Talking to Ya*.

It was lucky for me I got in with that gang, because as a boy down there on the West Side, I might easily have been mixed up with a different kind of mob.

So for me, and perhaps other Austin guys that got the music bug, jazz supplied the excitement we might otherwise have looked for among the illegal activities which flourished then in the neighbourhood.

For the white, middle-class, lower middle-class youngster (e.g. McPartland's father was a music teacher) who was to enter the jazz world as a performer, and in the process enlarge the dimensions of that world, jazz presented itself as a complex phenomenon. There was jazz as a form of music having a history. This was known about but not known in depth. In this context there was a sense of jazz constituting a genuine, indigenous folk music, and something which, in accordance with recognised practices in serious music, could be utilised to produce a unique American music (i.e. it could be utilised once modified). There was jazz as a universalised racy value, which the whole of the post-war Capitalist world was in on. There was jazz music, as something being spread by White Dixieland and its offshoots, the process being mediated by records and the radio. There was jazz music played by black musicians, which offered itself in two forms, the commercial form and the jam session, both forms arising for the most part in a gangster dominated, night-life scene. There was jazz music as symphonic jazz. These various aspects of jazz, like the total, social conception of jazz, presented themselves as liberation and excitement, as unrepressed 'really living'. To measure this it helps to contrast it with the social significance of jazz today.

Jazz as an activity for a small coterie of addicts, no doubt, is still thought of as 'real living' but this would not be its general social significance. It is to this general, social significance that the white, potential jazz musician of the 20s and 30s responded; the response being channelled through some or all of jazz's various interconnected and sometimes disconnected, evolving forms. What I wish to suggest is that all these living layers of jazz experience duplicate structurally (i.e. in the way the layers relate to each other) the original structure of New Orleans jazz (a less fragmented set of experiences) and that the lived, personal ambiguities in the New Orleans scene are lived out later as the social contrasts between the different layers (the layers themselves having associated with overlapping but differentiatable social groupings). The objective of the present line of discussion is to describe the modifying, repressive impulses of those making jazz, from the spreading jazz of the twenties up to the end of the Swing era, but this is something extremely complex to describe because of having to relate individuals to the proliferation of so many different but connected forms.

It makes sense to say that the early jazz was a social presentation of *disguised orgy* (sought out as debasing and, therefore, experienced as liberating). For reasons I have not gone into, Americans of the Jazz Age and beyond, were open to a general proliferation of some such experience. Jazz as music, dance and fashion was an appropriate vehicle for such a proliferation. However, the forms of disguise had to convince the various thresholds of social consciousness throughout America, and from this viewpoint it was as if New Orleans Jazz was naked orgy (totally unexpurgated filth). In general the taboo on social thought and actions were so great that to call any social event a *jazz event*, as long as it was not too obviously not a jazz event, was sufficient for commercial success (e.g. Al Jolson in the 'Jazz Singer'). However, there were other responses. There was the response of saving jazz, as naked orgy, by incorporating what were deemed its best elements into a thin conception of symphonic, orchestrated music. Socially this was a response having important repercussions because a great number of commercially successful ballroom orchestras, throughout the Western world, were modelled on orchestras like the Whiteman orchestra. Such orchestras might include a 'hot' musician for a few well-mannered jazz breaks, just as the Whiteman orchestra incorporated Beiderbecke for this purpose. In this music there was a concession to the American fear...of the corrupting influence of jazz. The musical form into which the jazz elements were slotted (one major transformative ingredient was light syncopation) was largely derived from nineteenth-century, romantic, 'serious', 'light serious' music. Another response was to recreate the original music only in sweetened form, or by emphasising its 'sweet' as opposed to 'hot' elements. This was a more open flirtation with the 'naked orgy' value of the music, but what was already disguised was further disguised. Finkelstein, in his excellent book *Jazz: a People's Music*, shows how the 'sweet', 'hot' contrast permeated New Orleans jazz and, thereby, adds weight to my argument about New Orleans jazz.

One of the characteristics of New Orleans music, contributing largely to its variety and beauty is the mixture of different musical language, the interplay of the 'hot' and 'sweet', blue and non-blue. This fazes the theorists of pure-blues jazz, who either ignore the mixture or assume that the non-blue elements were 'subconsciously' assimilated and immediately 'blued' or 'African-ised' by the performers. It reveals, rather, that the interplay of the two languages was a most sensitive, highly conscious musical operation, and it is precisely the artist who is most 'folk' (or musically 'pure' as the theory goes), who will often play a non-blue melody straight and with great pleasure in it.

In white Dixieland the 'blued' elements are 'sweetened', but the excitement is still there through the active working upon the contrasts (remember the contrast adds up to the feeling of the debauching of white values, and excitement is generated simply by playing with the contrasts). White Dixieland is a jazzy music for having a 'good time', but it has a more intellectual side as well. It attracts into it young, white Americans who are in, or have connections with, higher education. Here, we have backgrounds that make for some commitment to 'serious' music (the élitist European tradition). However, the kind of individuals of this order, who are drawn into jazz, tend, in serious music, to identify with the avant-garde music, the music which selfconsciously breaks with a settled tradition in European 'serious' music. This avant-garde European music is not only taken up because of its bohemian excitement, but also because of its consciousness of jazz, employing as it does some miniscule jazz influences in its compositions. This jazz tinge is one of its exciting properties. A passing and respectful knowledge of the revolutionary happenings in 'serious' music influences the kind of jazz that certain jazz musicians produce. In this, then, excitement results from taking up the original value *jazz* at some close proximity to its roots, and saving it, and oneself, by imposing certain refinements upon it, but imposing the refinements is, in itself, an excitement not only because of what is being refined by them, but also because the veneer, though being morally upright (connected with 'art') is new and revolutionary and a break from what would have been regarded as European stuffiness. In this way one saves oneself from the temptation of total immersion in American low-life (never a real psychological possibility for most of those who felt themselves exposed to the temptation) and at the same time one redeems the low life, by a presentation of it through a respectable (the art connection) but chic (new, unstuffy) veneer, like stripping down an old wooden chair, and coating it in a very modern, but tasteful lacquer. The net effect of such a life, lived by musicians, was to produce the sense that one was 'really living', where 'really living' was achieved by hovering between seamy America and art.

Beiderbecke is typical of this. He lives the dreamy, other worldly life of the artist at the same time as the dissolute good-time life of the jazz age. However, in describing this particular mode of modifying the jazz tradition (and this contribution to its evolution) certain strands still need to be woven into the account. Thus, the musicians I am describing did not singly look back to New Orleans jazz and set about modifying it. Jazz was an ongoing set of experiences, and it was a set of experiences having a pronounced commercial expression. The commercial expression was itself (as already discussed) a modification of original jazz or, perhaps better, a utilisation of some of its elements as racy modifications in their own right, of a popular idiom (popular classics simplified, and derivatives). Therefore, the jazz musicians I am describing operated in a market which demanded such a product. Their modifying inclinations were, then, exercised upon an already highly modified jazz (in fact most of it now would not be regarded as jazz, though at the time it certainly was). On top of all these interactions was the interacting presence of black jazz. Black jazz as orgy was not simply an actively recalled debauched Arcadia, which had taken place in New Orleans in a mythical past, it was more importantly for those in the know an existing 'hot', sexy music to be located in the night life of the underworld. It was a 'sweetening' of this that many white musicians were drawn into. To be part of that world but be apart from it. Of course, different musicians responded differently and some were more inclined to be a part of, than be apart from (e.g. Eddie Condon).

What I have tried to explain so far is how the proliferations of jazz occurred in 'sweetened', cleaned up and therefore highly modified form, and how this process answered the demands and desires of a white audience and white musicians who wanted to be jazzmen. What I have been trying to underline in this account is that the value *jazz* looming beneath all the modifications, was the infectious quality. To think of oneself as a jazzman, to dance to jazz, to be part of the jazz age, this was the contagion, which appeared in many disguises dependent upon the repressive needs of the participants. However, jazz was, despite its being a generalised notion, none the less a more specific social identification of a value than the more general, though still socially identifiable, objective of 'debauchery' upon which the seeking of the jazz experience was dependent. In time *jazz*, as a value, was to wane, whereas, the more general objective was slowly but continuously pursued, feeding off other things.

Jazz, then, is a presence, which is continuously surfacing in the various forms of commercial music of the period. It is a subterranean, unthinkable excitement which is revealed through its concealment. It is a deep flowing, foul river and the various forms of concealment are its artificially constructed irrigation ditches. Of course, it was not necessary that there should be some *actual*, deep base to the jazz-flavoured frolics of the period, this is to say it was not necessary to there being an active notion of it. However, such a large process in society, manifesting itself in a spectrum of attitudes, did give rise to an actual social form, which was easily interpretable, by those who sought such a base, as the required deep base for the total social experience of jazz. By this I mean there was locatable, in the depths of society, a distinct stratum which was black jazz. It is this which now requires description.

In the depths we do not find unambiguous sordidness. In order to achieve understanding it is necessary to rethink, for a moment, the significance of the early jazz for the black man. It was the project of not meaning what one was saying, and at the same time implying an undermining meaning which one did not say. This was the significance of the music for blacks. However, when we move on to the spreading of the jazz experience throughout the capitalist world, we find the jazz, required of the black man commercially, leaves scant space for the positive act of withdrawing from meaning what is said. This difficulty is not experienced all at once, but it is a gradually changing practice which is not offset socially by commercially acceptable examples of scat singing (e.g. Armstrong) of material in the popular idiom. The black musicians fulfil the original structure of the music by dividing it up, by a fragmentation of it. The fragmentation is not so much one of dividing up a given and determinate musical style, as one of, in one context saying the acceptable meaning while constructing (the inventive side) another context, which takes away the acceptable meaning as meant. The acceptable meaning is, of course, for whites the liberation from repressive ideology, though this meaning is for other forces in white society unacceptable (the threat to the social fabric). However, this acceptable meaning cannot satisfy black consciousness, for its problem is not one of achieving liberation from its own, anachronistic (i.e. economically) repressive ideology. Its problem is one of getting back at white society without getting beat for it. It can hardly gain satisfaction from what gives white society its kicks. The two contrasts are concretely specified by the commercial gig (whatever and whenever, though most often on the fringes of white social experience) and the jam session. The jam session is a way of saying that as a professional musician the negro jazz musician is not for real. However, the jam session is no more important than the gig because the two feed off each other. The point of the jam session is to point to the gig as not being for real. It is for this reason that, what has been seen as the puzzling phenomenon of the negro musician taking up the commercial music of his day as a basis for jazz, becomes explicable. Thus, it has been alleged (Finkelstein) that a lot of fine musical material is utilised in New Orleans jazz (e.g. 'Panama') and that the same cannot be said of material utilised in later jazz (e.g. 'Embraceable You'). The reason often offered for the change around is commercial pressure, but this by itself does not explain the intrusion of white, commercial music into the jam session. It is when the jam session is linked to the commercial setting that the use of white, commercial music becomes clearly intelligible. It is when what jazz is *is* living to imply the contrast between the contexts that the dropping of earlier standards (i.e. standard numbers) can be undertaken lightly. The ambiguity, which was written into one and the same music in New Orleans, later, is no less present, but it is present through social fragmentation. The jam session is not *what it is all about* except in the sense that the jam session is created explicitly to *mean* this is what it is all about, this is what is done for real and not the other thing.

Gene Roney provides a telling illustration of this in Reisner's book on Parker,

> They were jam sessions held every morning. The ones Bird and I attended faithfully were held at the Reno Club, where Count Basie was playing. Basie had a nine piece band and they worked a tough schedule – from 8.30 to 5.00 in the morning. After that the jam sessions would begin. (Reisner, *Bird: The Legend of Charlie Parker*)

To think oneself into this situation, as audience, is to feel the insult. Having paid for the excitement of jazz one finds that the musicians are hanging around waiting for you to go, whereupon the real thing gets underway. It's like going to a party where everyone is waiting for you to leave so that they can get on with the *real* party.

What actually happens, in the jam session, is distinguishable from New Orleans jazz in so far as the music being worked upon has different significances. Thus, white, commercial music is jazzy (what that implied, at the time, I have already tried to specify) and it is concerned with, what earlier I called, carnal romance. The looser, somewhat less uptight, white society is competed against in the jam session; the negro out-seduces the white crooner and turns the quickstep into orgy. But the meaning is not just seduction and the orgiastic, it is rather the competitive meaning. The whole point, when Lester Young or Coleman Hawkins blow 'Embraceable You', is that compared with standard, white renditions of the number their seductiveness is so much more expressive. This, at the time, is not obviously apparent to white ears because seductive overtures could only be tolerated where there was the safety of restraint.

The competing against white society was not realised within the black musicians' world as a collectivised, group project. The element of competition involved, also, the internal relationship within black, jazz music. The individual objective was to achieve success in being against white society. This did not mean refusing to identify with any white objectives or social goals. White society was itself internally gripped by economic competitiveness both on a personal and social basis. To seek the trappings (all the negro musician of the period was at all likely to get) of wealth (e.g. 'flash' clothes, money to throw around on girls etc.) was both to identify with the system of white, American society and, at the same time, compete against individual whites. It was also, however, to compete against other negroes. To be successful in white society's terms was, also, to be successful in competing against whites, and to be successful at this was to be successful as a negro. The 'flash' negro then, with an ultra seductive style, was the competitive negro. The more seductive were one's choruses the more one outdid white society and the more one succeeded, against other blacks, in the black project of outdoing whites. What I am trying to emphasise is the fact that there is, on the part of black jazzmen, a deep entering into the romantic sentimentality of the commercial music of the period. The notion that the music of the period was simply used by coloured players, as a vehicle for the tracing of musical arabesques, does not stand up to the reality of a coloured musician soloing (e.g. Ben Webster). To allow, however, for the fact of an entering into the spirit of the music is not to situate the black musician as a gullible absorber of white commercialism in music. The black musician competes at the level of the music's significance to the consumer (i.e. in the area of its liberating meaning). This is a side to the music missed in a dismissive musicological treatment. It is true there is a turning away from the straight-forward, melody line of the pieces played, and that the pieces are often used as a pattern of chord changes, but the style remains one of displaying seductive technique. The discarding of the melody and the fastening onto the chord pattern is, I am suggesting, part of the general project whereby there is a disassociation from the acceptable. White, commercial tunes are played but not played, and in not playing them they are rendered more seductive or more orgiastic. Between the commercial performance and the jam session we find the contrast between the acceptable and the unacceptable disproportionately exhibiting itself, depending upon how commercial, or how free and open the context. Of course, the contexts themselves, especially the commercially viable ones, are determined by them being contexts in which black musicians are accepted. The music demanded by these contexts is, then, already, by the general standards of American commercial music, unacceptable. It is the deep base against which all other jazz experiences measure themselves. However, its reality, as I have tried to indicate, does not compare with how, as a measure, it is used. As a measure it represents obscene excess, in reality (i.e. for the negro) it is an ambiguous expression signifying competitive but sarcastic compliance. However, in so far as it is a movement which elaborates a rejection of the white, musical form, and is thereby a rejection of what that form means socially, then it gathers to itself potential excitement for those intentionally rejected by the movement. The most exciting party is the one you are not allowed to go to.

To this point I have tried to sketch in the development of jazz up until the middle of the 1930s. It is clear that by the time we reach the 1930s, jazz is a distinguishable phenomenon from the early jazz in and around New Orleans, though it is something linked to what was earlier. My objectives in specifying this development have been various.

Firstly, there has been a methodological objective, namely that of indicating the complexity, and the kind of complexity it is, which has to be described. There has not been some essential thing, which is jazz, which has been described. An account which seeks jazz in this way works from a preferred definition as to what jazz is. In contrast, it seems to me preferable in specifying what jazz is, and was, to delineate what at different times social consciousness has designated as jazz. When this is done, for the period in question, we find a number of distinguishable social processes exhibiting similar structures and all of them interacting with each other in a multiplicity of ways. As this complex has emerged it has been my intention, and is my recommendation, not to reduce this complexity to some systematic formula, but rather to allow it to unfold as something lived by so many different individuals in many different ways. In a way, the methodology has been a rejection of method, and an insistence on the fact that what is lived and concrete is so tangled that it cannot be rendered by a point by point (a), (b), (c) sort of formula. This is not to say it cannot be known, but the knowing, which is possible, is not a definite knowledge, it is instead, an imaginative reliving of what was lived, and this leaves one with as many loose ends and dissatisfactions as the life lived and, therefore, known. However, this is not to excuse any sparsity of detail in the present account, this is excused differently by the scope of the enquiry. What I have tried to indicate is the way a more ample account should be conducted.

The second objective, which relates to the thematic centre of this essay, has concerned bringing into focus the first actual social processes in which a relationship between jazz and art gets posited. I think it is clear that this positing is quite distant from the different, sometimes opposed, strands within what, by the mid 1950s, has become the orthodoxy within jazz, i.e. that jazz is an art form. By the 1950s, a consciousness of jazz as art includes the belief that jazz is an art movement with an unrecognised (certainly by the general public and also by the established art fraternity) history. In this movement, the history of jazz is being sifted like some ancient civilization for its great works of art, and involvement in the movement includes, as a competitive motive, the desire to accumulate esoteric knowledge. The most straight-forward illustration of this is the growth of discography, as it concerns jazz (a growth which had been taking place since the middle of the 1930s), although the motive has a more complicated and more socially diffuse nature. The earlier appraisal of jazz as art was much more the view that jazz was a possible *art form*, or that jazz could be turned into art. The subsequent view was not the locating of successful attempts at achieving objectives prescribed by the earlier view. The earlier view was not, then, the sudden realisation that what lay all around one, namely jazz music, was, in fact, as yet unrecognised art music, rather it was the view that jazz was a music that could be turned into art by the creative efforts of schooled musicians. This view did not result from deep, aesthetic deliberations as to what could, or could not count as art; rather, for certain groups of people, it was a view which fitted what was specific to their position in society. Jazz is a form of life having a deep base, and the deep base, constituting the most authentic area of jazz as art, was not within the limits of the social consciousness which first drew the concepts of jazz and art together. In terms of this first view of jazz and art, jazz moved into art as it moved away from the deep base, and moved towards (as a set of musical techniques i.e. techniques formally definable) the world of art as normally constituted. This, then, as a movement, is not one which particularly involves the coloured player. The coloured player, as someone confined to the deep base, is obviously enough not enticed by this movement into a consciousness of his activity as art.

A third objective in setting up the account, as it has proceeded thus far, follows on from having specified the first stirrings of the art movement in jazz. Thus, we can see that the tradition, of regarding jazz as art, does not proceed, in the first place, from expert interpretation of a phenomenon which, until that time, had eluded intelligent assessment. Whether one agrees with my general account of jazz or not, no one today would accept the jazz/art view which predominated in America during the 20s and early 30s. In fact most of what was at that time produced under the jazz/art banner, would today count neither as art nor jazz. I have argued that later interpretations, of jazz as art, constitute misinterpretations of the actual jazz movement as social experience. Thus, the evidence accumulates for the view that the interpretations of jazz as art do not function as true knowledge of jazz (which is their ideological stance) but rather they function as unconscious, justifying disguises for entry into jazz experience (itself multifarious in nature and constantly changing) from various social bases. In time, as I shall try to indicate, the interpretation of jazz as art, though various in nature, takes over the reality of jazz, so that for those who make jazz and those who listen to it (and those for that matter who sell it) to be in jazz is to be concerned with art experience. As this becomes the prevailing conception of jazz, so jazz ceases to be a popular idiom and instead becomes increasingly complex and inaccessible. This is not to say that the value jazz had to previous generations disappears. There is no fundamental structural change affecting society which coincides with the immersion of jazz in art. The value jazz had to previous generations is still present, though appearing now under the label of Rhythm and Blues and its offshoots and derivatives, or rather R and B constitutes the deep base against which the popular idioms measure themselves. At this point jazz as the value it was dies.

Aesthetic judgement and sociological analysis

Janet Wolff (b.1924)

This reading links the concerns of Parts One and Two. Janet Wolff's approach to art is through sociology, and her claim is that the social history of art challenges Romantic notions of art and the artist. Like Pierre Macherey (Reading 11) she treats art as a form of production subject to ideological pressures and, like Roger Taylor (Reading 7), she feels that popular culture has been undervalued in relation to 'high art'. Making what she calls a 'sociological intervention' into the question of aesthetic value, Wolff provides a survey of the various ways in which aesthetic value has been constructed historically. Four main types of argument are identified: (a) segregationist, *which separates aesthetic value from social values; (b)* reductionist, *which reduces aesthetic value to ideological value (she singles out Terry Eagleton (Reading 12) as guilty of this); (c) arguments about the* transcendent *nature of art, which claim that art can transcend ideology; (d) arguments about the* specificity *of art, which see art as a specific 'discourse' within a given society and as having its own rules about the construction of value. Wolff's sympathies lie with (d), which she feels can be extended by use of the theories of the French philosopher, Michel Foucault (1926–84), one of the sources for what has come to be known as 'discourse theory'. Foucault saw discourses as arising from certain practices in society, and as organizing and codifying those practices into a system with its own concepts and specific use of language (a 'discourse'). Thus we could speak of the rise of the 'discourse of madness' in seventeenth- and eighteenth-century Europe, in which certain kinds of behaviour previously tolerated by society were classified as abnormal and those displaying them were hived off from society into institutions like lunatic asylums (see Michel Foucault,* Madness and Civilization, *1967, Tavistock Publications). 'Discourse theory' studies the broad social context from which discourses arise, as well as the rules and procedures governing each specific discourse. One problem that arises with 'discourse theory', as Wolff admits, is that it has little to say about 'aesthetic pleasure' (a criticism often levelled against Marxist aesthetics too).*

The sociology of art presents a challenge to aesthetics, a challenge which has so far not been satisfactorily met, nor even adequately acknowledged. Questions of aesthetic judgement are ignored by the sociologist of art, either because their relevance to sociology is not recognised, or because they are felt to belong to the discourse of philosophy of art, in which the sociologist is unwilling to engage. In this paper, I shall argue that the sociological study of the arts has quite important implications for aesthetics and aesthetic judgment, and that sociology, having mounted the challenge on the traditional discipline of aesthetics, must be prepared to follow through the consequences of this challenge. I begin by outlining the nature of the sociological challenge to aesthetics; I then go on to consider the implications for aesthetic judgment of this challenge; finally, I review some attempts to resolve the problem of 'aesthetic value' raised by sociology, and make some comparisons with the more familiar debate around the issue of 'truth' and relativism in the sociology of knowledge. (Some of the arguments in this paper are developed in more detail in... Wolff, 1983).

The sociological study of the arts has developed considerably in both Britain and the United States in the past fifteen years or so. The American work in this area has concentrated on the so-called 'production-of-culture' approach, and has occurred for the most part within the mainstream of sociology itself. The intention has been to identify and analyse the institutions and organisations of artistic production, in order to show how culture is 'produced' in social relations. (See, for example, Coser, 1978, and Peterson, 1976.) The trajectory of the sociology of the arts in Britain has been somewhat different, though in many ways it is complementary to the production-of-culture approach. The impetus has come as much from literary critics and art historians as from sociologists, and the work is accordingly inter-disciplinary in character. Compared with its American counterpart, it has also tended to be more strongly theoretical, and to have drawn very many of its conceptual tools and insights from Marxist and neo-Marxist analysis. (See Wolff, 1982, for a short summary of these developments.) One might say that work in the United States focusses on art as *production* whereas work in Britain focusses on art as *ideology*. The indications most recently, however, are of a certain convergence of interests and approach, with American scholars paying more attention to theoretical issues and to broader social and historical features of culture, and with British scholars moving from the more general or abstract areas of theory and ideology-critique to the concrete and detailed workings of the production of the arts. From the point of view of this paper, in any case, the main point is that both traditions feed into a new and anti-traditional view of art and, *a fortiori*, of aesthetics. Art, its production, its creators, and its assessors are necessarily demystified in the sociological perspective.

The implications of the sociological perspective for the traditional disciplines of art history, literary criticism, and the humanist study of culture in general have already been remarked, and the struggle over the contested terrain engaged (perhaps less so in art history than in the study of literature, at least in Britain). The sociology of art, or the social history of art, demonstrates the specific, historical, and arbitrary nature of the categories of 'art', 'artist' and 'work of art' themselves, by showing how these arose in particular historical circumstances in Western Europe, and developed in close connection with the rise of individualism in early capitalist society, and the notion of 'the individual' as a special category, distinct from his/her social attributes. The humanist perspective was, of course, reinforced by liberal philosophy and by classical political economy in the 18th century. In the 19th century, the notion of the artist as a peculiarly 'a-social' or special person was fuelled by the dual process of the decline of direct patronage in the arts, replaced by the reliance of the artist on the free market and the intermediary role of facilitators like dealers, critics, publishers, and so on; and the historical fact that artistic production, for whatever reasons (and these were complex and contradictory), managed to escape the fate of other forms of production during that century in Britain, namely that of falling under the law of profit, and of production under capitalist social relations. The artist/writer avoided the route of proletarianisation, retaining a specifically artisanal or petty bourgeois status in the production and sale of his/her work. Only in the 20th century do we see the widespread commercialisation of culture, including the 'high' arts, and the incorporation of artists into capitalist enterprise, as graphic designers, advertisers, copywriters, and other wage-labourers. (See Fuller, 1980a, and Vazquez, 1973.) So, particularly in the 19th century, the artist came to epitomise the idea of the 'free' creative worker, not subsumed under the factory system of commodity production, and following his/her own will. The original connection of artist and community, the nature of the artist as craftsperson, and the essential equivalence of artistic work and other forms of work were lost. The social history of art, then, challenges the Romantic notions of 'art' and of 'the artist', exposing the relative, and ideological, nature of such concepts.

Other aspects of artistic production are presented in a new light by the sociological intervention into the sacred arena. The essentially 'a-political' nature of 'great art' is thrown into question, by an analysis which insists on the ideological and political features of *any* cultural product. The view of works of art as the creation of a single, gifted individual, whether painter, writer, or film director, is challenged by an approach which carefully demonstrates the complex and multiple processes involved in the collective pro- duction of culture. The distinction between 'high art' and popular forms, or mass culture, is rendered problematic by a social-historical perspective which shows how such differentiation emerged, and examines its relationship to class and politics. All these issues have been noted by many others, and although the defenders of the old humanist disciplines of Literature and Art History continue to hold out against the inroads of the new critical approaches, I take it, that the validity and importance of the sociological intervention are firmly established. My task here is not to continue to enumerate the blows dealt by sociology to immanentist or transcendental notions of the arts which underlie those disciplines, however. I want, instead, to look at *aesthetics*, or the philosophy of art, and to consider the implications for this subject of the sociology of art. Aesthetics deals with questions concerning the nature of art, the nature of the aesthetic experience, and the nature of aesthetic judgment or evaluation. My argument is that sociology creates at least as many problems for this enquiry as it does for art history, and that, to date, these problems have barely been recognised, either by philosophers of art or by sociologists themselves. My main concern in this paper will be with the third kind of question of aesthetics, namely the nature of aesthetic judgment.

The first thing to point out is that there is by no means any agreement among philosophers as to the nature of aesthetic judgment (or, indeed, the nature of art or aesthetic experience). (See, for example, Osborne, 1972, and Hospers, 1969.) This is not the place or occasion to examine the various philosophical positions with regard to these questions – the phenomenological, the institu- tional, the physical-object-based analysis; nor am I qualified to adjudicate on such debates within philosophy. What I do argue, however, is that *any* discussion of aesthetic value needs to take account of the social history of art and of sociological analysis. There are a number of reasons for this, some more trivial than others. In the first place, the sociology of artistic consumption and taste demonstrates the relativity of judgment, and the transformations (socially, historically, and in other ways) of taste across time. The supposed universality of aesthetic judgment recommended by many philosophers who search for the intrinsic criteria of evaluation at least needs to confront the empirical fact of the variations of such judgments historically. Moreover, as the work of Pierre Bourdieu shows (Bourdieu, 1979 and 1980), aesthetic appreciation and assessment vary within a society and a period, being related to class position and educational achievement. So any aesthetics would have to be able to argue that the criteria for judgment and taste proposed as universal, or in some sense transcendent, overcome the relativism of time, place, and class.

Secondly, social history clarifies and locates the development of aesthetics itself, as a discipline. The separation of a distinct set of problems and experiences, and the recognition of these as worthy of study and investigation, dates from the 18th century, and the work of German philosophers like Baumgarten, Kant and Schiller. The development of aesthetics, of course, depended on the prior and accompanying constitution of 'art' itself as a self-contained discourse and practice, already illuminated by the social history of art. Aesthetics, in focussing attention on 'works of art', makes all the assumptions about art (for example, that the 'lesser' arts, crafts, and popular forms are not worthy of attention in the same way) made by those disciplines on which it is parasitic, such as art history. In other words, issues of value *are already assumed* by traditional aesthetics, by the very subject-matter it chooses to consider. The sociology *of* aesthetics, and particularly of its history and origins, illuminates many of the questions which are produced within its discourse.

Thirdly, and related to this point, the sociology of aesthetic judgment draws attention to the specific social and institutional location *of* such judgment. Those who accord 'value' to works of art and cultural products are empowered to do so by particular social and power relations in society, which situate them as critics and accreditors of art. They are to be found in establishments of higher education, departments of English Literature at universities, as reviewers and critics on certain prestigious journals, and as mediators or 'gate-keepers' in publishing and the art market. The criticism of art and literature is thus executed by a specific sector of the population, with its own particular social origins, orientations and ideologies; in England, at any rate, the class composition of this powerful minority is clearly unrepresentative of the population at large. As others have pointed out, criticism is never an innocent discipline (Eagleton, 1976: 11); it is produced in particular social relations, out of particular ideologies, and it is also closely integrated with the development of art and literature themselves, as ideological and political practices. At the very moment that criticism presents itself as 'pure' and timeless, its hidden ideological assumptions are asserted. An acceptable aesthetics, then, would need to be self-reflexive and not refuse examination of its own premises and prejudices. Again, the simple belief in universal standards of judgment is rendered more questionable.

The practices of criticism and aesthetic judgment, then, are subjected to deconstruction by sociology, and the notion of 'value' problematised. The sociology of art, which explores and identifies the essentially ideological nature of all cultural products, raises the pertinent question of whether *aesthetic* value is a chimera – a conception of timeless or universal beauty and worth which is itself entirely reducible to political/ideological/class values. In the rest of this paper, I want to look at some responses to the sociological challenge offered by a variety of people, all of whom have accepted to some extent the import of that challenge and the seriousness of its implications for aesthetic judgment. Their starting point is the recognition that (i) art is (amongst other things) ideological, (ii) criticism and aesthetic judgment are socially located, and (iii) aesthetics itself has a (social) history. The crucial question, then, is whether, and in what sense, we can continue to talk about 'aesthetic value' and 'aesthetic judgment', and what the relationship is between this and political-ideological value.

I think it is useful to identify four different responses to the sociology of art/aesthetics, which attempt to deal with the question of value. They might be referred to as (a) *segregationist* arguments, which insist on the separation of questions of origin and questions of validity of aesthetic judgment (in much the same way that some writers in the sociology of knowledge have argued for the independence of 'truth' from genesis of knowledge); (b) *reductionist* arguments, which collapse aesthetic into political-ideological value; (c) arguments about the *transcendent* nature of (great) art, which exempts it from social determination, or at least exempts that part of it which is 'valuable'; and (d) arguments about the *specificity* of art, which offer suggestions about the way in which we do discuss or accord merit to cultural products. As I shall argue, it is only the last of these four options which offers any real possibility for a sociological aesthetics.

An example of the first kind of resolution of the problem of relativism in art can be found in an essay by the art historian, Ernst Gombrich (1975). He argues that, although the social sciences are valuable in the study of art history, they have nothing to tell us as far as aesthetic value is concerned.

> It is when we come to this question concerning value, questions which are and will remain vital to the art historian, that the social scientist would, I think, have to refuse to be drawn...As a social scientist he (sic) must confine himself to social evidence, and this evidence can, in the nature of things, have no bearing on values. (Gombrich, 1975: 42)

That is to say, Gombrich believes that questions of value can, and indeed must, be *segregated* from questions of social origin. He goes on to conclude that the social scientist 'will have to rely on the art historian who is the keeper of the canon'. (Gombrich, 1975: 57.) The difficulty with this argument is that, as we have seen, this 'canon' is itself a problematic entity, which cannot be accepted uncritically. In general, the segregationist argument refuses to accept the full import of the sociological analysis of art and art criticism, by retaining the view that somehow criticism can be non-ideological, non-situated, and supra-historical. Aesthetics and art history cannot be preserved intact in this way from the insights of sociology, for their argument depends on a pre-critical conception of art and its practices.

The *reductionist* solution to the dilemma is, perhaps not surprisingly, more often encountered in the writings of sociologists than those of art historians, for the more philistine examples of sociological work in this area simply refuse to acknowledge problems concerned with the nature and quality of their subject-matter. Perhaps more surprisingly, we come across two rather prominent examples of reductionism in two influential texts in, respectively, the sociology of literature, and the social history of art, written in the 1970s by a marxist literary critic and a marxist art historian. Terry Eagleton, in his book *Criticism and Ideology* (1976) devotes a final chapter of a study of the ideological and social nature of literature to the question of 'aesthetic value'. His view is that such value is always *ideological* value.

> There is no 'immanent' value... Literary value is phenomenon
> which is *produced* in that ideological appropriation of the text,
> that 'consumptional production' of the work, which is the act of
> reading. It is always *relational* value... the histories of 'value' are
> a sub-sector of the histories of literary-ideological receptive
> practices. (Eagleton, 1976: 166–7. Emphasis in original.)

Although in his more recent work Eagleton does address the question of the specific nature of the aesthetic, as well as the problem of aesthetic 'pleasure' (e.g. Eagleton, 1981), in this text, which has been of great importance in the development of the sociology of literature, he appears to collapse aesthetic into political/ideological factors. Similarly, Nicos Hadjinicolaou, having demonstrated the ideological nature of visual art in interesting and suggestive ways, goes on to equate aesthetic judgments with ideological preferences.

> In practice this means that from now on the idealist question
> 'What is beauty?' or 'Why is this work beautiful?' must be replaced
> by the materialist question, 'By whom, when and for what reasons
> was this work thought beautiful?'. (Hadjinicolaou, 1978: 183.)

Beauty and aesthetic value are identical with aesthetic ideologies of particular social groups, and are inseparable from their wider political interests. Against both these accounts, I would argue that this equation cannot be so easily made, nor the translation from ideological content to aesthetic value so immediately effected. A reductionist account does not enable us to understand the nature of aesthetic *pleasure* produced in the experience of a work; nor is it demonstrated that ideological compatibility of recognition constitutes aesthetic judgment. For example, we would still want to differentiate between two works, of similar 'ideological' import, which appear to us to be of widely disparate 'quality'. This notion of 'quality', therefore, remains unexplored in the reductionist accounts.

The third type of argument asserts the social and ideological construction of art, but argues that art, or 'good' art, transcends its conditions of production. This willingness to exempt certain privileged categories of art from the grasp of sociology can be found also in the work of sociologists themselves, and not only, as might be expected, in that of literary and art scholars. An example of it occurs in Althusser's essays on art. (Althusser, 1971a and 1971b.) For him, art is somewhere between knowledge and ideology, exercising an ideological effect, and yet allowing us to 'feel the reality of the ideology' of the world (Althusser, 1971b: 204). As he says, 'I do not rank real art among the ideologies' (1971b: 203). He talks, too, of the 'privileged relation between (art) and ideology (1971a: 220), which enables the viewer to perceive ideology in some sense. This account seems to me to be both vague and unsatisfactory, particularly in the context of a theory which insists on a clear distinction between science and ideology. We might well still ask whether the role of art in enabling us to 'see' ideology renders art itself scientific or ideological (for, in Althusser's own terms, it must be one or the other). The question of the specific nature of art is both acknowledged and avoided in this account, by the device of an arbitrary discovery of an intermediate category of thought or knowledge. It is a surprisingly woolly compromise, as the reference to 'seeing', 'perceiving' and 'feeling' evidences, and an aside about aesthetic value does not make us any more confident that we can discover here a useful theory of art.

> Art (I mean authentic art, not works of an average or mediocre level) does not give us a knowledge... (Althusser, 1971b: 204.)

But it is precisely notions like 'authentic' and 'mediocre' which are problematic. The relationship between sociology and aesthetics cannot be dealt with by such a simple device as according a special epistemological status to art (much less 'great' or 'authentic' art). Althusser has an unusual companion in this attitude to the relationship between art and ideology, namely Herbert Marcuse. Throughout Marcuse's *œuvre*, at least from *Eros and Civilisation* (1969), we find a belief in the special power and status of art as the potential representative or key to freedom and against repression. In the late 1960s, he identified a (brief) possibility of oppositional culture and politics in the art and life-style of the student movement. In his last work, he asserts even more boldly the autonomy of art from its social relations, presenting the essay as a critique of 'Marxist orthodoxy'. Art remains here a 'dissenting force' (Marcuse, 1978: 8), as a result of its autonomy from social relations. The 'aesthetic dimension' somehow transcends the social and the processes of production *of* art. But we find here no attempt to explain how this can be possible. Marcuse's defence of his universalist, humanist stance is both idealist and metaphysical.

> By virtue of its transhistorical, universal truths, art appeals to a consciousness which is not only that of a particular class, but that of human beings as 'species beings', developing all their life-enhancing faculties. (Marcuse, 1978: 29.)

He avoids entirely an analysis of the production of art as ideology, and refuses to specify the nature of the transformation of art under different regimes and in different social conditions. On the question of aesthetic value, Marcuse's arguments are either circular or metaphysical.

> I term those works 'authentic' or 'great' which fulfill aesthetic criteria previously defined as constitutive of 'authentic' or 'great' art. In defense, I would say that throughout the long history of art, and in spite of changes in taste, there is a standard which remains constant. (1978:x)

By now it is hardly necessary to point out that it is this 'standard' which sociology calls into question. For Marcuse, the autonomy of art, and the criteria for aesthetic judgment, are defended by simply asserting them. He retreats from the challenge of elaborating a sociological aesthetics into the idealist categories of traditional aesthetics, in which art somehow *transcends* its conditions of production and reception.

Finally, I turn to accounts of culture which consider the *specificity* of art, in an attempt to deal with the ideological nature of art, and at the same time to identify its peculiar character, and the specific grounds of judgment involved in its assessment. These approaches recognise the need to avoid the extremes of segregationism and reductionism. There are three main sub-categories within this approach. First, the specificity of art is seen to consist in its *specific codes and conventions of representation,* and its techniques and skills. The contribution of structuralist and semiotic analyses has been considerable in enabling us to perceive the specificity of art and literature in this sense, as well as in refusing to allow us to collapse art into its social determinants, on the basis of a sort of 'reflection' theory, for we see that art *re*-produces ideology in a form worked through the particular codes and signs of the genre. Now it may be that there is some mileage with regard to the question of aesthetic judgment in the semiotic theory of art and culture, to the extent that a 'good' work is one which conforms to the rules and conventions of its genre, and/or is technically excellent. That is, one criterion for the assessment of a work is that of its success in meeting certain (identifiable) requirements for such work. However, this appears to me to be a somewhat limited account of aesthetic value; moreover, we can imagine saying of a work that it is technically excellent, but that despite that it 'fails' as a work of art (as well, of course, as that we don't like it). Conversely, the notion is logically possible of a 'good' work of art which is rather weak in terms of rules of narrative, structure, perspective, colour use, and so on.

The specificity of art is also invoked by certain writers who draw our attention to the *human universals* expressed in great works. Such accounts rest either on a philosophical anthropology (a theory of human nature), or on psychoanalytic theory. In his recent work, the Marxist literary critic, Raymond Williams, has resorted to anthropological assertions (following the arguments of the Italian writer, Timpanaro). Williams writes

> Even with the category of the aesthetic, I say it is wholly necessary to reject the notion of aesthetics as the special province of a certain kind of response, but we cannot rule out the possibility of rediscovering certain permanent configurations of a theoretical kind which answer to it. (1979: 325)

He says that in his own earlier writing, the problem of aesthetics had been particularly difficult, and that reading Timpanaro's work, stressing as it does the biological and material features of human existence, offered him some solution to this. For example,

> Many poems, many kinds of writing, indeed a lot of everyday speech communicate what is in effect a life rhythm and the interaction of these life rhythms is probably a very important part of the material process of writing and reading. (1979: 340)

The tentativeness of this account is obvious ('probably', 'cannot rule out', and so on). More importantly, it is never really specified what these 'permanent configurations' might be, nor how they are expressed in art. The kind of human universals which Timpanaro himself discusses are so general as to be of little use in 'explaining' art – love, death, sexuality. Moreover, it is less straight-forward a matter than it might seem to identify even these as pre-social or trans-historical. For example, Timpanaro reproduces uncritically a statement by Labriola, to the effect that 'we are born naturally male and female' (Timpanaro, 1975: 49). But as Foucault's work on sexuality demonstrates, and as psychoanalysis confirms, sex and gender are problematic concepts, and even the distinction between 'male' and 'female is produced in language and ideology. So any notion of 'biological constants' is fraught with difficulties. As ever, 'human universals' remain very elusive things. It is doubtful, anyway, how much they will illuminate the understanding of art for us. As far as psychoanalytic theory is concerned, my main comment would be that so far there is no satisfactory account (of which I am aware) which deals with the aesthetic. A recent book by Peter Fuller (1980b), which uses Kleinian theory to explain the continuing appeal of certain works of art (a problem recognised at least since Marx addressed the problem of how Greek art could continue to please contemporary audiences), produces a rather odd, and essentially unprovable, analysis of aesthetic experience (in terms of childhood experiences, and relation to the mother). The risk with psychoanalysis, including its Lacanian version, is that it will posit a-historical features of human experience, which ignore time, place, society and class (though Lacanian theory *has* been applied to the construction of gender difference with profitable results). Any such theory must also remain open to the fact of the social construction and historical variability of psychological processes. However, the promise of a psychoanalytic or psychologi-cal theory, in suitably sociological terms, may well be in a better position than other theories to deal with the issue of 'pleasure' raised by aesthetics. This need not be in terms of human universals, but simply in terms of the specific construction of particular (social) individuals. Such a promise remains to be fulfilled.

In this last section of the paper, I have been looking at approaches to aesthetic judgment which take on the implications of the sociology of art, and try at the same time to rescue a notion of the specifically aesthetic. For art is not just ideology, and its appreciation is not simply class-based cultural politics. Despite the variation of judgments across time and space, we still need to account for the *persistence* of value, and for the phenomenon of cross-cultural appeal (and without reducing *this* to statements about 'hegemony' or 'cultural imperialism', which seem to me to explain little about the nature of art and its reception). The final contender for a theory of the specificity of art which offers the beginnings of a promising analysis is *discourse theory*. If we apply the work of Foucault, developed by him in quite other connections, to the study of art, we can see art, art history, and art criticism as specific *discourses*, in which notions of value are constructed. By the same token, the 'rules' according to which we accord value are produced within the discourse. A criticism of discourse theory has been that it is a non-sociological, idealist approach, which allows total autonomy to language and discourse. But I would argue that the analysis of discourses is entirely compatible with a sociology of knowledge, which locates discourses, and shows that they are, in their turn, a product of material and social practices. In fact, in *The Archaeology of Knowledge* (1972), Foucault gives an indication of the lines on which an 'archaeology of art' might be undertaken, in terms of whether space, distance, depth, colour, light, etc. were 'considered, named, enunciated, and conceptualized in a discursive practice' (Foucault, 1972: 193–4). In such a framework, the auton-omy of art from social and ideological factors is automatically conceptualised. The criteria of judgment may be clearly specified. And the origins of the discourse itself can be spelled out, by a sociological analysis and historical enquiry. The weakness of discourse theory, with regard to aesthetics, is that it cannot engage with the problem of aesthetic pleasure, for this cannot be merely an effect of discourse. Like socio-psychoanalytical theories of art, discourse analysis offers the beginnings of a useful approach to a sociological aesthetics, though the exact form such an analysis might take has yet to be worked out.

It is interesting that the question of 'value' is now being posed in the sociology of art, at a time when equivalent issues in the sociology of knowledge are becoming less of a problem. The question of truth and relativism was always a problem in the classical sociology of knowledge. More recently, the demonstration that knowledge (including science) is interest-related, that the practices of scientists are, in one sense, arbitrary, and that knowledge has a 'provisional' nature, has been widely accepted among some sociologists of knowledge and science. Relativism has become respectable as one position within the sociology of knowledge. Conversely, for the sociology of the arts there appeared to be no such problem of 'truth', since art is not the kind of thing which may be 'true' or 'false'. Questions of epistemology therefore have not arisen in the same way in this area. But more recently, as I hope to have shown in this paper, the problem of 'truth' *has* emerged in a particular form in the sociology of art – namely, in terms of the question about 'true' or 'valid' assessments of works of art. It is now acknowledged that sociology raises numerous problems for aesthetic theory, and in particular for the issue of aesthetic judgment. In this paper, I have identified some of the implications for aesthetics which a sociology of art inevitably has, and considered some of the ways in which writers have attempted to confront, avoid, or deal with those implications. In conclusion, I would like to stress that the problem is not only one for philosophers of art. For although it is true that the categories of aesthetic discussion and aesthetic judgment have to be re-thought in post-sociological terms, it is equally true that sociology cannot pretend to aesthetic neutrality, as has been its practice to date. In choosing particular works or practices rather than others to study, for example, sociologists accept or re-affirm existing aesthetic judgments. (It is interesting that the major sociologists of art continue to discuss the 'great works' – George Eliot, Dickens, Thomas Mann, Conrad, Rembrandt, David). A new aesthetics is therefore an essential requirement not only for philosophy, but also for sociology itself.

References

ALTHUSSER, L. (1971a). 'Cremonini, painter of the abstract', in *Lenin and Philosophy and Other Essays*. London: New Left Books. pp.209–20.
ALTHUSSER, L. (1971b). 'A letter on art in reply to Andre Daspre', in *Lenin and Philosophy and Other Essays*. London: New Left Books. pp.203–8.
BOURDIEU, Pierre (1979). *La Distinction: Critique Sociale du Jugement*. Paris: Editions de Minuit.
BOURDIEU, Pierre (1980) 'The aristocracy of culture', *Media, Culture and Society*, Vol. 2, No. 3, pp.225–54.
COSER, Lewis (ed.) (1978) *The Production of Culture*, Social Research Vol. 45, No. 2.
EAGLETON, Terry (1976). *Criticism and Ideology*. London: New Left Books.
EAGLETON, Terry (1981) *Walter Benjamin, or Towards a Revolutionary Criticism*. London: New Left Books.
FULLER, Peter (1980a) 'The fine arts after modernism', *New Left Review* 119, pp.42–59.
FULLER, Peter (1980b) *Art and Psychoanalysis*. London: Writers and Readers Publishing Cooperative.
GOMBRICH, E.H. (1975). *Art History and the Social Sciences*. London: Oxford University Press.
HADJINICOLAOU, Nicos (1978) *Art History and Class Struggle*. London: Pluto.

HOSPERS, John (ed.) (1969) *Introductory Readings in Aesthetics* London: Collier-Macmillan.

MARCUSE, Herbert (1969) *Eros and Civilisation*. London: Sphere Books.

MARCUSE, Herbert (1978) *The Aesthetic Dimension: Toward a Critique of Marxist Aesthetics*. Boston: Beacon Press.

OSBORNE, Harold (ed.) (1972) *Aesthetics*. London: Oxford University Press.

PETERSON, Richard A. (ed.) (1976) *The Production of Culture*. London: Sage.

TIMPANARO, Sebastiano (1975) *On Materialism*. London: New Left Books.

VAZQUEZ, A.S. (1973) *Art and Society: Essays in Marxist Aesthetics*. London: Merlin Press.

WILLIAMS, Raymond (1979) *Politics and Letters: Interviews with New Left Review*. London: New Left Books.

WOLFF, Janet (1982) 'The problem of ideology in the sociology of art: a case study of Manchester in the nineteenth century', *Media, Culture and Society*, Vol. 4, No. 1, pp.63–75.

WOLFF, Janet (1983) *Aesthetics and the Sociology of Art*. London: Allen & Unwin.

The Republic

Plato (427–347 BC)

Plato continues his attack on poetry and the arts in this extract drawn from a later part of The Republic, *arguing that most poetry has no serious value or claim to truth and that it is potentially detrimental to public morality. Poetry, he maintains, cannot be true because it is a mere representation of ultimate reality, and its value can be called into question because it appeals to the lower, that is the emotional, part of our nature. The argument in the first case refers back to Plato's 'Theory of Forms', which holds that objects in the world are imitations or representations of a perfect form located outside the human realm. When poets talk about these objects, and when painters paint them, they are imitating an imitation, thus placing them at one further remove from the true 'form'. In the second case, Plato is led to be suspicious of poetry's ability to sway the emotions by the strength of his commitment to reason. There is a fear of what might happen if poetry were to cause us to relax control over our emotions, the assumption being that our subsequently unpredictable behaviour might threaten public order and morality. Plato establishes a clear link between aesthetic value and moral value, but mainly of a negative kind; poetry, he feels, is more likely to encourage immorality than morality, hence his continued defence of censorship.*

Part Ten [Book Ten] Theory of art

This part has the appearance of an appendix, written to justify against anticipated or actual criticism the attack on the poets in Books II and III (Part III). It has been suggested that it should not be taken too seriously, and should be read as an attack on the extravagant claims made for the poets by Greek opinion, rather than as a serious attempt to state a philosophy of art. It is true that the Greeks treated the works of Homer and the poets as their Bible, and true also, as we see from Plato's *Ion*, where Homer is claimed as a teacher of everything from carpentry to morals and generalship, that extravagant claims were made for them. But there is nothing to suggest that Plato is not serious, though he is often characteristically ironical; and the general contention in Section I that poetry is illusion fits well into the scheme of the Divided Line.

1 ART AND ILLUSION

The Greek word *mimesis*, 'representation', used in Part III to describe dramatic as opposed to narrative poetry, is now used to describe artistic creation as a whole, and interpreted to mean a rather unintelligent imitation.[1] The productions both of the painter and the poet are imitations of a life which has itself only secondary reality, and neither painter nor poet have any knowledge of what they imitate. Pictures and poems are second-hand, unreal, and tell us nothing about life.

'You know,' I said, 'among all the excellent features of our ideal state, there's none I rank higher than its treatment of poetry.'

'Why exactly?'

BK X 595

'Because it excluded all dramatic representation. Now that we have distinguished the various elements in the mind, we can see more clearly how essential it is to exclude it.'

'What do you mean?'

'Between ourselves – and you mustn't give me away to the tragedians and other dramatists – such representations definitely harm the minds of their audiences, unless they're inoculated against them by knowing their real nature.'

'What exactly have you in mind?'

'I must tell you, I suppose; yet the love and respect I've always had from a boy for Homer makes me hesitate – for I think he's the original master and guide of all the great tragic poets. But one must not respect an individual more than the truth, and so, as I say, I must tell you.'

'You must,' he said.

'Listen, then; or, rather, answer my questions.'

'Ask away.'

'Can you give me a general definition of representation? I'm not sure that I know, myself, exactly what it is.'

'Then it's not very likely I shall!'

'Oh, I don't know,' I said. 'Short sight is sometimes quicker than long sight.'

'True enough,' he replied. 'But with you here, if I did see anything, I shouldn't much want to say so. You must use your own eyes.'

'Then shall we start where we always do? You know that we always assume that there is a single essential Form corresponding to each class of particular things to which we apply the same name?'

'Yes, I know.'

'Then let us take an instance. For example, there are many particular beds and tables.'

'Yes.'

'But there are only two Forms, one of Bed and one of Table.'

'Yes.'

'Then we normally say that the maker of either of these kinds of furniture has his eye on the appropriate Form; and similarly with other things. For no one could possibly make the Form itself, could he?'

'No.'

'I wonder what you would call a man who could make all the objects produced by individual craftsmen?'

'He would be a remarkably clever man.'

'Just a minute, and you'll be more surprised still. For this same craftsman can not only make all artificial objects, but also create all plants and animals, himself included, and, in addition, earth and sky and gods, the heavenly bodies and the underworld.'

'An astonishing bit of craftsmanship!' he exclaimed.

'You don't believe me?' I asked. 'Tell me, do you think that a craftsman of this sort couldn't exist, or (in one sense, if not in another) create all these things? Do you know that there's a sense in which you could create them yourself?'

'What sense?'

'It's not difficult, and can be done in various ways quite quickly. The quickest way is to take a mirror and turn it round in all directions; before long you will create sun and stars and earth, yourself and all other animals and plants, and all the other objects we mentioned just now.'

'Yes, but they would only be reflections,' he said, 'not real things.'

'Quite right,' I replied, 'and very much to the point. For a painter is a craftsman of just this kind, I think. Do you agree?'

'Yes.'

'You may perhaps object that the things he creates are not real; and yet there *is* a sense in which the painter creates a bed, isn't there?'

'Yes,' he agreed, 'he produces an appearance of one.'

'And what about the carpenter? Didn't you agree that what he 597 produces is not the essential Form of Bed, the ultimate reality, but a particular bed?'

'I did.'

'If so, then what he makes is not the ultimate reality, but something that resembles that reality. And anyone who says that the products of the carpenter or any other craftsman are ultimate realities can hardly be telling the truth, can he?'

'No one familiar with the sort of arguments we're using could suppose so.'

'So we shan't be surprised if the bed the carpenter makes lacks the precision of reality?'

'No.'

'Then shall we try to define representation now, in the light of this illustration?'

'Yes, please.'

'We have seen that there are three sorts of bed. The first exists in the ultimate nature of things, and if it was made by anyone it must, I suppose, have been made by God. The second is made by the carpenter, the third by the painter.'

'Yes, that is so.'

'So painter, carpenter, and God are each responsible for one kind of bed.'

'Yes.'

'God created only one essential Form of Bed in the ultimate nature of things, either because he wanted to or because some necessity prevented him from making more than one; at any rate he didn't produce more than one, and more than one could not possibly be produced.'

'Why?'

'Because, suppose he created two only, you would find that they both shared a common character or form, and this common character would be the ultimate reality.'

'That's true.'

'And I suppose that God knew it, and as he wanted to be the real creator of a real Bed, and not just a carpenter making a particular bed, decided to make the ultimate reality unique.'

'I suppose so.'

'Then do you think we might call him author of the nature of things or some such name?'

'We could do so with justice; for all his creations are ultimate realities.'

'And what about the carpenter? Doesn't he manufacture the bed?'

'Yes.'

'And what about the artist? Does he make or manufacture?

'No.'

'Then what does he do?'

'I think that we may fairly say that he represents what the other two make.'

'Good,' said I. 'Then the artist's representation stands at third remove from reality?'

'It does.'

'So the tragic poet, whose art is representation, is third in succession to the throne of truth; and the same is true of all other artists.'

'So it seems.'

'We are agreed about representation, then. But, tell me, which does the painter try to represent? The ultimate reality or the things 598 the craftsman makes?'

'The things the craftsman makes.'

'As they are, or as they appear? There is still that distinction to make.'

'I don't understand,' he said.

'What I mean is this. If you look at a bed, or anything else, sideways or endways or from some other angle, does it make any difference to the bed? Isn't it merely that it looks different?'

'Yes, it's the same bed, but it looks different.'

'Then consider – does the painter try to represent the bed or other object as it is, or as it appears? Does he represent it as it is, or as it looks?'

'As it looks.'

'The artist's representation is therefore a long way removed from truth, and he is able to reproduce everything because he never penetrates beneath the superficial appearance of anything. For example, a painter can paint a portrait of a shoe-maker or a carpenter or any other craftsman without knowing anything about their crafts at all; yet, if he is skilful enough, his portrait of a carpenter may, at a distance, deceive children or simple people into thinking it is a real carpenter.'

'Yes, it may.'

'In all such cases,' I went on, 'we should be on our guard. When someone tells us that he has met someone who is a master of every craft and knows better than all the experts, we must tell him not to be silly, and not to let himself be taken in by a charlatan, whose apparent omniscience is due entirely to his own inability to distinguish knowledge and ignorance, reality and representation.'

'Very true.'

'We must go on to examine the claims of the tragedians and their chief, Homer. We are told that they are masters of all forms of skill, and know all about morality and religion; for – so the argument runs – a good poet must, if he's to write well, know all about his subject, otherwise he can't write about it. We must ask ourselves whether those who have met the poets, and read their works, have failed to perceive that these are representations at the third remove from reality, and easy to produce without any 599 knowledge of the truth, because they are shadows and not realities; or are they right, and do good poets really know about the subjects on which the public thinks they speak so well?'

'It's a question we should certainly examine.'

'Suppose, then, a man could produce both the original and the representation. Do you think he would devote himself to the manufacture of representations and make it the highest object in life?'

'No, I don't.'

'Of course not. If he really knew about the things he represented, he would devote himself to them and not to their representations; he would try to leave behind him the memory of things well done, and be more anxious to be praised for his actions than to write poems in praise of those of others.'

'I agree; the rewards and the reputations would both be greater.'

'We won't, then, expect Homer or any of the poets to explain medicine or any similar skilled activity to us; for example, if they claim to be real doctors and not merely to imitate doctor's talk, we won't ask them to name any poet, ancient or modern, who has performed cures like Aesculapius, or founded a school of medicine as he did. But we *have* a right to cross-question Homer when he tries to deal with matters of such supreme importance as military strategy, political administration and education. "My dear Homer," we shall say, "if our definition is wrong and you are not merely manufacturing shadows at third remove from reality, but are a stage nearer the truth about human excellence, and really capable of judging what kind of conduct will make the individual or the community better or worse, tell us any state whose constitution you have reformed, as Lycurgus did at Sparta and others have done elsewhere on a larger or smaller scale. What city owes the benefit of its legal system to you? Italy and Sicily owe theirs to Charondas, we owe ours to Solon. Tell us who is similarly indebted to you?"'

'I don't think,' said Glaucon, 'that Homer's most devoted admirers would claim there was anyone.'

'Well, then, is there any record of a successful war being fought 600 in Homer's day either under his command or with his advice?'

'No.'

'Then had he any practical skill? Did he invent any ingenious practical devices like Thales of Miletus or Anacharsis the Scythian?'

'He did nothing of that sort.'

'Well, if he did no public service, did he found a school of his own, where enthusiastic pupils came to hear him while he lived and to hand on a Homeric way of life to their successors? That was how Pythagoras got his great reputation, and his successors still talk of a Pythagorean way of life which distinguishes them in the eyes of the world from other people.'

'We hear nothing of that sort about Homer. Indeed, if the stories about Homer are true, his friend Creophylus is an even more absurd example of education than his name[2] suggests, as he is said to have paid very little attention to Homer in his own day, when he was still alive.'

'Yes, that's the story,' I said. 'But do you think, Glaucon, that if Homer had really had the knowledge to bring men the benefits of education, instead of merely representing it at second-hand, he would not have had many enthusiastic followers and admirers? Protagoras of Abdera and Prodicus of Ceos and a whole lot of other individual teachers have managed to persuade their contemporaries that no one who has not studied under *them* is fit to manage either private or public affairs; and they are so admired for this expert knowledge that their pupils are almost ready to carry them about shoulder-high. Would the contemporaries of Homer and Hesiod have let them continue as wandering minstrels, if they had really been able to make them better men? Wouldn't they have clung to them like solid gold and tried to keep them at home, and if they wouldn't stay, gone to school with them wherever they were till they had learnt what they could from them?'

'I think that's perfectly true, Socrates.'

'We may assume, then, that all the poets from Homer downwards have no grasp of reality but merely give us a superficial representation of any subject they treat, including human goodness. For example, as we said just now, the painter paints what looks like a shoemaker, though neither he nor his public know anything 601 about shoemaking, but judge merely by colour and form.'

'True.'

'In the same way the poet can use words as a medium to paint a picture of any craftsman, though he knows nothing except how to represent him, and the metre and rhythm and music will persuade people who are as ignorant as he is, and who judge merely from his words, that he really has something to say about shoemaking or generalship or whatever it may be. So great is the natural magic of poetry. Strip it of its poetic colouring, reduce it to plain prose, and I think you know how little it amounts to.'

'Yes, I've noticed that.'

'Like a face which relied on the bloom of youth for its charm, and had no real beauty.'

'Yes.'

'Here's another point. The artist who makes an image of a thing, knows nothing about the reality but only about the appearance – that was what we said, wasn't it?'

'Yes.'

'But that only takes us half-way.'

'Go on.'

'The painter may paint a picture of bit and bridle.'

'Yes.'

'But aren't they made by the harness-maker and smith?'

'Yes.'

'Then does the painter know what the bit and bridle ought to be like? Isn't this something that even the makers – the harness-maker and the smith – don't know, but only the horseman who knows how to use them?'

'True.'

'Isn't the same thing always true? You always have the three techniques – use, manufacture, and representation.'

'Yes.'

'And isn't the quality, beauty and fitness of any implement or creature or action judged by reference to the use for which man or nature intended it?'

'Yes.'

'It follows that the user must know about a thing and be able to tell the maker how well it has performed its function in use. For example, the flute player reports to the flute-maker on the performance of his flutes, and will give specifications for their manufacture which the flute-maker will follow.'

'Of course.'

'The player, in fact, knows about the merits and defects of his instruments, and the manufacturer will rely on the player's judgement?'

'Yes.'

'The user of an implement is therefore the man who knows about it; the manufacturer is compelled to take instructions from 602

---

him and rely on his knowledge, and is so able to form a correct opinion about its merits and defects.'

'That is so.'

'What about the artist and his representations? Has he the direct experience of the things he paints to enable him to know whether they are right or wrong? Or has he the correct opinion that springs from enforced reliance on the orders of someone who knows what he ought to paint?'

'He has neither.'

'So the artist has neither knowledge nor correct opinion about the goodness or badness of the things he represents.'

'Apparently not.'

'So the poet too, as artist, will be pretty ignorant about the subjects of his poetry.'

'Completely ignorant.'

'But he'll go on writing poetry, in spite of his ignorance of all he writes about, and will represent anything that pleases the ignorant multitude.'

'What else can he do?'

'Well,' I concluded, 'we seem to be pretty well agreed that the artist knows little or nothing about the subjects he represents and that his art is something that has no serious value; and that this applies to all tragic poetry, epic or dramatic.'

'Yes, entirely agreed.'

2   THE APPEAL OF ART AND POETRY

Art and poetry appeal to, and represent, the lower, less rational part of our nature.

'Now, look here,' I said; 'we have said that this process of representation deals with something at third remove from reality, haven't we?'

'Yes.'

'Then what part of the human being does it affect?'

'What do you mean by part?'

'Something like this. The apparent size of an object, as you know, varies with its distance from our eye.'

'Yes.'

'So also a stick will look bent if you put it in the water, straight when you take it out, and differences of shading can make the same surface seem to the eye concave or convex; and it's clearly all a matter of our mind being confused. It is on this natural weakness of ours that the scene-painter and conjuror and their fellows rely when they deceive us with their tricks.'

'True.'

'Measuring, counting, and weighing were invented to help us out of these difficulties, and to ensure that we should not be guided by apparent differences of size, quantity and heaviness, but by proper calculations of number, measurement, and weight – calculations which can only be performed by the element of reason in the mind.'

'Yes, that's true.'

'Yet when reason informs us, as the result of frequent measurements, that one thing is greater than or less than or equal to another, it may be contradicted by appearances.'

'It may be.'

'Yet we said that the same part of us cannot hold different opinions about the same thing at the same time.'

'And we were quite right.'

'So the part of the mind which contradicts the measurements 603 cannot be the same as the part which agrees with them.'

'No.'

'But the part which relies on measurement and calculation must be the best part of us, and the part which contradicts them an inferior one.'

'Inevitably.'

'That was the conclusion I had in mind when I said that the work of the painter and of all other artists was far removed from reality, and appealed to an element in us equally far removed from reason, a thoroughly unsound combination.'

'Thoroughly unsound.'

'So art is a poor child born of poor parents.'

'I suppose so.'

'And does this apply to the visual arts only, or also to the art which appeals to the ear, that is, poetry?'

'I should think it probably applies to poetry too.'

'We mustn't rely on probabilities drawn from painting,' I said, 'but consider the part of the mind to which dramatic poetry appeals, and ask how good or bad it is.'

Yes, that's what we should do,' he agreed.

'Then let us put it like this, 'I went on: 'drama represents human beings in action, either voluntary or compulsory; in that action they fare, as they think, well or ill, and experience joy or sorrow. Is that a fair summary?'

'Yes.'

'And does a man remain at unity in himself in all these experiences? We saw that there could be conflict and contradiction in the realm of vision; isn't there a similar conflict and contradiction in the realm of action? There is really no need to ask the question, because, as I remember, we have already agreed that our mind is full of innumerable conflicts of this sort.'

'We were quite right about that.'

'Yes, but there's an omission we ought to make good.'

'What is it?'

'Didn't we say[3] that a good man who loses his son, or anything else dear to him, will bear the misfortune more equably than other people?'

'Yes.'

'Now consider: is it because he will feel no grief? or is that impossible, and is it because he will moderate his sorrow?'

'The second alternative is nearer the truth.'

'Then tell me, will he be more inclined to resist and fight against 604 his grief when his fellows can see him, or when he is alone by himself?'

'Much more inclined when he's with others.'

'On the other hand, when he is alone he will not mind saying and doing things which he would be ashamed to let other people hear or see?'

'That is true.'

'His reason and his principles demand restraint, while his feeling of sorrow prompts him to give way to grief.'

'True.'

'And the simultaneous presence of opposite impulses implies that there are two elements in his nature.'

'Of course.'

'One of these is law-abiding, and ready to submit to the principles of conduct, which say that it is best, so far as we can, to bear misfortune patiently and without bitterness; for it may prove a blessing in disguise, and nothing is gained by impatience, nor is anything in human life of great consequence; besides, grief prevents us getting just the help we need.'

'And what is that?'

'The help of our reason,' I said, 'which reflects on what has happened and then chooses the best move that the fall of the dice allows. We must learn not to hold our hurts and waste our time crying, like children who've bumped themselves, but to train our mind to banish grief by curing our hurts and rectifying our mistakes as soon as it can.'

'That is the right way to deal with misfortune.'

'And the highest part of us is ready to proceed accordingly.'

'Yes, obviously.'

'The other part of us, which remembers our sufferings and is never tired of bemoaning them, we may, I think, call irrational and lazy and cowardly.'

'Yes, we may.'

'And this recalcitrant element in us gives plenty of material for dramatic representation; but the reasonable element and its unvarying calm are difficult to represent, and difficult to understand if represented, particularly by the motley audience in a theatre, who have no experience of it.'

'Very true.'

605

'The dramatic poet will not therefore naturally turn to this element, nor will his skill be directed to please it, if he wants to win a popular reputation; he will find material for his dramas in the character that is unstable and irritable.'

'Obviously.'

'Then we can fairly take the poet and set him beside the painter. He resembles him both because his works have a low degree of truth and because he appeals to the low element in the mind. We are therefore quite right to refuse to admit him to a properly run state, because he stirs up and encourages and strengthens the lower elements in the mind at the expense of reason, which is like giving power and political control to the worst elements in a state and ruining the better elements. The dramatic poet produces a similar state of affairs in the mind of the individual, by encouraging the unreasoning part of it, which cannot make distinctions of size and confuses large and small, and by creating images far removed from reality.'

'I agree.'

3 THE EFFECTS OF POETRY AND DRAMA

Poetry, dramatic poetry in particular, has a bad moral effect on its audiences, who learn to admire and imitate the faults it represents. We cannot, therefore, allow poetry in our ideal state.

'The gravest charge against poetry still remains. It has a terrible power to corrupt even the best characters, with very few exceptions.'

'It is indeed terrible if it can do that.'

'Then listen. When we hear Homer or one of the tragic poets

representing the sufferings of a great man and making him bewail them at length with every expression of tragic grief, you know how even the best of us enjoy it and let ourselves be carried away by our feelings; and are full of praises for the merits of the poet who can most powerfully affect us in this way.'

'Yes, I know.'

'Yet in our private griefs we pride ourselves on just the opposite, that is, on our ability to bear them in silence like men, and we regard the behaviour we admired on the stage as womanish.'

'Yes, I'm aware of that.'

'Then is it really right,' I asked, 'to admire, when we see him on the stage, a man we should ourselves be ashamed to resemble? Is it reasonable to feel enjoyment and admiration rather than disgust?'

'It seems most unreasonable,' he said.

'Particularly,' I added, 'if you look at it in this way.' 606

'How?'

'If you consider that the poet gratifies and indulges the natural instinct for tears and the desire to give full vent to our sorrows, both of which we restrain in our private misfortunes. Our better nature, being without adequate moral or intellectual training, relaxes its control, on the grounds that it is someone else's sufferings it is watching and that there's nothing wrong in praising and pitying another man with some claim to goodness, even though his grief is excessive; besides, it reckons the pleasure it gets as sheer gain, and would certainly not consent to be deprived of it by condemning the whole poem. For very few people are capable of realizing that our feelings for other people must influence ourselves, and that if we let ourselves feel excessively for the misfortunes of others it will be difficult to restrain our feelings in our own.'

'That is very true.'

'The same argument applies to laughter. For the effect is similar when you enjoy on the stage – or even in ordinary life – jokes that you would be ashamed to make yourself, instead of detesting their vulgarity. You are giving rein to your comic instinct, which your reason has restrained for fear you may seem to be playing the fool, and bad taste in the theatre may insensibly lead you into becoming a buffoon at home.'

'It may indeed.'

'Poetry has the same effect on us when it represents sex and anger, and the other desires and feelings of pleasure and pain which normally accompany our actions. It feeds them when they ought to be starved, and makes them control us when we ought, in the interests of our own welfare and happiness, to control them.'

'I can't deny it,' he said.

And so, Glaucon,' I continued, 'when you meet people who admire Homer as the educator of Greece, and who say that in social and educational matters we should study him and model our lives on 607 his advice, you must feel kindly towards them as good men within their limits, and you may agree with them that Homer is the best of poets and first of tragedians. But you will know that the only poetry that should be allowed in a state is hymns to the gods and paeans in praise of good men; once you go beyond that and admit the sweet lyric or epic muse, pleasure and pain become your rulers instead of law and the principles commonly accepted as best.'

'Quite true.'

'Our defence, then, when we are reminded that we banished poetry from our state, must be that reason demands it. But in case we are condemned for being insensitive and bad mannered, let us add that there is an old quarrel between philosophy and poetry. One can quote many examples of this ancient antagonism: remarks about the "bitch that growls and snarls at her master", and "a reputation among empty-headed fools", or "the crowd of heads that know too much" and the "subtle thinkers" who are "beggars" none the less.[4] However, let us freely admit that if drama and poetry written for pleasure can prove to us that they have a place in a well-run society, we will gladly admit them, for we know their fascination only too well; but it would be wicked to abandon what we believe to be the truth. I expect you feel the fascination of poetry yourself, don't you,' I asked, 'especially when it's Homer exercising it?'

'I do indeed.'

'It is only fair, then, that poetry should return, if she can make her defence in lyric or other metre.'

'Yes.'

'And we should give her defenders, men who aren't poets themselves but who love poetry, a chance of defending her in prose and proving that she doesn't only give pleasure but brings lasting benefit to human life and human society. And we will listen favourably, as we shall gain much if we find her a source of profit as well as pleasure.'

'Yes, we shall gain a lot.'

'But if they fail to make their case, then we shall have to follow the example of the lover who renounces a passion that is doing him no good, however hard it may be to do so. Brought up as we 608 have been, we are bound to love poetry, and we shall be glad if it proves to have a real value; but in the absence of such proof we shall, whenever we listen to it, recite this argument of ours to ourselves as a charm to prevent us falling under the spell of a passion most men have never outgrown. Our theme shall be that such poetry has no serious value or claim to truth, and we shall warn people against it for fear of its effects on their character, and tell them to adopt the view of poetry we have described.'

'I entirely agree.'

'Yes, my dear Glaucon,' I said, 'because the issues at stake, the choice of good and evil, are even greater than they appear, and neither honour nor wealth nor power, nor poetry itself, should tempt us to neglect the claims of justice and goodness.'

'I agree,' he said; 'your argument convinces me, as I think it would anyone else.'

Notes

1 In visual terms what we should call an extreme photographic realism. Such extreme realism, both in theory and practice, was not uncommon in the early fourth century, and is effectively criticized by Aristotle in the *Poetics*.

2 Beefeater is perhaps the nearest rendering in English. Adam quotes 'I am a great eater of beef, and I believe that does harm to my wits' (*Twelfth Night*, I, 3.90).

3 Cf. p.[23]

4 The sources of these quotations are unknown.

The philosophy of modern music

Theodor Adorno (1903–69)

Theodor Adorno was, along with his colleagues Herbert Marcuse and Max Horkheimer, one of the leading members of the highly influential, Marxist-oriented, Frankfurt School of Social Research, which flourished in Germany up until the Nazi takeover. Thereafter its members continued to work in Europe and the United States. Adorno reacted against the conservative bias of socialist realism, which in the main was hostile to experimental art, and championed the cause of modernism, particularly in music, on the grounds that radicalism in politics should be matched by a similar sense of radicalism in artistic practice. The extract that follows is taken from The Philosophy of Modern Music *(1948), and puts the case for Arnold Schoenberg, the inventor of twelve-tone music, being the more valuable composer than Igor Stravinsky, because the former's radical experimentalism represents a greater break with the past. Adorno, in common with Brecht and Benjamin (see Reading 4), sees art's value as lying in its ability to challenge tradition and the established order.*

Schoenberg and progress

DISTURBANCE OF THE WORK

The changes encountered in music during the last thirty years have yet to be comprehended in their full breadth. More is involved than the much discussed crisis – a condition of chaotic fermentation, that is, the end of which could be foreseen and which would restore order after disorder. The concept of some future renewal – whether in significant and highly polished works of art, or in the blissful harmony of music with society – simply denies events of the past and elements that can be suppressed, but not eradicated. Under the coercion of its own objective consequences music has critically invalidated the idea of the polished work and disrupted the collective continuity of its effect. To be sure, no crisis has been able to put a stop to public musical life – neither the economic crisis nor the cultural crisis, in whose concept the idea of prevailing reconstruction is already contained. Even in music the concept of the monopoly of the fittest has survived. Even in the face of highly cacophonous sound, which flees from the web of organized culture and its consumers, the fraud of today's culture becomes obvious. Its management suppresses the emergence of a more valid culture, placing the blame for this situation on the lack of 'achievement.' All those outside the sphere of management are path-finders, trail-blazers, and – above all – tragic figures. Those who come after them are to have a better lot; if they conform, they are granted entry. But these outsiders are in no sense the pioneers of future works. They challenge the concept of production and the works produced. The apologist of actual radical music – who would support his arguments by pointing to the prolific output of the Schoenberg school – already denies precisely what he wishes to support. Today the only works which really count are those which are no longer works at all...

The dream of permanent artistic possessions is not only destroyed from the outside by the threatening social condition; the historical tendency present in musical means renounces this dream. The procedural method of modern music questions what many progress-ives expect of it: structures perfected within themselves which might be exhibited for all time in museums of opera and concert.

INHERENT TENDENCY OF MUSICAL MATERIAL

The assumption of an historical tendency in musical material contradicts the traditional conception of the material of music. This material is traditionally defined – in terms of physics, or possibly in terms of the psychology of sound – as the sum of all sounds at the disposal of the composer. The actual compositional material, however, is as different from this sum as is language from its total supply of sounds. It is not simply a matter of the increase and decrease of this supply in the course of history. All its specific characteristics are indications of the historical process. The higher the degree of historical necessity present within these specific characteristics, the less directly legible they become as historical indications. In that very moment when the historical expression of a chord can no longer be aurally perceived, it demands that the sounds which surround it give a conclusive account of its historical implications. These implications have determined the nature of this expression. The meaning of musical material is not absorbed in the genesis of music, and yet this meaning cannot be separated from it. Music recognizes no natural law; therefore, all psychology of music is questionable. Such psychology – in its efforts to establish an invariant 'understanding' of the music of all times – assumes a constancy of musical subject. Such an assumption is more closely related to the constancy of the material of nature than psychological differentiation might indicate. What this psychology inadequately and noncommittally describes is to be sought in the perception of the kinetic laws of matter. According to these laws, not all things are possible at all times. To be sure, a unique ontological law is by no means to be ascribed either to the material of tones itself or to tonal material which has been filtered through the tempered system. This, for example, is the typical argumentation of those who – either from relationships of harmonic tones or from the psychology of the ear – attempt to deduce that the triad is the necessary and universally valid condition of all possible comprehension and that, therefore, all music must be dependent upon it. This argumentation, which even Hindemith has appropriated for himself, is nothing but a superstructure for reactionary compositional tendencies. Its deception is revealed by the observation that the trained ear is able to perceive harmonically the most complicated overtone relationships as well as less complex relationships. The listener, thereby, feels no particular urgency for a 'resolution' of the alleged dissonances, but rather spontaneously resists resolutions as a retrogression into less sophisticated modes of listening...

All the tonal combinations employed in the past by no means stand indiscriminately at the disposal of the composer today. Even the more insensitive ear detects the shabbiness and exhaustion of the diminished seventh chord and certain chromatic modulatory tones in the salon music of the nineteenth century. For the technically trained ear, such vague discomfort is transformed into a prohibitive canon. If all is not deception, this canon today excludes even the medium of tonality – that is to say, the means of all traditional music. It is not simply that these sounds are antiquated and untimely, but that they are false. They no longer fulfill their function. The most progressive level of technical procedures designs tasks before which traditional sounds reveal themselves as impotent clichés. There are modern compositions which occasionally scatter tonal sounds in their own context. It is precisely the triads which, in such context, are cacophonous and not the dissonances! As a substitute for dissonances, these triads at times might even be justified. Impure style is, however, not alone responsible for the impropriety of their employment. Rather the technical horizon, against which the tonal sounds are glaringly conspicuous, today encompasses all music. If a contemporary composer restricts himself exclusively to tonal sounds – in the manner of Sibelius – these sound just as false as if they were enclaves within the atonal field...

SCHOENBERG'S CRITICISM OF ILLUSION AND PLAY

Today this process has turned against the self-sufficient work of art and everything determined thereby. The illness which has befallen the idea of the work might well have its roots in a social condition which reflects nothing binding and affirmative enough to guarantee the internal harmony of the work sufficient unto itself. The prohibitive difficulties of the work are, however, evident not only in the reflection upon it, but in the dark interior of the work itself. If one thinks of the most conspicuous symptom – namely, the shrinking of the expansion in time – which in music is only an external factor of the work, then it must be stated that only individual impotence, incapacity for structural formulation – not sparseness – is to be made responsible for the lack of success of a given work. No works could exhibit greater concentration and consistency of formal structure than Schoenberg's and Webern's shortest movements. Their brevity is a direct result of the demand for the greatest consistency. This demand precludes the superfluous. In so doing this consistency opposes expansion in time, which has been the basis for the conception of the musical work since the eighteenth century, certainly since Beethoven. The work, the age, and illusion are all struck by a single blow. Criticism of the extensive scheme is interlocked with criticism of the content, in terms of phrase and ideology. Music, compressed into a moment, is valid as an eruptive revelation of negative experience. It is closely related to actual suffering. In this spirit of compression modern music destroys all decorative elements and, therewith, symmetrically extended works. Among the arguments which would attempt to relegate the disquieting phenomenon of Schoenberg into the past of Romanticism and individualism (in order to be able to serve the operations of modern collectives with a better conscience), the most widely spread is the one which brands him as an 'espressivo composer' and his music as an 'exaggeration' of a decayed mode of expression. It is neither necessary to deny his origin in the Wagnerian *espressivo* style nor to overlook the traditional *espressivo* elements in his earlier works. These compositions, nonetheless, prove their ability to come to terms with this barren emptiness. At the same time, Schoenberg's *espressivo* style since the break – if not from the very beginning, at least since the *Piano Pieces* [*opus* 11] and the George songs, *Das Buch der hängenden Gärten* [*opus* 15] – differs in quality from Romantic expression precisely by means of that intensification which thinks this *espressivo* though to its logical conclusion. The expressive music of the West, since the beginning of the seventeenth century, assumed an expressiveness which the composer allotted to his musical structures in much the same way as the dramatist did to his theatrical figures, without the expressed emotions claiming to have immediate presence and reality within the work. Dramatic music, just as true *musica ficta*, from Monteverdi to Verdi presented expression as stylized communication – as the representation of passions.[1] Whenever this music extended beyond this, laying claim to a substantiality beyond the appearance of expressed feelings, this claim hardly restricted itself to specific musical emotions, reflecting in turn such emotions of the soul. This claim was validated only by the totality of the form, which exercises control over the musical characters and their correlation. The process is totally different in the case of Schoenberg. The actual revolutionary moment for him is the change in function of musical expression. Passions are no longer simulated, but rather genuine emotions of the unconscious – of shock, of trauma – are registered without disguise through the medium of music. These emotions attack the taboos of form because these taboos subject such emotions to their own censure, rationalizing them and transforming them into images. Schoenberg's formal innovations were closely related to the change in the content of expression. These innovations serve the breakthrough of the reality of this content. The first atonal works are case studies in the sense of psychoanalytical dream case studies. In the very first publication on Schoenberg, Vassily Kandinsky called the composer's paintings 'acts of the mind'. The scars of this revolution of expression, however, are the blotches which have become fixed in his music as well as in his pictures, as the heralds of the id against the compositional will. They destroy the surface and are as little to be removed by subsequent correction as are the traces of blood in a fairy tale. Authentic suffering has implanted these in the work of art as a sign that the autonomy of the work is no longer recognized by this suffering. The heteronomy of the scars – and the blotches – challenges music's façade of self-sufficiency. This façade is based on the fact that in all traditional music the formally defined elements are employed as if they were the inviolable necessity of this one individual case; or that this façade appears as though it were identical with the alleged language of form. Since the beginning of the bourgeois era, all great music has founded its sufficiency in the illusion that it has achieved an unbroken unity and justified through its own individuation the conventional universal legality to which it is subject. This is contradicted by modern music. The criticism directed towards decorative elements, towards convention, and towards abstract universality of musical language are all of one mind. If music is privileged above all other forms by the absence of illusive imagery – the fact that it does not paint a picture – then it nonetheless has participated energetically in the illusory character of the bourgeois work of art; this it does by means of its specific interests with the domination of conventions. Schoenberg declared his independence from this type of art by seriously heeding precisely that expression whose inclusion in the universal trend towards conciliation determines the most basic principle of musical illusion. His music officially denies the claim that the universal and the specific have been reconciled. Regardless of the indebtedness of this music in its origins to parallel principles exhibited in nature, and regardless of the similarity of its formal irregularities to organic forms – in no way does it present an organic totality...

Stravinsky and restoration

THE FINAL TRICK

How treacherous that Stravinsky – as soon as he had stated his objective demands in positive terms – had to assemble his armature out of the supposedly pre-subjective phases of music. It would have been preferable if this formal language had primarily extended beyond the incriminated Romantic element therein by virtue of its own gravitational force. In this case, however, he was able to come to his own aid, in that he derived a stimulus from the inconsistency between the 'pre-Classic' formulae, and his own state of consciousness and the condition of material. In an ironic game, he then enjoyed the impossibility of restoration which he initiated. The subjective aestheticism of the objective attitude is unmistakable: it is reminiscent of Nietzsche who, in order to prove that he was cured of Wagner, claimed to love in Rossini, Bizet, and the journalistic Offenbach all of those elements which made a mockery of his own pathos and differentiation. Subjectivity was retained through the exclusion of it from the creative process, as, for example, in the somewhat graceful insult to Pergolesi in the *Pulcinella* suite. This has been the major accomplishment of Stravinsky in recent years. The work is, of course, lightly colored by speculation upon those listeners who wish their music to be familiar, but at the same time to be labeled modern. This indicates the willingness inherent in this music to be used as fashionable commercial music – similar to the willingness of surrealism to be used for shop-window decoration. The penchant for conciliation, which becomes ever more pressing, cannot find relief in the face of the contradiction between modernity and pre-Classicism. Stravinsky tries to balance this out in a double manner. On the one hand, the devices of the eighteenth century – to which this new style was restricted in the beginning and which, once taken from their context, are painfully dissonant both in the literal and figurative sense – are blended into the compositional idiom. They by no means protrude as foreign elements; rather the total musical inventory is developed therefrom. They are no longer evident, and with the mediation of their contradiction to the modern element, the musical language is increasingly toned down from work to work...

...Stravinsky's shock technique assumes a command of that musical world of images of the most recent past. This shock, however, loses its effectiveness with ever-increasing speed; today, for example, only twenty years after its compositon, *Le Baiser de la Fée* sounds honestly innocuous in spite of the lovely skirts of the ballerinas and the Swiss tourist costumes out of Andersen's day. At the same time, the increase in quotable musical goods gradually bridges the gap between past and present. The idiom, finally developed with such great effort, no longer shocks anyone: it is the very essence of everything approved and certified in the two hundred years of bourgeois music, treated according to the procedure of rhythmic tricks which has meanwhile found approval. As a revenant, healthy common sense is re-established to the right which it had forfeited long ago. The authoritarian character of today is, without exception, conformist; likewise the authoritarian claim of Stravinsky's music is extended totally and completely to conformism. In the final analysis, the music tends to become the style for everyone, because it coincides with the man-in-the-street style in which they have always believed and to which this music automatically directs them again. Its indifference, and its anemia – which becomes evident as soon as the last aggressive impulses are subdued – are the price which it must pay for its recognition of the consensus as the moment of authenticity...

...The formerly rough surface is now sealed and polished. Previously, expression had been cut off from the subject; now even the ominous secret of the sacrifice of the subject is concealed in silence. Those who long for the administration of society through direct domination by force continually acclaim the traditional values which they wish to preserve from ruin. From this point, in like manner, objectivistic music appears as the force of preservation, proclaiming its own recovery. Out of the disintegration of the subject it designs for itself the formula of the aesthetic integration of the world. It recoins in counterfeit the destructive law of society itself – of absolute power, that is – as the constructive law of authenticity. The farewell trick of Stravinsky – who otherwise, in an elegant gesture, renounced everything astonishing – is the enthroning of the self-forgotten negative as the self-conscious positive.

NEOCLASSICISM

Stravinsky's entire work has had this maneuver as its goal; in pursuing it, however, it becomes a modestly pompous event in the transition to neo-classicism. It is decisive that according to its purely musical nature, no distinction between infantile and neo-classic works can be discerned. The reproach that Stravinsky – in the manner of a German classicist – had developed from a revolutionary into a reactionary cannot be validated. All compositional elements of the neo-classic phase are not only implicitly contained in what preceded this phase, but in both cases they define the entire compositional inventory. Even the mask-like 'as if' of the first compositions of the new style coincides with the old process of writing music about music. There are works of the early nineteen-twenties – such as the *Concertino for String Quartet* and the *Wooodwind Octet* – which would be difficult to classify as either infantile or neo-classic. They are particularly successful because they preserve the aggressive fragmentation of infantilism without deforming a model in any obvious way: They neither parody nor celebrate. It would be a simple matter to compare the transition to neo-classicism to that from free atonality to twelve-tone technique, which Schoenberg completed at the very same time: both developments have in common the transformation of highly specifically designed and employed means into, as it were, disqualified, neutral material, severed from the original intention of its appearance. But the analogy is not valid beyond this point. The transformation of the vehicles of atonal expression into the expressive means of twelve-tone came to pass in Schoenberg out of specific compositional force itself. For this reason it has changed decisively the language of music as well as the essence of the individual compositions. In Stravinsky, there is no trace of this. To be sure, his regression to tonality gradually becomes less scrupulous, until the provocatively false is mellowed to the point that it is no more than a spice within the work – as, for example, the chorale contained in *L' Histoire du Soldat.* If there is any essential change, however, it is not the musical, but rather the literary aspect; it involves the claim made by the musical, or, it could almost be said – by its ideology. All of a sudden, music wishes to be taken literally. It is the idolatrously fixed grimace, which is revered as an image of the gods. The authoritarian principle of making-music-about-music is applied in such a way that all possible antiquated musical formulae are vindicated of their binding responsibility, which they have lost historically and which they seem to possess only when they actually no longer possess them. At the same time, the usurpatory element in authority is cynically underscored by means of arbitrary acts which inform the confused listener of the illegitimacy of the claim to authority without relenting from this claim in the slightest degree. Stravinsky's older jokes – which were often somewhat more discrete – ridicule the norm in the same breath in which they proclaim it: this norm is to be obeyed not for the sake of its own justice but merely because of the dictatorial powers which it possesses. This strategy of courteous terror takes the following technical course. There are passages in which the traditional language of music, particularly in the pre-classic practice of sequences, seems automatically to demand certain continuations as a matter of course. These continuations are, however, avoided. Instead a surprise – an *imprévu* – is offered, which amuses the listener by cheating him out of what he has been waiting for. The schema prevails, but the continuity of progress which it has promised is not developed. Thus Stravinsky's neo-classicism practices the old custom of joining brokenly disparate models together. It is traditional music combed in the wrong direction.

Notes

1 *Musica ficta*: In the music of the tenth to sixteenth centuries, the theory of the chromatic or, more properly, non-diatonic tones other than those in the diatonic scale. – Trans.

A theory of literary production

Pierre Macherey

Pierre Macherey is a disciple of the French structuralist Marxist philosopher Louis Althusser, and one of the major sources for what has become known as the 'reading against the grain' method of textual analysis. The method is outlined in Macherey's A Theory of Literary Production *(1966), an extract from which follows. Macherey's contention is that literary works of art reveal the internal contradictions of the ideology of their time. To both Althusser and Macherey ideology is, by definition, a belief-system marked by internal contradictions, and it is in the system's nature to try to disguise those contradictions in order to protect its authority. Thus capitalist ideology explains away the sense of alienation that Marx saw as a consequence of the division of labour and the domination of the profit motive in human affairs, by arguing that alienation is man's natural state in the world, simply part of 'the human condition'. Ideology, in other words, provides what Macherey calls 'a false resolution to a real debate'. Texts are held to make that false resolution, otherwise invisible to us in our spontaneous everyday dealings with each other, visible on the page. It is the point of 'reading against the grain' to identify those false resolutions and the real debate lying behind them. The value of literature is that it enables the Marxist critic to conduct a more detailed critique of ideology, and Macherey speaks of it being a critic's duty to 'interrogate' texts to make them yield up their false resolutions. 'Reading against the grain' has become one of the most widely used techniques of Marxist literary criticism. In this next extract Macherey examines the complex relationship between texts and ideology, elaborating on Lenin's various readings of Tolstoy.*

The image in the mirror

We have to re-analyse these critical texts from a new point of view; for the moment, we have an account of the work of Tolstoy which is complete in its own fashion, within the limits of its insufficiency.

Within the work of Tolstoy we know that we are looking for its relation to history; but we do not know how such a study might be pursued, nor do we know *what* materials we shall be practically concerned with. In the interpretation which has just been offered it is as though the text itself had been abolished for the sake of its content. We have accounted for everything except the works of Tolstoy in their specificity. Obviously a knowledge of these works is not the same as a knowledge of what they were made from.

From Lenin's account we must isolate what will define the work of the writer...

Mirror, reflection, expression – these are the key notions of the Lenin articles. Lenin gives us his definition of literature in the proposition that the work is a mirror (recalling that mirror on the highway which serves as the ritual emblem of a realist literature). But Lenin uses the mirror to refer to a concept rather than an image. It must, then, be limited by a definition at least. In fact, it is qualified immediately by the statement that the 'thing' is not there for its own sake: 'We can hardly call "mirror" that which does not give a precise reflection of the world.' Thus the mirror is only superficially a mirror, or at least it reflects in its own special way. We are not concerned with just any reflecting surface which would give a direct reproduction of any object. And rather than the facile notion of a distorting mirror, Lenin suggests a fragmented image. Could it be a broken mirror?

In effect, the relationship between the mirror and what it reflects (the historical reality) is *partial*: the mirror selects, it does not reflect everything. The selection is not fortuitous, it is symptomatic; it can tell us about the nature of the mirror. We already know the reasons for this selectivity; Tolstoy's version of his age is incomplete because of his personal and ideological relation to it. In particular, we know that he could not grasp its revolutionary characteristics; thus it is not because he reflected the revolution that he earned the title of mirror of the revolution. If the work is a mirror it is certainly not by virtue of any manifest relation with the period 'reflected'. Tolstoy 'did not manifestly understand' his age, he 'manifestly turned away from it'. What is seen in the mirror of the work is not quite what Tolstoy saw, both in himself and as an ideological spokesman. Thus the image of history in the mirror will not be a reflection in the precise sense of a reproduction or facsimile. Indeed, we know that such a reproduction is impossible. The fact that we can recognise Tolstoy's era in his work does not prove that he truly knew that era. Tolstoy's relationship to his mirror is analogous to that of certain workers to the revolution of their own period: they participated spontaneously – and perhaps effectively – in that revolution, without understanding either its scope or its origins.

Initially this can be explained by the complexity of the revolution – the fact that it is not a single conflict but a struggle articulated by a multiplicity of determinations (as in the above analysis); the historical process unfolds at several levels simultaneously and is intricately knotted. It is thus possible to participate at a single level, in ignorance of all the others (although this ignorance is vulnerable). Even in the 'great revolution' there is an important peasant element, by which Tolstoy and his work are situated in history: 'Tolstoy had to reflect at least *some* of the essential aspects of the revolution'. But it is not simply a case of one element; this immediate relation is necessarily incomplete, not only by its content but in its very form. All those who played a part in this revolution – and who did not? – were involved in an immediate relation with at least one element of the total situation; but this relation was only superficially immediate, for it was actually determined by the totality. So these ideas – 'element of a situation', 'part played in an event' – would indeed be deceptive if they were to tempt us into a *mechanical* analysis. The reflected element, with its apparent spontaneity, is actually determined by both short- and long-term factors, by its place in the complex structure. Its positive presence is less important than the fact that it is, as it were, inscribed from the outside (*creusé de l'extérieur*), inserted obliquely by all the conditions that have generated it. The work is perhaps a mirror precisely because it registers the partiality of its own reflections, the incomplete reality of simple elements. It is privileged because it does not have to elaborate the totality in order to display it; it can reveal just the necessity of that totality – a necessity which can be deciphered from the work. It is the task of scientific criticism to achieve such a reading. The mirror can reveal in this way because it is not a mechanical reproducer of images (blind images which would merit only condemnation) nor an instrument of knowledge – though knowledge has its own appropriate instruments. It is an indispensable *revelation*, a revealer, and it is criticism that helps us to decipher these images in the mirror.

The secret of the mirror is to be sought in the form of its reflections; how does it show historical reality, by what paradox does it make visible its own blindness without actually seeing itself?

The notion of the mirror takes on a new meaning once it is supplemented by the idea of the analysis which defines the partiality of its reflections. But this analysis is itself deceptive, since it tends to suggest that the real is the mechanical product of a *montage*. It must be interpreted in a way that does not sacrifice its real complexity. In actual fact, it is not enough to say that the mirror catches a fragmented reality; the very image in the mirror is itself fragmented. The image renders real discontinuities by means of its own complexities. Thus the work of Tolstoy is not homogeneous; it has not the limpid continuity of the reflected image; it is not all of a piece. To think that it is would be an idealisation, a refusal to understand such as liberal-bourgeois criticism might attempt. We return to the notion that the mirror is not a simple reflecting surface: the work of Tolstoy is itself an assemblage. And, just as Freud has established that a dream has to be deconstructed into its constitutive elements before it can be interpreted, Lenin states that the literary text must be studied in the same way – not in the pursuit of a factitious totality, but according to its real and necessary discontinuity.

The revolutionary, if he is to see himself mirrored in the work of Tolstoy, must be aware of the deceptions of reactionary *and* liberal criticism. Instead of trying to assimilate the whole of Tolstoy he must be able to identify the mirror within his work. Otherwise the literary work is merely being used as the pretext for a declaration of political or ideological faith. Just as it is not a complete reflection, neither is Tolstoy's work a primary reflection, simple and complete in itself. Confronted with the complexity of the historical process, we must be able to articulate the complexity of the text. 'The great Tolstoyan image was not cast in metal, a single unalloyed block. And all his bourgeois admirers rise to honour his memory not because he was all of a piece but precisely because he was not' (Lenin, *On Literature and Art*).

The bourgeois judgment of Tolstoy was not just incomprehension or ignorance. It was a significant misreading. The bourgeois reading of Tolstoy is implicit in Tolstoy's own works; it is an index of their imbalance...

...in his first article, of 1908, Lenin writes:

the contradictions in Tolstoy's views must be appraised not from the standpoint of the present-day working-class movement and present-day socialism (such an appraisal is, of course, needed, but it is not enough), but from the standpoint of protest against advancing capitalism, against the ruining of the masses, who are being dispossessed of their land – a protest which had to arise from the patriarchal Russian countryside. (Ibid., p.30...)

Two years later, in his second article, he writes:

> That is why a correct appraisal of Tolstoy can be made only from
> the viewpoint of the class which has proved, by its political role and
> its struggle during the first denouement of these contradictions, at
> a time of revolution, that it is destined to be the leader in the
> struggle for the people's liberty and for the emancipation of the
> masses from exploitation – the class which has proved its selfless
> devotion to the cause of democracy and its ability to fight against
> the limitations and inconsistency of bourgeois (including peasant)
> democracy; such a viewpoint is only possible from the viewpoint
> of the Social-Democratic proletariat. (Ibid., pp.50–1...)

At first sight, the contrast seems embarrassingly obvious: in fact,
Lenin is proposing to pass 'two exact judgments' on Tolstoy. The
first bears on the very point of view by which Tolstoy's gaze is
defined; the second, denying the false interiority of the work, reveals
the work by the expedient of a decisive confrontation. Nothing
enables us to choose between these two undertakings, which are
finally opposed only through their equivalence, their necessary
relation. Tolstoy proclaims himself a writer precisely by the work's
power to effect within itself a precise variation – precise because it
cannot be accused of ambiguity. The sliding of points of view within
the work of Tolstoy is not an 'either...or...' but a *both at once*,
exactly situated within their conflict. Once again we encounter the
notion of a double reading, though this time in a stronger sense,
since it is a question of two *exact* readings. In that case, perhaps
the exactitude results from their conjunction.

It is for this reason that the truth of Tolstoy's work – and there
must surely be some truth in it, something from which one could
know the truth – should be sought in the presence of a conflict:
more precisely, it might be said that the content of Tolstoy's work
has something to do with contradiction. Lenin in fact states that:
Tolstoy's work is great because it reflects the contradictions of the
epoch. Does this mean that it reflects, term for term, the elements
of the contradiction, producing or reproducing an image of the
contradiction? Such a notion is a denial of Tolstoy's work as such,
an appropriation for the sake of a too directly satisfying explanation.
It is obvious that the contradictions of the epoch are (and must
remain) external to the work, because they are of a different nature.
If there is a contradiction in the work it must thus be a different kind

of contradiction, obeying the laws of a more subtle transposition.

The critical question, as formulated by Lenin, is expressed thus: What do we see in the mirror? The answer: the object in the mirror has something to do with contradiction. This is because, once again, the mirror does not reflect *things* (in which case the relationship between the reflection and the object would be one of mechanical correspondence). The image in the mirror is deceptive: the mirror enables us to grasp only *relationships* of contradiction. By means of contradictory images the mirror represents and evokes the historical contradictions of the period, what Lenin calls 'the faults and weaknesses of our revolution'...

But what can the contradictions in Tolstoy's work be? And what is their relation to the real contradictions? Lenin devotes the whole of the third paragraph of his first article to an enumeration of the contradictions in Tolstoy's work ('work' being taken in the widest possible sense to include all that Tolstoy had *done*, that is to say the books as well as the doctrine and the influence):

1	great artist	landlord obsessed with Christ
	protest	quietism (in all its forms)
2	criticism	non-violence
	realism	preaching

The first contradiction relates Tolstoy's work, in so far as it is defined by aesthetic criteria, to Tolstoy's real situation, in so far as it defines the subject of his narratives (who is speaking?). But this second term of the contradiction is itself contradictory, since it implies the conflict between Tolstoy's natural situation (his relationship *by birth* to history) and his ideological situation (which allows him to *displace* his relation to history). The production of the books depends on this conflict, since Tolstoy has no other reason to change his relation to history except that of becoming a writer, and since his preaching remains essentially a preaching by means of books. Therefore, the first contradiction is between the book itself and the (contradictory) conditions of its production. The second contradiction, which remains the same, stated in three different forms, defines the very *content* of the work. The contradiction attacks the book from the interior and the exterior.

These contradictions are 'glaring': that is to say, they are obvious enough not to constitute a secret in the work. They are not manifest, however: Tolstoy's work communicates them to us without announcing them. They are *in* the work, but not as its explicit content; in this role we find only *some* of the real contradictions (for example, the contradiction between political violence and the comedy of justice denounced by Tolstoy). The contradictions structure the whole of the work; they shape its fundamental disparity. (For the image in the mirror we could perhaps here substitute the 'figure in the carpet' exemplified by a famous short story by Henry James.)

These contradictions define Tolstoy's work since they give it both its limits and its meaning – a meaning which is only intelligible when reckoned from those limits. The limits: Tolstoy could not have a complete knowledge of the historical process (and because his knowledge is incomplete it is not, precisely, a knowledge). The meaning: these limits are necessary if it is the case that 'the contradictions... are not accidental' (ibid., p.30...). This meaning defined by limits, this content determined from without, enables us to say that the work of Tolstoy is *expressive*, that it is defined by its relation to something other than itself. We rediscover, in an inverted form, something we already know: we have seen that the work cannot include an ideology – which by itself does not belong to it – unless it establishes that ideology in a relation of difference with itself; we now see that the work can only exist if it introduces into itself this alien term which precipitates an internal contradiction...

Because of the contradictory conditions in which it is produced, the literary work is *simultaneously* (and it is this conjunction which concerns us) a reflection and the absence of a reflection: this is why it is itself contradictory. It would therefore be incorrect to say that the contradictions of the work are the *reflection* of historical contradictions: rather they are the consequences of the absence of this reflection. Once again we see that there can be no mechanical correspondence between the object and its 'image'. Expression does not mean a direct reproduction (or even knowledge), but an indirect figuration which arises from the deficiencies of the reproduction. Thus the work has a self-sufficient meaning which does not require to be completed; this meaning results from the disposition of partial reflections within the work and from a certain impossibility of reflecting. The function of criticism is to bring this to light.

The concept of expression is therefore much less ambiguous than that of reflection, since it enables us to define the overall structure of the work: a contrast which is based on an absence. The contradiction or deficiency *fills* the work of Tolstoy; it delineates its general architecture. The dialectic *in* the book (we recall Brecht's notion of a dialectic of the theatre) arises from the dialectical relation between the book and the real dialectic of the historical process. The conflict or contradiction, as it appears in the book, is itself one of the terms of the real conflict. This is why the contradictions in the book cannot be those of reality; they are the product of that reality, the culmination of a process of dialectical elaboration, which involves the intervening mediation of the means peculiar to literature. The interpreter is at the centre of a relationship of exchange; through his work Tolstoy gives us access to history itself, but to accomplish this he places himself (or he *is* placed – it is the same thing) within the historical conflict. Placed thus at the centre of an exchange, he explores the paths of a new economy.

We have yet to grasp the workings of this interpretation, that is to say, to know the terms of the dialectic in the book. What are the terms of the contradiction which Tolstoy exposes? Several answers are given to this question: between ideology (as enclave) and the work (defined by its relation to literature); between the questions (ideally posed) and the answers (ideally given); between the data and the observation which restores them. But all these answers paradoxically converge in one answer: when Lenin speaks of the contradiction in Tolstoy's work it is the ideological contradiction which he always has in mind:

> the contradictions in Tolstoy's views are indeed a mirror of those contradictory conditions in which the peasantry had to play their historical part in our revolution. (Ibid., p. 30...)

At the same time as it establishes an ideological content the book presents the contradiction of that content: this content only exists enveloped in the form of a contestation. Thus we perceive that there can be both a contradiction in 'the ideas' and a contradiction between the ideas and the book which presents them...

If we examine the nature of ideology in general (see Louis Althusser's 'Marxism and Humanism' in *For Marx*) it is soon obvious that there can be no ideological contradiction, except if we put ideology in contradiction with itself, if we induce contradiction within the framework of a dialogue (which is also ideological). By definition, an ideology can sustain a contradictory debate, for ideology exists precisely in order to efface all trace of contradiction. Thus, an ideology, as such, breaks down only in the face of the real questions: but for that to come about, ideology must not be able to hear these questions; that is to say, ideology must not be able to translate them into its own language. In so far as ideology is the false resolution of a real debate, it is always adequate to itself *as a reply*. Obviously the great thing is that it can never answer the question. In that it succeeds in endlessly prolonging its imperfection, it is complete; thus it is always equally in error, pursued by the risk that it cannot envisage – *the loss of reality*. An ideology is loyal to itself only in so far as it remains inadequate to the question which is both its foundation and its pretext. Ideology's essential weakness is that it can never recognise for itself its own real limits: at best it can learn of these limits from elsewhere, in the action of a radical criticism, not by a superficial denunciation of its content; the criticism of ideology is then replaced by a *critique of the ideological.*

It is therefore correct to say that ideology, rather than being alienated or contradictory, is captive. But captured by what? If we reply that it is captive of itself, we lapse into fallacies, false contradiction. Ideology is, in fact, a captive of its own limits (which is not the same thing). Ideology is enclosed, finite, but it mistakenly proclaims itself to be unlimited (having an answer for everything) within its limits. It is for this reason that ideology cannot create a system, which would be the condition for contradiction. (There can only be contradiction within a structured system; otherwise, there is merely opposition.) Ideology is a false totality because it has not appointed its own limits, because it is unable to reflect the limitation of its limits. Ideology has received these limits, but it exists solely in order to forget that moment of origin. These abiding limits, which are both permanent and permanently latent, are the source of that dissonance which structures all ideology: the dissonance between its explicit openness and its implicit closure.

Thus the ideological background, which constitutes the real support of all forms of expression and all ideological manifestations, is fundamentally silent – one might say unconscious. But it must be emphasised that this unconscious is not a silent knowledge, but a total misrecognition of itself. If it is silent, it is silent on that about which it has nothing to say. We should therefore preserve the expression in all its ambiguity: it refers to that ideological horizon which conceals only because it is interminable, because there is always something more, but it refers also to that abyss over which ideology is built. Like a planet revolving round an absent sun, an ideology is made of what it does not mention; it exists because there are things which must not be spoken of. This is the sense in which Lenin can say that 'Tolstoy's silences are eloquent'.

Ultimately, by interrogating an ideology, one can establish the existence of its limits because they are encountered as an impassable obstacle; they are there, but they cannot be made to speak. To know what an ideology means, to express this meaning, we must therefore go beyond and outside ideology; we must attack it from the outside in an effort to give form to that which is formless. This is not an enterprise of description: the symptomatic weaknesses are not to be located in the answers, which can always contrive a display of impeccable logical coherence; they are to be located in the questions which are left unanswered.

Thus when Lenin tells us that 'the ideas of Tolstoy reflect weaknesses and inadequacies' (op cit., p.30...) this means that the status of the image in the mirror is not purely ideological. Between the ideology and the book which expresses it, something has happened; the distance between them is not the product of some abstract decorum. Even though ideology itself always sounds solid, copious, it begins to speak of its *own absences* because of its presence in the novel, its visible and determinate form. By means of the text it becomes possible to escape from the domain of spontaneous ideology, to escape from the false consciousness of self, of history, and of time. The text constructs a determinate image of the ideological, revealing it as an object rather than living it from within as though it were an inner conscience; the text explores ideology (just as Balzac explores the Paris of the *Comédie humaine*, for instance), puts it to the test of the written word, the test of that watchful gaze in which all subjectivity is *captured*, crystallised in objective form. The spontaneous ideology in which men live (it is not produced spontaneously, although men believe that they acquire it spontaneously) is not simply reflected by the mirror of the book; ideology is broken, and turned inside out in so far as it is transformed in the text from being a state of consciousness. Art, or at least literature, because it naturally scorns the credulous view of the world, establishes myth and illusion as *visible objects*.

Tolstoy's work is engaged in a sterile social critique; but behind that futile generosity there figures a historical question which is placed within our grasp. Thus the work is certainly determined by its relation to ideology, but this relation is not one of analogy (as would be a reproduction): it is always more or less contradictory. A work is established against an ideology as much as it is from an ideology. Implicitly, the work contributes to an exposure of ideology, or at least to a definition of it; thus the absurdity of all attempts to 'demystify' literary works, which are defined precisely by their enterprise of demystification.

But it would not be correct to say that the book initiates a dialogue with ideology (which would be the worst possible way of becoming caught up in its game). On the contrary, its function is to present ideology in a non-ideological form. To take up the classical distinction between form and content – although the use of this distinction could not be generalised – it could be said that the work has an ideological content, but that it endows this content with a specific form. Even if this form is itself ideological there is an internal displacement of ideology by virtue of this *redoubling*; this is not ideology contemplating itself, but the mirror-effect which exposes its insufficiency, revealing differences and discordances, or a significant incongruity.

Thus we can gauge the distance which separates the work of art from true knowledge (a scientific knowledge) but which also unites them in their common distance from ideology. Science does away with ideology, obliterates it; literature challenges ideology by using it. If ideology is thought of as a non-systematic ensemble of significations, the work proposes a *reading* of these significations, by combining them as signs. Criticism teaches us to read these signs.

We seem thus to have exhausted the meanings of the concept of the mirror: it is the meeting place of reflections which are shaped on the ground of a blind surface, just as colours, at the right moment, constitute a picture on the canvas. Lenin teaches us that it is not so simple to look in the mirror: he has undertaken a rigorous scrutiny of mirrors.

Criticism and ideology

Terry Eagleton (b.1943)

Terry Eagleton has been one of the leading Marxist literary critics and theorists writing in English in recent years. He has drawn inspiration from many continental thinkers, particularly the French philosophers Louis Althusser and Pierre Macherey (see Reading 11), the moving spirits behind the structuralist Marxist movement. Eagleton's work most clearly influenced by Althusser and Macherey is Criticism and Ideology *(1976), a section of which forms the next reading. Marxism has traditionally experienced problems with the concept of aesthetic value and Eagleton tackles this issue in the last chapter of* Criticism and Ideology. *For the Marxist, the main problem concerning aesthetic value is whether there is any way of judging it other than by crude political considerations. Eagleton's conclusions are very tentative; drawing on Brecht he sees aesthetic value as residing in the work's continuing ability to make us think, but finally decides that the socio-political conditions by which a Marxist theory of aesthetic value could be formulated do not yet obtain. This is a disappointing conclusion to reach and it indicates just how intractable a problem this remains to most Marxists. Politics seems to have the last word.*

Marxism and aesthetic value

Marxist criticism should indeed decisively intervene in the 'value-problem'; but nothing is to be gained by that form of literary ultra-leftism which dismisses received evaluations merely because they are the product of bourgeois criticism...

It would seem absurd for Marxist criticism to be silent on the qualitative distinction between say, Pushkin and Coventry Patmore. Yet such a theoretical prudery is in vogue within Marxist aesthetics. At its simplest level, it appears as an egalitarian unease about the 'élitism' of assigning certain works to second-class status: how patrician to prefer Blake to Betjeman. In its more sophisticated form, it presents itself as a rigorous scientificity hostile to the idealism of 'normative' judgement. The critic's task is not to range works upon an evaluative scale but to achieve scientific knowledge of the conditions of their historical possibility. Whether the work in question is to be approved or censured is irrelevant to that end; evaluation is thus evacuated from the realm of literary science, to be furtively cultivated, perhaps, as a private pleasure...

Politically counterproductive though both positions undoubtedly are, they are none the less considerably more valuable than the bourgeois aesthetics they oppose. For there is no question that the instalment of the 'value-question' at the heart of critical enquiry is a rampantly ideological gesture. The ideological unity between the old-fashioned school of 'appreciation', and the anti-academicist school of 'relevance', is nowhere more clearly revealed than in the priority they assign to problems of value, on which all else is made to turn. Whether it is translated as 'taste' or metaphysical commitment, private predilection or public conviction, intuitive sympathy or moral allegiance, the ideological function of the 'value-question' is to dissolve the materialist analysis of literary texts into abstract moralism, or into the existential moment of individual consumption. (We may leave aside the reformist moves towards 'readers' participation' predictable within such a problematic.) Criticism becomes a mutually supportive dialogue between two highly valorised subjects: the valuable text and the valuable reader. We do not need to ask how the value of each of these privileged subjects is established, any more than we need to ask how the value of a commodity is sealed. It is sealed by exchange: by that alienation of the historically specific which permits one lonely abstraction to encounter, and be equalised by, another, in a self-closing circle from which the material has been abolished. Valuable text and valuable reader are reversible: in a mutual complicity, such a text writes its reader and such a reader writes the text. The valuable reader is constituted as valuable by the texts which he constitutes as such; ideological value is projected into the Tradition to re-enter the present as metaphysical confirmation or critique. The name of this tautology is Literature – that historical invention whose ideological tyranny is more supple and deep-seated for us than that of any other art-form. For the art gallery, concert hall and opera house are flagrantly privileged spaces which flaunt themselves as such: the demarcation between initiate and ignorant is here taut and unmistakeable. This is not so of literature, for two reasons. First, the character of literary production in advanced social formations is such that it ceaselessly surpasses such cloistered, isolable spheres: literature is multiple and polycentric, saturating the very textures of our social life, pervasively present as consolation, information, persuasion, infatuation. Second, an advanced social formation demands that literacy also should be widely diffused, so that today its relatively marked absence even in such conditions is inevitably scandalous, signifying a loss of full humanity. In such a situation, Literature presents itself as threat, mystery, challenge and insult to those who, able to read, can nonetheless not 'read'. To be able to decipher the signs and yet remain ignorant: it is in this contradiction that the tyranny of Literature is revealed. Reading is at once the most natural and esoteric of acts, spontaneous and sacred, public facility and privileged cult. Its unnaturalness is thus enforced by its very naturalness, which is not the case with opera houses and concert halls. Whereas they are in principle out of reach, Literature is always that which can be reached for – an 'ordinary' phenomenon which is always alien. Sited somewhere on the ground of familiar language, Literature entices only to refuse, appears complicit only to cold-shoulder. Literature is always somewhere else: that which, being literate, we have not read or cannot read. Literacy admits us to reading so that we can take the full measure of our exclusion: its effect is to display the secretive knowledge which is always possible but never possessed.

It can be argued, of course, that the unreadability of Literature is precisely its radicalism – that the 'readable' text, in naturalising its signs, operates upon the reader an insidious mystification subverted by the modernist text which puts its modes of sense-production archly or candidly on show. Yet that 'radical' case has rarely been coupled with a critique of the social determinants which allow a mere few thousand access to such writing. It is then predictable that such purely gestural, shamefaced materialism will provoke its angry reaction...

Populism and theoreticism, in aesthetics as in politics, are familiar deformations of Marxist-Leninism, and the question of literary value is a crux of this debate. Yet if there can indeed be a 'science of value', it must differ from those familiar forms of historicism which regard the work as the 'expression' of a 'world view' which in turn expresses a privileged 'class-position' occupied by the individual or 'transindividual' author at a particular historical point. Such a conception merely dissolves the materiality of the text to the transparency of historical 'consciousness' or 'praxis'. Conversely, if the varieties of formalism have insisted that value (where they have admitted it) is the product of a certain play of significations, they have tended to isolate that process from the material matrix within which historicism, in however idealist a form, has tried to place it. A materialist approach to the problem of value must therefore appear as a double-refusal: of the expressive models of historicism, and of the reductive operations of formalism.

Moreover, in opposition to certain trends within bourgeois and even materialist criticism, such a method must re-enact the founding gesture of Marxist political economy and re-consider the question of value on the site of literary *production*. This is not, need one say, to ignore the spheres of textual circulation and consumption – to fetishise value as an immanent quality of the product, sublimely untainted by the ideological practices of literary reception. For there is no 'immanent' value – no value which is not *transitive*. Literary value is a phenomenon which is *produced* in that ideological appropriation of the text, that 'consumptional production' of the work, which is the act of reading. It is always *relational* value: 'exchange-value'. The histories of 'value' are a sub-sector of the histories of literary-ideological receptive practices – practices which are in no sense a mere 'consumption' of a finished product, but which must be studied as a determinate (re)production of the text. We read ('consume') what an ideology reads ('produces') for us; to read is to consume the determinate material of a text in a specific ideological production of it. For the literary text is always the text-for-ideology, selected, deemed readable and deciphered by certain ideologically governed conventions of critical receptivity to which the text itself contributes. Those conventions are embedded in the material apparatuses of 'culture' and education, and represent a conjuncture of 'general' ideological discourses and that specific, overdetermined instance of them which is the literary-aesthetic. If the text itself is the overdetermined product of a structural conjuncture, so indeed is the practice of reading; the problems of textual meaning and value pose themselves precisely in the series of historical conjunctures between these two moments. Reading is the operation whereby a particular historical ideology so puts to work the materials of the text as to fashion it into a readable product, an ideological object, a text-for-ideology. And as the text is itself a production of ideology, working now athwart, now in complicity with it, so reading, as an ideological production of the production of ideology, works now 'with', now 'athwart' the lines of the text, in a double-movement determined by its relation to the textual production of ideology ('textual ideology') and to the extra-textual ideology thus produced.

To re-consider the point of textual production, then, is not to surrender to some immanentist theory of value. As a determinate product, the text naturally presses its own modes of producibility upon the recipient, and in this sense may be said to produce its own consumption – not that it dictates a single sense to the reader, but that it generates a field of possible readings which, within the conjuncture of the reader's ideological matrix and its own, is necessarily finite. The text, it can be claimed, produces its own reader, even if only to be misread. But the text's own proffered modes of producibility are naturally constructed by the ideological act of reading; and there is no way out of this hermeneutical circle at the level of empirical reception. The theoretical importance of production for the value-question lies not at this level, where text and reading mutually produce each other in ideological complicity, but at the level of the text's own historical self-production in relation to its ideological environs. It is because this process can be scientifically analysed (rather than confined to some mythical limbo of lost origins) that a knowledge of the text is possible – a knowledge which, as I shall argue, embraces as one of its facets the question of value. Only by posing the problem in this way can we avoid at once that form of empiricism whereby the text naturalistically reproduces its meaning within the reader, and those modes of voluntarism in which the reader arbitrarily projects his meaning upon the text. Just as the relations between text and the ideology it produces are neither mechanistic nor gratuitous, so the same can be maintained for the relations between the text and a knowledge of it. If the text does not spontaneously enforce its immanent meaning on the reader, neither is it a mere gestural cue, a set of empty notations to be filled. The text is indeed irreducible to some single privileged significance intuitable across history; but it is equally indissoluble to a random splay of pluralist sense. For it is the determinations of that pluralism which count: this *découpage* of meaning rather than another, constituted by a determinate set of distances, breaks and redoublings whose source is to be found in its ideologically governed process of self-production. Both transcendentalist and pluralist cases end in mysticism: in the enigma of the concealed essence of meaning, or in the profound mystery of the purely phenomenal. The one is no more than the obverse of the other, in a shared problematic of essence/phenomenon, a coupling of idealism and empiricism. The critical sceptic sensually thrilling to the unfounded play of signs is the son of the metaphysical father rapt before the ritual of ultimate meaning.

If, then, a 'science of literary value' is an element of the science of ideologies, is value to be abandoned to some mere ideological relativism, some 'solipsism of the citizen' in which any discourse of 'objective merit' or 'false estimation' is to be jettisoned as immanentist and idealist? It is at this point that we need to re-open the question of textual production in relation to the problem of value. For if there can be a science of the ideologies of value, there may also be a science of the ideological conditions of the production of value. Such a science would not reinsert value 'within' the product, but would rather reinsert the conditions of textual production within the 'exchange relation' of value. On the question of aesthetic value, one must surely agree with Brecht:

> Anything that was worn out, trivial, or so commonplace that it *no longer made one think*, they did not like at all ('You get nothing out of it'). If one needed an aesthetic, one could find it here.[1]

When Shakespeare's texts cease to make us think, when we get nothing out of them, they will cease to have value. But *why* they 'make us think', why we 'get something out of them' (if only for the present) is a question which must be referred at once to the ideological matrix of our reading and the ideological matrix of their production. It is in the *articulation* of these distinct moments that the question of value resides [Eagleton goes on to criticize the belief that texts have either an autonomous 'moral' or 'aesthetic' level where they can be judged.] ...

... The relative autonomy of the aesthetic is not a question of some hierarchical division of levels within the work; it is a matter of the work's irreducibility to the historico-ideological of which it is the product. It is not that reductionism gives us a merely partial view of the artefact: it is that it abolishes it as an object and puts another in its place. It is not a question of 'suspending' the work's historical conditions of possibility, placing them in brackets (as Trotsky suggests) to attend to its 'aesthetic effect'; it is rather that its aesthetic effect is itself the index of a certain bracketing, whereby the work dissolves and distantiates the real to produce it as signification. The aesthetic is that which speaks of its historical conditions by remaining silent – inheres in them by distance and denial. The work 'shows' rather than 'states' those conditions in the nature of the productive relations it sets up to the ideological significations which found it. 'Real' history is cancelled by the text, but in the precise modes of that cancellation lies the text's most significant relation to history. The relation between 'aesthetic' and 'historical' is neither one between 'levels' within the text, nor between the work as aesthetic fact and its encircling historical conditions; it is rather that those historical conditions, in the form of the ideological, become the very determinant structure of that process of textual self-production which is, in its entirety, 'aesthetic'. We are concerned, in other words, with the specific operations whereby the ideological produces within itself that internal distantiation which is the aesthetic. It is not, *pace* Trotsky, a question of suspending the fact that Dante was a petty-bourgeois medieval Florentine; it is a matter of taking Trotsky's pertinent comments together with Engels's remarks in his Preface to the 1892 Italian edition of *The Communist Manifesto*:

> The close of the feudal Middle Ages and the onset of the modern capitalistic era are marked by a figure of grandiose stature: it is an Italian, Dante, who is both the last poet of the Middle Ages and the first modern poet. Today, just as it was around 1300, a new historical era is in the making. Will Italy provide us with a new Dante who will announce the birth of this new proletarian era?

It is not that Dante's work is valuable because it 'speaks of' an important historical era, or 'expresses the consciousness' of that epoch. Its value is an effect of the process whereby the complex ideological conjuncture in which it inheres so produces (internally distantiates) itself in a play of textual significations as to render its depths and intricacies vividly perceptible...

... *The Divine Comedy*, as Engels implies, belongs to the general history of class-society *by virtue* of occupying a particular moment in medieval Italy. And even an historically alien work may 'speak' to us in the present, for human animals ... share a biological structure even where they do not share a direct cultural heritage. Birth, nourishment, labour, kinship, sexuality, death are common to all social formations and to all literature; and it is no rebuttal of this to insert the correct but commonplace caveat that this biological 'infrastructure' is always historically mediated. So indeed it is; one merely repeats that what is variably mediated is a common biological structure.

It is not, of course, that art is necessarily more valuable when it evokes such transhistorical themes, any more than it is the case that only 'world-historical' conjunctures of the kind Engels identifies in Dante form the basis of literary achievement. Trotsky speaks of art as raising historically relative 'feelings and modes...above the limitations of the life of those days'; and this displaced 'universalism' can be traced throughout Marxist aesthetics as far as the later Lukács, who speaks in *The Peculiarity of the Aesthetic* of art as a suspension of heterogeneous life through which men enter momentarily into truly 'generic' being. What this 'materialist' position overlooks is that valuable art comes into being not *despite* its historical limitations (in some mystified Marcusean idealism) but *by virtue of* them. It is precisely this attitude which Marx adopts in his discussion of ancient Greek art in the *Grundrisse*; and it is not difficult to see in English literature how the value of, say, Jane Austen's fiction is indissociable from the dominative, drastically constricted class-practices and class-ethics which provide its problematic. The literary achievement of an Austen or a James is based on its reactionary conditions of class-formation, not a miracle which escapes them...

By some conjuncture of elements (class, sexuality, region, nationality and so on), these writers were contradictorily inserted into an hegemonic bourgeois ideology which had passed its progressive prime; and the relations here between historical fact and aesthetic value, overlooked by both formalist and sociologist, need to be enforced. Once more, it is not a question of some historicist 'expression' of certain privileged ideological sub-ensembles – an expression which bursts triumphantly through the fault-lines of 'orthodox' aesthetic and ideological modes to herald a new creation. It is a matter of a certain curvature in the ideological space in which the texts play – a curvature produced by the impaction of value upon value, signification upon signification, form upon form. It is not that a 'progressive' ideology thrusts through the constrictions of the hegemonic formation; there is little historically progressive about the ideological worlds of those major authors. It is rather that the hegemonic formation is produced from a particular dissentient conflictual position within it, and that the resulting problematic throws the 'fault-lines' of that formation into partial relief. One must examine this process simultaneously from the standpoint of textual production. In producing its meanings, such a text *produces* the ideological curvature of which I have spoken, inscribes it in its very substance. A particular line of sense, in order to preserve 'aesthetic' impact and consistency, will invert or modulate itself into an alternative 'ideological' register; or, to preserve 'ideological' purity, will be refracted into alternate forms of signification. It can be seen how the complex, intensive, pluralist play of senses thus constituted is relevant to the 'value-question' if one thinks of the work of a Trollope: work which bathes in a self-consistent, blandly undifferentiated ideological space...For the ideological matrix of Trollope's fiction (as with all writing) includes an ideology of the aesthetic – in Trollope's case, an anaemic, naïvely representational 'realism' which is merely a reflex of commonplace bourgeois empiricism...

...The text is a theatre which doubles, prolongs, compacts and variegates its signs, shaking them free from single determinants, merging and eliding them with a freedom unknown to history, in order to draw the reader into deeper experiential entry into the space thereby created. There are, of course, polar extremes here: the text which deliberately estranges by its 'excessive' parading of devices, and the text which woos us by a form of 'natural', 'innocent' writing with the seeming transparency of experience itself. But the literary work is more typically reducible to neither: it engages sympathy in proportion to its unreality. It is because its 'unreality' licenses a more-than-'natural' flexing and compacting of senses that we are made to see (and tempted to accept) the versions of historical reality it offers.

Yet it is precisely here that the question of value is engaged. For not every text 'flexes and compacts its senses' in the same mode or to the same degree as every other; nor does every text's 'versions of historical reality' count for much. All texts signify, but not all texts are significant. It is possible for a literary work so to produce a constricted ideology as to 'renew' it – so to 'estrange' its staled, threadbare significations, by virtue of its own 'second order' signifying labour, as to revivify the values and perceptions that ideology proffers. The converse is also familiar: a work may occlude and impoverish the elements of a positively enabling ideology by its textual operations. And there are, of course, other possibilities: we speak of the average love-story in a teenage magazine as 'inferior' literature because the withered ideological matrix within which it moves simply precludes that transformative textual pro-duction of such myths which might alone 'redeem' them. Yet it is too simple to speak of a 'first' and 'second' order of significations (ideology and text), as though these were both monistic systems. For each order is typically constituted by a complex ensemble of signs which belong to distinct ideological spheres; and the study of textual production, from the viewpoint of both meaning and value, is the study of the complex transactions between these sub-ensembles.

The value of a text, then, is determined by its double mode of insertion into an ideological formation and into the available lineages of literary discourse. It is in this way that the text enters into relation with an always partial range of the historically determined values, interests, needs, powers and capacities which surround it: not that it 'expresses' or 'reproduces' such things (for a text is made of words, not needs), but that it constructs itself in relation to the ideological signs which encode them. This is not to say, however, that the valuable text is always the bearer of 'progressive' values and capacities, or that it is the mere reflex of a progressive 'class-subject'. Take the contrast between Ben Jonson and Walter Savage Landor. Incongruously diverse as those writers are, they have in common a certain tradition of conservative classical humanism; but the positively enabling nature of that ideology in the first could not be in sharper contrast with its tepid, synthetic lifelessness in the second. By the time of Landor, such classical humanism has become a decorous academic withdrawal, an elaborate shell sucked of substance. In Jonson, however, such classicism combines with other elements to create a complex ideological space in which the experience of a limited but significant dialectic of historical interests is brought into sharp focus. It is not at all that Jonson's texts display a 'progressive class-ideology'; nor is it simply a matter of the ideological materials which those texts work. For classical humanism is an active determinant of the forms and significations of Jonson's drama, part of the aesthetic tradition into which his texts are inserted. In conjuncture with other traditions, it becomes the productive instrument by which a resourceful ideological world is so 'internally distantiated' as to yield up the wealth of its prejudices and perceptions. It is not that Jonson is 'exposed to history', and Landor is in flight from it – not that Jonson's texts resonate with 'real life', while Landor's smell of the study. While Landor was in full flight from history on the back of his bizarre epics, *The Prelude* was moving in a similar direction; but the contradiction and complexity of that movement in Wordsworth's case are a condition of superior value. It is a contradiction inscribed in the very form of Wordsworth's text: *The Prelude* is a poem about the poet's preparation to write an epic which turns out to be *The Prelude*. While Landor launches his exotic verse-tragedies and outlandish epics in cavalier disregard of the most basic question – how could such forms at such an historical conjuncture be anything but worthless? – *The Prelude* is creased and haunted by the aesthetic and ideological ambiguities of its moment. It is haunted by certain spiritual and historical possibilities, by the ghost of certain powers and values which its formal ideology is forced to censor; and it is in the rifts created by this radical lack of unity with itself that its play of meanings becomes most fertile. The work of a Landor or a Lamb, lacking for the most part access to such possibilities, relegates itself to irretrievably minor status.

It is necessary, then, to refuse a 'moralism' of literary value: to reunite the question of a work's quality with the question of its conditions of possibility. Men do not live by culture alone: far from it. But the claim of historical materialism is that, in effect, they will. Once emancipated from material scarcity, liberated from labour, they will live in the play of their mutual significations, move in the ceaseless 'excess' of freedom. In that process,the signs of sense and value by which previous societies have lived their life-conditions will still, no doubt, be relevant. Yet if Marxism has maintained a certain silence about aesthetic value, it may well be because the material conditions which would make such discourse fully possible do not as yet exist. The same holds for 'morality': if Marxism has had little to say directly about the 'moral', one reason for this obliquity is that one does not engage in moral debate with those for whom morality can only mean moralism. It is not a question of injecting a different content into these categories, but of transvaluating the categories themselves; and that cannot be done by a simple act of will. The 'aesthetic' is too valuable to be surrendered without a struggle to the bourgeois aestheticians, and too contaminated by that ideology to be appropriated as it is. It is, perhaps, in the provisional, strategic silence of those who refuse to speak 'morally' and 'aesthetically' that something of the true meaning of both terms is articulated.

Note

1   Brecht Against Lukács', *New Left Review* 84, March/April, 1974.

Art and authenticity

Nelson Goodman (b.1906)

The question of whether aesthetic value is closely tied up with a work of art's uniqueness has been keenly debated with respect to painting. Some philosophers have argued that it makes no difference at all aesthetically whether a work of art is authentic or a forgery, and that it ought to be judged on its beauty alone. In this extract, Nelson Goodman takes issue with such a view, arguing that knowledge of the authorship of a painting is part of the process by which we learn to discriminate between reproductions/forgeries and the authentic work of art, and thus to ascribe value. As Goodman points out in the case of Van Meegeren's forgeries of Vermeer, the aesthetic value of those forgeries has been downgraded as we have gained more knowledge in the interim of the 'minute perceptual differences' between them and authenticated Vermeers. Goodman makes it clear that the ability to appreciate aesthetic value involves a complex learning process and is not just a question of disinterested contemplation.

> ... the most tantalizing question of all: If a fake is so expert that even after the most thorough and trustworthy examination its authenticity is still open to doubt, is it or is it not as satisfactory a work of art as if it were unequivocally genuine?
>
> Aline B. Saarinen[1]

The Perfect Fake

Forgeries of works of art present a nasty practical problem to the collector, the curator, and the art historian, who must often expend taxing amounts of time and energy in determining whether or not particular objects are genuine. But the theoretical problem raised is even more acute. The hardheaded question why there is any aesthetic difference between a deceptive forgery and an original work challenges a basic premise on which the very functions of collector, museum, and art historian depend. A philosopher of art caught without an answer to this question is at least as badly off as a curator of paintings caught taking a Van Meegeren for a Vermeer.

The question is most strikingly illustrated by the case of a given work and a forgery or copy or reproduction of it. Suppose we have before us, on the left, Rembrandt's original painting *Lucretia* and, on the right, a superlative imitation of it. We know from a fully documented history that the painting on the left is the original; and we know from X-ray photographs and microscopic examination and chemical analysis that the painting on the right is a recent fake. Although there are many differences between the two – e.g., in authorship, age, physical and chemical characteristics, and market value – we cannot see any difference between them; and if they are moved while we sleep, we cannot then tell which is which by merely looking at them. Now we are pressed with the question whether there can be any aesthetic difference between the two pictures; and the questioner's tone often intimates that the answer is plainly *no*, that the only differences here are aesthetically irrelevant.

We must begin by inquiring whether the distinction between what can and what cannot be seen in the pictures by 'merely looking at them' is entirely clear. We are looking at the pictures, but presumably not 'merely looking' at them, when we examine them under a microscope or fluoroscope. Does merely looking, then, mean looking without the use of any instrument? This seems a little unfair to the man who needs glasses to tell a painting from a hippopotamus. But if glasses are permitted at all, how strong may they be, and can we consistently exclude the magnifying glass and the microscope? Again, if incandescent light is permitted, can violet-ray light be ruled out? And even with incandescent light, must it be of medium intensity and from a normal angle, or is a strong raking light permitted? All these cases might be covered by saying that 'merely looking' is looking at the pictures without any use of instruments other than those customarily used in looking at things in general. This will cause trouble when we turn, say, to certain miniature illuminations or Assyrian cylinder seals that we can hardly distinguish from the crudest copies without using a strong glass. Furthermore, even in our case of the two pictures, subtle differences of drawing or painting discoverable only with a magnifying glass may still, quite obviously, be aesthetic differences between the pictures. If a powerful microscope is used instead, this is no longer the case; but just how much magnification is permitted? To specify what is meant by merely looking at the pictures is thus far from easy; but for the sake of argument, let us suppose that all these difficulties have been resolved and the notion of 'merely looking' made clear enough.

Then we must ask who is assumed to be doing the looking. Our questioner does not, I take it, mean to suggest that there is no aesthetic difference between two pictures if at least one person, say a cross-eyed wrestler, can see no difference. The more pertinent question is whether there can be any aesthetic difference if nobody, not even the most skilled expert, can ever tell the pictures apart by merely looking at them. *But notice now that no one can ever ascertain by merely looking at the pictures that no one ever has been or will be able to tell them apart by merely looking at them.* In other words, the question in its present form concedes that no one can ascertain by merely looking at the pictures that there is no aesthetic difference between them. This seems repugnant to our questioner's whole motivation. For if merely looking can never establish that two pictures are aesthetically the same, something that is beyond the reach of any given looking is admitted as constituting an aesthetic difference. And in that case, the reason for not admitting documents and the results of scientific tests becomes very obscure.

The real issue may be more accurately formulated as the question whether there is any aesthetic difference between the two pictures *for me* (or for x) if I (or x) cannot tell them apart by merely looking at them. But this is not quite right either. For I can never ascertain merely by looking at the pictures that even I shall never be able to see any difference between them. And to concede that something beyond any given looking at the pictures by me may constitute an aesthetic difference between them *for me* is, again, quite at odds with the tacit conviction or suspicion that activates the questioner.

Thus the critical question amounts finally to this: is there any aesthetic difference between the two pictures for x at t, where t is a suitable period of time, if x cannot tell them apart by merely looking at them at t? Or in other words, can anything that x does not discern by merely looking at the pictures at t constitute an aesthetic difference between them for x at t?

The answer

In setting out to answer this question, we must bear clearly in mind that what one can distinguish at any given moment by merely looking depends not only upon native visual acuity but upon practice and training. Americans look pretty much alike to a

Chinese who has never looked at many of them. Twins may be indistinguishable to all but their closest relatives and acquaintances. Moreover, only through looking at them when someone has named them for us can we learn to tell Joe from Jim upon merely looking at them. Looking at people or things attentively, with the knowledge of certain presently invisible respects in which they differ, increases our ability to discriminate between them – and between other things or other people – upon merely looking at them. Thus pictures that look just alike to the newsboy come to look quite unlike to him by the time he has become a museum director.

Although I see no difference now between the two pictures in question, I may learn to see a difference between them. I cannot determine now by merely looking at them, or in any other way, that I *shall* be able to learn. But the information that they are very different, that the one is the original and the other is the forgery, argues against any inference to the conclusion that I *shall not* be able to learn. And the fact that I may later be able to make a perceptual distinction between the pictures that I cannot make now constitutes an aesthetic difference between them that is important to me now.

Furthermore, to look at the pictures now with the knowledge that the left one is the original and the other the forgery may help develop the ability to tell which is which later by merely looking at them. Thus, with information not derived from the present or any past looking at the pictures, the present looking may have a quite different bearing upon future lookings from what it would otherwise have. The way the pictures in fact differ constitutes an aesthetic difference between them for me now because my knowledge of the way they differ bears upon the role of the present looking in training my perceptions to discriminate between these pictures, and between others.

But that is not all. My knowledge of the difference betweeen the two pictures, just because it affects the relationship of the present to future lookings, informs the very character of my present looking. This knowledge instructs me to look at the two pictures differently now, even if what I see is the same. Beyond testifying that I may learn to see a difference, it also indicates to some extent the kind of scrutiny to be applied now, the comparisons and contrasts to be made in imagination, and the relevant associations to be brought to bear. It thereby guides the selection, from my past experience, of items and aspects for use in my present looking. Thus not only later but right now, the unperceived difference between the two pictures is a consideration pertinent to my visual experience with them.

In short, although I cannot tell the pictures apart merely by looking at them now, the fact that the left-hand one is the original and the right-hand one a forgery constitutes an aesthetic difference between them for me now because knowledge of this fact (1) stands as evidence that there may be a difference between them that I can learn to perceive, (2) assigns the present looking a role as training toward such a perceptual discrimination, and (3) makes consequent demands that modify and differentiate my present experience in looking at the two pictures.

Nothing depends here upon my ever actually perceiving or being able to perceive a difference between the two pictures. What informs the nature and use of my present visual experience is not the fact or the assurance that such a perceptual discrimination is within my reach, but evidence that it may be; and such evidence is provided by the known factual differences between the pictures. Thus the pictures differ aesthetically for me now even if no one will ever be able to tell them apart merely by looking at them.

But suppose it could be *proved* that no one ever will be able to see any difference? This is about as reasonable as asking whether, if it can be proved that the market value and yield of a given U.S. bond and one of a certain nearly bankrupt company will always be the same, there is any financial difference between the two bonds. For what sort of proof could be given? One might suppose that if nobody – not even the most skilled expert – has ever been able to see any difference between the pictures, then the conclusion that I shall never be able to is quite safe; but, as in the case of the Van Meegeren forgeries (of which, more later), distinctions not visible to the expert up to a given time may later become manifest even to the observant layman. Or one might think of some delicate scanning device that compares the color of two pictures at every point and registers the slightest discrepancy. What, though, is meant here by 'at every point'? At no mathematical point, of course, is there any color at all; and even some physical particles are too small to have color. The scanning device must thus cover at each instant a region big enough to have color but at least as small as any perceptible region. Just how to manage this is puzzling since 'perceptible' in the present context means 'discernible by merely looking,' and thus the line between perceptible and nonperceptible regions seems to depend on the arbitrary line between a magnifying glass and a microscope. If some such line is drawn, we can never be sure that the delicacy of our instruments is superior to the maximal attainable acuity of unaided perception. Indeed, some experimental psychologists are inclined to conclude that every measurable difference in light can sometimes be detected by the naked eye. And there is a further difficulty. Our scanning device will examine color – that is, reflected light. Since reflected light depends partly upon incident light, illumination of every quality, of every intensity, and from every direction must be tried. And for each case, especially since the paintings do not have a plane surface, a complete scanning must be made from every angle. But of course we cannot cover every variation, or even determine a single absolute correspondence, in even one respect. Thus the search for a proof that I shall never be able to see any difference between the two pictures is futile for more than technological reasons.

Yet suppose we are nevertheless pressed with the question whether, if proof *were* given, there would then be any aesthetic difference for me between the pictures. And suppose we answer this farfetched question in the negative. This will still give our questioner no comfort. For the net result would be that if no difference between the pictures can in fact be perceived, then the existence of an aesthetic difference between them will rest entirely upon what is or is not proved by means other than merely looking at them. This hardly supports the contention that there can be no aesthetic differences without a perceptual difference.

Returning from the realm of the ultra-hypothetical, we may be faced with the protest that the vast aesthetic difference thought to obtain between the Rembrandt and the forgery cannot be accounted for in terms of the search for, or even the discovery of, perceptual differences so slight that they can be made out, if at all, only after much experience and long practice. This objection can be dismissed at once; for minute perceptual differences can bear enormous weight. The clues that tell me whether I have caught the eye of someone across the room are almost indiscernible. The actual differences in sound that distinguish a fine from a mediocre performance can be picked out only by the well-trained ear. Extremely subtle changes can alter the whole design, feeling, or expression of a painting. Indeed, the slightest perceptual differences sometimes matter the most aesthetically; gross physical damage to a fresco may be less consequential than slight but smug retouching.

All I have attempted to show, of course, is that the two pictures can differ aesthetically, not that the original is better than the forgery. In our example, the original probably is much the better picture, since Rembrandt paintings are in general much better than copies by unknown painters. But a copy of a Lastman by Rembrandt may well be better than the original. We are not called upon here to make such particular comparative judgments or to formulate canons of aesthetic evaluation. We have fully met the demands of our problem by showing that the fact that we cannot tell our two pictures apart merely by looking at them does not imply that they are aesthetically the same – and thus does not force us to conclude that the forgery is as good as the original.

The example we have been using throughout illustrates a special case of a more general question concerning the aesthetic significance of authenticity. Quite aside from the occurrence of forged duplication, does it matter whether an original work is the product of one or another artist or school or period? Suppose that I can easily tell two pictures apart but cannot tell who painted either except by using some devices like X-ray photography. Does the fact that the picture is or is not by Rembrandt make any aesthetic difference? What is involved here is the discrimination not of one picture from another but of the class of Rembrandt paintings from the class of other paintings. My chance of learning to make this discrimination correctly – of discovering projectible characteristics that differentiate Rembrandts in general from non-Rembrandts – depends heavily upon the set of examples available as a basis. Thus the fact that the given picture belongs to the one class or the other is important for me to know in learning how to tell Rembrandt paintings from others. In other words, my present (or future) inability to determine the authorship of the given picture without use of scientific apparatus does not imply that the authorship makes no aesthetic difference to me; for knowledge of the authorship, no matter how obtained, can contribute materially toward developing my ability to determine without such apparatus whether or not any picture, including this one on another occasion, is by Rembrandt.

Incidentally, one rather striking puzzle is readily solved in these terms. When Van Meegeren sold his pictures as Vermeers, he deceived most of the best-qualified experts; and only by his confession was the fraud revealed. Nowadays even the fairly knowing layman is astonished that any competent judge could have taken a Van Meegeren for a Vermeer, so obvious are the differences. What has happened? The general level of aesthetic sensibility has hardly risen so fast that the layman of today sees more acutely than the expert of twenty years ago. Rather, the better information now at hand makes the discrimination easier. Presented with a single unfamiliar picture at a time, the expert had to decide whether it was enough like known Vermeers to be by the same artist. And every time a Van Meegeren was added to the corpus of pictures accepted as Vermeers, the criteria for acceptance were modified thereby; and the mistaking of further Van Meegerens for Vermeers became inevitable. Now, however, not only have the Van Meegerens been subtracted from the precedent-class for Vermeer, but also a precedent-class for Van Meegeren has been established. With these two precedent-classes before us, the characteristic differences become so conspicuous that telling other Van Meegerens from Vermeers offers little difficulty. Yesterday's expert might well have avoided his errors if he had had a few known Van Meegerens handy for comparison. And today's layman who so cleverly spots a Van Meegeren may well be caught taking some quite inferior school-piece for a Vermeer.

In answer the questions raised above, I have not attempted the formidable task of defining 'aesthetic' in general, but have simply argued that since the exercise, training, and development of our powers of discriminating among works of art are plainly aesthetic activities, the aesthetic properties of a picture include not only those found by looking at it but also those that determine how it is to be looked at. This rather obvious fact would hardly have needed underlining but for the prevalence of the time-honored Tingle-Immersion theory, which tells us that the proper behavior on encountering a work of art is to strip ourselves of all the vestments of knowledge and experience (since they might blunt the immediacy of our enjoyment), then submerge ourselves completely and gauge the aesthetic potency of the work by the intensity and duration of the resulting tingle. The theory is absurd on the face of it and useless for dealing with any of the important problems of aesthetics; but it has become part of the fabric of our common nonsense.

Note

1   *New York Times Book Review*, July 30, 1961, p. 14.

The act of creation

Arthur Koestler (1905–83)

The author Arthur Koestler, best known for books such as Darkness at Noon *(1970),* The Sleepwalkers *(1968) and* The Act of Creation *(1969), takes a very different attitude towards the relationship of authenticity and aesthetic value from Goodman (Reading 13). Koestler believes that one's aesthetic appreciation should not be affected by the authenticity or non-authenticity of the work of art. In the extract below, Koestler argues that the aesthetic qualities of a Van Meegeren 'Vermeer' are the same before and after its unmasking as a forgery, and he attributes the difference in our reaction mainly to snobbery. Authenticity, Koestler claims, is 'extraneous to aesthetic value', although he concedes that we find it 'well-nigh impossible' to separate them. The demand for authenticity, which Goodman sees as an entirely justifiable part of the process by which we arrive at aesthetic value, is dismissed by Koestler as being little better than 'fetish-worship'.*

Confusion and sterility

THE AESTHETICS OF SNOBBERY

In 1948, a German art restorer named Dietrich Fey, engaged in reconstruction work on Lübeck's ancient St Marien Church, stated that his workmen had discovered traces of Gothic wall-paintings dating back to the thirteenth century, under a coating of chalk on the church walls. The restoration of the paintings was entrusted to Fey's assistant, Lothar Malskat, who finished the job two years later. In 1950 Chancellor Adenauer presided over the ceremonies marking the completion of the restoration work, in the presence of art experts from all parts of Europe. Their unanimous opinion, voiced by Chancellor Adenauer, was that the twenty-one thirteenth-century Gothic saints on the church walls were 'a valuable treasure and fabulous discovery of lost masterpieces'.

None of the experts on that or any later occasion expressed doubt as to the authenticity of the frescoes. It was Herr Malskat himself who, two years later, disclosed the fraud. He presented himself on his own initiative at Lübeck police headquarters, where he stated that the frescoes were entirely his own work undertaken by order of his boss, Herr Fey; and he asked to be tried for forgery. The leading German art experts, however, stuck to their opinion; the frescoes, they said, were without doubt genuine, and Herr Malskat was merely seeking cheap publicity. An official Board of Investigation was appointed, and came to the conclusion that the restoration of the wall-paintings was a hoax – but only after Herr Malskat had confessed that he had also manufactured hundreds of Rembrandts, Watteaus, Toulouse-Lautrecs, Picassos, Henri Rousseaus, Carots, Chagalls, Vlamincks, and other masters, and sold them as originals – some of which were actually found by the police in Herr Fey's house. Without this *corpus delicti*, it is doubtful whether the German experts would ever have admitted having been fooled.

My point is not the fallibility of the experts. Herr Malskat's exploit is merely one of a number of similarly successful hoaxes and forgeries – of which the most fabulous were probably van Meegeren's faked Vermeers. The disturbing question which they raise is whether the Lübeck saints are less beautiful, and have ceased to be 'a valuable treasure of masterpieces', simply because they had been painted by Herr Malskat and not by somebody else? And furthermore, if van Meegeren can paint Vermeers as good as Vermeer himself, why should they be taken off the walls of the Dutch and other National Galleries? If even the experts were unable to detect the difference, then surely the false Vermeers must procure as much aesthetic pleasure to the common run of Museum visitors as the authentic ones. All the curators would have to do is to change the name on the catalogue from Vermeer to van Meegeren.

There are several answers to this line of argument, but before going into them I want to continue in the part of the devil's advocate by considering an example of a forgery in a different field: Macpherson's *Ossian*. The case is so notorious that the facts need only be briefly mentioned. James Macpherson (1736–96), a Scottish poet and adventurer, alleged that in the course of his wanderings in the Highlands he had discovered some ancient Gaelic manuscripts. Enthusiastic Scottish *littérateurs* put up a subscription to enable Macpherson to pursue his researches, and in 1761 he published *Fingal, an ancient Epic Poem in Six Books, together with several other poems composed by Ossian, the Son of Fingal*. Ossian is the legendary third-century hero and bard of Celtic literature. *Fingal* was soon followed by the publication of a still larger Ossianic epic called *Temora*, and this by a collected edition, *The Works of Ossian*. The authenticity of Macpherson's text was at once questioned in England, particularly by Dr Johnson (whom Macpherson answered by sending him a challenge to a duel), and to his death Macpherson refused, under various unconvincing pretexts, to publish his alleged Gaelic originals. By the turn of the century the controversy was settled; it was established that while Macpherson had used fragments of ancient Celtic lore, most of the 'Ossianic texts' were of his own making.

Yet here again the question arises whether the poetic quality of the work itself is altered by the fact that it was written not by Ossian the son of Fingal, but by James Macpherson? The 'Ossianic' texts were translated into many languages, and had a considerable influence on the literature and cultural climate of Europe in the late eighteenth and early nineteenth centuries. This is how the *Encyclopaedia Britannica* sums up its evaluation of Macpherson (my italics):

> The varied sources of his work and its worthlessness as a transcript of actual Celtic poems do not alter the fact that he produced a work of art which... *did more than any single work to bring about the romantic movement in European, and especially in German, literature...* Herder and Goethe... were among its profound admirers.

These examples could be continued indefinitely. Antique furniture, Greek tanagra figures, Gothic madonnas, old and modern masters are being forged, copied, counterfeited all the time, and the value we set on the object is not determined by aesthetic appreciation and pleasure to the eye, but by the precarious and fallible judgement of experts. And it will always be fallible for the good and simple reason that genius consists not in the perfect exercise of a technique, but in its invention; once the technique is established, diligent pupils and imitators can produce works in the master's idiom which are often indistinguishable, and sometimes technically more accomplished than his.

Some years ago, at a fancy-dress ball – in Monte Carlo, I believe – a competition was held to decide which among the dozen or so guests masquerading as Charlie Chaplin came nearest to the original. Chaplin himself happened to be among them – and got only the third prize. In 1962, the Fogg museum of Harvard arranged a private exhibition for connoisseurs, where some of the exhibits were fakes, others genuine; the guests were to decide which was which. Included were, among other items, an original portrait by Annibale Caracci, one of the most influential painters of the Italian baroque, and a contemporary copy therof; also an original Picasso drawing of a Mother and Child, and two forgeries thereof. The result was similar to that of the Chaplin competition; among those who plumped for one of the forgeries were the chairman of Princeton's Art Department and the Secretary of the Fogg; the director of the Metropolitan Museum refused to submit to the test, while other experts 'scored themselves on sheets of paper, compared their verdicts with the officially announced facts, and quietly crumpled their papers'.

Let me repeat: the principal mark of genius is not perfection, but originality, the opening of new frontiers; once this is done, the conquered territory becomes common property. The fact that even professional experts are unable to point out the difference in artistic merit between the true and the false Picasso, Caracci, or Vermeer, is conclusive proof that no such difference can be registered by the layman's eye. Are we, then, all snobs to whom a signature, an expert testimony based on X-ray photography, or the postmark of a period is more important than the intrinsic beauty of the object itself? And what about the contested works of Shakespeare and Johann Sebastian Bach? Are their dramatic and poetic and harmonic qualities dependent on the technical controversies between specialists?

The answer, I believe, can be summed up in a single sentence: our appraisal of a work of art or literature is hardly ever a unitary act, and mostly the result of two or more independent and simultaneous processes which interfere with and tend to distort each other. Let me illustrate this by a story which I have told elsewhere at greater length.

A friend of mine, whom I shall call Catherine, was given as a present by an unobtrusive admirer a drawing from Picasso's classical period; she took it to be a reproduction and hung it in her staircase. On my next visit to her house, it was hanging over the mantelpiece in the drawing-room: the supposed reproduction had turned out to be an original. But as it was a line-drawing in ink, black contour on white paper, it needed an expert, or at least a good magnifying lens, to show that it was the original and not a lithograph or reproduction. Neither Catherine, nor any of her friends, could tell the difference. Yet her appreciation of it had completely changed, as the promotion from staircase to drawing-room showed. I asked her to explain the reason for her change of attitude to the thing on the wall which in itself had not changed at all; she answered, surprised at my stupidity, that of course the thing had not changed, but that she *saw* it differently since she knew that it was done by Picasso himself and 'not just a reproduction'. I then asked what considerations determined her attitude to pictures in general, and she replied with equal sincerity that they were, of course, considerations of aesthetic quality – 'composition, colour, harmony, power, what have you.' She honestly believed to be guided by purely aesthetic value-judgements based on those qualities; but if that was the case, since the qualities of the picture had not changed, how could her attitude to it have changed?

I was labouring a seemingly obvious point, yet she was unable to see that she was contradicting herself. It proved quite useless repeating to her that the origin and rarity-value of the object did not alter its qualities – and, accordingly, should not have altered her appreciation of it, if it had really been based on purely aesthetic criteria as she believed it to be. In reality, of course, her attitude was determined not by those criteria, but by an accidental bit of information – which might be right or wrong, and was entirely extraneous to the question of aesthetic value. Yet she was by no means stupid; in fact there is something of her confusion in all of us. We all tend to believe that our attitude to an object of art is determined by aesthetic considerations alone, whereas it is decisively influenced by factors of a quite different order. We are unable to see a work of art isolated from the context of its origin or history; and if Catherine were to learn that her Picasso was after all a reproduction, her attitude would again change according to the changed context. Moreover, most people get quite indignant when one suggests to them that the origin of a picture has nothing to do with its aesthetic value as such. For, in our minds, the question of period, authorship, and authenticity, *though in itself extraneous to aesthetic value*, is so intimately mixed up with it, that we find it well-nigh impossible to unscramble them. The phenomenon of snobbery, in all its crude and subtle variants, can always be traced back to some confusion of this type.

Thus Catherine would *not* be a snob if she had said: 'A reproduction of this line-drawing is to all practicable purposes indistinguishable from the original, and therefore just as beautiful as the original. Nevertheless, one gives me a greater thrill than the other, for reasons which have nothing to do with beauty.' But alas, she is incapable of disentangling the two different elements which determine her reactions, and to a greater or lesser extent we are all victims of the same confusion. The change in our attitude, and in the art dealer's price, when it is discovered that a cracked and blackened piece of landscape displaying three sheep and a windmill, bears the signature of Broeckendael the Elder, has nothing to do with beauty, aesthetics, or what have you. And yet, God help us, the sheep and the mill and the brook *do* suddenly look different and more attractive – even to the hard-boiled dealer. What happened was that a bit of incidental information cast a ray of golden sunlight on those miserable sheep; a ray emitted not by the pigment but by the cerebral cortex of the art-snob.

THE PERSONAL EMANATION

Let me now present the case for the defence. The appraisal of a work of art is generally the result of two or more independent processes which interact with each other. One complex process constitutes the aesthetic experience as such... it implies a system of values, and certain criteria of excellence, on which we believe our judgement to be based. But other processes interfere with it, with their different systems of values, and distort our judgements. I shall mention two types of such interfering systems.

The first is summed up in the statement of a little girl of twelve, the daughter of a friend of mine, who was taken to the Greenwich Museum, and when asked to name the most beautiful thing she had seen there, declared without hesitation: 'Nelson's shirt.' When asked what was so beautiful about it, she explained: 'That shirt with blood on it was jolly nice. Fancy real blood on a real shirt which belonged to somebody really historic.'

Her sense of values, unlike Catherine's, was still unspoilt. The emotion that she had experienced was derived from the same kind of magic that emanates from Napoleon's inkpot, the relic of the saint carried in the annual procession, the rope by which a famous murderer was hanged, the galley-proof corrected by Tolstoy's hand. Our forebears believed that an object which had been in the possession of a person became imbued with his emanations, and in turn emanated something of his substance. 'There is, I am sure,' a columnist wrote in the *Daily Express*, 'for most of us a special pleasure in sinking your teeth into a peach produced on the estate of an Earl who is related to the Royal Family.' You might even come to feel that you are a member of the family if you persist long enough in this somewhat indirect method of transubstantiation.

We can no more escape the pull of magic inside us than the pull of gravity. Its manifestations may take a more or less dignified form; but the value we set on the peach from the Earl's estate or the splinter from the saint's bone, on Dickens's quill or Galileo's telescope, is derived from the same source of sympathetic magic. It is, as the little girl said, jolly nice to behold a fragment of a marble by Praxiteles – although it has been battered out of human shape, with a leper's nose and broken ears. The contact with the master's hand has imbued it with a kind of effluvium which has lingered on, and emanates the same thrill as the real blood on Nelson's shirt – or the real ink from Picasso's pen.

The inordinate importance that we attribute to the original and authenticated, even in those borderline cases where only the expert can decide on questions of authenticity, has its unconscious roots in this particular kind of fetish-worship. Hence its compelling power – who would not cherish a lock from an Egyptian mummy's head? Yet, as every honest art dealer will admit, borderline cases are so frequent as to be almost the rule. I am no longer referring to forgeries, but to the classical practice of the master letting his pupils, apprenticed to his workshop, assist in the execution of larger undertakings; and 'assistance' could mean anything from the filling in of background and minor details, to the painting of a whole picture after the master's sketch. We are made to realize how common this practice was by the emphasis which Michelangelo's admiring contemporaries put on the fact that he painted the ceiling of the Sistine Chapel 'alone and unaided'. If we remember that even the experts were at a loss to tell the Caracci portrait from its contemporary copy – probably by a pupil – we must conclude that for the great majority of mortals, including connoisseurs, the difference between an authenticated masterpiece, a doubtful attribution, and a work 'from the school of', is in most cases not discernible. But the fact remains that an 'attribution', perfect in its genre but not authenticated, is held in lower esteem than a work of lesser perfection, guaranteed to have come from the ageing master's hand. It is not the eye that guides the museum visitor, but the magic of names. The English nation forked out a million pounds to prevent the sale to America of a Leonardo sketch to which it had never paid any attention; and the hundreds of thousands of good citizens who queued to see it could not have told it from a page in an art-student's sketch-book; they went to see Nelson's shirt.

THE ANTIQUARIAN FALLACY

The second 'interfering system' is period consciousness. A Byzantine icon, or a Pompeian fresco is not enjoyed at its face value, but by a part-conscious attunement of the mind to the values and techniques of the time. Even in paintings from periods whose idiom is much closer to ours – a Holbein portrait, for instance – such externals as costume and headdress drive it mercilessly home to us that the man with the unforgettable, timeless face belonged to the court of Henry VIII. The archetypal quality is there, but period-consciousness intrudes; and the danger is that it may dominate the field.

Thus we look at an old picture through a double frame: the solid gilt frame which isolates it from its surroundings and creates for it a hole in space; and the period-frame in our minds which creates for it a hole in time, and assigns its place on the stage of history. Each time we think we are making a purely aesthetic judgement according to our lights, the stage-lights interfere. When we contemplate the Gothic wall-paintings on the church in Lübeck for the first time, believing them to be authentic, and then a second time, knowing that they were made by Herr Malskat, our experience will indeed be completely changed, although the frescoes are the same as at the time when they were hailed as masterpieces. The period-frame has been changed, and with it the stage-lights.

Apart from being unavoidable, this relativism of aesthetic judgement has its positive sides: by entering into the spirit and climate of the period, we automatically make allowances for its crudities of technique, for its conventions and blind spots; we bend over the past with a tender antiquarian stoop. But this gesture degenerates into antiquarian snobbery at the point where the period-frame becomes more important than the picture, and perverts our scale of values. The symptoms are all too familiar: indiscriminate reverence for anything classified as Italian Primitive or Austrian Baroque (including its mass-produced puffy, chubby, winged little horrors); collective shifts of period-consciousness (from anti-Victorian to pro-Victorian in recent years); the inanities of fashion (Fra Angelico is 'in', Botticelli is 'out').

What is wrong with a forgery?

Alfred Lessing (b.1936)

More discussion of the Van Meegeren affair, and the issues it raises concerning aesthetic value, is contained in the following extract from The Forger's Art *(1983) by Alfred Lessing. Like Koestler (Reading 14), Lessing argues that aesthetic value is independent of authenticity, and that genuineness versus forgery is a 'nonaesthetic standard of judgement'. He sees forgery as being against the spirit of art, in the sense that the forger is laying claim to an originality which can only belong to the artist who inspires the copy. Van Meegeren 'Vermeers' therefore 'lack integrity', although that does not mean that they also lack aesthetic value. Aesthetic experience and aesthetic value remain for Lessing completely independent of the question of authenticity.*

This chapter attempts to answer the simple question: What is wrong with a forgery? It assumes, then, that something *is* wrong with a forgery. This is seen to be a reasonable assumption when one considers that the term *forgery* can be defined only in reference to a contrasting phenomenon which must somehow include the notion of genuineness or authenticity. When thus defined there can be little doubt that the concept of forgery is a normative one. It is clear, moreover, that it is a negative concept implying the absence or negation of value. But a problem arises when we ask what kind of value we are speaking of. It appears to be generally assumed that in the case of artistic forgeries we are dealing with the absence or negation of *aesthetic* value. If this were so, a forgery would be an aesthetically inferior work of art. But this, as I will show, is not the case. Pure aesthetics cannot explain forgery. Considering a work of art aesthetically superior because it is genuine, or inferior because it is forged, has little or nothing to do with aesthetic judgment or criticism. It is rather a piece of snobbery.[1]

It is difficult to make this position convincing to a person who is convinced that forgery *is* a matter of aesthetics. If a person insists that for him the aesthetic value (i.e., the beauty) of a work of art is affected by the knowledge that it is or is not genuine, there is little one can say to make that fact unreal for him. At most one can try to show that in the area of aesthetics and criticism we are easily confused and that his view, if carried through, leads to absurd or improbable conclusions. It is important that we do this because it is impossible to understand what is wrong with a forgery unless it be first made quite clear that the answer will not be in terms of its aesthetic worth.

Somehow critics have never understood this and have again and again allowed themselves to be forced into an embarrassing position upon the discovery of some forgery or other. Perhaps the classic, certainly the most celebrated case in point, was that of Han van Meegeren, who in 1945 disturbed the complacent tranquility of the world of art and art critics by confessing that he was the artist responsible for eight paintings, six of which had been sold as legitimate Vermeers and two as de Hooghs. It is not hard to in.agine the discomfort felt by critics at that time, especially when we recall how thoroughly successful van Meegeren was in perpetrating his fraud. His *Disciples at Emmaus* was subjected to the very highest praise by the noted critic and scholar Abraham Bredius...as one of Vermeer's finest achievements, and it hung in the Boymans Museum for seven years. During that time thousands upon thousands admired and praised the painting. There was no doubt in anyone's mind that this was one of the greatest of Vermeer's paintings and, indeed, one of the most beautiful works of art in the world. It was undoubtedly this universal judgment of aesthetic excellence which accounts largely for the sensational effects of van Meegeren's confession in 1945.

It is of course embarrassing and irritating for an expert to make a mistake in his field. And it *was*, as it turned out, a mistake to identify the painting as a Vermeer. But it should be obvious from the words of Bredius that there is more involved here than a mere matter of misidentification. 'The colors are magnificent,' he writes. 'The highest art...this magnificent painting...*the* masterpiece of Vermeer': this is more than identification. This clearly is aesthetic praise. And it is just the fact that the critics heaped such lavish praise on a picture which turned out to have been painted by a second-rate contemporary artist that made the van Meegeren case such a painful affair for them. To their way of thinking, which I am trying to show was not very logical, they were now apparently faced with the dilemma of either admitting that they had praised a worthless picture or continuing to do so.

This was, of course, precisely the trap that van Meegeren had laid for the critics. It was, in fact, the whole *raison d'être* of his perpetrating the fraud. He deliberately chose this extreme, perhaps pathological, way of exposing what he considered to be false aesthetic standards of art critics. In this respect his thinking was no more logical than that of the critics. His reasoning, at least about his first forgery, *The Disciples*, was in effect as follows: 'Once my painting has been accepted and admired as a genuine Vermeer, I will confess publicly to the forgery and thus force the critics either to retract their earlier judgments of praise, thereby acknowledging their fallibility, or to recognize that I am as great an artist as Vermeer.' The dilemma as stated contains a difficulty to which we shall return later. What is important historically is that the critics accepted van Meegeren's dilemma as a genuine one (thereby becoming the dupes of a logical forgery as well as an artistic one), although in the public outburst of indignation, condemnation, praise, blame, analysis, investigation, and discussion which followed van Meegeren's confession, it is difficult to determine which horn of this dilemma the critics actually chose to be impaled on.

There existed, in fact, a small group of critics who never for a moment accepted van Meegeren's claim to have painted *The Disciples at Emmaus*. They argued vehemently that whereas all the other paintings in question are easily shown to be forgeries, no convincing evidence had been produced to prove that *The Disciples* (as well as one other painting entitled *The Last Supper*) was not by Vermeer and that, in fact, all evidence pointed to the conclusion that it was a genuine Vermeer. Subsequent laboratory tests using more modern techniques have finally settled the issue against these critics, but that need not concern us.

What should concern us is the fact that aesthetically it would seem to make no difference whatever whether *The Disciples* is a Vermeer or a van Meegeren. Needless to say, this is not the view of the critics. To them apparently it makes all the difference in the world. Consider, for example, the words of J. Decoen, who was one of that aforementioned group of critics that held that *The Disciples* was a genuine Vermeer:

> I must recall that the moment of greatest anguish for me was when the verdict [of van Meegeren] was being considered. The Court might, according to an ancient Dutch Law, have ordered the destruction of *all* the pictures. One shudders at the thought that one could, officially, have destroyed two of the most moving works which Vermeer has created. During the trial, at the moment

of his indictment, the Public Prosecutor stated that there was in Court a man who claimed that a number of the paintings were not by van Meegeren. He made this statement because, ever since 1945, he must have realized that my perseverance had not faltered, that my conviction was deep, and that I had never changed my original statements in any respect whatsoever. These words may possibly have influenced the decision of the Court with regard to the application of the Law. If this be so, I should consider myself amply repaid for my efforts and pains, for my tenacity may possibly have ultimately rescued two capital works of the Dutch school of the seventeenth century.[2]

But what does it matter that Decoen is wrong? Could he no longer take pride in having prevented the destruction of these 'capital' paintings even though they are products of the twentieth instead of the seventeenth century? The answers, it seems to me, are almost self-evident. What, after all, makes these paintings 'capital works'? Surely it is their purely aesthetic qualities, such as the ones mentioned by Bredius in his description of *The Disciples*. But if this is so, then why, even if this painting is a forgery, should Decoen not be justified in his actions, since he has preserved a painting which is aesthetically important for the only reason that a painting can be aesthetically important – namely, its beauty? Are we any more justified in destroying capital paintings of the twentieth century than those of the seventeenth? To this question we are usually given the answer that the one is after all a forgery while the other is genuine. But our question is precisely: What is the difference between a genuine Vermeer and a van Meegeren forgery? It is of no use to maintain that one need but look to see the difference. The fact that *The Disciples* is a forgery (if indeed it is) cannot, so to speak, be read off from its surface, but can finally be proved or disproved only by means of extensive scientific experiments and analyses. Nor are the results of such scientific investigations of any help in answering our question, since they deal exclusively with nonaesthetic elements of the picture, such as its chemical composition, its hardness, its crackle, and so on. The truth is that the difference between a forgery and a genuine work of art is by no means as obvious as critics sometimes make out. In the case of *The Disciples*, at least, it is certainly not a matter of but needing to look in order to see. The actual history of *The Disciples* turns all such attempted *post facto* explanations into a kind of academic sour grapes.

The plain fact is that aesthetically it makes no difference whether a work of art is authentic or a forgery, and, instead of being embarrassed at having praised a forgery, critics should have the courage of their convictions and take pride in having praised a work of beauty. Perhaps if critics did respond in this way we should be less inclined to think that so often their judgments are historical, biographical, economical, or sociological instead of aesthetic. For in a sense, of course, van Meegeren proved his point. Perhaps it is a point for which such radical proof was not even necessary. We all know very well that it is just the preponderance in the art world of nonaesthetic criteria such as fame of the artist and the age or cost of the canvas which is largely responsible for the existence of artistic forgeries in the first place. We all know that a few authentic pen and ink scratches by Picasso are far more valuable than a fine landscape by an unknown artist. If we were offered a choice between an inferior (but genuine) Degas sketch and a beautiful Jones or Smith or X, how many of us would choose the latter? In a museum that did not label its paintings, how many of us would not feel uneasy lest we condemn one of the greats or praise an unknown? But, it may be argued, all this we know. It is simply a fact and, moreover, probably an unavoidable, understandable – even a necessary – fact. Is this so serious or regrettable? The answer, of course, is that it is indeed serious and regrettable that the realm of art should be so infested with nonaesthetic standards of judgment that it is often impossible to distinguish artistic from economic value, taste or fashion from true artistic excellence, and good artists from clever businessmen.

This brings us to the point of our discussion so far. The matter of genuineness versus forgery is but another nonaesthetic standard of judgment. The fact that a work of art is a forgery is an item of information about it on a level with such information as the age of the artist when he created it, the political situation in the time and place of its creation, the price it originally fetched, the kind of materials used in it, the stylistic influences descernible in it, the psychological state of the artist, his purpose in painting it, and so on. All such information belongs to areas of interest peripheral at best to the work of art as aesthetic object, areas such as biography, history of art, sociology, and psychology. I do not deny that such areas of interest may be important and that their study may even help us to become better art appreciators. But I do deny that the information which they provide is of the essence of the work of art or of the aesthetic experience which it engenders.

It would be merely foolish to assert that it is of no interest whatsoever to know that *The Disciples* is a forgery. But to the man who has never heard of either Vermeer or van Meegeren and who stands in front of *The Disciples* admiring it, it can make no difference whether he is told that it is a seventeenth-cetury Vermeer or a twentieth-century van Meegeren in the style of Vermeer. And when some deny this and argue vehemently that, indeed, it does make a great deal of difference, they are only admitting that *they* do know something about Vermeer and van Meegeren and the history of art and the value and reputation of certain masters. They are only admitting that *they* do not judge a work of art on purely aesthetic grounds but also take into account when it was created, by whom, and how great a reputation it or its creator has. And instead of seeking justification in the fact that in truth it is difficult to make a pure, aesthetic judgment, unbiased by all our knowledge of the history and criticism of art, they generally confuse matters of aesthetics even more by rationalizing that it is the complexity of the aesthetic experience which accounts for the difference made by the knowledge that a work of art is a forgery. That the aesthetic experience is complex I do not deny. But it is not so complex that such items of information as the place and date of creation or the name of the creator of a work of art have to be considered. The fact that *The Disciples* is a forgery is just that, a fact. It is a fact *about* the painting which stands entirely apart from it as an object for aesthetic contemplation. The knowledge of this fact can neither add anything to nor subtract anything from the aesthetic experience (as aesthetic), except insofar as preoccupation with it or disappointment on its account may in some degree prevent us from having an aesthetic experience at all. Whatever the reasons for the removal of *The Disciples* from the walls of the Boymans Museum in Rotterdam, they were assuredly not aesthetic.

And yet, we can all sympathize with, or at least understand, why *The Disciples* was removed. It was, after all, a forgery, and even if we grant that it is not a matter of aesthetics, it still seems self-evident that forgery remains a normative term implying a defect or absence in its object. In short, we still need to answer our question: What is wrong with a forgery?

The most obvious answer to this question, after the aesthetic one, is that forgery is a moral or legal normative concept, and that it thus refers to an object which, if not necessarily aesthetically inferior, is always morally offensive. Specifically, the reason forgery is a moral offense, according to this view, is of course that it involves *deception*. Reasonable as this view seems at first, it does not, as I will try to show, answer our question adequately.

Now it cannot be denied, I think, that we do in fact often intend little more than this moral connotation when we speak of forgery. Just because forgery is a normative concept we implicitly condemn any instance of it because we generally assume that it involves the breaking of a legal or moral code. But this assumption is only sometimes correct. It is important to note this because historically by far the majority of artistic fakes or forgeries have not been legal forgeries. Most often they have been the result of simple mistakes, misunderstandings, and lack of information about given works of art. We can, as a point of terminology, exclude all such instances from the category of forgery and restrict the term to those cases involving deliberate deception. There is, after all, a whole class of forgeries, including simple copies, misattributions, composites, and works 'in the manner of' some reputable artist, which represent deliberate frauds. In these cases of forgery, which are undoubtedly the most notorious and disconcerting, someone, e.g., artist or art dealer, has passed off a work of art as being something which it is not. The motive for doing soo is almost always economic, but occasionally, as with van Meegeren, there is involved also a psychological motive of personal prestige or revenge. In any case, it seems clear that – if we leave out of consideration the factor of financial loss, which can of course be considerable, as again the van Meegeren case proved – such deliberate forgeries are condemned by us on moral grounds, that is, because they involve conscious deception.

Yet as a final answer to our question as to what is wrong with a forgery, this definition fails. The reason is the following: Although to some extent it is true that passing *anything* off as *anything* that it is not constitutes deception and is thus an undesirable or morally repugnant act, the case of deception we have in mind when we define forgery in terms of it is that of passing off the inferior as the superior. Although, strictly speaking, passing off a genuine de Hoogh as a Vermeer is also an immoral act of deception, it is hard to think of it as a forgery at all, let alone a forgery in the same sense as passing off a van Meegeren as a Vermeer is. The reason is obviously that in the case of the de Hoogh a superior work is being passed off as a superior work (by another artist), while in the van Meegeren case a presumably inferior work is passed off as a superior work.

What is needed, then, to make our moral definition of forgery more accurate is the specification 'passing off the inferior as the superior.' But it is just at this point that this common-sense definition of artistic forgery in moral terms breaks down. For we are now faced with the question of what is meant by superior and inferior in art. The moral definition of forgery says in effect that a forgery is an inferior work passed off as a superior one. But what is meant here by inferior? We have already seen the forgery is not necessarily *aesthetically* inferior. What, then, does it mean? Once again, what is wrong with a forgery?

The attempt to define forgery in moral terms fails because it inevitably already assumes that there exists a difference between genuine works of art and forgeries which makes passing off the latter as the former an offense against a moral or legal law. For only if such a difference does in fact exist can there be any rationale for the law. It is, of course, precisely this assumed real difference which we are trying to discover in this chapter.

It seems to me that the offense felt to be involved in forgery is not so much against the spirit of beauty (aesthetics) or the spirit of the law (morality) as against the spirit of art. Somehow, a work such as *The Disciples* lacks artistic integrity. Even if it is beautiful and even if van Meegeren had not forged Vermeer's signature, there would still be something wrong with *The Disciples*. *What*? is still our question.

We may approach this problem by considering the following interesting point. The concept of forgery seems to be peculiarly inapplicable to the performing arts. It would be quite nonsensical to say, for example, that the man who played the Bach suites for unaccompanied cello and whom at the time we took to be Pablo Casals was in fact a forger. Similarly, we should want to argue that the term *forgery* was misused if we should read in the newspaper that Margot Fonteyn's performance in *Swan Lake* last night was a forgery because as a matter of fact it was not Margot Fonteyn who danced last night, but rather some unknown person whom everyone mistook for Margot Fonteyn. Again, it is difficult to see in what sense a performance of, say *Oedipus Rex* or *Hamlet* could be termed a forgery.

Here, however, we must immediately clarify our point, for it is easily misunderstood. There is, of course, a sense in which a performance of *Hamlet* or *Swan Lake* or the Bach suites could be called a forgery. If, for example, someone gave a performance of *Hamlet* in which every gesture, every movement, every vocal interpretation had been copied or imitated from the performance of *Hamlet* by Laurence Olivier, we could, I suppose, call the former a forgery of the latter. But notice that in that case we are interpreting the art of acting not as a performing art but as a creative art. For what is meant is that Olivier's interpretation and performance of *Hamlet* is itself an original and creative work of art which can be forged. Similar comments would apply to Margot Fonteyn's *Swan Lake* and Casals's Bach suites and, in fact, to every performance.

My point is, then, that the concept of forgery applies only to the creative and not to the performing arts. It can be denied, of course, that there is any such ultimate distinction between creative and performing arts. But we shall still have to admit, I think, that the duality on which it is based – the duality of creativity or originality on the one hand and reproduction or technique on the other – is real. We shall have to admit that originality and technique are two elements of all art; for it can be argued not only that a performance requires more than technique, namely originality, but also that the creation of a work of art requires more than originality, namely technique.

The truth of the matter is probably that both performances and works of art vary greatly and significantly in the degree to which they possess these elements. In fact, their relative presence in works of art and performances makes an interesting way of categorizing the latter. But it would be wrong to assert that these two elements are inseparable. I can assure the reader that a portrait painted by me would be technically almost totally incompetent, and yet even I would not deny that it might be original. On the other hand, a really skillful copy of, for example, a Rembrandt drawing may be technically perfect and yet lack all originality. These two examples establish the two extreme cases of a kind of continuum. The copy of Rembrandt is, of course, the forgery *par excellence.* My incompetent portrait is as far removed from being a forgery as any work can be. Somewhere in between lies the whole body of legitimate performances and works of art.

The implications of this long and devious argument are as follows: Forgery is a concept that can be made meaningful only by reference to the concept of originality, and hence only to art viewed as a *creative*, not as a reproductive or technical, activity. The element of performance or technique in art cannot be an object for forgery because technique is not the kind of thing that can be forged. Technique is, as it were, public. One does or does not possess it or one acquires it or learns it. One may even pretend to have it. But one cannot forge it because in order to forge it one must already possess it, in which case there is no need to forge it.

It is not Vermeer's technique in painting light which van Meegeren forged. That technique is public and may be had by anyone who is able and willing to learn it. It is rather Vermeer's discovery of this technique and his use of it, that is, Vermeer's originality, which is forged. The light, as well as the composition, the color, and many other features, of course, were original with Vermeer. They are not original with van Meegeren. They are forged.

At this point our argument could conclude were it not for the fact that the case which we have used throughout as our chief example, *Christ and the Disciples at Emmaus*, is not in fact a skillful copy of a Vermeer but a novel painting in the style of Vermeer. This threatens our definition of forgery since this particular forgery (always assuming it *is* a forgery) obviously possesses originality in some sense of the word.

The problem of forgery, in other words, is a good deal more complex than might at first be supposed, and before we can rest content with our definition of forgery as the lack of originality in works of art, we must show that the concept of originality can indeed account for the meaning of forgery as an untrue or objectionable thing in all instances, including even such a bizarre case as van Meegeren's *Disciples at Emmaus*. It thus becomes important to examine the various possible meanings that the term *originality* may have in the context of art in order to determine in what sense *The Disciples* does and does not possess it, and hence in what sense it can meaningfully and justifiably be termed a forgery.

1 A work of art may be said to be original in the sense of being a particular object not identical with any other object. But this originality is trivial since it is a quality possessed by all things. *Particularity* or *self-identity* would be better names for it.

2 By originality in a work of art we may mean that it possesses a certain superficial individuality which serves to distinguish it from other works of art. Thus, for example, a certain subject matter in a particular arrangement painted in certain colors may serve to identify a painting and mark it as an original work of art in the sense that its subject matter is unique. Probably the term *individuality* specifies this quality more adequately than *originality*.

It seems safe to assert that this quality of individuality is a necessary condition for any work of art to be called original in any significant sense. It is, however, not a necessary condition for a work to be called beautiful or to be the object of an aesthetic experience. A good reproduction or copy of a painting may be the object of aesthetic contemplation yet lack all originality in the sense which we are here considering. Historically many forgeries are of this kind, i.e., more or less skillful copies of existing works of art. They may be described as being forgeries just because they lack this kind of originality and hence any other kind of originality as well. Notice that the quality which makes such a copy a forgery, i.e., its lack of individuality, is not a quality which exists in the work of art as such. It is a fact about the work of art which can be known only by placing the latter in the context of the history of art and observing whether any identical work predates it.

As we said above, it is not this kind of originality which is lacking in *The Disciples.*[3]

3 By originality in art we may mean the kind of imaginative novelty or spontaneity which is a mark of every good work of art. It is the kind of originality which attaches to individual works of art and which can be specified in formal or technical terms such as composition, balance, color intensity, perspective, harmony, rhythm, tempo, texture, rhyme, alliteration, suspense, character, plot, structure, choice of subject matter, and so on. Here again, however, in order for this quality to be meaningfully called originality, a reference must be made to a historical context in terms of which we are considering the particular work of art in question, e.g., this work of art is original because the artist has done something with the subject and its treatment which has never been done before, or this work is not original because many others just like it predate it.

In any case, *The Disciples* does, by common consent, possess this kind of originality and is therefore, in this sense at least, not a forgery.

4 The term *originality* is sometimes used to refer to the great artistic achievement of a specific work of art. Thus we might say that whereas nearly all of Milton's works are good and original in the sense of (3) above, *Paradise Lost* has a particularly profound originality possessed only by really superlative works of art. It is hard to state precisely what is meant by this use of the term *originality*. In justifying it we should probably point to the scope, profundity, daring, and novelty of the conception of the work of art in question as well as to the excellence of its execution. No doubt this kind of originality differs from that discussed under (3) above only in degree.

It is to be noted that it cannot be the lack of this kind of originality which defines a forgery since, almost by definition, it is a quality lacking in many – maybe the majority of – legitimate works of art. Moreover, judging from the critical commentary with which *The Disciples* was received at the time of its discovery – commentary unbiased by the knowledge that it was a forgery – it seems reasonable to infer that the kind of originality meant here is in fact one which *The Disciples* very likely possesses.

5   Finally, it would seem that by originality in art we can and often do mean the artistic novelty and achievement not of one particular work of art but of the totality of artistic productions of one man or even one school. Thus we may speak of the originality of Vermeer or El Greco or Mozart or Dante or Impressionism or the Metaphysical Poets or even the Greeks or the Renaissance, always referring, I presume, to the artistic accomplishments achieved and embodied in the works of art belonging to the particular man, movement, or period. In the case of Vermeer we may speak of the originality of the artist's sense of design in the genre picture, the originality of his use of bright and pure colors, and of the originality of his treatment and execution of light.

We must note first of all that this meaning of originality, too, depends entirely on a historical context in which we are placing and considering the accomplishment of one man or one period. It would be meaningless to call Impressionism original, in the sense here considered, except in reference to the history of art which preceded it. Again, it is just because Vermeer's sense of pictorial design, his use of bright colors, and his mastery of the technique of painting light are not found in the history of art before him that we call these things original in Vermeer's work. Originality, even in this more profound sense, or rather especially in this more profound sense, is a quality definable only in terms of the history of art.

A second point of importance is that while originality as here considered is a quality which attaches to a whole corpus or style of works of art, it can be considered to exist in one particular work of art in the sense that that work of art is a typical example of the style or movement to which it belongs and therefore embodies the originality of that style or movement. Thus we may say that Vermeer's *A Painter in His Studio* is original because in this painting (as well as in several others, of course) we recognize those characteristics mentioned earlier (light, design, color, etc.) which are so typical of Vermeer's work as a whole and which, when we consider the whole of Vermeer's work in the context of the history of art, allow us to ascribe originality to it.

Turning our attention once more to *The Disciples*, we are at last in a position to provide an adequate answer to our question as to the meaning of the term forgery when applied to a work of art such as *The Disciples*. We shall find, I think, that the fraudulent character of this painting is adequately defined by stating that it lacks originality in the fifth and final sense which we have here considered. Whatever kinds of originality it can claim – and we have seen that it possesses all the kinds previously discussed – it is *not* original in the sense of being the product of a style, period, or technique which, when considered in its appropriate historical context, can be said to represent a significant achievement. It is just this fact which differentiates this painting from a genuine Vermeer! The latter, when considered in its historical context, i.e., the seventeenth century, possesses the qualities of artistic or creative novelty which justify us in calling it original. *The Disciples*, on the other hand, in *its* historical context, i.e., the twentieth century, is not original, since it presents nothing new or creative to the history of art even though, as we have emphasized earlier, it may well be as beautiful as the genuine Vermeer pictures.

It is to be noted that in this definition of forgery the phrase 'appropriate historical context' referes to the date of production of the particular work of art in question, not the date which in the history of art is appropriate to its style or subject matter.[4] In other words, what makes *The Disciples* a forgery is precisely the disparity or gap between its stylistically appropriate features and its actual date of production. It is simply this disparity which we have in mind when we say that forgeries such as *The Disciples* lack integrity.

It is interesting at this point to recall van Meegeren's reasoning in perpetrating the Vermeer forgeries. 'Either,' he reasoned, 'the critics must admit their fallibility or else acknowledge that I am as great an artist as Vermeer.' We can see now that this reasoning is not sound. For the notion of greatness involved in it depends on the same concept of historical originality which we have been considering. The only difference is that we are now thinking of it as an attribute of the artist rather than of the works of art. Van Meegeren's mistake was in thinking that Vermeer's reputation as a great artist depended on his ability to paint beautiful pictures. If this were so, the dilemma which van Meegeren posed to the critics would have been a real one, for his picture is undeniably beautiful. But, in fact, Vermeer is *not* a great artist only because he could paint beautiful pictures. He is great for that reason plus something else. And that something else is precisely the fact of his originality, i.e., the fact that he painted certain pictures in a certain manner *at a certain time in the history and development of art.* Vermeer's art represents a genuine creative achievement in the history of art. It is the work not merely of a master craftsman or technician but of a creative genius as well. And it is for the latter rather than for the former reason that we call Vermeer great.

Van Meegeren, on the other hand, possessed only craftsmanship or technique. His works lack the historical originality of Vermeer's and it is for this reason that we should not want to call him great as we call Vermeer great.[5] At the same time it must be recalled that van Meegeren's forgeries are not forgeries *par excellence. The Disciples,* though not original in the most important sense, possesses, as we have seen, degrees of originality generally lacking in forgeries.

In this connection it is interesting to speculate on the relations between originality and technique in the creative continuum which we came upon earlier. A totally original work is one which lacks all technique. A forgery *par excellence* represents the perfection of technique with the absence of all originality. True works of art are somewhere in between. Perhaps the really great works of art, such as Vermeer's, are those which embody a maximum of both originality and technique: van Meegeren's forgeries can never be in this last category, for, as we have seen, they lack the most important kind of originality.

Finally, the only question that remains is why originality is such a significant aspect of art. Now we need to note, of course, that the concern with originality is not a universal characteristic of art or artists. Yet the fact that the search for originality is perhaps typical only of modern Western art tends to strengthen the presumption of its fundamental relation to the concept of forgery. For it is also just in the modern Western tradition that the problem of forgery has taken on the kind of economic and aesthetic significance which warrants our concern with it here. But why, even in modern Western art, should the importance of originality be such that the concepts of greatness and forgery in art are ultimately definable only by reference to it? The answer is, I believe, not hard to find. It rests on the fact that art has and must have a history. If it did not, if artists were concerned only with making beautiful pictures, poems, symphonies, etc., the possibilities for the creation of aesthetically pleasing works of art would soon be exhausted. We would (perhaps) have a number of lovely paintings, but we should soon grow tired of them, for they would all be more or less alike. But artists do not seek merely to produce works of beauty. They seek to produce *original* works of beauty. And when they succeed in achieving this originality we call their works great not only because they are beautiful but because they have also unlocked, both to artists and to appreciators, unknown and unexplored realms of beauty. Men like Leonardo, Rembrandt, Haydn, Goethe, and Vermeer are great not merely because of the excellence of their works but also because of their creative originality which goes on to inspire other artists and leads through them to new and aesthetically valuable developments in the history of art. It is, in fact, this search for creative originality which insures the continuation and significance of such a history in the first place.

It is for this reason that the concept of originality has become inseparable from that of art. It is for this reason too that aesthetics has traditionally concerned itself with topics such as the inspiration of the artist, the mystery of the creative act, the intense and impassioned search of the artist, the artist as the prophet of his times, the artistic struggle after expression, art as the chronicle of the emotional life of a period in history, art as a product of its time, and so on. All such topics are relevant not to art as the production of works of beauty but to art as the production of *original* works of beauty, or, more accurately, works of original beauty. As such they are perfectly legitimate topics of discussion. But we must not forget that the search for originality is, or ought to be, but the means to an end. That end is, presumably, the production of aesthetically valuable or beautiful works of art; that is, works which are to become the object of an aesthetic experience. That experience is a wholly autonomous one. It does not and cannot take account of any entity or fact which is not aesthetically perceivable in the work of art itself. The historical context in which that work of art stands is just such a fact. It is wholly irrelevant to the pure aesthetic appreciation and judgment of the work of art. And because the fact of forgery – together with originality and greatness – can be ultimately defined only in terms of this historical context, it too is irrelevant to the aesthetic appreciation and judgment of *The Disciples at Emmaus* or any other work of art. The fact of forgery is important historically, biographically, perhaps legally, or, as the van Meegeren case proved, financially; but not, strictly speaking, aesthetically.

In conclusion, let us consider the following paradoxical result. We have seen in what sense Vermeer is considered to be a great artist. We have also seen that although *The Disciples* is indistinguishable from a genuine Vermeer, van Meegeren cannot be thus called great. And yet we would suppose that Vermeer's greatness is somehow embodied in his work, that his paintings are proof of and monuments to his artistic genius. What are we to say, then, of this van Meegeren forgery which hung in a museum for seven years as an embodiment and proof of Vermeer's genius? Are we to say that it now no longer embodies anything at all except van Meegeren's skillful forging technique? Or are we to grant after all that this painting proves van Meegeren's greatness as Vermeer's paintings do his? The answer is, I think, surprising but wholly appropriate. Paradoxically, *The Disciples at Emmaus* is as much a monument to the artistic genius of Vermeer as are Vermeer's own paintings. Even though it was painted by van Meegeren in the twentieth century, it embodies and bears witness to the greatness of the seventeenth-century art of Vermeer.

Notes

1 Cf. Arthur Koestler, 'The Anatomy of Snobbery,' *The Anchor Review* 1 (Garden City: Doubleday Anchor Books, 1955): 1–25.

2 J. Decoen, *Vermeer-Van Meegeren, Back to the Truth*, trans. E.J. Labarre (London: Donker, 1951), p.60.

3 A slightly more complex case is offered by forgeries (including probably some of van Meegeren's less carefully executed Vermeer forgeries) which are not simple copies of other paintings but which are composites of other paintings. While such forgeries clearly have a measure of individuality totally lacking in the simple copy, I should want to maintain that they lack only superficially the kind of originality here discussed.

4 To avoid all ambiguity in my definition of forgery, I need to specify whether 'actual date of production' refers to the completion of the finished, concrete work of art or only to the productive means of such works. This question bears on the legitimacy of certain works in art forms where the means of production and the finished product are separable. Such works include lithographs, etchings, woodcuts, cast sculptures, etc. What, for example, are we to say of a modern bronze cast made from a mold taken directly from an ancient bronze cast or a modern print made from an eighteenth-century block? Are such art objects forgeries? The answer, it seems to me, is largely a matter of convenience and terminology. Assuming that there is no moral fraud, i.e., deception, involved, whether or not to call such cases instances of forgery becomes an academic question. It depends entirely on what we take to be 'the work of art.' In the case of lithography or etching there may be some ambiguity about this. I myself would define 'the work of art' as the finished concrete product and hence I would indeed call modern prints from old litho stones forgeries, though, assuming no deception is involved, forgeries of a peculiarly amoral, nonoffensive sort. In other arts, such as music, there is little or no ambiguity on this point. Clearly, no one would want to label the first performance of a newly discovered Beethoven symphony a forgery. In still other, e.g., the literary, arts, due to the absolute inseparability of the concrete work of art and the means of its production, this problem cannot arise at all.

5 Unless it be argued that van Meegeren derives *his* greatness from the originality of his works when considered in the context not of the history of art but of the history of forgery!

The concept of authentic performance

James O. Young (b.1943)

Aesthetic value is a particularly complex issue when it comes to the performing arts. The question of whether aesthetic value depends on the manner of performance has been much debated in classical music circles in recent years, with a determined lobby claiming that authentic performance (on period instruments, for example) is necessary to realize the true value of older compositions. James O. Young examines these claims in the next extract, concluding that authentic performance is neither attainable nor an ideal worth attaining: we cannot recapture past conditions or attitudes, nor does it seem desirable to Young to do so. Aesthetic value in music, he holds, depends on 'successful' rather than authentic performance. He argues that there are many different possible ways of performing a piece successfully.

> If you feel the seriousness of a tune, what are you perceiving? – Nothing that could be conveyed by reproducing what you heard.
>
> Wittgenstein, *Investigations*, p.210e.

Interest in early music has increased dramatically in recent years. Anyone at all cognizant of music is aware of a constant stream of books, journals, concerts, workshops, conferences and recordings devoted to early music. The extent of interest in early music is indicated by the fact that in Britain alone there are well over one-hundred professional ensembles engaged in the performance of early music.[1] The early music movement is not so much concerned with a period of music as with an artistic ideal. Within the movement's purlieu falls the music of all periods from classical antiquity through the middle ages, the renaissance, the baroque, classical and romantic periods to the early twentieth century. 'Modern' musicians, however, interpret much of this same repertoire. What distinguishes the advocates of early music is that they aim at 'authentic performance'.[2]

There can be no doubt that the early music movement has been of enormous value. Members of the movement have, however, been insufficiently reflective about the concept of authentic performance.[3] They believe that it is possible to give performances which are 'authentic'. These performances have, moreover, more than antiquarian interest. Authentic performance is supposed to represent an attractive artistic ideal. That is, an authentic performance is an artistically successful interpretation of a composition. However, had advocates of early music paused to reflect, they would have realized that authentic performance cannot be characterized in such a way that it represents an ideal which is both attainable and worth attaining. There are principled, not merely practical, reasons why authentic performance is not a realizable artistic ideal. Reflection on these reasons will provide insight into the nature of music and the experience of music.

Members of the early music movement tend to regard the quest for authentic performance as a process of solving musicological difficulties of a practical nature. They begin by compiling scores which are faithful to composers' manuscripts or to early editions. Performers of early music pay particular attention to scoring. They perform on authentic instruments and do so with an ensemble of the authentic size. Having determined a score and selected their instruments, performers of early music proceed to perform in accordance with authentic performance techniques, the techniques contemporary with a piece's composition. They also ensure that their instruments are tuned as they would have been at the time of composition. So, for example, a Beethoven piano concerto will be performed on a fortepiano (either an 'original instrument' or an authentic copy) and not on a modern concert grand. The stringed instruments will be strung in gut and the wind instruments will have fewer keys and otherwise differ from modern instruments. The orchestra will be much smaller than is now common and there will be a greater balance between the strings and winds. The fast movements will be played at a tempo slower than is now common and the slow movements will be rather faster. The A above middle C will be tuned to 435 cycles per second and not to the now-standard 440. If all practical questions of score, instrumentation, tuning, and performance techniques could be resolved, performers of early music believe, authentic performance is possible.

Of course, as advocates of authentic performance recognize, some practical obstacles to authentic performance will never be overcome. We will never know precisely how bowed instruments were used to accompany medieval songs. No scores have survived since the accompaniment was improvised. There are insurmountable practical obstacles to giving an authentic performance of even such a familiar piece as Mozart's Clarinet Concerto. As is well known, the piece was written for Anton Stadler. What is less well known is that he did not play a clarinet at all but a basset clarinet. Precisely what sort of instrument Stadler would have played is unknown and, in all probability, will remain unknown. Moreover, the manuscript of Mozart's concerto does not survive. In the first printed edition of the concerto, published ten years after Mozart's death, the basset clarinet part is rewritten so as to be playable on a clarinet. It is possible to reconstruct the original score but not with complete accuracy. But the concept of authentic performance is not problematic for practical reasons. Imagine that there is an Omniscient Musicologist, a musicologist than whom no greater can be conceived. Such a musicologist would know everything about original scores, instruments, performance techniques and tuning. But the concept of authentic performance would still be problematic.

Suppose that, with the aid of the Omniscient Musicologist, all of the practical difficulties of the early music movement are overcome. It would then be possible to give the first characterization of authentic performance:

(1) An authentic performance is a performance which reproduces music as it was heard at the time of its composition.

There are good reasons to suppose that authentic performances, so characterized, could not be given. But it should be apparent that, when conceived of in this manner, authentic performance does not even represent an artistic ideal worth attaining.[4]

The first point worth noting is that there are moral obstacles which should prevent the authentic performance of certain compositions. Consider the authentic performance of eighteenth-century opera.[5] Many of the parts were written for, and performed by, castrati. Now, the tone colour of a castrato's voice differs from that of a female alto or soprano. But not even the most committed advocate of early music will think that the ideal of authentic performance would justify the mutilation of pre-pubescent boys. This is, perhaps, an extreme example but it serves to demonstrate that there are moral constraints which should prohibit the realization of the ideal of the authentic performance of all music.

There are, however, no moral obstacles facing the authentic performance of many compositions. These compositions, it might be thought, could be heard as they were at the time of their composition. A problem, however, immediately presents itself. If (1) is accepted, there will be a question about how to give an authentic performance of pieces which were not performed at the time of their composition. And there certainly are pieces which were not so performed. The performance of such pieces cannot reproduce how the music sounded at the period of their composition. Or, rather, the only authentic performance is non-performance – which is scarcely an attractive artistic ideal. But most compositions were heard within a short time of their composition. It is not clear, however, why anyone would want to hear them that way again.

Music must often have sounded perfectly atrocious at the time of its composition. The instruments on which music was performed were often in very bad repair. While in the service of Esterházy, Haydn had to contend with oboes in rotten condition.[6] In 1770 Charles Burney travelled throughout France and Italy collecting material for his history of music. He wrote that 'All the keyed instruments I have yet heard on the continent, except some of the organs[,] are very bad'. Of the spinets he heard in Italy he wrote that 'the keys are so noisy and tone so feeble one hears more wood than wire'.[7] If authentic performance is to reproduce music as it was originally heard, performers of early music are committed to playing Haydn's early symphonies on rotten oboes and to performing eighteenth-century Italian domestic music on decrepit harpsichords. Surely this is enough to render unappealing authentic performance as characterized in (1).

But it gets worse. Not only were the instruments of the eighteenth century often of a poor quality, but often the musicians were as well. Many of the best-known pieces of the eighteenth century were originally performed by amateurs. Handel's Chandos Anthems were first played by the Duke of Chandos' domestic staff. One of the players was recommended because 'He shaves very well & hath an excellent hand on the violin & all necessary languages'.[8] However good his hand may have been on the violin, it is unlikely that he played as well as a modern professional. Even the professional musicians of the period were not up to present standards. The difficulties which Mozart had with his players were, of course, legion. Mind you, he often did not make things easy for them. He often provided them with scores only a few days or even a few hours before a performance. So, if we accept (1) as the characterization of authentic performance, it seems that performers of early music must not allow themselves to become too accomplished and must, in some cases, take care not to rehearse their parts.

Of course, not every original performance was given by poor musicians on bad instruments. But the fact that many were is enough to render (1) untenable. Authentic performance should be characterized in such a way that artistically attractive authentic performances can be given of any piece, regardless of how it may originally have sounded. Moreover, it should be clear that (1) is not in accord with the actual practices of performers of early music. In deciding how to play a composition they do not attempt to determine whether the piece was played well or poorly. Rather, they attempt to decide how the composition *should* sound. Talk about how early music should sound suggests another account of authentic performance.

Recognizing that standards of musicianship and of instrument making have not always been what they now are, one might characterize authentic performance in terms of the intentions of composers.[9] One might adopt the following account of authentic performance.

(2) An authentic performance is one in which a composition sounds the way its composer intended it to sound.

This characterization will avoid many of the objections to which (1) is subject. Unfortunately, if authentic performance is so characterized, there is no way to determine which performances are authentic. And it is not even clear that (2) represents an ideal worth attaining.

The second account of authentic performance fails because of our inability to determine all of a composer's intentions. Certainly it is possible to know with a fair degree of certainty what some of a composer's intentions were. No doubt he intended that his compositions should sound as they do when played on the instruments available at the time of composition. And, no doubt, he intended that the instruments should be tuned as was customary in the period. The Omniscient Musicologist will be able to tell us a great deal about how a composer intended his works to sound. But there is a great deal that not even an Omniscient Musicologist can know. The totality of possible musicological evidence will underdetermine the selection of one performance as more authentic than another.

There is no possible evidence which will determine precisely what a composer's intentions were with respect to all aspects of the interpretation of a piece. The possible evidence could take one of two forms. Musicologists could discover a composer's instructions about how to play a piece and reports may survive about how he actually performed one of his compositions. In practice, of course, even this evidence is often unavailable. But if it were available to an Omniscient Musicologist, it would still not determine which performances are authentic. Even complete reports of a composer's own performance of a solo piece would not be decisive evidence. There is no guarantee that even a composer's own performance realized his intentions. Not even a composer's own reports would be decisive evidence. The knowledge of how a piece is to be interpreted is, in large measure, practical knowledge, a knowledge of how something is to be done. Such knowledge, like the knowledge of how to ride a bicycle, cannot be fully captured in propositional terms. Not even the composer will be able to describe precisely what his intentions were. If we cannot know what a composer's intentions were, we cannot determine which performances are authentic and which are not and (2) is unsatisfactory.

Even if authentic performance could be characterized in terms of composers' intentions, it is not clear that, so characterized, it would be an attractive artistic ideal. Composers may not be the best interpreters of their own compositions. Once a piece has been composed, the composer's views on how it is best performed are no better than those of any qualified musician. And they may be worse. Frescobaldi left very detailed instructions on how to perform his keyboard compositions.[10] These instructions do not, of course, determine the choice of authentic performances. But even if they did, performers might be wise to disregard them. Many musicians, including those interested in authentic performance, disregard Frescobaldi's instructions simply because they believe that following them does not result in very successful interpretations.

Performers of early music might encourage another account of authentic performance by noting that they never aimed to realize the intentions of a single individual but, rather, to perform in the style of some period. The performers of some period, perhaps, never succeeded in perfectly realizing the style of their time. However, had these musicians been properly trained and had they been possessed of good instruments, the recreation of how their music sounded would be a more attractive artistic goal. These reflections give rise to the third account of authentic performance.[11]

(3) An authentic performance makes a piece sound as it would have sounded at the period of its composition, had conditions been ideal.

This characterization of authentic performance is immune to many of the objections which cripple (1) and (2). It is, however, subject to the objection that music cannot sound to us as it would have sounded to earlier listeners, even under ideal conditions. And it is still not clear that we should want music to sound as it would have sounded under ideal conditions.

As Wittgenstein recognized, just as there is a distinction between seeing and seeing as, so there is a distinction between hearing and hearing as. All observers see the same thing when they look at a picture of a duck-rabbit.[12] And yet the picture looks one way to someone who only sees it as a rabbit and another to someone who only sees it as a duck. Moreover, the beliefs of viewers have an impact on how things look to them. Someone who has no knowledge of rabbits will not see the duck-rabbit as a rabbit. Gombrich relates a story which indicates that the same points can be made about hearing as can be made about seeing.[13] During the Second World War he was engaged in monitoring broadcasts. Many of the monitored transmissions were barely audible. Even though two listeners heard the same sounds they often heard them as different things. Any beliefs about what was being said in the broadcasts were sure to have an impact on what listeners would hear them as saying. There is no more an innocent ear than there is an innocent eye.

Suppose that listeners of some period were to hear a composition of their time performed under ideal conditions. And suppose that listeners of our time were to hear an authentic performance (as defined in (3)) of the same piece. The two groups of listeners would, on these suppositions, here the same (or similar) sounds. But they would not hear them as the same. A few examples will make this point clear. Some invervals which are now heard as consonant were in the past heard as dissonant. In the middle ages a third was a dissonant interval. Medieval listeners hearing (under ideal conditions) a composition which contained a third would hear the interval as dissonant. Now, of course, thirds are no longer heard as dissonant. Modern listeners hearing the same medieval composition will hear the thirds as consonant. The same piece will sound quite different to modern and medieval ears, even under ideal conditions. Having been exposed (subjected?) to the music of the twentieth century almost nothing sounds dissonant any longer. It is even difficult for us to hear the dissonances of the eighteenth and nineteenth centuries.

The experience of music has changed in more fundamental ways as well. Eighteenth-century people had many beliefs which we do not have. These beliefs had an enormous impact on how they experienced music. Unlike those who first heard Lully's operas, we do not hear the trumpet flourishes as the trumpets of the Sun King. Lully's operas shamelessly flattered Louis XIV and we cannot but hear them as affected and sycophantic. But the courtiers at Versailles heard them quite differently. They knew the sound of ceremonial trumpets and they believed sycophancy to be normal behaviour. In the eighteenth century the rustic bagpipe and shepherd flute were still familiar. Audiences would have heard many passages for oboe or flute in Bach or Handel as recalling these instruments. Modern listeners can hear the same sounds as eighteenth-century listeners would have heard under ideal conditions. But the sounds are not heard as possessed of rustic associations.[14] Of course, we can and do learn that period listeners heard certain sounds as rustic or regal. But it is one thing to know that others heard them thus and quite another to hear them so ourselves.

Hearing, like other forms of perception, is not a passive process but an active process of interpreting vibrations of air. The music of the past could not sound to us as it did to listeners of earlier eras, we could not hear it as they heard it, unless we could interpret it as they did. We could not so interpret the music of earlier listeners unless we shared the beliefs which enabled them to hear as they did. Our experiences of music, of society and of nature are very different from the experiences of, say, listeners in the eighteenth century and so our beliefs and our interpretation of music must differ. Since our interpretation must differ so must how the music sounds to us. By listening to a great deal of their music we share some of their experiences and come to have some of their beliefs – but not all of them. Which is just as well – to do so we would have to live in an absolute monarchy – but our inability to share their beliefs makes it impossible for us to hear music of earlier periods as it was heard.

Paraphrasing Wittgenstein we might ask, if some period audience heard the regality of a tune, what were they perceiving? – nothing that could be conveyed by reproducing what they heard, or would have heard under ideal conditions. Authentic performance as characterized in (3) requires that there be authentic listeners who hear music as it was heard during an earlier period. We are not and cannot be such listeners. Since the music of earlier periods cannot sound to us as it sounded to period listeners, or would have sounded to them under ideal conditions, (3) must be rejected. Authentic performance as characterized in (3) is an unattainable goal.

There is a sense in which no listener ever hears music precisely as another does. But the experience and beliefs of two similarly educated twentieth-century listeners will be substantially the same and it is reasonable to suppose that they hear music very much as the other does. But even within the twentieth century not all listeners hear music as others do. Listening to Oriental music is, for many Westerners, like listening to a foreign language. They may, for example, fail to discern something as simple as whether a song is happy or sad. Oriental listeners, in contrast, will immediately hear a song as happy or as sad. The song sounds differently to them. The distinction between this case and that of early music is that it is possible for Westerners to acquire the experiences and beliefs which would enable them to hear as Orientals do.

It might be thought that, even if we cannot hear music as an early listener heard it, perhaps in the 'mind's ear' music could sound to us as it sounded in the mind's ear of the early listener. There is, however, no more an innocent mind's ear than there is an innocent ear. Indeed, the psychological evidence indicates that mental images are even more conceptualized, even more interpreted, than sensory images. The beliefs of subjects have an enormous impact on how mental images seem to them.[15]

It is not possible for musicians to give a performance which would sound to us as it would have sounded to period listeners. It is not even clear that this would be a worthwhile artistic goal if it were possible. There is much early music which we would not want to hear as it would have sounded, under ideal conditions, to period audiences. Much great music was poorly regarded by early listeners. Burney merely reported prevailing sentiments when he found 'a manifest inferiority in design, invention, grace, elegance and every captivating requisite' in Handel's late operas.[16] It is not at all desirable to hear Handel's late operas as contemporaries heard them, or would have heard them under ideal conditions. We now hear Handel's late operas as full of every captivating requisite and a performance which does not let us hear them this way holds little allure...

It is now possible to see why the quest for an authentic performance was misguided. The problem is that the concept of authentic performance suggests that there is an ideal performance of every composition. That is, there is a suggestion that there is a single best interpretation of any piece and this is its authentic performance. It is, however, necessary for all listeners and musicians to hear and play music in their own fashion. They cannot play or hear music as people in the past may have done. Just as each generation must interpret Shakespeare in its own way, so must each age interpret Bach for itself. There is no ideal performance of a composition but, rather, many.

Authentic performance cannot be characterized in such a way that it represents an artistic ideal which is both attainable and worth attaining. The conclusion to be drawn is that the concept is not a useful one. It does not follow that the early music movement is without value. On the contrary, the movement has enormously enriched musical experience. It has done this, however, not by giving authentic performances but by giving successful ones. That is, an early music performance is valuable not because it bears some relation to past performances but because present listeners find it artistically appealing. The playing of authentic scores on authentically tuned authentic instruments in accordance with authentic performance techniques will not result in authentic performances. But performances by modern performers of early music can, and often do, attain the artistic goals of present listeners.[17]

Notes

1   See the *Directory of British Early Music Groups* (London: Early Music Centre, 1981).

2   Robert Donington, a distinguished authority on early music, writes, for example, that 'if you want the best that any music has to offer, you do well to go at it in the authentic way'. 'Why early music?' *Early Music*, 11 (1983), p.45.

3   But see three recent articles, one by a musician, one by a music critic and one by a philosopher. Ton Koopman, 'Some Thoughts on Authenticity', *Musick*, Vol. 8, No. 3 (1987). pp.2–6; Will Crutchfield, 'The Meanings of "Authenticity"', *Oberlin Alumni Magazine*, Vol. 82, No. 4 (1986), pp.4–9; and Stephen Davies, 'Authenticity in Musical Performance', *British Journal of Aesthetics*, 27 (1987), pp.39–40.

4   See Davies, pp.41–2. Davies reaches this conclusion for reasons similar to those given here.

5   This same example is used by Davies, p.49, n.2.

6   This is reported in Christopher Hogwood, *Music at Court* (London: The Folio Society, 1977), p.112.

7   Charles Burney, *Music, Men, and Manners in France and Italy 1770* (London: The Folio Society, 1969), p.69.

8   Quoted in Christopher Hogwood, *Handel* (London: Thames and Hudson, 1984), p.73.

9   The harpsichordist Ralph Kirkpatrick reports that his aim is to perform 'harpsichord and clavichord music in a manner as close as possible to what could be ascertained of the intentions of the composers'. 'Fifty years of harpsichord playing', *Early Music*, 11 (1983), p.31.

10   Selections from Frescobaldi's instructions are found in *Composers on Music*, ed. Sam Morgenstern (New York: Pantheon, 1956), pp.24–6.

11   This is essentially the account of authentic performance given by Davis, p.45. He writes that 'a performance will be more rather than less authentic if it successfully (re)creates the sound of a performance of the work in question as could be given by good musicians playing good instruments under good conditions (of rehearsal time etc.), where "good" is relativized to the best of what was known by the composer to be available at the time, whether or not those resources were available for the composer's use'. My talk of ideal conditions can be taken as shorthand for Davies's definition and the following argument will still work.

12   For a discussion and a drawing of a duck-rabbit see Ludwig Wittgenstein, *Philosophical Investigations* (Oxford: Basil Blackwell, 1963), pp.194ff.

13   E. H. Gombrich, *Art and Illusion* (Princeton U.P., 1969), pp.204–5.

14   These examples are taken from Hogwood, *Music at Court*, pp.59f. Hogwood would not draw the same conclusions.

15   For a discussion of the conceptualized nature of mental images see Zenon Pylyshyn, 'Imagery and Artificial Intelligence', in *Readings in Philosophy of Psychology*, Vol. 2, ed. Ned Block (Cambridge, Massachusetts: Harvard U.P., 1981), pp.170–94. Pylyshyn mainly discusses visual mental imagery but there is no reason to suppose that auditory imagery would be any different.

16   Quoted in Hogwood, *Handel*, p.101.

17   In the course of writing this essay I profited from the comments of Bill Eastman, D.D. Todd, Sheldon Wein and, especially, Charles Morgan. Special thanks are due to Rosemary Mountain of the School of Music, University of Victoria and an anonymous referee.

Art and the aesthetic

George Dickie (b.1936)

*Theories of aesthetic value can be constructed in a variety of ways
and for many different reasons, but there is a question that often
needs to be asked beforehand: what are the criteria involved in
deciding whether an object qualifies as an artwork, and thus can be
said to have aesthetic value? The question becomes particularly
important in the case of works like Marcel Duchamp's 'ready-made'
sculptures (the urinal exhibited under the title 'Fountain', for
example), which have aroused considerable controversy in art circles.
'Fountain' has no aesthetic value in its usual habitat: how then can
it suddenly acquire it in an art gallery? The 'institutional theory of
art' propounded by George Dickie is one way of trying to deal with
such problem cases. According to this theory, the 'artworld' (a network
of systems consisting of theatre, painting, sculpture, literature, and
so on) has the authority to confer the status of 'work of art' on
objects. Art is an 'institutional concept', Dickie argues, and a work
of art is an artefact which a representative of the social institution
we call the 'artworld' deems worthy of appreciation. In effect, it is
the artworld's prerogative to decide which objects will be considered
to have aesthetic value. Although Dickie insists that the conferring
of status is no simple matter, the theory has a certain arbitrary
quality to it and has been widely criticized.*

What is art? An institutional analysis

The attempt to define 'art' by specifying its necessary and sufficient
conditions is an old endeavour. The first definition – the imitation
theory – despite what now seem like obvious difficulties, more or
less satisfied everyone until some time in the nineteenth century.
After the expression theory of art broke the domination of the
imitation theory, many definitions purporting to reveal the necessary and sufficient conditions of art appeared. In the mid-1950s,
several philosophers, inspired by Wittgenstein's talk about concepts,
began arguing that there are no necessary and sufficient conditions

for art. Until recently, this argument had persuaded so many philosophers of the futility of trying to define art that the flow of definitions had all but ceased. Although I will ultimately try to show that 'art' can be defined, the denial of that possibility has had the very great value of forcing us to look deeper into the concept of 'art.' The parade of dreary and superficial definitions that had been presented was, for a variety of reasons, eminently rejectable. The traditional attempts to define 'art,' from the imitation theory on, may be thought of as Phase I and the contention that 'art' cannot be defined as Phase II. I want to supply Phase III by defining 'art' in such a way as to avoid the difficulties of the traditional definitions and to incorporate the insights of the later analysis. I should note that the imitation theory of the fine arts seems to have been adopted by those who held it without much serious thought and perhaps cannot be considered as a self-conscious theory of art in the way that the later theories can be.

The traditional attempts at definition have sometimes failed to see beyond prominent but accidental features of works of art, features that have characterized art at a particular stage in its historical development. For example, until quite recently the works of art clearly recognizable as such were either obviously representational or assumed to be representational. Paintings and sculptures were obviously so, and music was widely assumed in some sense also to be representational. Literature was representational in that it described familiar scenes of life. It was, then, easy enough to think that imitation must be the essence of art. The imitation theory focused on a readily evident relational property of works of art, namely, art's relation to subject matter. The development of nonobjective art showed that imitation is not even an always-accompanying property of art, much less an essential one.

The theory of art as the expression of emotion has focused on another relational property of works of art, the relation of a work to its creator. The expression theory also has proved inadequate, and no other subsequent definition has been satisfactory. Although not fully satisfying as definitions, the imitation and expression theories do provide a clue: both singled out *relational* properties of art as essential. As I shall try to show, the two defining characteristics of art are indeed relational properties, and one of them turns out to be exceedingly complex.

I

The best-known denial that 'art' can be defined occurs in Morris Weitz's article 'The Role of Theory in Aesthetics.'[1] Weitz's conclusion depends upon two arguments which may be called his 'generalization argument' and his 'classification argument.' In stating the 'generalization argument' Weitz distinguishes, quite correctly, between the generic conception of 'art' and the various subconcepts of art such as tragedy, the novel, painting, and the like. He then goes on to give an argument purporting to show that the subconcept 'novel' is open, that is, that the members of the class of novels do not share any essential or defining characteristics. He then asserts without further argument that what is true of novels is true of all other subconcepts of art. The generalization from one subconcept to all subconcepts may or may not be justified, but I am not questioning it here. I do question, however, Weitz's additional contention, also asserted without argument, that the generic conception of 'art' is open. The best that can be said of his conclusion about the generic sense is that it is unsupported. All or some of the subconcepts of art may be open and the generic conception of art still be closed. That is, it is possible that all or some of the subconcepts of art, such as novel, tragedy, sculpture, and painting, may lack necessary and sufficient conditions and at the same time that 'work of art,' which is the genus of all the subconcepts, can be defined in terms of necessary and sufficient conditions. Tragedies may not have any characteristics in common which would distinguish them from, say, comedies *within the domain of art*, but it may be that there are common characteristics that works of art have which distinguish them from nonart. Nothing prevents a 'closed genus/open species' relationship. Weitz himself has recently cited what he takes to be a similar (although reversed) example of genus-species relationship. He argues that 'game' (the genus) is open but that 'major league baseball' (a species) is closed.[2]

His second argument, 'the classification argument,' claims to show that not even the characteristic of artifactuality is a necessary feature of art. Weitz's conclusion here is something of a surprise, because it has been widely assumed by philosophers and nonphilosophers alike that a work of art is necessarily an artifact. His argument is simply that we sometimes utter such statements as 'This piece of driftwood is a lovely piece of sculpture,' and since such utterances are perfectly intelligible, it follows that some nonartifacts such as certain pieces of driftwood are works of art (sculptures). In other words, something need not be an artifact in order to be correctly classified as a work of art. I will try to rebut this argument shortly.

Recently, Maurice Mandelbaum has raised a question about Wittgenstein's famous contention that 'game' cannot be defined and Weitz's thesis about 'art.'[3] His challenge to both is based on the charge that they have been concerned only with what Mandelbaum calls 'exhibited' characteristics and that consequently each has failed to take account of the nonexhibited, relational aspects of games and art. By 'exhibited' characteristics Mandelbaum means easily perceived properties such as the fact that a ball is used in a certain kind of game, that a painting has a triangular composition, that an area in a painting is red, or that the plot of a tragedy contains a reversal of fortune. Mandelbaum concludes that when we consider the nonexhibited properties of games, we see that they have in common 'the potentiality of... [an]... absorbing non-practical interest to either participants or spectators.'[4] Mandelbaum may or may not be right about 'game,' but what interests me is the application of his suggestion about nonexhibited properties to the discussion of the definition of art. Although he does not attempt a definition of 'art,' Mandelbaum does suggest that feature(s) common to all works of art may perhaps be discovered that will be a basis for the definition of 'art,' if the nonexhibited features of art are attended to.

Having noted Mandelbaum's invaluable suggestion about definition, I now return to Weitz's argument concerning artifactuality. In an earlier attempt to show Weitz wrong, I thought it sufficient to point out that there are two senses of 'work of art,' an evaluative sense and a classificatory one; Weitz himself distinguishes these in his article as the evaluative and the descriptive senses of art. My earlier argument was that if there is more than one sense of 'work of art,' then the fact that 'This piece of driftwood is a lovely piece of sculpture' is intelligible does not prove what Weitz wants it to prove. Weitz would have to show that 'sculpture' is being used in the sentence in question in the classificatory sense, and this he makes no attempt to do. My argument assumed that once the distinction is made, it is obvious that 'sculpture' is here being used in the evaluative sense. Richard Sclafani has subsequently noted that my argument shows only that Weitz's argument is inconclusive and that Weitz might still be right, even though his argument does not prove his conclusion. Sclafani, however, has constructed a stronger argument against Weitz on this point.[5]

Sclafani shows that there is a third sense of 'work of art' and that 'driftwood cases' (the nonartifact cases) fall under it. He begins by comparing a paradigm work of art, Brancusi's *Bird in Space*, with a piece of driftwood which looks very much like it. Sclafani says that it seems natural to say of the piece of driftwood that it is a work of art and that we do so because it has so many properties in common with the Brancusi piece. He then asks us to reflect on our characterization of the driftwood and the *direction* it has taken. We say the driftwood is art because of its resemblance to some paradigm work of art or because the driftwood shares properties with several paradigm works of art. The paradigm work or works are of course always artifacts; the direction of our move is from paradigmatic (artifactual) works of art to nonartifactual 'art.' Sclafani quite correctly takes this to indicate that there is a primary, paradigmatic sense of 'work of art' (my classificatory sense) and a derivative or secondary sense into which the 'driftwood cases' fall. Weitz is right in a way in saying that the driftwood is art, but wrong in concluding that artifactuality is unnecessary for (the primary sense of) art.

There are then at least three distinct senses of 'work of art': the primary or classificatory sense, the secondary or derivative, and the evaluative. Perhaps in most uses of Weitz's driftwood sentence example, both the derivative and the evaluative senses would be involved: the derivative sense if the driftwood shared a number of properties with some paradigm work of art and the evaluative sense if the shared properties were found to be valuable by the speaker. Sclafani gives a case in which only the evaluative sense functions, when someone says, 'Sally's cake is a work of art.' In most uses of such a sentence 'work of art' would simply mean that its referent has valuable qualities. Admittedly, one can imagine contexts in which the derivative sense would apply to cakes. (Given the situation in art today, one can easily imagine cakes to which the primary sense of art could be applied.) If, however, someone were to say, 'This Rembrandt is a work of art,' both the classificatory and the evaluative senses would be functioning. The expression 'this Rembrandt' would convey the information that its referent is a work of art in the classificatory sense, and 'is a work of art' could then only reasonably be understood in the evaluative sense. Finally, someone might say of a sea shell or other natural object which resembles a man's face but is otherwise uninteresting, 'This shell (or other natural object) is a work of art.' In this case, only the derivative sense would be used.

We utter sentences in which the expression 'work of art' has the evaluative sense with considerable frequency, applying it to both natural objects and artifacts. We speak of works of art in the derived sense with somewhat less frequency. The classificatory sense of 'work of art,' which indicates simply that a thing belongs to a certain category of artifacts, occurs, however, very infrequently in our discourse. We rarely utter sentences in which we use the classificatory sense, because it is such a basic notion: we generally know immediately whether an object is a work of art, so that generally no one needs to say, by way of classification, 'That is a work of art,' although recent developments in art such as junk sculpture and found art may occasionally force such remarks. Even if we do not often talk about art in this classificatory sense, however, it is a basic concept that structures and guides our thinking about our world and its contents.

II

It is now clear that artifactuality is a necessary condition (call it the genus) of the primary sense of art. This fact, however, does not seem very surprising and would not even be very interesting except that Weitz and others have denied it. Artifactuality alone, however, is not the whole story and another necessary condition (the differentia) has to be specified in order to have a satisfactory definition of 'art.' Like artifactuality, the second condition is a nonexhibited property, which turns out to be as complicated as artifactuality is simple. The attempt to discover and specify the second condition of art will involve an examination of the intricate complexities of the 'artworld.' W.E. Kennick, defending a view similar to Weitz's, contends that the kind of approach to be employed here, following Mandelbaum's lead, is futile. He concludes that 'the attempt to define Art in terms of what we do with certain objects is as doomed as any other.'[6] He tries to support this conclusion by referring to such things as the fact that the ancient Egyptians sealed up paintings and sculptures in tombs. There are two difficulties with Kennick's argument. First, that the Egyptians sealed up paintings and sculptures in tombs does not show that they regarded them differently from the way in which we regard them. They might have put them there for the dead to appreciate or simply because they belonged to the dead person. The Egyptian practice does not establish so radical a difference between their conception of art and ours that a definition subsuming both is impossible. Second, one need not assume that we and the ancient Egyptians share a common conception of art. It would be enough to be able to specify the necessary and sufficient conditions for the concept of art which we have (we present-day Americans, we present-day Westerners, we Westerners since the organization of the system of the arts in or about the eighteenth century – I am not sure of the exact limits of the 'we'). Kennick notwithstanding, we are most likely to discover the differentia of art by considering 'what we do with certain objects.' Of course, nothing guarantees that any given thing we might do or an ancient Egyptian might have done with a work of art will throw light on the concept of art. Not every 'doing' will reveal what is required.

Although he does not attempt to formulate a definition, Arthur Danto in his provocative article, 'The Artworld,' has suggested the direction that must be taken by an attempt to define 'art.'[7] In reflecting on art and its history together with such present-day developments as Warhol's *Brillo Carton* and Rauschenberg's *Bed*, Danto writes, 'To see something as art requires something the eye cannot descry – an atmosphere of artistic theory, a knowledge of history of art: an artworld'[8] Admittedly, this stimulating comment is in need of elucidation, but it is clear that in speaking of 'something the eye cannot descry' Danto is agreeing with Mandelbaum that nonexhibited properties are of great importance in constituting something as art. In speaking of atmosphere and history, however, Danto's remark carries us a step further than Mandelbaum's analysis. Danto points to the rich structure in which particular works of art are embedded: he indicates *the institutional nature of art*.[9]

I shall use Danto's term 'artworld' to refer to the broad social institution in which works of art have their place.[10] But is there such an institution? George Bernard Shaw speaks somewhere of the apostolic line of succession stretching from Aeschylus to himself. Shaw was no doubt speaking for effect and to draw attention to himself, as he often did, but there is an important truth implied by his remark. There is a long tradition or continuing institution of the theater having its origins in ancient Greek religion and other Greek institutions. That tradition has run very thin at times and perhaps even ceased to exist altogether during some periods, only to be reborn out of its memory and the need for art. The institutions associated with the theater have varied from time to time: in the beginning it was Greek religion and the Greek state; in medieval times, the church; more recently, private business and the state (national theater). What has remained constant with its own identity throughout its history is the theater itself as an established way of doing and behaving, what I shall call ... the primary convention of the theater. This institutionalized behavior occurs on both sides of the 'footlights': both the players and the audience are involved and go to make up the institution of the theater. The roles of the actors and the audience are defined by the traditions of the theater. What the author, management, and players present is art, and it is art because it is presented within the theater-world framework. Plays are written to have a place in the theater system and they exist as plays, that is, as art, within that system. Of course, I do not wish to deny that plays also exist as literary works, that is, as art within the literary system: the theater system and the literary system overlap. Let me make clear what I mean by speaking of the artworld as an institution. Among the meanings of 'institution' in *Webster's New Collegiate Dictionary* are the following: '3. That which is instituted as: a. An established practice, law, custom, etc. b. An established society or corporation.' When I call the artworld an institution I am saying that it is an established practice. Some persons have thought that an institution must be an established society or corporation and, consequently, have misunderstood my claim about the artworld.

Theater is only one of the systems within the artworld. Each of the systems has had its own origins and historical development. We have some information about the later stages of these developments, but we have to guess about the origins of the basic art systems. I suppose that we have complete knowledge of certain recently developed subsystems or genres such as Dada and happenings. Even if our knowledge is not as complete as we wish it were, however, we do have substantial information about the systems of the artworld as they currently exist and as they have existed for some time. One central feature all of the systems have in common is that each is a framework for the *presenting* of particular works of art. Given the great variety of the systems of the artworld it is not surprising that works of art have no exhibited properties in common. If, however, we step back and view the works in their institutional setting, we will be able to see the essential properties they share.

Theater is a rich and instructive illustration of the institutional nature of art. But it is a development within the domain of painting and sculpture – Dadaism – that most easily reveals the institutional essence of art. Duchamp and friends conferred the status of art on 'ready-mades' (urinals, hatracks, snow shovels, and the like), and when we reflect on their deeds we can take note of a kind of human action which has until now gone unnoticed and unappreciated – the action of conferring the status of art. Painters and sculptors, of course, have been engaging all along in the action of conferring this status on the objects they create. As long, however, as the created objects were conventional, given the paradigms of the times, the objects themselves and their fascinating exhibited properties were the focus of the attention of not only spectators and critics but of philosophers of art as well. When an artist of an earlier era painted a picture, he did some or all of a number of things: depicted a human being, portrayed a certain man, fulfilled a commission, worked at his livelihood, and so on. In addition he also acted as an agent of the artworld and conferred the status of art on his creation. Philosophers of art attended to only some of the properties the created object acquired from these various actions, for example, to the representational or to the expressive features of the objects. They entirely ignored the nonexhibited property of status. When, however, the objects are bizarre, as those of the Dadaists are, our attention is forced away from the objects' obvious properties to a consideration of the objects in their social context. As works of art Duchamp's 'ready-mades' may not be worth much, but as examples of art they are very valuable for art theory. I am not claiming that Duchamp and friends invented the conferring of the status of art; they simply used an existing institutional device in an unusual way. Duchamp did not invent the artworld, because it was there all along.

The artworld consists of a bundle of systems: theater, painting, sculpture, literature, music, and so on, each of which furnishes an institutional background for the conferring of the status on objects within its domain. No limit can be placed on the number of systems that can be brought under the generic conception of art, and each of the major systems contains further subsystems. These features of the artworld provide the elasticity whereby creativity of even the most radical sort can be accommodated. A whole new system comparable to the theater, for example, could be added in one fell swoop. What is more likely is that a new subsystem would be added within a system. For example, junk sculpture added within sculpture, happenings added within theater. Such additions might in time develop into full-blown systems. Thus, the radical creativity, adventuresomeness, and exuberance of art of which Weitz speaks is possible within the concept of art, even though it is closed by the necessary and sufficient conditions of artifactuality and conferred status.

Having now briefly described the artworld, I am in a position to specify a definition of 'work of art.' The definition will be given in terms of artifactuality and the conferred status of art or, more strictly speaking, the conferred status of candidate for appreciation. Once the definition has been stated, a great deal will still remain to be said by way of clarification: A work of art in the classificatory sense is (1) an artifact (2) a set of the aspects of which has had conferred upon it the status of candidate for appreciation by some person or persons acting on behalf of a certain social institution (the artworld).

The second condition of the definition makes use of four variously interconnected notions: (1) acting on behalf of an institution, (2) conferring of status, (3) being a candidate, and (4) appreciation. The first two of these are so closely related that they must be discussed together. I shall first describe paradigm cases of conferring status outside the artworld and then show how similar actions take place within the artworld. The most clear-cut examples of the conferring of status are certain legal actions of the state. A king's conferring of knighthood, a grand jury's indicting someone, the chairman of the election board certifying that someone is qualified to run for office, or a minister's pronouncing a couple man and wife are examples in which a person or persons acting on behalf of a social institution (the state) confer(s) *legal* status on persons. The congress or a legally constituted commission may confer the status of national park of monument on an area or thing. The examples given suggest that pomp and ceremony are required to establish legal status, but this is not so, although of course a legal system is presupposed. For example, in some jurisdictions common-law marriage is possible – a legal status acquired without ceremony. The conferring of a Ph.D. degree on someone by a university, the election of someone as president of the Rotary, and the declaring of an object as a relic of the church are examples in which a person or persons confer(s) nonlegal status on persons or things. In such cases some social system or other must exist as the framework within which the conferring takes place, but, as before, ceremony is not required to establish status: for example, a person can acquire the status of wise man or village idiot within a community without ceremony.

Some may feel that the notion of conferring status within the artworld is excessively vague. Certainly this notion is not as clear-cut as the conferring of status within the legal system, where procedures and lines of authority are explicitly defined and incorporated into law. The counterparts in the artworld to specified procedures and lines of authority are nowhere codified, and the artworld carries on its business at the level of customary practice. Still there *is* a practice and this defines a social institution. A social institution need not have a formally established constitution, officers, and bylaws in order to exist and have the capacity to confer status – some social institutions are formal and some are informal. The artworld could become formalized, and perhaps has been to some extent in certain political contexts, but most people who are interested in art would probably consider this a bad thing. Such formality would threaten the freshness and exuberance of art. The core personnel of the artworld is a loosely organized, but nevertheless related, set of persons including artists (understood to refer to painters, writers, composers), producers, museum directors, museum-goers, theater-goers, reports for newspapers, critics for publications of all sorts, art historians, art theorists, philosophers of art, and others. These are the people who keep the machinery of the artworld working and thereby provide for its continuing existence. In addition, every person who sees himself as a member of the artworld is thereby a member. Although I have called the persons just listed the core personnel of the artworld, there is a minimum core within that core without which the artworld would not exist. This essential core consists of artists who create the works, 'presenters' to present the works, and 'goers' who appreciate the works. This minimum core might be called 'the presentation group,' for it consists of artists whose activity is necessary if anything is to be presented, the presenters (actors, stage managers, and so on), and the goers whose presence and cooperation is necessary in order for anything to be presented. A given person might play more than one of these essential roles in the case of presentation of a particular work. Critics, historians, and philosophers of art become members of the artworld at some time after the minimum core personnel of a particular art system get that system into operation. All of these roles are institutionalized and must be learned in one way or another by the participants. For example, a theater-goer is not just someone who happens to enter a theater; he is a person who enters with certain expectations and knowledge about what he will experience and an understanding of how he should behave in the face of what he will experience.

Assuming that the existence of the artworld has been established or at least made plausible, the problem is now to see how status is conferred by this institution. My thesis is that, in a way analogous to the way in which a person is certified as qualified for office, or two persons acquire the status of common-law marriage within a legal system, or a person is elected president of the Rotary, or a person acquires the status of wise man within a community, so an artifact can acquire the status of candidate for appreciation within the social system called 'the artworld.' How can one tell when the status has been conferred? An artifact's hanging in an art museum as part of a show and a performance at a theater are sure signs. There is, of course, no guarantee that one can always know whether something is a candidate for appreciation, just as one cannot always tell whether a given person is a knight or is married. When an object's status depends upon nonexhibited characteristics, a simple look at the object will not necessarily reveal that status. The nonexhibited relation *may* be symbolized by some badge, for example, by a wedding ring, in which case a simple look will reveal the status.

The more important question is that of how the status of candidate for appreciation is conferred. The examples just mentioned, display in a museum and a performance in a theater, seem to suggest that a number of persons are required for the actual conferring of the status. In one sense a number of persons are required but in another sense only one person is required: a number of persons are required to make up the social institution of the artworld, but only one person is required to act on behalf of the artworld and to confer the status of candidate for appreciation. In fact, many works of art are seen only by one person – the one who creates them – but they are still art. The status in question may be acquired by a single person's acting on behalf of the artworld and *treating an artifact as a candidate for appreciation.* Of course, nothing prevents a group of persons from conferring the status, but it is usually conferred by a single person, the artist who creates the artifact. It may be helpful to compare and contrast the notion of conferring the status of candidate for appreciation with a case in which something is simply presented for appreciation: hopefully this will throw light on the notion of status of candidate. Consider the case of a salesman of plumbing supplies who spreads his wares before us. 'Placing before' and 'conferring the status of candidate for appreciation' are very different notions, and this difference can be brought out by comparing the salesman's action with the superficially similar act of Duchamp in entering a urinal which he christened *Fountain* in that now-famous art show. The difference is that Duchamp's action took place within the institutional setting of the artworld and the plumbing salesman's action took place outside of it. The salesman could do what Duchamp did, that is, convert a urinal into a work of art, but such a thing probably would not occur to him. Please remember that *Fountain*'s being a work of art does not mean that it is a good one, nor does this qualification insinuate that it is a bad one either. The antics of a particular present-day artist serve to reinforce the point of the Duchamp case and also to emphasize a significance of the practice of naming works of art. Walter de Maria has in the case of one of his works even gone through the motions, no doubt as a burlesque, of using a procedure used by many legal and some nonlegal institutions – the procedure of licensing. His *High Energy Bar* (a stainless-steel bar) is accompanied by a certificate bearing the name of the work and stating that the bar is a work of art only when the certificate is present. In addition to highlighting the status of art by 'certifying' it on a document, this example serves to suggest a significance of the act of naming works of art. An object may acquire the status of art without ever being named but giving it a title makes clear to whomever is interested that an object is a work of art. Specific titles function in a variety of ways – as aids to understanding a work or as a convenient way of identifying it, for example – but any title at all (even *Untitled*) is a badge of status.[11]

The third notion involved in the second condition of the definition is candidacy: a member of the artworld confers the status of candidate for appreciation. The definition does not require that a work of art actually be appreciated, even by one person. The fact is that many, perhaps most, works of art go unappreciated. It is important not to build into the definition of the classificatory sense of 'work of art' value properties such as actual appreciation: to do so would make it impossible to speak of unappreciated works of art. Building in value properties might even make it awkward to speak of bad works of art. A theory of art must preserve certain central features of the way in which we talk about art, and we do find it necessary sometimes to speak of unappreciated art and bad art. Also, not every aspect of a work is included in the candidacy for appreciation; for example, the color of the back of a painting is not ordinarily considered to be something which someone might think it appropriate to appreciate. The problem of which aspects of a work of art are to be included within the candidacy for appreciation is a question I shall pursue later in Chapter 7 [not reproduced here] in trying to give an analysis of the notion of aesthetic object. The definition of 'work of art' should not, therefore, be understood as asserting that every aspect of a work is included within the candidacy for appreciation.

The fourth notion involved in the second condition of the definition is appreciation itself. Some may assume that the definition is referring to a special kind of *aesthetic* appreciation. I shall argue later...that there is no reason to think that there is a special kind of aesthetic consciousness, attention, or perception. Similarly, I do not think there is any reason to think that there is a special kind of aesthetic appreciation. All that is meant by 'appreciation' in the definition is something like 'in experiencing the qualities of a thing one finds them worthy or valuable,' and this meaning applies quite generally both inside and outside the domain of art. Several persons have felt that my account of the institutional theory of art is incomplete because of what they see as my insufficient analysis of appreciation. They have, I believe, thought that there are different kinds of appreciation and that the appreciation in the appreciation of art is somehow typically different from the appreciation in the appreciation of nonart. But the only sense in which there is a difference between the appreciation of art and the appreciation of nonart is that the appreciations have different *objects*. The institutional structure in which the art object is embedded, not different kinds of appreciation, makes the difference between the appreciation of art and the appreciation of nonart.

In a recent article[12] Ted Cohen has raised a question concerning (1) candidacy for appreciation and (2) appreciation as these two were treated in my original attempt to define 'art.'[13] He claims that in order for it to be possible for candidacy for appreciation to be conferred on something that it must be possible for that thing to be appreciated. Perhaps he is right about this; in any event, I cannot think of any reason to disagree with him on this point. The possibility of appreciation is one constraint on the definition: if something cannot be appreciated, it cannot become art. The question that now arises is: is there anything which it is impossible to appreciate? Cohen claims many things cannot be appreciated; for example, 'ordinary thumbtacks, cheap white envelopes, the plastic forks given at some drive-in restaurants.'[14] But more importantly, he claims that *Fountain* cannot be appreciated. He says that *Fountain* has a point which can be appreciated, but that it is Duchamp's gesture that has significance (can be appreciated) and not *Fountain* itself. I agree that *Fountain* has the significance Cohen attributes to it, namely, that it was a protest against the art of its day. But why cannot the ordinary qualities of *Fountain* – its gleaming white surface, the depth revealed when it reflects images of surrounding objects, its pleasing oval shape – be appreciated. It has qualities similar to those of works by Brancusi and Moore which many do not balk at saying they appreciate. Similarly, thumbtacks, envelopes, and plastic forks have qualities that can be appreciated if one makes the effort to focus attention on them. One of the values of photography is its ability to focus on and bring out the qualities of quite ordinary objects. And the same sort of thing can be done without the benefit of photography by just looking. In short, it seems unlikely to me that any object would not have some quality which is appreciatable and thus likely that the constraint Cohen suggests may well be vacuous. But even if there are some objects that cannot be appreciated, *Fountain* and the other Dadaist creations are not among them.

I should note that in accepting Cohen's claim I am saying that every work of art must have some minimal *potential* value or worthiness. This fact, however, does not collapse the distinction between the evaluative sense and the classificatory sense of 'work of art.' The evaluative sense is used when the object it is predicated of is deemed *to be* of substantial, actual value, and that object may be a natural object. I will further note that the appreciatability of a work of art in the classificatory sense is *potential* value which in a given case may never be realized.[15]

The definition I have given contains a reference to the artworld. Consequently, some may have the uncomfortable feeling that my definition is viciously circular. Admittedly, in a sense the definition is circular, but it is not viciously so. If I had said something like 'A work of art is an artifact on which a status has been conferred by the artworld' and then said of the artworld only that it confers the status of candidacy for appreciation, then the definition would be viciously circular because the circle would be so small and *uninformative*. I have, however, devoted a considerable amount of space in this chapter to describing and analyzing the historical, organization, and functional intricacies of the artworld, and if this account is accurate the reader has received a considerable amount of *information* about the artworld. The circle I have run is not small and it is not uninformative. If, in the end, the artworld cannot be described independently of art, that is, if the description contains references to art historians, art reporters, plays, theaters, and so on, then the definition strictly speaking is circular. It is not, however, viciously so, because the whole account in which the definition is embedded contains a great deal of information about the artworld. One must not focus narrowly on the definition alone: for what is important to see is that art is an institutional concept and this requires seeing the definition in the context of the whole account. I suspect that the 'problem' of circularity will arise frequently, perhaps always, when institutional concepts are dealt with.

III

The instances of Dadaist art and similar present-day developments which have served to bring the institutional nature of art to our attention suggest several questions. First, if Duchamp can convert such artifacts as a urinal, a snow shovel, and a hatrack into works of art, why can't natural objects such as driftwood also become works of art in the classificatory sense? Perhaps they can if any one of a number of things is done to them. One way in which this might happen would be for someone to pick up a natural object, take it home, and hang it on the wall. Another way would be to pick up a natural object and enter it in an exhibition. I was assuming earlier, by the way, that the piece of driftwood referred to in Weitz's sentence was in place on a beach and untouched by human hand or at least untouched by any human intention and therefore was art in the evaluative or derivative sense. Natural objects which become works of art in the classificatory sense are artifactualized without the use of tools – artifactuality is conferred on the object rather than worked on it. This means that natural objects which become works of art acquire their artifactuality at the same time that the status of candidate for appreciation is conferred on them, although the act that confers artifactuality is not the same act that confers the status of candidate for appreciation. But perhaps a similar thing ordinarily happens with paintings and poems; they come to exist as artifacts at the same time that they have the status of candidate for appreciation conferred on them. Of course, being an artifact and being a candidate for appreciation are not the same thing – they are two properties which may be acquired at the same time. Many may find the notion of artifactuality being conferred rather than 'worked' on an object too strange to accept and admittedly it is an unusual conception. It may be that a special account will have to be worked out for exhibited driftwood and similar cases.

Another question arising with some frequency in connection with discussions of the concept of art and seeming especially relevant in the context of the institutional theory is 'How are we to conceive of paintings done by individuals such as Betsy the chimpanzee from the Baltimore Zoo?' Calling Betsy's products paintings is not meant to prejudge that they are works of art, it is just that some word is needed to refer to them. The question of whether Betsy's paintings are art depends upon what is done with them. For example, a year or two ago the Field Museum of Natural History in Chicago exhibited some chimpanzee and gorilla paintings. We must say that these paintings are not works of art. If, however, they had been exhibited a few miles away at the Chicago Art Institute they would have been works of art – the paintings would have been art if the director of the Art Institute had been willing to go out on a limb for his fellow primates. A great deal depends upon the institutional setting: one institutional setting is congenial to conferring the status of art and the other is not. Please note that although paintings such as Betsy's would remain her paintings even if exhibited at an art museum, they would be the *art* of the person responsible for their being exhibited. Betsy would not (I assume) be able to conceive of herself in such a way as to be a member of the artworld and, hence, would not be able to confer the relevant status. Art is a concept which necessarily involves human intentionality. These last remarks are not intended to denigrate the value (including beauty) of the paintings of chimpanzees shown at natural history museums or the creations of bower birds, but as remarks about what falls under a particular concept.

Danto in 'Art Works and Real Things' discusses defeating conditions of the ascriptivity of art.[16] He considers fake paintings, that is, copies of original paintings which are attributed to the creators of the original paintings. He argues that a painting's being a fake prevents it from being a work of art, maintaining that originality is an analytical requirement of being a work of art. That a work is derivative or imitative does not, however, he thinks, prevent it from being a work of art. I think Danto is right about fake paintings, and I can express this in terms of my own account by saying that originality in paintings is an antecedent requirement for the conferring of the candidacy for appreciation. Similar sorts of things would have to be said for similar cases in the arts other than painting. One consequence of this requirement is that there are many works of nonart which people take to be works of art, namely, those fake paintings which are not known to be fakes. When fakes are discovered to be fakes, they do not lose that status of art because they never had the status in the first place, despite what almost everyone had thought. There is some analogy here with patent law. Once an invention has been patented, one exactly like it cannot be patented – the patent for just that invention has been 'used up.' In the case of patenting, of course, whether the second device is a copy or independently derived is unimportant, but the copying aspect is crucial in the artistic case. The Van Meegeren painting that was not a copy of an actual Vermeer but a painting done in the manner of Vermeer with a forged signature is a somewhat more complicated case. The painting with the forged signature is not a work of art, but if Van Meegeren had signed his own name the painting would have been.

Strictly speaking, since originality is an analytic requirement for a painting to be a work of art, an originality clause should be incorporated into my definition of 'work of art.' But since I have not given any analysis of the originality requirement with respect to works other than paintings, I am not in a position to supplement the definition in this way. All I can say at this time is what I said just above, namely, that originality in paintings is an antecedent requirement for the conferring of the candidacy for appreciation and that considerations of a similar sort would probably apply in the other arts.

Weitz charges that the defining of 'art' or its subconcepts forecloses on creativity. Some of the traditional definitions of 'art' *may* have and some of the traditional definitions of its subconcepts probably *did* foreclose on creativity, but this danger is now past. At one time a playwright, for example, may have conceived of and wished to write a play with tragic features but lacking a defining characteristic as specified by, say, Aristotle's definition of 'tragedy.' Faced with this dilemma the playwright might have been intimidated into abandoning his project. With the present-day disregard for established genres, however, and the clamor for novelty in art, this obstacle to creativity no longer exists. Today, if a new and unusual work is created and it is similar to some members of an established type of art, it will usually be accommodated within that type, or if the new work is very unlike any existing works then a new subconcept will probably be created. Artists today are not easily intimidated, and they regard art genres as loose guidelines rather than rigid specifications. Even if a philosopher's remarks were to have an effect on what artists do today, the institutional conception of art would certainly not foreclose on creativity. The requirement of artifactuality cannot prevent creativity, since artifactuality is a necessary condition of creativity. There cannot be an instance of creativity without an artifact of some kind being produced. The second requirement involving the conferring of status could not inhibit creativity; in fact, it encourages it. Since under the definition anything whatever may become art, the definition imposes no restraints on creativity.

The institutional theory of art may sound like saying, 'A work of art is an object of which someone has said, "I christen this object a work of art."' And it is rather like that, although this does not mean that the conferring of the status of art is a simple matter. Just as the christening of a child has as its background the history and structure of the church, conferring the status of art has as its background the Byzantine complexity of the artworld. Some may find it strange that in the nonart cases discussed, there are ways in which the conferring can go wrong, while that does not appear to be true in art. For example, an indictment might be improperly drawn up and the person charged would not actually be indicted, but nothing parallel seems possible in the case of art. This fact just reflects the differences between the artworld and legal institutions: the legal system deals with matters of grave personal consequences and its procedures must reflect this; the artworld deals with important matters also but they are of a different sort entirely. The artworld does not require rigid procedures; it admits and even encourages frivolity and caprice without losing its serious purpose. Please note that not all legal procedures are as rigid as court procedures and that mistakes made in conferring certain kinds of legal status are not fatal to that status. A minister may make mistakes in reading the marriage ceremony, but the couple that stands before him will still acquire the status of being married. If, however, a mistake cannot be made *in* conferring the status of art, a mistake can be made *by* conferring it. In conferring the status of art on an object one assumes a certain kind of responsibility for the object in its new status – presenting a candidate for appreciation always allows the possibility that no one will appreciate it and that the person who did the conferring will thereby lose face. One *can* make a work of art out of a sow's ear, but that does not necessarily make it a silk purse.

Notes

1 *Journal of Aesthetics and Art Criticism*, September 1956, pp.27–35. See also Paul Ziff's 'The Task of Defining a Work of Art,' *Philosophical Review*, January 1953, pp.58–78; and W.E. Kennick's 'Does Traditional Aesthetics Rest on a Mistake?' *Mind*, July 1958, pp.317–334.

2 'Wittgenstein's Aesthetics,' in *Language and Aesthetics*, Benjamin R. Tilghman, ed. (Lawrence, Kans., 1973), p.14. This paper was read at a symposium at Kansas State University in April 1970. Monroe Beardsley has pointed out to me that the relationship between 'game' and 'major league baseball' is one of class and member rather than of genus and species.

3 'Family Resemblances and Generalizations Concerning the Arts,' *American Philosophical Quarterly*, July 1965, pp.219–228; reprinted in *Problems in Aesthetics*, Morris Weitz, ed., 2d ed. (London, 1970), pp.181–197.

4 *Ibid.*, p.185 in the Weitz anthology.

5 '"Art" and Artifactuality,' *Southwestern Journal of Philosophy*, Fall 1970, pp.105–108.

6 'Does Traditional Aesthetics Rest on a Mistake?' *Mind*, p.330.

7 *Journal of Philosophy*, October 15, 1964, pp.571–585.

8 *Ibid.*, p.580.

9 Danto does not develop an institutional account of art in his article nor in a subsequent related article entitled 'Art Works and Real Things,' *Theoria*, Parts 1–3, 1973, pp.1–17. In both articles Danto's primary concern is to discuss what he calls the Imitation Theory and the Real Theory of Art. Many of the things he says in these two articles are consistent with and can be incorporated into an institutional account, and his brief remarks in the later article about the ascriptivity of art are similar to the institutional theory. The institutional theory is one possible version of the ascriptivity theory.

10 This remark is not intended as a definition of the term 'artworld,' I am merely indicating what the expression is used to *refer* to. 'Artworld' is nowhere defined in this book, although the referent of the expression is described in some detail.

11 Recently in an article entitled 'The Republic of Art' in *British Journal of Aesthetics*, April 1969, pp.145–56, T.J. Diffey has talked about the status of art being conferred. He, however, is attempting to give an account of something like an evaluative sense of 'work of art' rather than the classificatory sense, and consequently the scope of his theory is much narrower than mine.

12 'The Possibility of Art: Remarks on a Proposal by Dickie,' *Philosophical Review*, January 1973, pp.69–82.

13 'Defining Art,' *American Philosophical Quarterly*, July 1969, pp.253–256.

14 'The Possibility of Art,' p.78.

15 I realized that I must make the two points noted in this paragraph as the result of a conversation with Mark Venezia. I wish to thank him for the stimulation of his remarks.

16 Pages 12–14.

But is it art?

B.R. Tilghman (b.1927)

*The institutional theory of art comes under attack in the next extract,
taken from* But is it Art? *(1984) by B.R. Tilghman. Tilghman
considers the case of conceptual art – art in which it is the artist's
intent to convey a concept rather than to create an art object, as in
the work of Andy Warhol and Claes Oldenburg – and concludes that
the institutional theory cannot comprehend it, since conceptual art
involves a repudiation of aesthetics. One of the criteria that Tilghman
would want to build into an aesthetic theory of value is aesthetic
intention on the part of the artist, and where that intention is absent,
as it conspicuously and deliberately is in conceptual art, there can
be no aesthetic value. The best that Tilghman can say of conceptual
art is that it has a negative value in showing us what art is* not.

The shock of the new

A persistent feature of the last hundred and more years of art
history has been the seasonal recurrence of what Ian Dunlop has
labeled *The Shock of the New*.[1] On any number of occasions during
this period the artworld has been shocked by the appearance of
avant garde movements that have seemed to challenge artistic
traditions and prevailing conceptions of art. One thinks immediately
of the impact made by the first impressionist showings, the fauves,
the post-impressionist, the surrealists, and so on. Professional critics
and casual gallerygoers alike have been disturbed and puzzled by
these new developments that they did not know what to make of.
The new works did not seem to accommodate themselves to what
art was thought to be like and frequently the motives of the artists
were themselves impugned. This sort of thing is still very much
with us and has been especially exacerbated by a number of
movements of the very recent past including some manifestations
of pop art, minimal art, arte povera, conceptual art, and the
like. One need only think of Andy Warhol's *Brillo Box*, Claes
Oldenburg's *Placid Civic Monument*, the hole he had dug in Central

Park behind the Metropolitan Museum and then filled in again or the piece that Robert Barry offered for Lucy Lippard's Seattle World's Fair show which consisted simply of the remark 'All the things I know but of which I am not at the moment thinking – 1:36 P.M.; 15 June 1969, New York'...

When faced with this sort of thing the plight of our plain gentleman, described in chapter 3 [not reproduced here], evokes sympathy. But what exactly is his plight? It is not that he thinks the work before him is bad; after all, he doesn't know what is relevant to the assessment of its worth and in this respect he is like the man who doesn't see the point of the joke and doesn't know where to look for it. His first reaction might be to dismiss the business out of hand as a kind of nonsense or as a prank or joke, and not a very good one at that. But he is reluctant to thus dismiss it out of hand. A great many allegedly serious people do take it seriously and he thinks of those traditional critics who proved to be the laughing stock of later generations for making mock of the impressionists, the post-impressionists and all the others we now rank among the modern masters. He has grounds for his reluctance.

How can he be brought to understand this new material and be shown that there is something to it after all or, as may be, verify his original suspicions? We can approach this task and at the same time get a clearer view of our man's situation by examining in some detail an actual case of new works of art shocking the artworld and producing what may be described as a crisis in criticism and appreciation. The case I want to examine is that of those painters for whom Roger Fry coined the name 'Post-Impressionist' in 1910. This case is instructive because we now have an advantageous historical perspective from which to view it and also because Fry's critical defense of those painters is an excellent example of how a new movement can be sympathetically understood and judged.

Roger Fry was well known in Edwardian Britain as an art historian and critic and was popular as a public lecturer on the arts. He also had a modest reputation as a painter in his own right. In 1910 he organized the first exhibition of post-impressionist painting at the Grafton Gallery in London. The exhibition included works by Manet, Cézanne, Gauguin, Van Gogh, Vlaminck, Derain, Seurat, Signac, Matisse, Rouault, and Picasso, to name only the more important. The great majority of these works were new both to British artists as well as to the British public. Critical and public reaction was generally one of outrage. When they were not simply laughed at, the paintings were called indecent and pornographic.

The tendency was for critics to regard it all as destructive of artistic tradition and of the artistic values so laboriously developed from the renaissance on. It was especially puzzling that a man such as Roger Fry who could write and lecture eloquently on the likes of Bellini and Botticelli could at the same time perpetrate a thing like the Grafton show.

The critical reaction to the exhibition is made comprehensible by the state of the arts and artistic taste at that time, that is, by the culture of the period, the Edwardian artworld. This state of things has been described for us in some detail.[2] The 'old masters' of the high renaissance were still much admired and the popular academic painters of the nineteenth century, Alma-Tadema, Leighton, and Landseer, for example, were thought of as carrying on that tradition. Some artists and collectors had begun to make their peace with impressionism and if the impressionists were not exactly in vogue, at least they were no longer despised. Whatever group of painters passed for avant garde in Britain, it was a pretty tame crowd; there was nothing that could properly be called bohemia where radical ideas were fermenting. Although a number of British painters had studied in France, they had confined themselves to the more reputable *ateliers*, and had apparently not penetrated into *la vie bohème* whence came the makings of the Grafton show.

Against this background it is easy to understand the reception of the post-impressionists and why neither critics nor public knew what to make of them. There was no problem in describing and evaluating a new painting done in the familiar traditions. Here one knew what to look for, literary and historical content, drawing, space composition, perspective, color, atmospheric rendering, and so on and there was no great problem in telling the painter who had learned his lessons from the inept who couldn't make it all come off. With the post-impressionists, however, none of the familiar categories seemed to apply. No wonder they were seen as either hopelessly unskilled and doing very badly what the academic painters did very well or as deliberately, and perhaps even maliciously, kicking over all that was of value.

In an article in *The Nation*[3] Fry defended the post-impressionists in the following way. He admitted that although 'they were in revolt against the photographic vision of the nineteenth century, and even against the tempered realism of the last four hundred years', nevertheless they are the most traditional of recent artists. They represent a rather successful attempt to get behind 'the too elaborate pictorial apparatus which the Renaissance established in painting. In short they are the true Pre-Raphaelites.' He then went on to develop this point.

> We think of Giotto as a preparation for a Titianesque climax, forgetting that with every piece of representational mechanism which the artist acquired, he both gained new possibilities of expression and lost other possibilities. When you draw like Tintoretto, you can no longer draw like Giotto, or even Piero della Francesca. You have lost the power of expression which the bare recital of elementary facts of mass, gesture, and movement gave, and you have gained whatever a more intricate linear system and chiaroscuro may provide. (p.332)

Fry's argument is in essence a rejection of the view of art history associated with Vasari that understands Giotto as doing in a crude and clumsy beginner's way what Leonardo, Michaelangelo, and Titian did superbly well. With such a picture of art history in mind it is also possible to see Cézanne and the others as doing very badly what the nineteenth century academics did very skillfully. There are, however, other ways to look at Giotto; he has his own values of form, design, and expression that tended to get submerged in the later development of renaissance techniques of representation. Now, Fry tells us, don't look at Cézanne as you look at the nineteenth century academics; see him, instead, as doing the kind of thing that Giotto was doing. (Fry also compares Cézanne to Mantegna and Piero.) To understand the post-impressionists the reference point must be Giotto rather than Raphael.

I have spoken of Fry's *argument*, but something wants saying about the use of the word. Fry's conclusions about Cézanne and the other post-impressionists could no doubt be accommodated as a formal exercise by some such scheme as that set out in chapter 1 [not reproduced here] with his basic 'assumptions' about artistic value made explicit and all the rest. But the force of what Fry has to tell us about post-impressionism does not depend upon any relation of entailment by previously accepted premises. That Cézanne is good and worth looking at is not arrived at deductively – and it is certainly not rendered inductively probable by any marshalling of evidence either. What Fry is actually doing is showing us how to look at Cézanne so that we will see his value for ourselves. He helps us to do this by pointing out likenesses between his work and aspects of the artistic tradition with which we are already familiar despite those aspects having been neglected in the then prevalent view of art history.

This kind of pointing out is double-edged in an interesting way. For if Fry can show us that Cézanne is like Giotto, then surely we can also see that Giotto is like Cézanne with the result that the kind of formal values common to the two are brought much more forcefully to our attention and this neglected aspect of the tradition can henceforth become another focus of appreciative and critical awareness. Something rather similar had been suggested sometime earlier by Degas when he exclaimed 'O Giotto! teach me to see Paris, and you, Paris, teach me to see Giotto.'[4] In such ways the tradition is thus modified and expanded.

Very much the same kind of aesthetic commerce between the current and the past is instanced in an example drawn from literary criticism. In a brief essay on Kafka, Jorge Luis Borges calls attention to the existence of Kafkaesque themes in earlier writers. He then goes on to conclude that:

> Kafka's idiosyncrasy, in greater or less degree, is present in each of these writings, but if Kafka had not written we would not perceive it; that is to say, it would not exist. The poem 'Fears and Scruples' by Robert Browning is like a prophecy of Kafka's stories, but our reading of Kafka refines and changes our reading of the poem perceptibly... The fact is that each writer creates his precursors. His work modifies our conception of the past, as it will modify the future.[5]

Although it is surely an exaggeration to say that Cézanne created Giotto, as if we had to have seen Cézanne before we could appreciate Giotto, nevertheless there is a point here well taken. The work of Cézanne and his contemporaries of the late nineteenth and early twentieth century has indeed modified our conception of art history and artistic tradition. With the move toward abstraction and expressionism, Byzantine art and primitive art, for example, as well as a unique figure such as El Greco, cannot possibly look the same to us. The new developments are sometimes, to be sure, the result of the influence of a tradition, but they need not be linked to that tradition merely by historical ties; sometimes it is the new works themselves that help mark out just what that tradition is.

The major accomplishment of Fry's critical work was to show the artistic public how to look at the new painting. His importance lies not so much in any theory he developed, but in the critical and appreciative practice that he encouraged. It is in the light of all this that we can gain a different understanding of what is going on logically in the theory of art as 'significant form' that Clive Bell worked out as a result of his experience with and his thought about post-impressionism largely under the influence of Roger Fry. If the theory is taken as an attempt to explain the meaning of the word 'art' or to lay down the necessary and sufficient conditions for its application, the result is the sheerest nonsense. It is better understood, I believe, as an expression of how Bell and Fry looked at the post-impressionists and as an instrument in the critical and interpretive labor that they took up on their behalf in the context of Edwardian taste. This allows us to appreciate Morris Weitz's apt characterization of the theory.

> What gives it its aesthetic importance is what lies behind the formula: In an age in which literary and representational elements have become paramount in painting, return to the plastic ones since these are indigenous to painting. Thus, the role of the theory is not to define anything but to use the definitional form, almost epigrammatically, to pinpoint a crucial recommendation to turn our attention once again to the plastic elements in painting.[6]

There is a pattern in this history of Fry and the post-impressionists that now needs to be made explicit. This pattern is composed of four elements. (1) There is the culture of the period, the background of artistic life, traditions, and practices, the artworld, against which works of art are understood, described, and evaluated. (2) Something is offered as a work of art that apparently cannot be accommodated by the tradition and that cannot be described and evaluated in terms of familiar categories and standards, with the result that the critics as well as the general public are puzzled, if not outraged in addition. (3) The new work is defended by the demonstration of a connection, however unsuspected, with some aspect of the familiar tradition. The connection is established by showing the likeness that is to be seen between the new and the already familiar. The demonstration thus provides a way to understand and assess the new work. (4) The result of all this is that the relevant aspect of the tradition is given an importance it did not have previously and the tradition is thereby modified and enlarged. It remains to be seen whether the conceptual pattern revealed in the criticism of Roger Fry has any application to the critical and appreciative concerns that surround Oldenburg's *Monument*, Barry's 'All the things I know...'...

There is one feature of our present day artistic life that is quite different from that of Britain in 1910. We are now habituated to artistic change and aesthetic experimentation and new artistic movements are the order of the day. We are no longer disturbed simply because something is new and unlike what we are familiar with; in this respect we are undoubtedly much more tolerant and open than the Edwardians. We are also much more sophisticated with respect to art history; we are aware of a vast historical and contemporary range of artistic styles and intentions and we know that these can make quite different demands on our appreciative faculties. Put in another way, this means that we have a wider and richer vocabulary for artistic description at our disposal than did that older generation that Fry had to contend with. Not only can we talk about the traditional values of representation and draftsmanship, but also about the formal values that Fry called our attention to and abstract values of color and texture as well, not to mention more recent styles and movements such as cubism, expressionism, and surrealism that provide us with additional ways to categorize and describe both twentieth century art and that of the past.

I have already suggested that puzzlement in the face of a new kind of art is marked by not knowing how to describe the things in question and this inability to describe is logically one with not knowing how to appreciate the work, not knowing how to look at the new painting, read the new poetry, listen to the new music and so on. I want to bring out the importance of this now. We know how to describe a Raphael as, say, a madonna and as an example of high renaissance space composition. Fry's British public made the mistake of trying to describe a Cézanne or Matisse as an example of academic composition. They looked at Cézanne and Matisse as if they were trying to do the same kinds of thing as the academic painters such as Leighton and Alma-Tadema were doing and it is thus not at all surprising that they had to describe them as making singularly inept essays in that direction. How, then, is our plain gentleman to describe Oldenburg, Barry, or any of our other curiosities? Presumably it won't do – despite the obvious temptation – merely to say that Oldenburg has flung a spadeful of dirt in the face of a gullible public, but what is *Placid Civic Monument* other than a filled-in hole in the ground?

Let us note the problems in giving a satisfactory answer to that last question. In the first place, the thing is strikingly devoid of aesthetic properties. When it was still just a hole in the ground before it was filled in, it wasn't much to look at. It was of no interest as a formal design and after it was filled whatever possibilities there may have been in that direction were effectively closed off; now there is nothing to see at all. Oldenburg tells us that the thing includes all that is related to the event of digging and filling the hole, but did not happen at the spot of the event, such as the deliberations of the Park Board. The whole park and its connections are supposed to enter into it and he also tells us that it is open to any interesting interpretation.[7] A work of art is not the sort of thing we think of as open to just *any* interpretation, interesting or otherwise. In fact, the way that Oldenburg talks about *Monument* makes it perilously close to being a starting point for an exercise in free association. Typically a work of art is a focus where, by means of its form and organization certain attitudes, beliefs, feelings, or expressive features are concentrated to the exclusion of others. In Giotto's Arena Chapel *Deposition* the limp and ashen body of the dead Christ is the dramatic center of the composition. The attitudes of the mourners are concentrated there and the barren and desicated landscape in the background reinforces the whole atmosphere of the painting. The painting is about suffering, death, and sorrow and is not about any number of other aspects of human experience. That other notable hole in the ground, Ophelia's grave, is the cockpit of Hamlet's agony and the ironies and tensions found there mirror those in the castle and do not connect with just anything that happens to be going on in Denmark. Such remarks as these are commonplaces about art, but are commonplaces that remind us that not just any description or interpretation can be true of, or relevant to, a work of art, or anything else, for that matter. The subject of any interpretation is the subject of no interpretation. The object of this kind of critical generosity has no value; anything whatsoever would do just as well.

The kind of move that Fry made in defense of post-impressionism is not available to anyone wishing to defend and explain something like *Placid Civic Monument*. Fry's critical maneuvering took place within a context of aesthetic concerns; he was concerned with the aesthetic properties of visual art and our perception of those properties. The notion of an aesthetic property is vague enough, but fortunately not hopelessly so. I am convinced that a theoretical definition of the aesthetic is out of the question and have no desire even to offer any general characterization of it short of a definition; it is enough for our purposes to have a catalogue of illustrative examples. Under the heading of aesthetic qualities we can include such things as design and composition, space, line, mass, color, and subject matter in the visual arts; plot structure, character development, rhyme scheme, imagery, and metaphor in literature; melody, harmony, and tonality in music, and so on. These are all the things that I earlier referred to as the particulars of the various art forms and that Mandelbaum would doubtless include among the exhibited properties of art. There are also other properties that can be called aesthetic that one may hesitate to describe as 'directly exhibited'; I am thinking of properties that are the result of certain relations between works of art such as style, allusion, pastiche, and parody. Exactly where the line is drawn between the aesthetic and the non-aesthetic properties of art is of no great matter for the present issue. Be that as it may, Fry can be understood as advising the British public, in effect, to pay more attention to certain of those properties – the formal ones – and less attention to certain others – the ones having to do with subject matter. An influential strain within the conceptual art movement to which Oldenburg's *Monument* belongs, by contrast, has declared the entire range of the aesthetic to be irrelevant, a declaration manifested in the critical slogans of the seventies that spoke of the 'dematerialization' of the art object and of the 'deaestheticization' of art.

The conceptual art of the latter sixties and the early seventies was a rather diffuse movement about which it may be dangerous to generalize. It is regarded by many as the spiritual descendant of Marcel Duchamp and his readymades. Ted Cohen had criticized Dickie's institutional definition of a work of art as a candidate for appreciation by offering the example of Duchamp's notorious *Fountain* as a work of art that cannot be appreciated.[8] Dickie responded to this with the counter-contention that *Fountain* does indeed have many qualities that can be appreciated, 'its gleaming white surface',[9] for example. Dickie is quite right about this and Cohen is, I think, mistaken. Like almost any other object in the world the utensil has some aesthetic character although the thing is by no means a triumph of industrial design. The dispute, however, is altogether beside the point as it bears on the status of *Fountain* as art. In a conversation in 1967 Duchamp said of his readymades that:

> I had to be careful to avoid the 'look' [of being art]. It's very difficult to choose an object, because after two weeks you either

love it or hate it. You have to become so indifferent that you have no aesthetic feeling. The choice of Readymades is always founded on visual indifference and a total lack of good or bad taste.[10]

Can we take Duchamp as a reliable guide to his own work? Perhaps we are not justified in doing so, but whether we are or not, the important thing for our present concern is the persistence of the belief that art can be disconnected from all consideration of aesthetics.

In recent years at least two reasons have been offered for this radical distinction between art and aesthetics. One is a professed surfeit of objects. Douglas Huebler expressed this when he said that 'The world is full of objects, more or less interesting; I do not wish to add any more.'[11] Something more like an argument was presented by Joseph Kossuth when he said that 'It is necessary to separate aesthetics from art because aesthetics deal with opinions on perception of the world in general.'[12] If there is an argument in this, it is that since other things have aesthetic character in addition to works of art, aesthetic character has nothing to do with art. The argument as it stands is a transparent *non sequitur* and only points out the truism that aesthetics is a wider notion than art; i.e. having aesthetic character cannot be a sufficient condition for art; it shows neither that aesthetics is unnecessary to art nor that it is irrelevant to art.

Virtually all description and discussion of art has traditionally been carried on in terms of the aesthetic properties of art. It is the repudiation of aesthetic character as irrelevant to art that is largely responsible for generating the puzzlement of our plain gentleman. This repudiation, in effect, deprives him of his artistic vocabulary and puts him quite literally at a loss for words for he has been deprived of the entire set of concepts in terms of which he knows how to talk about and understand art. And this allows us to see very clearly how the pattern manifested in Roger Fry's defense and justification of post-impressionism can have no application in the task of educating the public to the appreciation of conceptual art since Fry was concerned to demonstrate *aesthetic* connections between the new and the old. It is also worth noting in passing that if readymades and conceptual art are indeed to be recognized as genuine art forms, then they are counter-examples to Dickie's institutional theory. Dickie's definition describes a work of art as something offered for appreciation, but it is clear from his discussion that the appreciation Dickie refers to is the appreciation of the aesthetic character of things and where aesthetic character has been repudiated there is no room for its appreciation. The institutional theory cannot comprehend conceptual art.

There are four themes that run through much of the thinking and writing of conceptual artists and their critic touts that it is important to call attention to. The first of these is the rejection of the aesthetic that we have been discussing. Having disconnected aesthetics from art as beside the point, conceptual art claims that the important thing is, instead of objects and the looks of objects, i.e. their aesthetic character, the concept of the idea behind it all. The word 'concept' however, seems to be used in more than one way in the writings of those that think of themselves as conceptual artists. Sometimes the word is used to suggest that the work of art is itself a 'concept', some kind of imaginary, hypothetical, or theoretical object such as Barry's 'All the things I know...' rather than anything tangible hanging on the wall or standing on a pedestal. Kosuth seems to have had this sense of concept in mind when he exhibited a series of photostats of the dictionary definition of water for he explained what he was about with the statement 'I was interested in just representing the *idea* of water.'[13] Kosuth's remark suggests that he believes that there is something called 'the idea of water' that can be identified and thought about in independence of any context in which either the word 'idea' or 'water' may have a use. We may be tempted to ponder the merits of, say, a new 'idea for conserving water', but I can only assume the artist would disclaim any interest in that on the grounds that he wants to entertain only the idea of water *simpliciter*. Needless to add, we are still owed an account of what that might be.

Kosuth, however, also has another view of the matter in which he understands the notion of the artist's concepts to refer to his intentions. Speaking of the work of Donald Judd, he says

One could say that if one of Judd's box forms was seen filled with debris, seen placed in an industrial setting, or even merely sitting on a street corner, it would not be identified as art. It follows then that understanding and consideration of it as an artwork is necessary a priori to viewing it in order to 'see' it as a work of art. Advance information about the concept of art and about the artist's concept is necessary to the appreciation and understanding of contemporary art.[14]

It is by no means clear, I should point out, how it follows that the key to identifying it as art is information about the artist's concepts, that is, intentions. But setting that difficulty aside, according to him it is the intention that makes something a work of art and not the nature of the object itself, if, indeed, there is an object at all. Kosuth is thus led to conclude that the only value in, say, a cubist painting is the idea of cubism and not the painting itself. He likens such a painting in a museum to Lindbergh's *Spirit of St Louis* in the Smithsonian Museum; it is now no more than an historical curiosity.

For all the importance conceptual art attaches to concepts, ideas, and intentions the literature of the movement is singularly lacking in descriptions of conceptual artists' intentions and, furthermore, from the way these intentions are talked about one suspects that conceptual art is confused about the very idea of an intention. If this latter contention is true, it may explain why so few details are forthcoming about particular intentions. An investigation of this will help us see the issues in a clearer light.

The notion of an intention belongs to a family of notions that include such things as plans, designs, projects, schemes, purposes, and motives. It is not necessary at this stage in the discussion to pause to sort out the many differences in import and implication of these words, that, for example, 'motive' often suggests something ulterior and 'scheme' something untoward. What I do want to insist upon as central is that the description of an intention is one with the description of the thing intended. The intention, the concept, the plan behind the *Spirit of St Louis*, conceived by Lindbergh and the engineers at Ryan, was to build an aircraft capable of flying the Atlantic and 'aircraft capable of flying the Atlantic' is a description eminently true of the *Spirit of St Louis*. Likewise, the intention of the cubist artist was doubtless to represent the girl and the mandolin as a series of interestingly interrelated planes and that is just what the painting is.

Conceptual artists have written as if it were possible to 'dematerialize' and hence 'deaestheticize' art by skimming off the work of art itself and leaving the intention behind, performing, as it were, a Cheshire cat kind of operation. Skimming off the cat to leave the grin behind is a transparent piece of nonsense and the idea of an intention essentially disconnected from the deed intended is also a piece of nonsense although not quite so transparent. An intention is an intention to do something and our understanding of intentions is logically linked to our understanding of carrying them out. This is shown in the fact that the only way to describe an intention is by means of the description of the thing intended. To be sure, many intentions, especially good ones, are never carried out and for a variety of reasons are frustrated or abortive and it is this that doubtless contributes to the belief that the conceptual distance between intention and execution is greater than it in fact is. Many plans and projects are never executed; indeed, many plans were never intended to be executed. We think of the projects assigned to architectural students as school exercises and proposals for various works that are no more than flights of fancy. We must remember, however, that our understanding of these unachieved proposals, plans, and projects is really parasitic upon our understanding of the standard case of the carried-out intention. In all these other instances there is a reason the project was not actually undertaken, e.g. there was no money, it was badly conceived, the selection committee didn't like it, it was only a schooling exercise for those who will later carry their designs to completion, and so on. What conceptual art is asking us to entertain, by contrast, is the idea of an intention that is essentially severed from any execution. To speak of an intention whose nature it is never to be acted upon can only be incoherent.[15]

There is an additional difficulty. Kosuth says that the only value in a cubist painting is the idea of cubism. But what is that idea? It is, no doubt, the idea to use paint in a certain way, to represent objects as interrelated planes, to construct just these color combinations, in a word, to paint in the fashion that we know as cubism. Kosuth's notion of a concept or intention thus trades upon our previous familiarity with artistic intentions. Traditionally artistic intentions have all been *aesthetic* intentions where the modifier 'aesthetic' goes proxy for all those properties and relations I have been calling the particulars of the various art forms. If we are to take the proposal to deaestheticize art seriously, we must be prepared to understand the concept of an artistic intention that is not an aesthetic intention and I must confess to being at a loss to know what such an intention might be.

Kosuth may well be correct in pointing out that Lindbergh's plane is now merely an historic curiosity and important only for its concept. That is to say, we would not use it now, even if it were in flying condition, for transatlantic travel; the thing is obsolete and the job it was designed to do is done much better by the jets although we cannot deny its pioneering influence and its importance as a portent of things to come. The assimilation of our understanding and appreciation of art to that of technological development is the saddening part of all of this. It is almost as if Kosuth had reverted to Vasari's picture of art history that represented Giotto, as a primitive Titian (the *Spirit of St Louis* as a primitive 747, cubism as primitive conceptual art) or perhaps Kosuth was so engrossed in his own preoccupations that he was unable to admit the value in anything that did not have a direct influence on his own work. The attitudes manifested by Kosuth are perfectly possible ones; there is nothing incoherent or logically awry in taking such a stance toward cubism or any other movement or particular work of art; in this respect it is not like the idea of a concept or intention just discussed. This stance is not something to be deplored. It is simply too bad that there are people who cannot enjoy and appreciate a work of art in the way that so many of us do.

The third feature of conceptual art to be noted is the idea that something can be declared a work of art. This idea seems to have had its beginnings with Duchamp and his ready-mades. Duchamp took ordinary objects, a bottle rack, snow shovel, a urinal and entered them in exhibitions declaring them to be works of art. The conceptual artists are fond of repeating the slogan that art is whatever an artist says is art or is whatever is presented in an art 'ambience', a museum, studio, or theater. This aspect of conceptual art is obviously consonant with that part of Dickie's institutional theory that speaks of conferring status on things on behalf of the artworld. I would assume that Duchamp's entering of *Fountain* in the exhibition was a paradigm case of status conferral.

Some perspective can perhaps be gotten on this aspect of conceptual art by means of a parable. In his *Memoir* of Wittgenstein Malcolm tells how Wittgenstein and he took frequent long walks that usually involved intense and exhausting discussion, although on occasion Wittgenstein could display a playful countenance. On one of these occasions he 'gave' Malcolm each tree that they passed with the reservation that Malcolm was not to cut it down or do anything with it, or prevent the previous owners from doing anything with it, but with these reservations it was henceforth Malcolm's. Wittgenstein is, of course, offering a gentle conceptual joke. It is the kind of joke that consists in uttering an expression solemnly just as if it had a job to do except that it is uttered in the absence of all the usual conditions of application or in such a way that those conditions are effectively stripped away. In the hands of someone like Wittgenstein, however, we are not left simply with the absurdity of an utterance hopelessly out of place, for the joke also serves as a reminder of what the role of the expression really is. One does not make a gift simply by saying 'This is yours' or in circumstances where all rights of ownership were set aside.

The application of the parable should be obvious. A work of art is not created simply by designating anything whatever while saying 'This is my work of art'. We may be tempted to conclude on the basis of this that much of conceptual art is an extended conceptual joke, but I think it would be a mistake to suppose this is how it is intended. There was more than plenty of the jokester in Duchamp as his fascination with puns, if nothing else, makes clear. It has been suggested that his *Fountain* be understood as a gesture – of cocking a snook at an overly pompous establishment of galleries, critics, and juries, I suppose – but such a gesture is at best a one-off exercise that doesn't wear well with repetition. Nor are his puns essentially conceptual; 'LHOOQ' is clever, but merely irreverant and doesn't direct attention to the logic of anything. The writing of recent conceptual artists gives no hint that they understand themselves as making jokes; the almost comic serious-ness with which they pursue, unsyntactically, lame conclusions belies that possibility.

From another point of view, however, we can understand this facet of recent activity by analogy with Wittgenstein giving trees to Malcolm. This performative side of the business can be taken as an unwitting conceptual joke that serves to remind us who look at it all from the outside what art really is, or at least where that part of the landscape is in which it is to be found, by calling attention to what it is not and in this light much of the conceptual art movement thus appears as an intellectual confusion unintentionally engaged in showing itself up for what it is.

Notes

1 *The Shock of the New* (New York, St Louis, San Francisco: American Heritage Press, 1972).

2 See Dunlop's chapter on the post-impressionists; Virginia Woolf, *Roger Fry: A Biography* (London: Hogarth Press, 1940); and Frances Spaulding, *Roger Fry: Art and Life* (Berkeley and Los Angeles: University of California Press, 1980).

3 'The Grafton Gallery – I', *The Nation* (London, Nov. 19, 1910), pp.31ff.

4 'Shop Talk', in Elizabeth Gilmore Holt, *From the Classicists to the Impressionists* vol. III of *A Documentary History of Art* (Garden City NJ: Doubleday, 1966), p.404.

5 'Kafka and his Precursors', in his *Other Inquisitions* (Austin: University of Texas Press, 1964), p.108.

6 'The Role of Theory in Aesthetics', p.35.

7   Barbara Haskell, *Claes Oldenburg: Object into Monument* (Pasadena, Calif.: Pasadena Art Museum, 1971), p.62.

8   'The Possibility of Art: Remarks on a Proposal by Dickie', *The Philosophical Review*, 82, (1973), p.78.

9   *Art and the Aesthetic: An Institutional Analysis* (Ithaca and London: Cornell University Press, 1974), p.42.

10   Pierre Cabanne, *The Brothers Duchamp* (Boston: New York Graphic Society, 1976), p.141.

11   Quoted by Lucy R. Lippard, *Six Years: The Dematerialization of the Art Object from 1966 to 1972* (New York and Washington: Praeger Publishers, 1973), p.74.

12   'Art after Philosophy', *Studio International* 178 (Nov. 1969), p.134.

13   Arthur Rose, 'Four Interviews with Barry, Huebler, Kosuth, and Weiner', *Arts Magazine* (Feb. 1968), p.23.

14   'Art after Philosophy', p.137.

15   Lawrence Weiner appended the following to the description of a number of his 'works': '1. The artist may construct the piece. 2. The piece may not be fabricated. 3. The piece need not be built.' He later added 'As to construction, please remember...there is no correct way to construct the piece as there is no incorrect way to construct it.' (Quoted by Lucy R. Lippard, *Six Years*, pp.73–4).

PART THREE CRITICISM AND INTERPRETATION

Deciding about art

Timothy Binkley (b.1943)

*According to the institutional theory, works acquire aesthetic value
when a member of the artworld designates them as worthy of
appreciation. Timothy Binkley, while in general agreement with the
theory, wants a more precise requirement: that the member of the
artworld in question should be the artist. It is the artist's intention
that counts in this variant of the institutional theory. Where Dickie
speaks of aesthetic status being conferred on a work, Binkley speaks
of it being created by a decision on the part of the artist. All that is
required to create a work of art is for the artist to specify what the
artwork is: this is what Binkley calls 'piece-specification', and he feels
it is less open to abuse than Dickie's 'status-conferral' procedure. It
could be objected that all Binkley has done is to be more precise
about who is allowed to make arbitrary decisions as to what counts
as an object of aesthetic value.*

1   Is it art?

2   For example, Lucy Lippard recently put together a show of
women conceptual artists. It was called 'c. 7500' and I saw it at the
Moore College of Art in Philadelphia. Photographs, statements,
various documents decorated the walls of the gallery; a number of
pieces in binders commanded two tables. Upon arriving at the first
table I picked up the most eyecatching piece, bound in synthetic
grass and filled with words in numbered squares. The other pieces
were more modestly bound, though their contents were no less
interesting. While going through the table pieces I came upon a
small brown spiral notebook. Most of its pages were empty, though
some here and there had statements or poems or fragments thereof
written on them. Some loose sheets had been torn out, folded, and
slipped back in between the pages. Eventually I turned to the front
page which was filled with words in blue ink. In bold red letters at
the top was the statement 'NOT PART OF THE EXHIBITION'.

3   My first reaction was to drop the notebook and look about

sheepishly to see if anyone witnessed my blunder. But I began to wonder. I had reacted too quickly. The simple fact that someone wrote in the book a statement denying its membership in the show did not prove it was not part of the show. (Remember, this is conceptual art. Why not?) So I found myself in a quandary: Is the notebook part of the show or isn't it? I scrutinized the table.

(a)   All the other pieces lying there had substantial bindings and most of them had their pages protected against human fingers by sturdy plastic coverings. The spiral notebook looked naked and vulnerable by comparison. It was not decked out for travelling. (The show travelled.)

(b)   Several tags, each bearing the name of an artist and a work, were mounted on the wall next to the table. There were more pieces than tags and no tag supported the brown spiral.

(c)   An empty cigarette pack relaxed among the busy binders. Surely the notebook, like the cigarette pack, was a joke or perhaps an expression of contempt. I pictured three or four people in the gallery playing the game of who could make the best laugh or the worst insult.

(d)   The other binders on the table had some organization to their contents. The spiral seemed unstructured and uninteresting. Too unsophisticated. A botched job... Yet why shouldn't this be the finishing touch on a piece intended to appear spurious?

4.   At last I put my insecurity to a somewhat fitful rest. I didn't think the brown spiral was part of the show, and the evidence I had pointed in that direction. But there was still sufficient room between my inclination and certainty for the brown spiral to squeeze through and claim the status of *bona fide* member of the show. A change in perspective could reverse the weight of the evidence.

A few days later I returned to the gallery, hoping to find the object of my distress gone. It was still there.

By chance I later met the director of the gallery who assured me that the notebook was not part of the show. That clinched it. She should know. 'Not part of the exhibition.'

5   Now the lurking ponderous question. Is the brown spiral notebook art?

Had the thing turned out to be part of the show, there would be no difficulty assigning it the status of art object (or at least artwork). But what now? Would something have to *make* it art? Would Lucy Lippard have to see it and like it enough to keep it in the show or at least write about it? Would someone have to grant the notebook its art credentials in an official forum in order to save it from being nothing but a little joke among a handful of people who saw the show in Philadelphia? Yet why couldn't the brown spiral be art just as it stands? Perhaps it is an artwork witnessed by only a few persons. Why can't a joke about art be art? Marcel Duchamp did it years ago; why shouldn't anonymous do it today? Duchamp's urinal called 'Fountain' was submitted and suppressed; the brown spiral seized its place without prior consent. Does forcible entry cancel art status?

These questions are not settled as easily and as tidily as the first. There is no easy appeal to authority. Especially if the person who authored the book demurs in the absence of philosophical proclivities.

6   It did not occur to me to wonder whether the piece bound in synthetic grass is an artwork.

<h1 style="text-align:center">I</h1>

1   The perplexed decider wants relief. Perhaps a dashing definition of art will come to the rescue. Scenario: The decider's distress is relieved in short order by seeing whether the resistant object meets the demands of the definition. If it fits, it's art; if not, no.

Even if a definition does not settle the issue, it could be helpful nonetheless. It would formulate a set of essential features of art by means of which questionable entities could be compared with unquestionable art and unquestionable non-art. The status of the problematic item would be elucidated if not decisively fixed.

Unfortunately, reliance upon definition does not appear to be a viable alternative. Consider the following argument.

2   Art cannot be defined. This proposition is demonstrated by explaining how to construct a counter-example to any particular definition of art. A formula will be given for producing artworks which stand as counter-examples to specific definitions of art claiming to distinguish art from what is not art. Any proposed definition is disproved by being subjected to the formula.

Before presenting the formula, it would be useful first to mention the Readymade tradition, which gives some rationale for the workings of the formula. Duchamp took several common objects (a shovel, a typewriter cover, a hatrack) and simply converted them unchanged into artworks. These pieces he called Readymades. One thing Duchamp demonstrated with these artworks is that in order to 'create' a work of art it is necessary only to *specify* what the artwork is. An artist may specify as a piece an object he has designed, but that is not a *sine qua non* of arthood. In establishing this fact, Duchamp severed aesthetics from art. Aesthetics presupposes that to create an artwork is to bring into being aesthetic qualities, such as beauty and expressiveness, which are aspects of the appearance of an object or an event.[1] These qualities are found in the look of a painting, the sound of a sonata, etc., and they do secure one way of specifying an artwork. But it is not the only way. Anything can be art if it is indexed or catalogued as art. All one need do is make clear what he intends the piece to be. Artists since Duchamp have revelled in this realization.

The notions of specifying and indexing which have been introduced here need further discussion, and they will be examined later on. Let us return to the argument under way.

The formula. The formula gives instructions for making a piece, Pi, with reference to a definition of art, Di. So let Di be any definition of art. Appeal to a defender of Di to exhibit an example of something which, according to the definition, is not art. If no defender can be found, a volunteer may select an example of non-art using the definition. If no volunteer can be found, you may do it yourself. The piece, Pi, will consist of this example of non-art.

The formula has roughly three steps for arriving at the artwork Pi. (1) Secure a definition of art, Di; (2) Find an example, Ei, of non-art on the basis of criteria articulated by Di; (3) The piece, Pi, is specified to be the example, Ei: $Pi = Ei$.

Although the 'creative act' is signalized and accomplished by the declaration '$Pi = Ei$,' any 'creativity' in the piece results from the groundwork for (3) constructed in (1) and (2). It is also worth noting for future reference that (3) does not involve taking something which is not art and christening it art. I am an artist. I want to make a piece. I avail myself of the formula. (3) says not 'Ei is a work of art,' or 'I hereby declare Ei a work of art.' (3) says the piece I am now making is Ei. Not *a* piece, *the* piece. The question of the art status of Ei need not explicitly arise. I am going to make a piece, Pi. The question '*Is* Pi a work of art?' does not arise in the course of applying the formula. The question is '*What* is the piece, the artwork?', and the answer is supplied by (3), which finalizes the creation of the work of art Pi.

Consider a specific example of how the formula is used. I shall demonstrate that Susanne Langer's proposed definition of art does not define art. This I will do by making a piece (of art) which will be called 'P-One,' and which will both (a) be an artwork and (b) not conform to Langer's definition. I begin with Langer's definition: art is significant form, by which she means form isomorphic to human feeling.[2] Now, according to this definition, the number one seems not to be artwork since it has no form isomorphic to human feeling. So I specify my piece, 'P-One,' to be the number one. It is an artwork which is not judged to be an artwork by Langer's definition. Reservations about whether 'P-One' is indeed a work of art will be addressed shortly.

As if to assure ourselves that the counter-example to the definition, Di, is not just an anomaly, the formula may be used to construct a matrix of pieces, Pij, where 'i' indexes the definition and 'j' the number of times the formula has been applied to the definition. Then we've got indefinitely many counter-examples to indefinitely many definitions of art. There could even be indefinitely many matrices, if one is so inclined. The matrix could be 'performed,' each performance yielding a different array of artworks.

The only circumstance under which this argument against definition fails is where no examples of non-art can be found, i.e. where Di defines everything, including the null set, to be art.

3   Many questions arise. It might be useful to point out the relative unimportance of some misgivings. The fact that we have a formula and not actual pieces need create no special problems. The pieces could be executed (or whatever the word should be – created, specified, made...) and stand witness against the definitions. I do not pretend to know in general what it would take for such pieces to be executed successfully, but I suspect that if they were done by a recognized artist, for example, only those who balk at this kind of art in general would feel they were being served tripe for art. (The rest of us know that tripe can be art too.) One cannot describe generally what would have to happen before the items in the matrix became actual artworks, but I can suggest several specific methods of execution which have been used by artists and which would undoubtedly meet with success in creating artworks. One method would be to publish the pieces somewhere (in the classified section of a newspaper, in an art journal, in a book...). One could explain the pieces, specify the definitions, and list the examples of non-art which constitute the Pij, the elements of the matrix. Another method would be to convince the director of a gallery to allow space and time for the documentation of the pieces. Pictures or descriptions of each piece could be mounted on the gallery walls, along with an explanation of the project. The fact that the artworks would have to be supported by some linguistic act does not distinguish them from a great deal of recent art.[3] Either of these two methods, I claim, would be sufficient to establish the proposed

pieces as actual works of art, because these methods have already been employed successfully by artists.[4] I could even go so far as to execute a matrix of pieces in this paper, but I won't go that far. What it would take to make such a matrix an artistic success, or even noticed, I will not attempt to say. Such things are difficult to explain even for traditional art.

4   Next a somewhat harder question whose answer has already been suggested. Are the pieces so proposed *really* art? The only response I can muster is that they certainly are, or could be when executed, if much of what currently passes as art is art indeed. I am thinking, for example, of a piece by Robert Barry: 'All the things I know but of which I am not at the moment thinking – 1:36 P.M.; 15 June 1969, New York.'[5] If this and similar 'Conceptual' pieces are art, there is no reason why the proposed counter-definition pieces cannot be art. The only potential impediment is that they are created with an ulterior philosophical motive. But it would be simple enough to imagine them occurring in a more artistic context and serving a more artistic purpose, insofar as artistic and philosophical aims can be distinguished.

The only question left concerning the artistic status of the pieces in the matrix is whether Conceptual pieces such as Barry's are art. And I don't know what to say except that they are made (created, realized, or whatever) by people considered artists, they are treated by critics as art, they are talked about in books and journals having to do with art, they are exhibited in or otherwise connected with art galleries, and so on. Conceptual art, like all art, is situated within a cultural tradition out of which it has developed. Transitions from one kind of art to another are sometimes smooth and sometimes rough. But conceptual art, like any other radical development in art, has not simply appeared out of nowhere. It is within a long artistic tradition that this type of art has been accepted as art. The same critics who write about Picasso and Manet write about Duchamp and Barry. The same journals that publish articles about Abstract Expressionism publish articles about Conceptualism. The same people who made Pollock's drips and splashes objects of derision scoff at Barry's acts of specification.

It does not appear that one can deny the proposed pieces Pij the status of art unless a convincing argument is offered discounting the *prima facie* evidence for accepting Conceptual art as art. No such argument has been forthcoming. When we philosophize about art we initially decide what to talk about by looking to artists, critics, and audiences, just as in the philosophy of science we initially decide what to study by looking to scientists, or in the philosophy of law we determine what to study by examining the actual practice of law. Needless to say, we can reserve the right to reject some purported art or science or law at a later time, but rarely find the need to exercise this right.

II

1   So art cannot be defined. This conclusion is nothing new, I hear you cry. There is a familiar and much touted argument against the definability of art. Presuming to follow in the footsteps of Wittgenstein, Morris Weitz asserts that those things we call 'art', like those things we call 'games', do not exhibit some set of common properties by virtue of which they are called art (or games), but rather share a complicated network of 'family resemblances' which ties them together under the single concept. 'Art' according to Weitz, is an 'open concept':

> A concept is open if its conditions of application are emendable and corrigible; i.e., if a situation or case can be imagined or secured which would call for some sort of DECISION on our part to extend the use of the concept to cover this, or to close the concept and invent a new one to deal with the new case and its new property. If necessary and sufficient conditions for the application of a concept can be stated, the concept is a closed one.[6]

Weitz argues that 'art' does not fall into the latter category.

> 'Art'... is an open concept. New conditions (cases) have constantly arisen and will undoubtedly constantly arise; new art forms, new movements will emerge, which will demand decisions on the part of those interested, usually professional critics, as to whether the concept should be extended or not.[7]

In the first place, Weitz's claim turns out to say surprisingly little since he believes only the concepts of logic and mathematics are closed. The indefinability of art is the indefinability of almost every concept we use. By contrast, the indefinability argued above is unique to the concept 'art.' To appreciate this fact, it will be useful to explore several shortcomings in Weitz's account.

2   In the world of art, we are told, just as in the world of games, there are continually new items presented to us which are like old

art or old games in some respects, but unlike them in others, so that we need decide whether to include them within the concept – whether to 'extend' the concept.[8] I think this makes the situation with respect to art look far too tidy. It fails to capture the unique way in which art is indefinable. The concept 'art' is not just open, along with most other concepts; it is radically open, radically indefinable.

To see what I mean by calling art a 'radically open' concept, consider what effect the anti-definition argument has on Weitz's portrayal of 'art' as a family resemblance concept. Alluding to Wittgenstein's development of the notion of family resemblances in discussing the concept 'game' Weitz says

> The problem of the nature of art is like that of the nature of games, at least in these respects: If we actually look and see what it is that we call 'art', we will also find no common properties – only strands of similarities. Knowing what art is is not apprehending some manifest or latent essence but being able to recognize, describe, and explain those things we call 'art' in virtue of these similarities.[9]

In other words, art is a family; no one property adheres to all art objects; they are related through a network of similarities or family resemblances.

The anti-definition argument defeats the family resemblance account of art as perfunctorily as it defeats a definition proposing necessary and sufficient conditions. Presumably the family resemblances structuring the concept of art act in some way to discriminate clear cases of non-art: some entities will conspicuously fail to be members of the art family. Suppose one of these entities is Ei. My piece will be Ei. Q.E.D. Family resemblances have no more power than necessary conditions to distinguish art from what is not. The artist in the house has license to lodge any vagabond or renegade he takes a liking to. This is because properties of objects are fundamentally irrelevant to art status, a point which might be made by saying that arthood is a relation, not a property. To be an artwork is not to share by identity or consanguinity properties which delineate 'art,' but to be catalogued as an artwork, a piece. The family resemblance approach to art falters at the same step which brings down definitions: both make the fundamental error of aesthetics, which is to suppose that arthood is a function of (aesthetic) properties of objects. Family resemblances are at best a heuristic for discerning arthood.

3   Compare art with games. Weitz would say that cases arise in which we find ourselves having to make a decision about whether the concept 'game' ought to cover new and different items. He says the same about art: 'New conditions (cases) have constantly arisen and will undoubtedly constantly arise.' This is probably an accurate description of the status of the concept 'game' but the function of Weitz's 'undoubtedly' is far too weak for 'art.' What makes art different is that cases do not simply *arise* which force us to shuffle about trying to update our system of concepts. The artist is free consciously to create a work – an *art*work – which calls into question or flagrantly violates some salient feature of the concept 'art' as it stood prior to the creation of the work. If art can be conceptual, the concept 'art' is grist for its mill. The history of recent art is the pyrotechnic pageant of one after another familiar feature of art being purposely called into question and deleted or exalted in the creation of works of art. The radical openness of the concept 'art' is the artist's freedom to discuss and challenge the concept itself in his artworks.

Whether a strange new activity should be included under the concept 'game' is probably decided, as Weitz says, by comparing it with what currently falls under the concept and searching for relevant similarities, or family resemblances. Not so with art. One reason for art's imperviousness has already been noted: similarities among objects are at best a tenuous guide to arthood. A reproduction of the *Mona Lisa* looks more like 'art' than Duchamp's urinal, but the former is not an artwork, while the latter is. Here is where any aesthetic approach to art founders. Aesthetics is a study of aesthetic qualities, and aesthetic qualities are neither a necessary nor a sufficient condition of arthood. Aesthetic qualities can be ascertained in things which are not works of art. They underlie the pursuit of Beauty in both art and nature, and hence establish no guarantee of the presence of arthood. They are not sufficient proof of art status. Neither are they necessary, as Duchamp has demonstrated with the Readymade. When he removed an ordinary snow shovel from the hardware store and titled it 'In Advance of the Broken Arm,' no aesthetic qualities were changed. The work of art and the work of industry preceding it have identical aesthetic qualities which have nothing to do with the emergence of art. Furthermore, some works of art, such as the Barry piece mentioned above, lack aesthetic qualities altogether because they fall outside the category of things which *can* have aesthetic qualities.

Weitz's family resemblance account of art is also flawed by its emphasis upon decision. By the time an artist proffers something as an artwork, the decision about its art status has already been made. The artist says 'Here is an artwork,' not 'Here is something bizarre; tell me if it's art.' Sometimes a type of decision is called for; witness the brown spiral notebook. Yet the reason it is hard to say whether the notebook is a work of art is that it is unclear what the intentions of its author(s) were regarding art status, making it difficult for us to 'read' the piece. Ultimately the power to decide about arthood rarely rests with the audience. The concept 'art' changes because it is changed by artists, and not by professional critics as Weitz would have it. Although not without power, critics are frequently just as overwhelmed by the onslaught of art as the rest of us. It is not as though we find the meticulous need to fit our concepts to intriguing and original data which keep surfacing.

It might now appear as though the responsibility for arthood has devolved upon the artist *qua* artist, but anyone can be an artist, even in his spare time. What is crucial is the act of specifying a piece, and the artist is simply the specifier. Success at specifying is not a question of whether you're an artist, but rather of whether you know and can use existing specifying conventions, or else can establish new ones.

4. The radical openness of the concept 'art' made possible the argument against definability presented in Part I. No similar argument could be constructed to prove the indefinability of 'game'. There is nothing about games, nothing about making up and playing games, which demands that the concept be open. The concept 'game' could be applied to a more restricted set of things and defined with necessary and sufficient conditions without thereby seriously affecting our ability to do what we now do with the concept. A slight change in boundaries and the invention of a few new terms would be necessary. The only reason the concept is open is that it takes in too wide a variety of things in order for there to be a single feature found in them all. This is undoubtedly true of art too, but it does not tell us anything about the unique indefinability of 'art.' What makes 'art' different is that it is centrally involved with the creation of new instances of the concept, while it is possible that no new games be invented in the future without seriously harming the concept 'game.' In other words, unlike 'game,' there is something about 'art' which makes it *really* an open concept. This is what I am calling radical openness. It is not a matter of the concept taking in too wide a range of things for necessary and

sufficient conditions to be produced, but rather a matter of the concept including the feature that what falls under it has the freedom to question and expand it without prior permission from the prelate of concepts. Art determines what art is and we must see where it goes. Art, like philosophy, has the ability to be self-referential and self-critical, though the artist has an even freer hand than the philosopher in using his power.[10] If a DeKooning can be art, so can an erased DeKooning. And if an artist presented a DeKooning painting as an 'unerased DeKooning', the piece would be different from the painting 'unerased' to make the work. This underscores the elusiveness of 'art.' Artists are not bound by definitions of art. They have the license to violate them if only they have the ingenuity. Extending and changing the concept 'art' is the business of art today, and not merely the by-product of the creative genius of a few people.

5   Weitz worries that defining art (i.e. closing the concept) will stifle creativity. I think he has it reversed. Creativity stifles definition. And family resemblances as well.

III

1   There is a purported definition of art which seems to escape the clutches of the anti-definition argument given above. I am thinking of George Dickie's 'Institutional Definition', which goes as follows:

> A work of art... is (1) an artifact (2) a set of aspects of which has had conferred upon it the status of candidate for appreciation by some persons acting on behalf of a certain social institution (the artworld).[11]

Donald Judd has said, 'if someone calls it art, it's art',[12] and with this idea Dickie circumvents the logic of the anti-definition argument by characterizing art in terms of what seems to be the act required to transform the examples of non-art into art. In producing the matrix of pieces, something without art status is granted that status, thereby awarding it the essential feature of art for the Institutional Definition. Any definition relevantly similar to Dickie's is not defeated by the matrix of counter-definition pieces. However, the most crucial part of the Institutional Definition, the notion of status-conferral, proves inadequate. But first let us see why status-conferral is the most crucial part of the Definition.

2   The artifactuality requirement is probably the most suspicious

part of Dickie's definition. Consider the construction of the counter-definition matrix. Suppose a definer proposes as non-art the Black Forest and his grandmother's arthritis. Each of these things is transformed into art by the formula. According to Dickie, each becomes an artifact in the process. Henceforth we count the Black Forest and the definer's grandmother's arthritis as artifacts. Cristo could make an artifact by wrapping the Black Forest, but is christening enough? We could imagine the perplexed tourist standing before Yosemite Falls wondering whether he is feasting upon the wonders of nature or artifice – wondering not whether the Falls works by a hidden man-made mechanism, but simply whether some artist has made it into his piece yet. But then what happens to the concept of artifactuality? It becomes useless, and to no apparent purpose outside securing a place for an artifactuality requirement in a definition.

3   The next feature of the Institutional Definition which may give us cause to wonder is the concept of candidacy for appreciation. Dickie explains the meaning of the term 'appreciation' as follows: 'In experiencing the qualities of a thing one finds them worthy or valuable.'[13] Most art requests our 'appreciation'. Yet must this 'appreciation' be oriented toward the experience of valuable qualities? The experience of boredom while watching one of Andy Warhol's early films may be valuable in the absence of any experienced qualities which are found to be valuable. And then again, maybe the boredom lacks value altogether. There may be nothing of value in the *experience of qualities* of *Chelsea Girls* without the film thereby lacking both interest and importance as a work of art. In other words, an artist need not show his art with the implicit hope that someone will appreciate valuable qualities lodged in it. An artwork need not even be a *candidate* for appreciation, in Dickie's sense. If an artist has contempt for his audience and purposely tries to create art which frustrates attempts to experience valuable qualities, he may be immoral, but his ability to create art is unaffected.

Because of its initial orientation toward perception, aesthetics assumes that a certain kind of experience is essential to art. But can we *experience* the knowledge making up Robert Barry's piece? – how could we experience what he knows but is not thinking about at a particular moment? Do we need to experience any of the counter-definition pieces in order for them to be approached properly as works of art? I think not. Some experience is required in order to find out what the pieces are; but for a great deal of contemporary art experience is but a mode of access to the art, much as the experience of reading a calculus book is a mode of access to the mathematics. This non-experiential facet of art has been especially prominent since Duchamp. Whether the experience of the art is discomforting or pleasurable matters only secondarily, as it does in mathematics. If we grant that thinking is a kind of experience, then perhaps experience is essential to all art, just as it is to all mathematics. This would be an admission of the failure of aesthetics to cope with art, however, since such experience is not an ingredient of art, but merely a handle on it.

4   Having the status of candidate for appreciation does not appear to be a necessary condition for being a work of art. Neither is it sufficient, even if joined with the artifactuality stipulation. A brief biography of an artist mounted on the gallery wall beside his works is (1) an artifact (2) a set of aspects of which has had conferred upon it the status of candidate for appreciation by some person or persons acting on behalf of the artworld. The director of the gallery is acting in his or her official capacity as a member of the artworld in 'exhibiting' the biographical sketch to be appreciated by visitors to the gallery. We appreciate knowing something about the person who made the art. But the biographical note is not a work of art. It is not indexed as a work of art, but rather as an item of interest.

Consider also the brown spiral notebook. There is a sense in which, here too, someone has acted on behalf of the artworld to confer the status of candidate for appreciation. But that doesn't settle the issue of arthood. We still have to ask, as we do of the biography, Is the thing intended for 'artistic consumption?' A biography hung on a gallery wall as a piece by a conceptual artist is a 'candidate for appreciation' perhaps, but it is also an artwork. What makes the difference between the artistic biography and the non-artistic one? What is the difference between treating the brown spiral as art and treating it as nothing but a joke or an insult?

One way out of the problem would be to introduce a distinction between artistic appreciation and other kinds of appreciation. As suggested already, this would be an arduous, if possible, chore since no obvious distinction volunteers itself. There is no conspicuous type of 'appreciation' common to the *Mona Lisa*, Duchamp's *Fountain*, and Barry's piece, but absent from all non-art. Traditionally, a uniquely *aesthetic* (perceptual) appreciation was thought to mark the difference. Dickie denies that a special aesthetic experience exists.[14] I am inclined to say that even if it does exist, it is not something which pertains only to art objects. Here we confront the old problem of separating aesthetic experiences of nature from aesthetic experiences of art. The impediment to discovering any difference is that aesthetics is fundamentally about the perception of aesthetic qualities, not about art, and hence is not equipped with resources for characterizing specifically artistic endeavors.

5   What is left of the Institutional Definition once we excise reference to artifactuality and appreciation?

> A work of art is something upon which some person or persons acting on behalf of a certain social institution (the artworld) has conferred the status of work of art.

As it stands now, this refined form of the Definition is circular: an artwork is something granted the status of artwork. Dickie recognizes that his definition is circular, but argues that it is not viciously circular since the circle is mediated by his discussion of 'the historical, organizational, and functional intricacies of the artworld'.[15] The circle is indeed informative since it displays the material vacuity of the indexical concept 'artwork'. To be an artwork is like being thought about by someone; artworks share no common properties or even a network of similarities, but only a 'place' in the artworld. The question we must return to now is whether Dickie's notion of status conferral accurately designates how something achieves a place in the index of artworks.

6   In making the pieces Pij, I do not engage in an explicit act of conferral; rather I avail myself of a versatile convention for making artworks which is widely countenanced by artists today. This convention might be termed the 'Specification Rubric', and its general form is 'I hereby specify the piece (I am now making) to be ____,' where the blank can be filled in by a specification of anything whatever as the piece. Methods of specification are varied, but they all are used to 'create' and identify specific pieces. The Rubric established a piece-making or piece-specifying convention, and not a status-conferring convention. The difference can be seen in the number of distinct actions required to achieve conferral and specification. A conferral happens in two stages. First, the item on which status is going to be conferred needs to be specified, then the actual conferral of status can take place. When art is created, however, a single act of specification appears sufficient for 'imparting arthood'. I hesitate at using the word 'impart', because the kind of specification involved in making art differs from that preceding the

act of conferral. Status conferral commences with the identification of a thing which does not yet have the status it will be given when the conferral takes place. For art, on the other hand, the specification does not usually isolate something which *will be granted arthood*; rather the specification isolates *the piece*. Art status is gratuitous. The question 'What is the piece?' and, once the piece is discerned, the question 'So what?' totally eclipses the question 'Is it art (yet)?'

Artworks are created, not by christening things to be art, but rather by specifying pieces. Arthood is not a property something can have without its being *a* piece, *an* artwork. One can make a piece without explicit conferral, but one cannot confer art status without explicitly making (specifying) a piece. Endowing something with a status is not enough; one must create by bringing a new piece into existence. The artist does not 'make this X into an artwork', he 'makes (creates) this artwork Y', where 'Y' tells what the piece is.

The weakness of the conferral model for arthood is shown in the way it singles out artworks extensionally. Consider Dickie's analogues for art-status conferral:

> My thesis is that, in a way analogous to the way in which a person is certified as qualified for office, or two persons acquire the status of common law marriage within a legal system, or a person is elected president of the Rotary, or a person acquires the status of wise man within a community, so an artifact can acquire the status of candidate for appreciation within the social system called 'the artworld'.[16]

In all of Dickie's examples, the conferral of status occurs within an extensional context. If Harry Haller is certified or elected, and if Harry Haller happens to be the loneliest man in the country, then it is true that the loneliest man in the country is certified or elected. Artworks, on the other hand, need to be designated intensionally. To see why, suppose that at 1:36 P.M. on the 15th June, 1969, Robert Barry was not thinking about anything he knows. Then the following two declarations made by Barry will be equivalent:

> (1) I hereby confer art status on everything I know but am not at the moment thinking – 1:36 P.M., 15 June 1969, New York.
> (2) I hereby confer art status on everything I know.

If Barry was, for example, daydreaming at the specified moment, (1) and (2) should establish the art status of the same entity and one merely duplicate the other. However, (2) cannot be used by Barry to create the piece discussed earlier. This is because 'Everything I know but am not at the moment thinking...' and 'Everything I know' specify two different *pieces*. The former piece contains reference to a specific moment in time, while the latter does not, and this could be a major artistic difference.

Moreover, two (or more) different pieces can be housed in the same extensional entity. Duchamp painted 'The King and Queen Surrounded by Swift Nudes' on the back of a canvas on which he had already painted 'Paradise'.[17] One artifact, two artworks. A conferral of status is not refined enough to take notice of the difference. This point could be taken a step further. Suppose Andy Warhol makes a piece he specifies to be 'All the things Robert Barry knows but was not thinking about at 1:36 P.M., 15 June 1969.' If arthood is a matter of conferral, Warhol cannot make his piece since Barry has pre-empted him. But Warhol can make his piece and it is different from Barry's. For one thing, it is Warhol's, not Barry's. For another, the two pieces were created at different times. Most important, the two works of art can hardly avoid having entirely different meanings. The interpretation of one will be read in the context of Barry's *oeuvre*, the interpretation of the other in the context of Warhol's.[18]

Dickie might attempt to take account of these problematic cases with appropriate reference to the 'set of aspects' mentioned in his definition. The role of this set of aspects is somewhat unclear in Dickie's argument. He says in his definition that the set of aspects has conferred on it the status of candidate for appreciation, but he frequently speaks as though it is the artifact itself which receives the conferral, as he does in the last passage quoted. Moreover, he seems to use 'conferral of arthood' and 'conferral of status of candidate for appreciation' interchangeably. In any event, Dickie would presumably try to differentiate the Warhol piece from the extensionally equivalent Barry piece by saying that different *sets of aspects* of the same entity (All the things Barry knows...) receive a conferred status, thereby allowing two works to have a common basis. The weakness of this gambit is that it would tend to violate Dickie's model of status-conferral. The sets of aspects singled out to differentiate the two artworks would have to refer in some way to the particular circumstances of the purported 'status-conferral'. In other words, the aspects which separate the Warhol and the

Barry works are determined in part by the fact that one was done by Barry and the other by Warhol. This means that *what* receives the conferred status would be identified through details of the individual acts of conferral. And then it begins to look as though we don't have a genuine conferral of status, but something else. Dickie's examples of conferral all forbid this type of peculiarity. At one point he likens art-making to christening. What or who is christened in no way depends upon the particulars of the christening act itself – upon whether, for example, the individual is christened by one person or another, or whether he is christened at one time or another. Moreover, once christened is enough. Persons are christened, not aspects of persons; a person cannot be christened again under some other aspect unless a different status is conferred. Christening has an extensional logic. In response to 'Who was christened?', any reply extensionally equivalent to a true response will fit. This is not true of questions such as, 'What is the artwork?' or 'What became an artwork?' Dickie's failure to note this distinction makes his theory incapable of explaining an important difference:

> Some may find it strange that in the nonart cases discussed, there are ways in which the conferring can go wrong, while that does not appear to be true in art. For example, an indictment might be improperly drawn up and the person charged would not actually be indicted, but nothing parallel seems possible in the case of art. This fact just reflects the differences between the artworld and legal institutions: the legal system deals with matters of grave personal consequences and its procedures must reflect this; the artworld deals with important matters also, but they are of a different sort entirely. The artworld does not require rigid procedures; it admits and even encourages frivolity and caprice without losing serious purpose.[19]

But once the difference between the status-conferral and piece-specification are clarified, the laxity of artworld conventions has a simple explanation. Status-conferral is a *changing* convention, piece-specification is a *creating* convention. The point of status-conferral is to award a new status to an antecedently identified entity. Thus the conventions of status-conferral articulate rules to be followed in order to affix the new status to the old entity. If the rules are not followed, the status does not adhere. The purpose of piece-specifying, on the other hand, is to create new entities – new pieces –

which need not be isolated and identified prior to their becoming pieces. The conventions of specifying are simply the recognized means of identifying pieces. The reason piece-specifying cannot fail in the way status-conferring can is that once the piece is specified with the appropriate means of specification, it is a piece; but status-conferring requires something beyond specification – a procedure for conferring the status on the antecedently identified (specified) entity. This mechanism of conferral can malfunction. No corresponding fallible procedure is a component of a piece-specification.

The Specification Rubric reflects the intensionality of artistic creation by formulating a model for piece-making instead of status-conferring. The following two declarations are not equivalent:

(3) I hereby specify my piece to be everything I know but am not at the moment thinking – 1:36 P.M., 15 June 1969.
(4) I hereby specify my piece to be everything I know.

From the fact that someone has created the piece specified in (3) it does not follow that the piece specified in (4) is also a work of art, even if the two are extensionally the same. It may be true of Barry's piece that it is everything he knows, but this cannot be said to be the piece.

A piece usually has an author, an individual denoted by the 'I' in (3) and (4). However, the 'I' in (1) and (2) simply refers to a role; it makes no difference who confers status if the point is status conferral. Unless we are willing to give up the concept of an author as a person whose intentions are relevant to what we understand the piece to be, something other than status conferral must serve as a model for artistic creation.

To make a work of art is not to christen something art, but to index it under 'art pieces.' To do that is to specify a piece within an artistic indexing convention. Indexes list their items intensionally, and artistic indexing conventions provide means for intensionally specifying pieces. These conventions have existed at least since the Renaissance, when our current conception of 'art' was born. When Leonardo took up palette and brush, he did not first make a painting and then christen it art if he liked it. The mere fact that he used the artistic convention of painting on canvas assured that what he specified as the piece would be art. With this convention, the piece is specified when Leonardo stops painting and says 'that's it' (as opposed to stopping painting and throwing the thing out or setting it aside for completion at a later time). The history of art since the Renaissance, and especially since Duchamp, has been gradual liberalization of the conventions for piece-specification, until artists embraced the idea that it is nothing other than specification, by whatever means, which assures arthood. This realization freed art of aesthetics by making it unnecessary to specify a piece using aesthetic qualities. Any means of (intensional) specification will work.

The reason Dickie highlights conferral is probably that he has in mind the Readymade as a schematic model of the achievement of arthood, since it seems to strip artistic creation bare of all superfluities. However, it is as *a piece* that any Readymade bears artistic interest, and it is in becoming a piece that any Readymade becomes art. What makes it appear that Duchamp conferred art status on the Readymades is the way they conspicuously reject the aesthetic principle that dictates the coincidence of arthood and created aesthetic qualities. They do this by passing unaltered through the portals of art. But it is not status conferral that makes them art. Their dramatic entrance into the gallery is utilized not to make art, but rather to make a point. And that point is that piece-making is an act of specification within indexing conventions. The Readymade is the point in the history of art where the Specification Rubric was openly espoused. The reason status-conferral seems to take place is that the Rubric was supported with an implicit declaration 'This is art too.' But this declaration did not make the Readymades art, it simply called attention to the fact that they are works of art by being specified as pieces. It asserted the validity of the Rubric. Duchamp bypassed the indexing conventions superimposed on art by aesthetics. These conventions are, in effect, the media of art which connect physical materials and aesthetic qualities. Duchamp demonstrated that an artist's intention need not be imprisoned in the aesthetic qualities of a medium and that a simple piece-specification convention is sufficient for artistic creation. He didn't confer art status on anything; he avowed new conventions.

7 Dickie's definition, though not explicitly defeated by the matrix of pieces, is implicitly countered by the means of creation employed. If I had conferred status in making 'P-One', it would automatically be true that '5/5' is a work of art. But since I specified a piece, '5/5' is not the artwork I created. A work of art is a piece specified within artistic indexing conventions. This is not a definition of 'work of art', however. It is a description of the current state of

artistic institutions. *A priori* limits cannot be set for creativity, especially when the materials of creation are the concepts and conventions of art itself.

The Institutional Definition of art, which first appeared as a way of getting around the indefinability of art, turns out to be a disappointment, especially for the decider hoping to relieve his uncertainty about the brown spiral notebook. Yet it does highlight important features of the concept 'artwork.' As Arthur Danto says, 'To see something as art requires something the eye cannot de[s]cry – an atmosphere of artistic theory, a knowledge of the history of art: an artworld.'[20] This is why, when searching for support in counting Barry's piece as an artwork, I appealed to how it is treated within certain artistic institutions. And this is why I first turned to artistic conventions in trying to evaluate the status of the brown notebook. If I had found a tag stating its title and naming the artist, its role as a member of the show and as an artwork would have been secured. Part of the trouble we have in deciding whether it is art is that there are no clear conventions governing renegades.

Notes

1   For an insightful discussion of aesthetic qualities, see M. C. Beardsley 'What Is An Aesthetic Quality?', *Theoria* 39 (1973): 50–70.

2   See S. Langer, *Feeling and Form*, N.Y. 1953.

3   Cf. H. Rosenberg 'Art and Words', *The De-definition of Art*, N.Y. 1972.

4   See, e.g., L. Lippard *Six Years: The Dematerialization of the Art Object from 1966 to 1972*, N.Y. 1973.

5   Ibid.: 112. Lippard's book contains numerous examples, similar to this one, where an artist 'creates' a work simply by specifying some entity as his piece.

6   M. Weitz, 'The Role of Theory in Aesthetics', rep. in F. J. Coleman (ed) *Contemporary Studies in Aesthetics*, N.Y. 1968: 89. My reservations about Weitz's use of Wittgenstein are explained in *Wittgenstein's Language*, The Hague 1973.

7   Weitz, ibid.: 90.

8   If the concept were genuinely 'open', why do we need to 'extend' it? Also, is Weitz's description of the situation accurate? Do we hold a hearing? Do critics actually have to decide whether to extend the concept? Perhaps a concept without necessary and sufficient conditions could still fail to be 'open' because we don't need to decide to extend the concept.

9   Weitz, op. cit.: 89.

10   C. Greenberg characterizes 'Modernist' painting in terms of self-criticism. See his 'Modernist Painting', rep. in G. Battcock *The New Art*, N.Y. 1966: 100–110. Perhaps it is this self-scrutiny which makes 'art' an 'essentially contested concept'. See W. B. Gallie 'Essentially Contested Concepts', *Proc. Aris Soc.* 56 (1955–56).

11   G. Dickie, 'What is Art?', above: 23.

12   See J. Kosuth 'Art After Philosophy', rep. in U. Meyer *Conceptual Art*, N.Y. 1972: 155–170.

13   Dickie, above: 27. For some relevant criticism of Dickie's position on this and other points, see T. Cohen 'The Possibility of Art', *Phil Rev* 82 (1973): 69–82.

14   Ibid., passim.

15   Ibid.: 28.

16   Above: 25.

17   See *Marcel Duchamp*, catalogue for the show organized by the Philadelphia Museum of Art and the Modern Museum of Art (1973): 248. It is interesting that the 'paintings' are upside down with respect to each other, so that not both can be shown properly at the same time.

18   A. Danto gives a similar example in 'The Artworld', above: 15f.

19   Dickie, above: 31f.

20   Danto: 16.

Of the standard of taste

David Hume (1711–76)

The empiricist philosopher David Hume is best known nowadays for his researches into the nature of knowledge, causality, self and personal identity in A Treatise of Human Nature *(1739–40) and the* Enquiry Concerning Human Understanding *(1748), but he also wrote widely on other topics, including aesthetics. In the following essay, 'Of the standard of taste' (1757), he considers whether there can be general principles of taste. This was a keenly debated issue in eighteenth-century intellectual circles. Hume feels there is such a standard and that some judgements of taste can be considered superior to others (a preference for the poetry of Milton over that of Ogilby, for example). There are, he claims, 'common sentiments of human nature' (note that in eighteenth-century usage 'sentiment' means something more like 'sensation' nowadays) on which the rules of art are founded, and which can be discovered by observation (Hume invariably lays great stress on the role of observation in philosophical enquiry). The appreciation of beauty is just such a common sentiment for Hume – as 'benevolence' is held to be in his moral philosophy – and anyone who deviates from the standard judgements regarding beauty (who, for instance, prefers Ogilby to Milton) reveals himself to be 'absurd and ridiculous'. It might be cited against Hume that another of his empirically observed preferences, for the prose of the essayist Addison over that of Bunyan, has now been largely reversed among the literary establishment. Whether this can be explained away as a temporary deviation from the norm is a moot point. Hume's reliance on custom and practice as a basis for aesthetic judgement would strike most modern critics as very restrictive: criticism now is more likely to be concerned with challenging received opinion than with upholding norms.*

The great variety of Taste, as well as of opinion, which prevails in the world, is too obvious not to have fallen under every one's observation. Men of the most confined knowledge are able to

remark a difference of taste in the narrow circle of their acquaintance, even where the persons have been educated under the same
government, and have early imbibed the same prejudices. But those
who can enlarge their view to contemplate distant nations and
remote ages, are still more surprised at the great inconsistence and
contrariety. We are apt to call *barbarous* whatever departs widely
from our own taste and apprehension; but soon find the epithet of
reproach retorted on us. And the highest arrogance and self-conceit
is at last startled, on observing an equal assurance on all sides, and
scruples, amidst such a contest of sentiment, to pronounce positively
in its own favor.

As this variety of taste is obvious to the most careless inquirer,
so will it be found, on examination, to be still greater in reality
than in appearance. The sentiments of men often differ with regard
to beauty and deformity of all kinds, even while their general
discourse is the same. There are certain terms in every language
which import blame, and others praise; and all men who use the
same tongue must agree in their application of them. Every voice
is united in applauding elegance, propriety, simplicity, spirit in
writing; and in blaming fustian, affectation, coldness, and a false
brilliancy. But when critics come to particulars, this seeming
unanimity vanishes; and it is found, that they had affixed a very
different meaning to their expressions. In all matters of opinion
and science, the case is opposite; the difference among men is there
often found to lie in generals than in particulars, and to be less in
reality than in appearance. An explanation of the terms commonly
ends the controversy: and the disputants are surprised to find that
they had been quarrelling, while at bottom they agreed in their
judgment.

Those who found morality on sentiment, more than on reason,
are inclined to comprehend ethics under the former observation,
and to maintain, that, in all questions which regard conduct and
manners, the difference among men is really greater than at first
sight it appears. It is indeed obvious, that writers of all nations and
all ages concur in applauding justice, humanity, magnanimity,
prudence, veracity; and in blaming the opposite qualities. Even
poets and other authors, whose compositions are chiefly calculated
to please the imagination, are yet found, from Homer down to
Fenelon,[1] to inculcate the same moral precepts, and to bestow their
applause and blame on the same virtues and vices. This great
unanimity is usually ascribed to the influence of plain reason,
which, in all these cases, maintains similar sentiments in all men,

and prevents those controversies to which the abstract sciences are so much exposed. So far as the unanimity is real, this account may be admitted as satisfactory. But we must also allow, that some part of the seeming harmony in morals may be accounted for from the very nature of language. The word *virtue*, with its equivalent in every tongue, implies praise, as that of *vice* does blame; and no one, without the most obvious and grossest impropriety, could affix reproach to a term, which in general acceptation is understood in a good sense: or bestow applause, where the idiom requires disapprobation. Homer's general precepts, where he delivers any such, will never be controverted; but it is obvious, that, when he draws particular pictures of manners, and represents heroism in Achilles, and prudence in Ulysses, he intermixes a much greater degree of ferocity in the former, and of cunning and fraud in the latter, than Fenelon would admit of. The sage Ulysses, in the Greek poet, seems to delight in lies and fictions, and often employs them without any necessity, or even advantage. But his more scrupulous son, in the French epic writer, exposes himself to the most imminent perils, rather than depart from the most exact line of truth and veracity.

The admirers and followers of the Alcoran[2] insist on the excellent moral precepts interspersed throughout that wild and absurd performance. But it is to be supposed, that the Arabic words, which correspond to the English, equity, justice, temperance, meekness, charity, were such as, from the constant use of that tongue, must always be taken in a good sense: and it would have argued the greatest ignorance, not of morals, but of language, to have mentioned them with any epithets, besides those of applause and approbation. But would we know, whether the pretended prophet had really attained a just sentiment of morals, let us attend to his narration, and we shall soon find, that he bestows praise on such instances of treachery, inhumanity, cruelty, revenge, bigotry, as are utterly incompatible with civilized society. No steady rule of right seems there to be attended to; and every action is blamed or praised, so far only as it is beneficial or hurtful to the true believers.

The merit of delivering true general precepts in ethics is indeed very small. Whoever recommends any moral virtues, really does no more than is implied in the terms themselves. That people who invented the word *charity*, and used it in a good sense, inculcated more clearly, and much more efficaciously, the precept, *Be charitable*, than any pretended legislator or prophet, who should insert such a *maxim* in his writings. Of all expressions, those which, together with their other meaning, imply a degree either of blame or approbation, are the least liable to be perverted or mistaken.

It is natural for us to seek a *Standard of Taste*; a rule by which the various sentiments of men may be reconciled; at least a decision afforded confirming one sentiment and condemning another.

There is a species of philosophy, which cuts off all hopes of success in such an attempt, and represents the impossibility of ever attaining any standard of taste. The difference, it is said, is very wide between judgment and sentiment. All sentiment is right; because sentiment has a reference to nothing beyond itself, and is always real, wherever a man is conscious of it. But all determinations of the understanding are not right; because they have a reference to something beyond themselves, to wit, real matter of fact; and are not always conformable to that standard. Among a thousand different opinions which different men may entertain of the same subject, there is one, and but one, that is just and true: and the only difficulty is to fix and ascertain it. On the contrary, a thousand different sentiments, excited by the same object, are all right; because no sentiment represents what is really in the object. It only marks a certain conformity or relation between the object and the organs or faculties of the mind; and if that conformity did not really exist, the sentiment could never possibly have being. Beauty is no quality in things themselves: it exists merely in the mind which contemplates them; and each mind perceives a different beauty. One person may even perceive deformity, where another is sensible of beauty; and every individual ought to acquiesce in his own sentiment, without pretending to regulate those of others. To seek the real beauty, or real deformity, is as fruitless an inquiry, as to pretend to ascertain the real sweet or real bitter. According to the disposition of the organs, the same object may be both sweet and bitter; and the proverb has justly determined it to be fruitless to dispute concerning tastes. It is very natural, and even quite necessary, to extend this axiom to mental, as well as bodily taste; and thus common sense, which is so often at variance with philosophy, especially with the sceptical kind, is found, in one instance at least, to agree in pronouncing the same decision.

But though this axiom, by passing into a proverb, seems to have attained the sanction of common sense; there is certainly a species of common sense, which opposes it, at least serves to modify and restrain it. Whoever would assert an equality of genius and elegance between Ogilby and Milton, or Bunyan and Addison, would be thought to defend no less an extravagance, than if he had maintained a mole-hill to be as high as Teneriffe, or a pond as extensive as the ocean. Though there may be found persons, who give the preference to the former authors; no one pays attention to such a taste; and we pronounce, without scruple, the sentiment of these pretended critics to be absurd and ridiculous. The principle of the natural equality of tastes is then totally forgot, and while we admit it on some occasions, where the objects seem near an equality, it appears an extravagant paradox, or rather a palpable absurdity, where objects so disproportioned are compared together.

It is evident that none of the rules of composition are fixed by reasonings *a priori*, or can be esteemed abstract conclusions of the understanding, from comparing those habitudes and relations of ideas, which are eternal and immutable. Their foundation is the same with that of all the practical sciences, experience; nor are they any thing but general observations, concerning what has been universally found to please in all countries and in all ages. Many of the beauties of poetry, and even of eloquence, are founded on falsehood and fiction, on hyperboles, metaphors, and an abuse or perversion of terms from their natural meaning. To check the sallies of the imagination, and to reduce every expression to geometrical truth and exactness, would be the most contrary to the laws of criticism; because it would produce a work, which, by universal experience, has been found the most insipid and disagreeable. But though poetry can never submit to exact truth, it must be confined by rules of art, discovered to the author either by genius or observation. If some negligent or irregular writers have pleased, they have not pleased by their transgressions of rule or order, but in spite of these transgressions: they have possessed other beauties, which were conformable to just criticism; and the force of these beauties has been able to overpower censure, and give the mind a satisfaction superior to the disgust arising from the blemishes. Ariosto[3] pleases; but not by his monstrous and improbable fictions, by his bizarre mixture of the serious and comic styles, by the want of coherence in his stories, or by the continual interruptions of his narration. He charms by the force and clearness of his expression, by the readiness and variety of his inventions, and by his natural pictures of the passions, especially those of the gay and amorous kind: and, however his faults may diminish our satisfaction, they are not able entirely to destroy it. Did our pleasure really arise from those parts of his poem, which we denominate faults, this would be no objection to criticism in general: it would only be an objection to those particular rules of criticism, which would establish such circumstances to be faults, and would represent them as universally blamable. If they are found to please, they cannot be faults, let the pleasure which they produce be ever so unexpected and unaccountable.

But though all the general rules of art are founded only on experience, and on the observation of the common sentiments of human nature, we must not imagine that, on every occasion, the feelings of men will be conformable to these rules. Those finer emotions of the mind are of a very tender and delicate nature, and require the concurrence of many favorable circumstances to make them play with facility and exactness, according to their general and established principles. The least exterior hinderance to such small springs, or the least internal disorder, disturbs their motion, and confounds the operations of the whole machine. When we would make an experiment of this nature, and would try the force of any beauty or deformity, we must choose with care a proper time and place, and bring the fancy to a suitable situation and disposition. A perfect serenity of mind, a recollection of thought, a due attention to the object; if any of these circumstances be wanting, our experiment will be fallacious, and we shall be unable to judge of the catholic and universal beauty. The relation, which nature has placed between the form and the sentiment, will at least be more obscure; and it will require greater accuracy to trace and discern it. We shall be able to ascertain its influence, not so much from the operation of each particular beauty, as from the durable admiration which attends those works that have survived all the caprices of mode and fashion, all the mistakes of ignorance and envy.

The same Homer who pleased at Athens and Rome two thousand years ago, is still admired at Paris and at London. All the changes of climate, government, religion, and language, have not been able to obscure his glory. Authority or prejudice may give a temporary vogue to a bad poet or orator; but his reputation will never be durable or general. When his compositions are examined by posterity or by foreigners, the enchantment is dissipated, and his faults appear in their true colors. On the contrary, a real genius, the longer his works endure, and the more wide they are spread, the more sincere is the admiration which he meets with. Envy and jealousy have too much place in a narrow circle; and even familiar acquaintance with his person may diminish the applause due to his performances: but when these obstructions are removed, the beauties, which are naturally fitted to excite agreeable sentiments, immediately display their energy; and while the world endures, they maintain their authority over the minds of men.

It appears, then, that amidst all the variety and caprice of taste, there are certain general principles of approbation or blame, whose influence a careful eye may trace in all operations of the mind. Some particular forms or qualities, from the original structure of the internal fabric are calculated to please, and others to displease; and if they fail of their effect in any particular instance, it is from some apparent defect or imperfection in the organ. A man in a fever would not insist on his palate as able to decide concerning flavors; nor would one affected with the jaundice pretend to give a verdict with regard to colors. In each creature there is a sound and a defective state; and the former alone can be supposed to afford us a true standard of taste and sentiment. If, in the sound state of the organ, there be an entire or a considerable uniformity of sentiment among men, we may thence derive an idea of the perfect beauty; in like manner as the appearance of objects in daylight, to the eye of a man in health, is denominated their true and real color, even while color is allowed to be merely a phantasm of the senses.

Many and frequent are the defects in the internal organs, which prevent or weaken the influence of those general principles, on which depends our sentiment of beauty or deformity. Though some objects, by the structure of the mind, be naturally calculated to give pleasure, it is not to be expected that in every individual the pleasure will be equally felt. Particular incidents and situations occur, which either throw a false light on the objects, or hinder the true from conveying to the imagination the proper sentiment and perception.

One obvious cause why many feel not the proper sentiment of beauty, is the want of that *delicacy* of imagination which is requisite to convey a sensibility of those finer emotions. This delicacy every one pretends to: every one talks of it; and would reduce every kind of taste or sentiment to its standard. But as our intention in this Essay is to mingle some light of the understanding with the feelings of sentiment, it will be proper to give a more accurate definition of delicacy than has hitherto been attempted. And not to draw our philosophy from too profound a source, we shall have recourse to a noted story in Don Quixote.[4]

It is with good reason, says Sancho to the squire with the great nose, that I pretend to have a judgment in wine: this is a quality hereditary in our family. Two of my kinsmen were once called to give their opinion of a hogshead, which was supposed to be excellent, being old and of a good vintage. One of them tastes it, considers it; and, after mature reflection, pronounces the wine to be good, were it not for a small taste of leather which he perceived in it. The other, after using the same precautions, gives also his verdict in favor of the wine; but with the reserve of a taste of iron, which he could easily distinguish. You cannot imagine how much they were both ridiculed for their judgment. But who laughed in the end? On emptying the hogshead, there was found at the bottom an old key with a leathern thong tied to it.

The great resemblance between mental and bodily taste will easily teach us to apply this story. Though it be certain that beauty and deformity, more than sweet and bitter, are not qualities in objects, but belong entirely to the sentiment, internal or external, it must be allowed, that there are certain qualities in objects which are fitted by nature to produce those particular feelings. Now, as these qualities may be found in a small degree, or may be mixed and confounded with each other, it often happens that the taste is not affected with such minute qualities, or is not able to distinguish all the particular flavors, amidst the disorder in which they are presented. Where the organs are so fine as to allow nothing to escape them, and at the same time so exact as to perceive every ingredient in the composition, this we call delicacy of taste, whether we employ these terms in the literal or metaphorical sense. Here then the general rules of beauty are of use, being drawn from established models, and from the observation of what pleases or displeases, when presented singly and in a high degree; and if the same qualities, in a continued composition, and in a smaller degree, affect not the organs with a sensible delight or uneasiness, we exclude the person from all pretensions to this delicacy. To produce these general rules or avowed patterns of composition, is like finding the key with the leathern thong, which justified the verdict of Sancho's kinsmen, and confounded those pretended judges who had condemned them. Though the hogshead had never been emptied, the taste of the one was still equally delicate, and that of the other equally dull and languid; but it would have been more difficult to have proved the superiority of the former, to the conviction of every bystander. In like manner, though the beauties of writing had never been methodized, or reduced to general principles; though no excellent models had ever been acknowledged, the different degrees of taste would still have subsisted, and the judgment of one man been preferable to that of another; but it would not have been so easy to silence the bad critic, who might always insist upon his particular sentiment, and refuse to submit to his antagonist. But when we show him an avowed principle of art; when we illustrate this principle by examples, whose operation, from his own particular taste, he acknowledges to be conformable to the principle; when we prove that the same principle may be applied to the present case, where he did not perceive or feel its influence: he must conclude, upon the whole, that the fault lies in himself, and that he wants the delicacy which is requisite to make him sensible of every beauty and every blemish in any composition or discourse.

It is acknowledged to be the perfection of every sense or faculty, to perceive with exactness its most minute objects, and allow nothing to escape its notice and observation. The smaller the objects are which become sensible to the eye, the finer is that organ, and the more elaborate its make and composition. A good palate is not tried by strong flavor, but by a mixture of small ingredients, where we are still sensible of each part, notwithstanding its minuteness and its confusion with the rest. In like manner, a quick and acute perception of beauty and deformity must be the perfection of our mental taste; nor can a man be satisfied with himself while he suspects that any excellence or blemish in a discourse has passed him unobserved. In this case, the perfection of the man, and the perfection of the sense of feeling, are found to be united. A very delicate palate, on many occasions, may be a great inconvenience both to a man himself and to his friends. But a delicate taste of wit or beauty must always be a desirable quality, because it is the source of all the finest and most innocent enjoyments of which human nature is susceptible. In this decision the sentiments of all mankind are agreed. Wherever you can ascertain a delicacy of taste, it is sure to meet with approbation; and the best way of ascertaining it is, to appeal to those models and principles which have been established by the uniform consent and experience of nations and ages.

But athough there be naturally a wide difference, in point of delicacy, between one person and another, nothing tends further to increase and improve this talent, than *practice* in a particular art, and frequent survey or contemplation of a particular species of beauty. When objects of any kind are first presented to the eye or imagination, the sentiment which attends them is obscure and confused; and the mind is, in a great measure, incapable of pronouncing concerning their merits or defects. The taste cannot perceive the several excellences of the performance, much less distinguish the particular character of each excellency, and ascertain its quality and degree. If it pronounce the whole in general to be beautiful or deformed, it is the utmost that can be expected; and even this judgment, a person so unpractised will be apt to deliver with great hesitation and reserve. But allow him to acquire experience in those objects, his feeling becomes more exact and nice: he not only perceives the beauties and defects of each part, but marks the distinguishing species of each quality, and assigns it suitable praise or blame. A clear and distinct sentiment attends him through the whole survey of the objects; and he discerns that very degree and kind of approbation or displeasure which each part is naturally fitted to produce. The mist dissipates which seemed formerly to hang over the object; the organ acquires greater perfection in its operations, and can pronounce, without danger of mistake, concerning the merits of every performance. In a word, the same address and dexterity which practice gives to the execution of any work, is also acquired by the same means in the judging of it.

So advantageous is practice to the discernment of beauty, that, before we can give judgment on any work of importance, it will even be requisite that that very individual performance be more than once perused by us, and be surveyed in different lights with attention and deliberation. There is a flutter or hurry of thought which attends the first perusal of any piece, and which confounds the genuine sentiment of beauty. The relation of the parts is not discerned: the true characters of style are little distinguished. The several perfections and defects seem wrapped up in a species of confusion, and present themselves indistinctly to the imagination. Not to mention, that there is a species of beauty, which, as it is florid and superficial, pleases at first; but being found incompatible with a just expression either of reason or passion, soon palls upon the taste, and is then rejected with disdain, at least rated at a much lower value.

It is impossible to continue in the practice of contemplating any order of beauty, without being frequently obliged to form *comparisons* between the several species and degrees of excellence, and estimating their proportion to each other. A man who has had no opportunity of comparing the different kinds of beauty, is indeed totally unqualified to pronounce an opinion with regard to any object presented to him. By comparison alone we fix the epithets of praise or blame, and learn how to assign the due degree of each. The coarsest daubing contains a certain lustre of colors and exactness of imitation, which are so far beauties, and would affect the mind of a peasant or Indian with the highest admiration. The most vulgar ballads are not entirely destitute of harmony or nature; and none but a person familiarized to superior beauties would pronounce their members harsh, or narration uninteresting. A great inferiority of beauty gives pain to a person conversant in the highest excellence of the kind, and is for that reason pronounced a deformity; as the most finished object with which we are acquainted is naturally supposed to have reached the pinnacle of perfection, and to be entitled to the highest applause. One accustomed to see, and examine, and weigh the several performances, admired in different ages and nations, can alone rate the merits of a work exhibited to his view, and assign its proper rank among the productions of genius.

But to enable a critic the more fully to execute this undertaking, he must preserve his mind free from all *prejudice* and allow nothing to enter into his consideration, but the very object which is submitted to his examination. We may observe, that every work of art, in order to produce its due effect on the mind, must be surveyed in a certain point of view, and cannot be fully relished by persons whose situation, real or imaginary, is not conformable to that which is required by the performance. An orator addresses himself to a particular audience, and must have a regard to their particular genius, interests, opinions, passions, and prejudices; otherwise he hopes in vain to govern their resolutions, and inflame their affections. Should they even have entertained some prepossessions against him, however unreasonable, he must not overlook this disadvantage; but, before he enters upon the subject, must endeavor to conciliate their affection, and acquire their good graces. A critic of a different age or nation, who should peruse this discourse, must have all these circumstances in his eye, and must place himself in the same situation as the audience, in order to form a true judgment of the oration. In like manner, when any work is addressed to the public, though I should have a friendship or enmity with the author, I must depart from this situation, and, considering myself as a man in general, forget, if possible, my individual being, and my peculiar circumstances. A person influenced by prejudice complies not with this condition, but obstinately maintains his natural position, without placing himself in that point of view which the performance supposes. If the work be addressed to persons of a different age or nation, he makes no allowance for their peculiar views and prejudices; but, full of the manners of his own age and country, rashly condemns what seemed admirable in the eyes of those for whom alone the discourse was calculated. If the work be executed for the public, he never sufficiently enlarges his comprehension, or forgets his interest as a friend or enemy, as a rival or commentator. By this means his sentiments are perverted; nor have the same beauties and blemishes the same influence upon him, as if he had imposed a proper violence on his imagination, and had forgotten himself for a moment. So far his taste evidently departs from the true standard, and of consequence loses all credit and authority.

It is well known, that, in all questions submitted to the understanding, prejudice is destructive of sound judgment, and perverts all operations of the intellectual faculties: it is no less contrary to good taste; nor has it less influence to corrupt our sentiment of beauty. It belongs to *good sense* to check its influence in both cases; and in this respect, as well as in many others, reason, if not an essential part of taste, is at least requisite to the operations of this latter faculty. In all the nobler productions of genius, there is a mutual relation and correspondence of parts; nor can either the beauties or blemishes be perceived by him whose thought is not capacious enough to comprehend all those parts, and compare them with each other, in order to perceive the consistence and uniformity of the whole. Every work of art has also a certain end or purpose for which it is calculated; and is to be deemed more or less perfect, as it is more or less fitted to attain this end. The object of eloquence is to persuade, of history to instruct, of poetry to please, by means of the passions and the imagination. These ends we must carry constantly in our view when we peruse any performance; and we must be able to judge how far the means employed are adapted to their respective purposes. Besides, every kind of composition, even the most poetical, is nothing but a chain of propositions and reasonings; not always, indeed, the justest and most exact, but still plausible and specious, however disguised by the coloring of the imagination. The persons introduced in tragedy and epic poetry must be represented as reasoning, and thinking, and concluding, and acting, suitably to their character and circumstances; and without judgment, as well as taste and invention, a poet can never hope to succeed in so delicate an undertaking. Not to mention, that the same excellence of faculties which contributes to the improvement of reason, the same clearness of conception, the same exactness of distinction, the same vivacity of apprehension, are essential to the operations of true taste, and are its infallible concomitants. It seldom or never happens, that a man of sense, who has experience in any art, cannot judge of its beauty; and it is no less rare to meet with a man who has a just taste without a sound understanding.

Thus, though the principles of taste be universal, and nearly, if not entirely, the same in all men; yet few are qualified to give judgment on any work of art, or establish their own sentiment as the standard of beauty. The organs of internal sensation are seldom so perfect as to allow the general principles their full play, and produce a feeling correspondent to those principles. They either labor under some defect, or are vitiated by some disorder; and by that means excite a sentiment, which may be pronounced erroneous. When the critic has no delicacy, he judges without any distinction, and is only affected by the grosser and more palpable qualities of the object: the finer touches pass unnoticed and disregarded. Where he is not aided by practice, his verdict is attended with confusion and hesitation. Where no comparison has been employed, the most frivolous beauties, such as rather merit the name of defects, are the object of his admiration. Where he lies under the influence of prejudice, all his natural sentiments are perverted. Where good sense is wanting, he is not qualified to discern the beauties of design and reasoning, which are the highest and most excellent. Under some or other of these imperfections, the generality of men labor; and hence a true judge in the finer arts is observed, even during the most polished ages, to be so rare a character: strong sense, united to delicate sentiment, improved by practice, perfected by comparison, and cleared of all prejudice, can alone entitle critics to this valuable character; and the joint verdict of such, wherever they are to be found, is the true standard of taste and beauty.

But where are such critics to be found? By what marks are they to be known? How distinguish them from pretenders? These questions are embarrassing; and seem to throw us back into the same uncertainty from which, during the course of this Essay, we have endeavored to extricate ourselves.

But if we consider the matter aright, these are questions of fact, not of sentiment. Whether any particular person be endowed with good sense and a delicate imagination, free from prejudice, may often be the subject of dispute, and be liable to great discussion and inquiry: but that such a character is valuable and estimable, will be agreed in by all mankind. Where these doubts occur, men can do no more than in other disputable questions which are submitted to the understanding: they must produce the best arguments that their invention suggests to them; they must acknowledge a true and decisive standard to exist somewhere, to wit, real existence and matter of fact; and they must have indulgence to such as differ from them in their appeals to this standard. It is sufficient for our present purpose, if we have proved, that the taste of all individuals is not upon an equal footing, and that some men in general, however difficult to be particularly pitched upon, will be acknowledged by universal sentiment to have a preference above others.

But, in reality, the difficulty of finding, even in particulars, the standard of taste, is not so great as it is represented. Though in speculation we may readily avow a certain criterion in science, and deny it in sentiment, the matter is found in practice to be much more hard to ascertain in the former case than in the latter. Theories of abstract philosophy, systems of profound theology, have prevailed during one age: in a successive period these have been universally exploded: their absurdity has been detected: other theories and systems have supplied their place, which again gave place to their successors: and nothing has been experienced more liable to the revolutions of chance and fashion than these pretended decisions of science. The case is not the same with the beauties of eloquence and poetry. Just expressions of passion and nature are sure, after a little time, to gain public applause, which they maintain for ever. Aristotle, and Plato, and Epicurus, and Descartes, may successively yield to each other: but Terence and Virgil maintain an universal, undisputed empire over the minds of men. The abstract philosophy of Cicero has lost its credit: the vehemence of his oratory is still the subject of our admiration.

Though men of delicate taste be rare, they are easily to be distinguished in society by the soundness of their understanding, and the superiority of their faculties above the rest of mankind. The ascendant, which they acquire, gives a prevalence to that lively approbation with which they receive any productions of genius, and renders it generally predominant. Many men, when left to themselves, have but a faint and dubious perception of beauty, who yet are capable of relishing any fine stroke which is pointed out to them. Every convert to the admiration of the real poet or orator, is the cause of some new conversion. And though prejudices may prevail for a time, they never unite in celebrating any rival to the true genius, but yield at last to the force of nature and just sentiment. Thus, though a civilized nation may easily be mistaken in the choice of their admired philosopher, they never have been found long to err, in their affection for a favorite epic or tragic author.

But notwithstanding all our endeavors to fix a standard of taste, and reconcile the discordant apprehensions of men, there still remain two sources of variation, which are not sufficient indeed to confound all the boundaries of beauty and deformity, but will often serve to produce a difference in the degrees of our approbation or blame. The one is the different humors of particular men; the other, the particular manners and opinions of our age and country. The general principles of taste are uniform in human nature: where men vary in their judgments, some defect or perversion in the faculties may commonly be remarked; proceeding either from prejudice, from want of practice, or want of delicacy: and there is just reason for approving one taste, and condemning another. But where there is such a diversity in the internal frame or external situation as is entirely blameless on both sides, and leaves no room to give one the preference above the other; in that case a certain degree of diversity in judgment is unavoidable, and we seek in vain for a standard, by which we can reconcile the contrary sentiments.

A young man, whose passions are warm, will be more sensibly touched with amorous and tender images, than a man more advanced in years, who takes pleasure in wise, philosophical reflections, concerning the conduct of life, and moderation of the passions. At twenty, Ovid may be the favorite author, Horace at forty, and perhaps Tacitus at fifty. Vainly would we, in such cases, endeavor to enter into the sentiments of others, and divest ourselves of those propensities which are natural to us. We choose our favorite author as we do our friend, from a conformity of humor and disposition. Mirth or passion, sentiment or reflection; whichever of these most predominates in our temper, it gives us a peculiar sympathy with the writer who resembles it.

One person is more pleased with the sublime, another with the tender, a third with raillery. One has a strong sensibility to blemishes, and is extremely studious of correctness; another has a more lively feeling of beauties, and pardons twenty absurdities and defects for one elevated or pathetic stroke. The ear of this man is entirely turned towards conciseness and energy; that man is delighted with a copious, rich, and harmonious expression. Simplicity is affected by one; ornament by another. Comedy, tragedy, satire, odes, have each its partisans, who prefer that particular species of writing to all others. It is plainly an error in a critic, to confine his approbation to one species or style of writing, and condemn all the rest. But it is almost impossible not to feel a predilection for that which suits our particular turn and disposition. Such performances are innocent and unavoidable, and can never reasonably be the object of dispute, because there is no standard by which they can be decided.

For a like reason, we are more pleased, in the course of our reading, with pictures and characters that resemble objects which are found in our own age and country, than with those which describe a different set of customs. It is not without some effort that we reconcile ourselves to the simplicity of ancient manners, and behold princesses carrying water from the spring, and kings and heroes dressing their own victuals. We may allow in general, that the representation of such manners is no fault in the author, nor deformity in the piece; but we are not so sensibly touched with them. For this reason, comedy is not easily transferred from one age or nation to another. A Frenchman or Englishman is not pleased with the *Andria* of Terence, or *Clitia* of Machiavel; where the fine lady, upon whom all the play turns, never once appears to the spectators, but is always kept behind the scenes, suitably to the reserved humor of the ancient Greeks and modern Italians. A man of learning and reflection can make allowance for these peculiarities of manners; but a common audience can never divest themselves so far of their usual ideas and sentiments, as to relish pictures which nowise resemble them.

But here there occurs a reflection, which may, perhaps, be useful in examining the celebrated controversy concerning ancient and modern learning; where we often find the one side excusing any seeming absurdity in the ancients from the manners of the age, and the other refusing to admit this excuse, or at least admitting it only as an apology for the author, not for the performance. In my opinion, the proper boundaries in this subject have seldom been fixed between the contending parties. Where any innocent peculiarities of manners are represented, such as those above mentioned, they ought certainly to be admitted; and a man who is shocked with them, gives an evident proof of false delicacy and refinement. The poet's *monument more durable than brass*,[5] must fall to the ground like common brick or clay, were men to make no allowance for the continual revolutions of manners and customs, and would admit of nothing but what was suitable to the prevailing fashion. Must we throw aside the pictures of our ancestors, because of their ruffs and farthingales? But where the ideas of morality and decency alter from one age to another, and where vicious manners are described, without being marked with the proper characters of blame and disapprobation, this must be allowed to disfigure the poem, and to be a real deformity. I cannot, nor is it proper I should, enter into such sentiments; and however I may excuse the poet, on account of the manners of his age, I can never relish the composition. The want of humanity and of decency, so conspicuous in the characters drawn by several of the ancient poets, even sometimes by Homer and the Greek tragedians, diminishes considerably the merit of their noble performances, and gives modern authors an advantage over them. We are not interested in the fortunes and sentiments of such rough heroes; we are displeased to find the limits of vice and virtue so much confounded; and whatever indulgence we may give to the writer on account of his prejudices, we cannot prevail on ourselves to enter into his sentiments, or bear an affection to characters which we plainly discover to be blamable.

The case is not the same with moral principles as with speculative opinions of any kind. These are in continual flux and revolution. The son embraces a different system from the father. Nay, there scarcely is any man, who can boast of great constancy and uniformity in this particular. Whatever speculative errors may be found in the polite writings of any age or country, they detract but little from the value of those compositions. There needs but a certain turn of thought or imagination to make us enter into all the opinions which then prevailed, and relish the sentiments or conclusions derived from them. But a very violent effort is requisite to change our judgment of manners, and excite sentiments of approbation or blame, love or hatred, different from those to which the mind, from long custom, has been familiarized. And where a man is confident of the rectitude of that moral standard by which he judges, he is justly jealous of it, and will not pervert the sentiments of his heart for a moment, in complaisance to any writer whatsoever.

Of all speculative errors, those which regard religion are the most excusable in compositions of genius; nor is it ever permitted to judge of the civility or wisdom of any people, or even of single persons, by the grossness or refinement of their theological principles. The same good sense that directs men in the ordinary occurrence of life, is not hearkened to in religious matters, which are supposed to be placed altogether above the cognizance of human reason. On this account, all the absurdities of the Pagan system of theology must be overlooked by every critic, who would pretend to form a just notion of ancient poetry; and our posterity, in their turn, must have the same indulgence to their forefathers. No religious principles can ever be imputed as a fault to any poet, while they remain merely principles, and take not such strong possession of his heart as to lay him under the imputation of *bigotry or superstition.* Where that happens, they confound the sentiments of morality, and alter the natural boundaries of vice and virtue. They are therefore eternal blemishes, according to the principle above mentioned; nor are the prejudices and false opinions of the age sufficient to justify them.

It is essential to the Roman Catholic religion to inspire a violent hatred of every other worship, and to represent all Pagans, Mahometans, and heretics, as the objects of divine wrath and vengeance. Such sentiments, though they are in reality very blamable, are considered as virtues by the zealots of that communion, and are represented in their tragedies and epic poems as a kind of divine heroism. This bigotry has disfigured two very fine tragedies of the French theatre, POLIEUCTE and ATHALIA;[6] where an intemperate zeal for particular modes of worship is set off with all the pomp imaginable, and forms the predominant character of the heroes. 'What is this,' says the sublime Joad to Josabet, finding her in discourse with Mathan the priest of Baal, 'Does the daughter of David speak to this traitor? Are you not afraid lest the earth should open, and pour forth flames to devour you both? Or lest these holy walls should fall and crush you together? What is his purpose? Why comes that enemy of God hither to poison the air, which we breathe, with his horrid presence?' Such sentiments are received with great applause on the theatre of Paris; but at London the spectators would be full as much pleased to hear Achilles tell Agamemnon, that he was a dog in his forehead, a deer in his heart; or Jupiter threaten Juno with a sound drubbing, if she will not be quiet.

Religious principles are also a blemish in any polite composition, when they rise up to superstition, and intrude themselves into every sentiment, however remote from any connection with religion. It is no excuse for the poet, that the customs of his country had burdened life with so many religious ceremonies and observances, that no part of it was exempt from that yoke. It must for ever be ridiculous in Petrarch to compare his mistress, Laura, to Jesus Christ.[7] Nor is it less ridiculous in that agreeable libertine, Boccace, very seriously to give thanks to God Almighty and the ladies, for their assistance in defending him against his enemies.[8]

Notes

1 François Fénelon (1651–1715), French prelate and writer, was appointed by Louis XIV as tutor to his grandson, the Duc de Bourgogne; Hume refers to Fénelon's *Télémaque*, composed for his pupil's instruction.

2 That is, the Koran.

3 Ludovico Ariosto (1474–1533), whose best-known work is the chivalric epic poem *Orlando Furioso* (1516).

4 Cervantes, *Don Quixote*, Part II, chapter 13.

5 Horace, *Carmina* III. 30. 1.

6 Hume refers here to Pierre Corneille's tragedy *Polyeucte* (1641) and to Jean-Baptiste Racine's religious tragedy *Athalie* (1691). The scene between Joad and Josabet, which Hume goes on to describe, takes place in *Athalie*, Act III, scene 5.

7 Probably Sonnet III. Francesco Petrarch, *Rime* (Naples, 1951).

8 Hume probably refers to the *Decameron*, preface to the Fourth Day, where Boccacio says to the ladies: '... armed with the help of God and your support, in which I rely, I shall go onward with this work, my back to this wind [of his enemies' criticism], letting it rage as it will.' Tr. Frances Winwar (New York: The Modern Library, 1955).

Logic and appreciation

Stuart Hampshire (b.1914)

Many philosophers have seen significant parallels between ethics and aesthetics, arguing that in each case value judgements are made and that general principles can, and should, be established by which we can make and defend those value judgements. Preferences, in other words, must come with logical reasons attached. In the next extract, Stuart Hampshire takes issue with this view and argues that there is no necessity for value judgements or general principles in criticism. That necessity only applies when we are responding to a problem – a moral dilemma, for example – and a work of art, Hampshire insists, is not a response to a problem: there is no requirement to decide for or against a work of art. Criticism, to Hampshire, is a question of paying close attention to an object, not of applying a theory to it. His view contrasts sharply with the continental aesthetic theorists of Readings 29–31.

When there are unavoidable problems, a rational man looks for some general method of solving them; a rational man may be defined as a man who adheres to general methods, allotting to each type of problem its own method of solution. Unless general methods of solution are recognized, there can be no grounds for distinguishing a valid from an invalid step in any argument in support of any solution. To be irrational is either to have no reasons at all for preferring one solution to another, or to give utterly different reasons in different cases of the same type; to refuse any general method of solving problems of a particular type is to accept either caprice or inconsistency in that domain. 'Must there be some general method of solving problems of conduct?' Or 'Must to act rightly be to act rationally and consistently?' – these have always been the principal questions in moral philosophy. Aristotle, the most accurate of moral philosophers, gave a carefully ambiguous answer, Kant an unambiguous 'Yes', Hume a qualified 'No'; for Hume held that morality was ultimately a matter of the heart and not of the head, of sympathy and not of consistency. But none of these philosophers denied that it always makes sense to ask for the reasons behind any practical decision; for constant ends may be served by a variety of different means. Actions (unlike works of art) do not bear their justification on the face of them; one must first inquire into reasons and purposes. Even if it is not necessary, at least it is always possible, to adopt some general ends of action, or (it is ultimately the same) to acknowledge some universal principles. Since any action susceptible of moral judgment can be viewed as the solution of a problem presented, one can always criticize and compare different methods of solution. Consistent policies are needed in order to meet common human predicaments; men may discuss the reasons which have inclined them to solve the same problem in different ways. Their arguments (since arguments must be consistent) will lead them to general principles; anyone, therefore, who moralizes necessarily generalizes; he 'draws a moral'; in giving his grounds of choice, he subsumes particular cases under a general rule. Only an aesthete in action would comfortably refuse to give any grounds of decision; he might refer the questioner to the particular qualities of the particular performance; precisely this refusal to generalize would be the mark of his aestheticism. Virtue and good conduct are essentially repeatable and imitable, in a sense in which a work of art is not. To copy a right action is to act rightly; but a copy of a work of art is not necessarily or generally a work of art.

In a moralizing climate there will always be a demand, based on analogy, for principles of criticism, parallel with principles of conduct. But this analogy must be false. Where it makes sense to speak of a problem, it makes sense to speak of a solution of it; and where solutions are offered, it makes sense to ask for reasons for preferring one solution to another; it is possible to demand consistency of choice and general principles of preference. But if something is made or done gratuitously, and not in response to a problem posed, there can be no question of preferring one solution to another; judgment of the work done does not involve a choice, and there is no need to find grounds of preference. One may, as a spectator, prefer one work to another, but there is no *necessity* to decide between them; if the works themselves are regarded as free creations, to be enjoyed or neglected for what they are, then any grading is inessential to the judgment of them; if they are not answers to a common problem, they do not compete and neither need be rejected, except on its own merits. A critical judgment is in this sense non-commital and makes no recommendation; the critic may reject the work done without being required to show what the artist ought to have done in place of the work rejected. But the moralist who condemns an action must indicate what ought to have been done in its place; for something had to be done, some choice between relative evils made. All practical decision is choice between relative evils or relative goods; if what was done was wrong, the agent must have failed to do what he ought to have done. Any moral comment has therefore some force of recommendation and is itself a practical judgment. A moral censor must put himself in the place of the agent and imaginatively confront the situation which the agent confronted; the censor and the agent censored have so far the same problem. But a critic is not another artist, as the moral censor is another agent; he is a mere spectator and he has the spectator's total irresponsibility; it is only required that he should see the object exactly as it is. Nothing which he says in judgment and description necessarily carries any exclusions with it, or necessarily reflects upon the merit of other work; the possible varieties of beautiful and excellent things are inexhaustible. He may therefore discuss any work on its merits alone, in the most strict sense of this phrase; he need not look elsewhere and to possible alternatives in making his judgment. On the contrary, his purpose is to lead people *not* to look elsewhere, but to look here, at precisely this unique object; not to see the object as one of a kind, but to see it as individual and unrepeatable.

One engages in moral argument in order to arrive at a conclusion – what is to be done or ought to have been done; one had the practical problem to begin with, and the conclusion ('this is better than that') is always more important than the route by which one arrives at it; for one *must* decide one way or the other. But a picture or poem is not created as a challenge or puzzle, requiring the spectator to decide for or against. One engages in aesthetic discussion for the sake of what one might see on the way, and not for the sake of arriving at a conclusion, a final verdict for or against; if one has been brought to see what there is to be seen in the object, the purpose of discussion is achieved. Where the logicians' framework of problem and conclusion does not apply, the notion of 'reason' loses some of its meaning also; it is unnatural to ask '*why* is that picture or sonata good?' in parallel with 'why was that the right thing to do?' There are no reasons why some object is ugly in the sense that there are reasons why some action is wrong. Perhaps it may be said that there are particular features of the particular object which *make* it ugly or beautiful, and these can be pointed out, isolated, and placed in a frame of attention; and it is the greatest service of the critic to direct attention in this analytical way. But when attention is directed to the particular features of the particular object, the point is to bring people to see these features, and not simply to lead them to say: 'That's good'. There is no point in arguing that the object is good *because* it possesses these qualities, if this involves the generalization that all objects similar in this respect are good; for if one generalizes in this manner, one looks away from the particular qualities of the particular thing, and is left with some general formula or recipe, useless alike to artist and spectator. One does not need a formula or recipe unless one needs repetitions; and one needs repetitions and rules in conduct, but not in art; the artist does not need a formula of reproduction and the spectator does not need a formula of evaluation.

The spectator-critic in any of the arts needs gifts precisely the opposite of the moralist's; he needs to suspend his natural sense of purpose and significance. To hold attention still upon any particular thing is unnatural; normally, we take objects – whether perceived by sight, touch, hearing, or by any combination of the senses – as signs of possible actions and as instances of some usable kind; we look through them to their possible uses, and classify them by their uses rather than by sensuous similarities. The common vocabulary, being created for practical purposes, obstructs any disinterested perception of things; things are (in a sense) recognized before they are really seen or heard. There is no practical reason why attention should be arrested upon a single object, framed and set apart; attention might always be practical attention, and therefore always passing from one thing to the next; in the sense in which thunder 'means' rain, almost everything means something else; 'what does it mean?' is the primitive reaction which prevents perception. One may always look through a picture as if it were a map, and look through a landscape towards a destination; for everything presented through the senses arouses expectations and is taken as a signal of some likely reaction. Nothing but holding an object still in attention, by itself and for its own sake, would count as having an aesthetic interest in it. A great part of a critic's work, in any of the arts, is to place a frame upon the object and upon its parts and features, and to do this by an unnatural use of words in description. Perception, of any kind and on any level, has degrees; some perceive more than others, and it is difficult to see and hear all that there is to see and hear. There is a metaphysical prejudice that the world consists of so many definite objects possessing so many definite qualities, and that, if we perceive and attend to the objects, we necessarily notice their qualities; as if the things and their qualities were somehow already isolated and labelled for us, ready for the camera-brain to record. So it seems that in principle a vast inventory might be made of all the things in the world with their qualities, passively received and recorded; when one had gone through the inventory of literal description, any further statements about the furniture of the world would be subjective impression and metaphor. There is the prejudice that things really do have colours and shapes, but that there do not exist, literally and objectively, concordances of colours and perceived rhythms and balances of shapes; these are supposed to be added by the mind. It seems that the more recondite qualities of form, expression, style, atmosphere, cannot properly be entered in the inventory of the world, alongside the weights and measures of things; the relations of stress and balance between masses in sculpture or building cannot *really* be seen in any literal sense; the expression of a voice is not as much a perceptible reality as its loudness. The qualities which are of no direct practical interest are normally described metaphorically, by some transference of terms from the common vocabulary; and the common vocabulary is a vocabulary of action, classifying by use and function. The assumption is that only these literal descriptions are descriptions of realities; so descriptions of aesthetic qualities become subjective impressions. But a colony of aesthetes, disengaged from practical needs and manipulations, would single out different units of attention (things), and they would see different resemblances and make different comparisons (qualities). Descriptions of aesthetic qualities, which for us are metaphorical, might seem to them to have an altogether literal and familiar sense. They might find complete agreement among themselves in the use of a more directly descriptive vocabulary, singling out different units of attention. A critic in any one of the arts is under the necessity of building such a vocabulary in opposition to the main tendency of his language; he needs somehow to convince himself that certain isolated objects of his attention really do have the extraordinary qualities which they seem to have; to this end he will need to discuss his perceptions with others, and to try to bring others to notice these qualities. He may have seen (in the wider sense of 'see') more than there is to be seen; and the only test of whether the qualities are really there must be some agreement among careful and disinterested observers. This is the point at which an aesthetic judgment is made – what are the relationships of elements here? What pattern or arrangement of elements is there to be seen, when öne attends to the thing carefully and disinterestedly? Anything may be seen or heard or read in many different ways, and as an arrangement of any number of elements of different kinds. The picking out of the elements and of their pattern, in defiance of habit and practical interest, is a work of practice and skill; and the use of words in description is an aid to this perception. Anything whatever may be picked out as an object of aesthetic interest – anything which, when attended to carefully and apart altogether from its uses, provides, by the arrangement of its elements and their suggestion to the imagination, some peculiar satisfaction of its own. An aesthetic judgment has to point to the arrangement of elements, and to show what constitutes the originality of the arrangement in this particular case; what one calls originality in one case may bear little analogy to originality found elsewhere; for there was no common problem to be solved and the achievements were essentially different.

But a moralist in criticism (and there exist such critics) will always be making unnecessary choices and laying down principles of exclusion, as a moralist must. He will make 'value judgments', and a value judgment is essentially a grading of one thing as better than another. If the judgment is an assessment of the particular excellences of works which are very similar, it may be enlightening and useful; but there can be larger comparisons of scale and greatness between things which are in themselves very different. Judgments of this second kind may be taken as practical advice that certain things ought to be read, seen, and heard, and the advice must involve some reference to the whole economy of human needs and purposes; but at this point the critic has actually become a moralist, and the arguments supporting his recommendations are the subject-matter of ethics. 'Is this thing more worth attention than other objects of its kind?' is one question, and 'What is the peculiar arrangement of elements here and what are the effects of this arrangement?' is another. Most aesthetic theories have involved a confusion of answers to these two very different questions; no positive answer to the second by itself entails any answer to the first. One would need to add some further premises about changing human needs and interests; and there is no reason to assume that all works of art satisfy the same needs and interests at all times and for all people. The objects themselves, and the artists who made them, make no unavoidable claim on the spectator's interest, and anyone may neglect the work done when it is of no interest to him. But the peculiar features of particular objects, with their own originality of arrangement, remain constant and unaffected by the spectator's choices and priorities; and there can be no place for exclusive theories and general principles in identifying their originality; they must be seen as they are, individually, and not judged as contestants in a single race called Art or The Novel or Painting.

I conclude that everyone needs a morality to make exclusions in conduct; but neither an artist nor a critical spectator unavoidably needs an aesthetic; and when in Aesthetics one moves from the particular to the general, one is travelling in the wrong direction.

Does traditional aesthetics rest on a mistake?

William E. Kennick (b.1923)

In the next extract, William E. Kennick takes a very similar line to Stuart Hampshire's (Reading 21) concerning the essential 'gratuitousness' of works of art, and the consequent fruitlessness of seeking to establish general principles for criticism. The main thrust of Kennick's argument is directed against the assumption that criticism presupposes aesthetic theory. Kennick sees no such necessary connection. Criticism can do quite well without general principles and criteria, and has no need to be grounded in a philosophical theory. Our tendency to assume the necessary connection above, he argues, merely demonstrates a mistaken analogy we make between aesthetic and moral judgements.

It rests, I think, on at least two of them, and the purpose of this paper is to explore the claim that it does.

By 'traditional aesthetics' I mean that familiar philosophical discipline which concerns itself with trying to answer such questions as the following: What is Art? What is Beauty? What is the Aesthetic Experience? What is the Creative Act? What are the criteria of Aesthetic Judgement and Taste? What is the function of Criticism? To be sure, there are others, like: Are the aesthetic object and the work of art the same? or, Does art have any cognitive content? – but these questions are commonly taken to be subordinate to those of the first group, which might be called the 'basic questions' of traditional aesthetics.

1   *The Basic Questions as Requests for Definitions.* If someone asks me 'What is helium?' I can reply: 'It's a gas' or 'It's a chemical element' or 'It's a gaseous element, inert and colourless, whose atomic number is 2 and whose atomic weight is 4.003'. A number of replies will do, depending upon whom I am talking to, the aim of his question, and so on. It is a pretty straightforward business; we get answers to such questions every day from dictionaries, encyclopedias, and technical manuals.

Now someone asks me 'What is Space?' or 'What is Man?' or 'What is Religion?' or 'What is Art?' His question is of the same form as the question 'What is helium?' but how vastly different! There is something very puzzling about these questions; they cannot be answered readily by appealing to dictionaries, encyclopedias, or technical manuals. They are philosophical questions, we say, giving our puzzlement a name, although we should not think of calling 'What is helium?' a philosophical question. Yet we expect something of the same sort of answer to both of them. There's the rub.

We say that questions like 'What is Space?' or 'What is Art?' are requests for information about the nature or essence of Space or of Art. We could say that 'What is helium?' is a request for information about the nature or essence of helium, but we rarely, if ever, do; although we do use questions like 'What is helium?' as analogues of questions like 'What is Space?' to show the sort of reply we are looking for. What we want, we say, is a definition of Space or Art, for as Plato and Aristotle taught us long ago, 'definition is the formula of the essence'. So, just as the traditional metaphysicians have long sought for the nature or essence of Space and of Time, of Reality and of Change, the traditional aesthetician has sought for the essence of Art and of Beauty, of the Aesthetic Experience and the Creative Act. Most of the basic questions of traditional aesthetics are requests for definitions; hence the familiar formulae that constitute the results of traditional aesthetic inquiry: 'Art is Expression' (Croce), 'Art is Significant Form' (Clive Bell), 'Beauty is Pleasure Objectified' (Santayana), and so on. Given these definitions we are supposed to know what Art is or what Beauty is, just as we are supposed to know what helium is if someone tells us that it is a chemical element, gaseous, inert, and colourless, with an atomic number of 2 and an atomic weight of 4.003. F. J. E. Woodbridge once remarked that metaphysics searches for the nature of reality and finds it by definition. We might say that traditional aesthetics searches for the nature of Art or Beauty and finds it by definition.

But why should it be so difficult to discern the essence of Art or Beauty? Why should it take so much argument to establish or defend such formulae as 'Art is Expression'? And once we have arrived at such formulae or have been given them in answer to our question, why should they be so dissatisfying?

To come closer to an answer to these questions, we must look at what it is the aesthetician expects of a definition of Art or Beauty. De Witt Parker has stated with unusual clarity the 'assumption' of the aesthetician in asking and answering such questions as 'What is Art?'; at the beginning of his essay on 'The Nature of Art' (note the title) he says:

> The assumption underlying every philosophy of art is the existence of some *common nature* present in all the arts, despite their differences in form and content; something the *same* in painting and sculpture; in poetry and drama; in music and architecture. Every single work of art, it is admitted, has a unique flavour, a *je ne sais quoi* which makes it incomparable with every other work; nevertheless, there is some mark or set of marks which, if it applies to any work of art, applies to *all* works of art, *and to nothing else* – a common denominator, so to say, which constitutes the definition of art, and serves to separate . . . the field of art from other fields of human culture.[1]

What we are after, it should be clear, is what the traditional logic texts calls a 'definition *per genus et differentiam*' of Art and Beauty.
2   *The Assumption Questioned; the First Mistake.* The assumption that, despite their differences, all works of art must possess some common nature, some distinctive set of characteristics which serves to separate Art from everything else, a set of necessary and sufficient conditions for their being works of art at all, is both natural and disquieting, and constitutes what I consider to be the first mistake on which traditional aesthetics rests. It is natural, because, after all, we do use the word 'art' to refer to a large number of very different things – pictures and poems and musical compositions and sculptures and vases and a host of other things; and yet the word is one word. Surely, we are inclined to say, there must be something common to them all or we should not call them all by the same name. *Unum nomen; unum nominatum.*

Yet the assumption is disquieting when we come to search for the common nature which we suppose all works of art to possess. It is so elusive. We ought to be able to read a poem by Donne or by Keats, a novel by George Eliot or Joseph Conrad, or a play by Sophocles or Shakespeare, to listen to Mozart and Stravinsky, and to look at the pictures of Giotto and Cezanne and the Chinese masters and *see* what Art is. But when we look we do not see what Art is. So we are inclined to suppose that its essence must be something hidden, something that only an aesthetician can see, like the sounds that only a dog can hear, or else, as Parker, for example, supposes, that it must be something very complex, involving many characteristics (*op. cit.* p.93). This explains why an adequate definition of Art is so hard to arrive at, why it is so much harder to answer questions like 'What is Art?' than it is to answer questions like 'What is helium?' Perhaps this also explains why there is a Philosophy of Art when there is no Philosophy of Helium?

But this explanation will not do. It will not do, that is, to suppose simply that the essence or nature of Art is elusive, very hard to detect, or very complex. It suggests that what we are faced with is a problem of scrutinizing, that what we have to do is to look long and hard at works of art, examine them carefully and diligently, and *voila*! we shall *see*. But no amount of looking and scrutinizing gives us what we want. All we see is this poem and that play, this picture and that statue, or some feature of them that catches our attention; and if we find some resemblances between poems or plays or pictures, or even between poems *and* pictures, pictures *and* musical compositions, these resemblances quickly disappear when we turn to other poems and plays and pictures. That is why in aesthetics it is best not to look at too many works of art and why, incidentally, aesthetics is best taught without concrete examples; a few will do. We can readily believe that we have seen the essence of Art when we have selected our examples properly; but when we range farther afield we lose it.

Despite the temptation to think that if we look long enough and hard enough at works of art we shall find the common denominator in question, after all the fruitless scrutinizing that has already been done, it is still more tempting to think that we are looking for something that is not there, like looking for the equator or the line on the spectrum that separates orange from red. No wonder that in aesthetics we soon begin to feel the frustration of St. Augustine when he asked himself 'What is Time?': 'If I am not asked, I know; if I am asked, I know not'. Something must be wrong.

What is wrong, as I see it, has nothing to do with the nature or essence of Art at all; that is, there is neither anything mysterious nor anything complicated about works of art which makes the task of answering the question 'What is Art?' so difficult. Like St. Augustine with Time, we do know quite well what Art is; it is only when someone asks us that we do not know. The trouble lies not in the works of art themselves but in the concept of Art. The word 'art', unlike the word 'helium', has a complicated variety of uses, what is nowadays called a complex 'logic'. It is not a word coined in the laboratory or the studio to name something that has hitherto escaped our attention; nor is it a relatively simple term of common parlance like 'star' or 'tree' which names something with which we are all quite familiar. As Professor Kristeller has shown us[2] it is a word with a long, involved, and interesting history; a complicated concept indeed, but not for the reasons which the aestheticians suppose. Any good dictionary will indicate some of its many meanings, some of the variety of uses which the word 'art' has; but no dictionary will give us the kind of formula which the aestheticians seek. That is why we suppose that the nature of Art is a philosophical problem and why there is a Philosophy of Art but no Philosophy of Helium. It is the complicated concepts like those of Space, Time, Reality, Change, Art, Knowledge, and so on that baffle us. Dictionaries and their definitions are of use in making short shrift of questions of the form 'What is X?' only in relatively simple and comparatively trivial cases; in the hard and more interesting cases they are frustrating and disappointing.

Doubtless there is an answer to this, and it might run somewhat as follows: 'We know that the word 'Art' has a variety of uses in English. Most commonly it is used to refer to pictures alone; when we visit an art museum or consult an art critic, we expect to see pictures or to hear pictures talked about. We say that painting, painting pictures, *not* painting houses or fences, is *an* art, that cooking and sewing and basket-weaving, bookbinding and selling are *arts*, but only some pictures do we call *works* of art, and rarely do we refer to dishes or garments or baskets as works of art, except honorifically. We speak of the liberal arts and the industrial arts and of the art of war. But all of this is beside the point. As aestheticians we are interested only in what are sometimes called the "fine arts", or what Collingwood calls "art proper" – works of art. Surely all of these have something in common, else how should we be able to separate those paintings and drawings and poems and plays, musical compositions and buildings which are works of art from those which are not?'

To answer the last question first and make a long story short: we are able to separate those objects which are works of art from those which are not, because we know English; that is, we know how correctly to use the word 'art' and to apply the phrase 'work of art'. To borrow a statement from Dr. Waismann and change it to meet my own needs, 'If anyone is able to use the word "art" or the phrase "work of art" correctly, in all sorts of contexts and on the right sort of occasions, he knows "what art is", and no formula in the world can make him wiser'.[3] 'Art proper' is simply what is properly called 'art'. The 'correctly' and 'properly' here have nothing to do with any 'common nature' or 'common denominator' of all works of art; they have merely to do with the rules that govern the actual and commonly accepted usage of the word 'art'.

Imagine a very large warehouse filled with all sorts of things – pictures of every description, musical scores for symphonies and dances and hymns, machines, tools, boats, houses, churches and temples, statues, vases, books of poetry and of prose, furniture and clothing, newspapers, postage stamps, flowers, trees, stones, musical instruments. Now we instruct someone to enter the warehouse and bring out all of the works of art it contains. He will be able to do this with reasonable success, despite the fact that, as even the aestheticians must admit, he possesses no satisfactory definition of Art in terms of some common denominator, because no such definition has yet been found. Now imagine the same person sent into the warehouse to bring out all objects with Significant Form, or all objects of Expression. He would rightly be baffled; he knows a work of art when he sees one, but he has little or no idea what to look for when he is told to bring an object that possesses Significant Form.

To be sure, there are many occasions on which we are not sure whether something is a work of art or not; that is, we are not sure whether to call a given drawing or musical composition a work of art or not. Are 'Nearer My God to Thee' and the political cartoons of Mr. Low works of art? But this merely reflects the systematic vagueness of the concepts in question, or what Dr. Waismann on another occasion has called their 'open texture'; a vagueness, note, which the definitions of the aestheticians do nothing at all to remove. On such occasions we can, of course, tighten the texture, remove some of the vagueness, by making a decision, drawing a line; and perhaps curators and purchasing committees of art museums are sometimes forced for obvious practical reasons to do this. But in doing so, they and we are not discovering anything about Art.

We do know what art is when no one asks us what it is; that is, we know quite well how to use the word 'art' and the phrase 'work of art' correctly. And when someone asks us what art is, we do *not* know; that is, we are at a loss to produce any simple formula, or any complex one, which will neatly exhibit the logic of this word and this phrase. It is the compulsion to reduce the complexity of aesthetic concepts to simplicity, neatness, and order that moves the aesthetician to make his first mistake, to ask 'What is Art?' and to expect to find an answer like the answer that can be given to 'What is Helium?'

What I have said about Art in this section applies, *mutatis mutandis*, to Beauty, the Aesthetic Experience, the Creative Act, and all of the other entities with which traditional aesthetics concerns itself.

Where there is no mystery, there is no need for removing a mystery and certainly none for inventing one.

3 *Common Denominators and Similarities.* Is the search for common characteristics among works of art, then, a fool's errand? That depends upon what we expect to find. If we expect to find some common denominator in Parker's sense, we are bound to be disappointed. We shall get ourselves enmeshed in unnecessary difficulties, and the definitions which we hope will free us from the net will be specious at best. If we say 'Art is Significant Form' we may feel momentarily enlightened; but when we come to reflect upon what we mean by 'significant form' we shall find ourselves entangled again. For the notion of Significant Form is clearly more obscure than is that of Art or Beauty, as the example of the warehouse above amply illustrates; the same holds for Expression, Intuition, Representation, and the other favoured candidates of the aestheticians. Nor will it do to say, as Professor Munro does,[4] that 'art is skill in providing stimuli to satisfactory aesthetic experience'. This has merely a scientific *sound*, and this sound is about as close as the effort to make aesthetics scientific comes to science. The notion of aesthetic experience is fraught with the same difficulties as the notion of art. To put it dogmatically, there is no such thing as *the* Aesthetic Experience; different sorts of experiences are properly referred to as aesthetic. Do not say they must all be contemplative. Does that really help at all?

There is, however, a fruitful and enlightening search for similarities and resemblances in art which the search for the common denominator sometimes furthers, the search for what, to torture a phrase of Wittgenstein's, we can call 'family resemblances'. When we squint we can sometimes see features of an object which otherwise we should miss. So in aesthetics, when we narrow our view, when in the search for the common denominator we carefully select our examples and restrict our sight, we may not see what we are looking for, but we may see something of more interest and importance. The simplifying formulae of the aestheticians are not to be scrapped merely because they fail to do what they are designed to do. What fails to do one thing may do another. The mistake of the aestheticians can be turned to advantage. The suspicion that aesthetics is not nonsense is often justified. For the idea that there is a unity among the arts, properly employed, can lead to the uncovering of similarities which, when noticed, enrich our commerce with art. Croce's supposed discovery that Art is Expression calls our attention to, among other things, an interesting feature of some, if not all, works of art, namely, their indifference to the distinction between the real and the unreal.

Or, to take examples from critics, when F. R. Leavis says of Crabbe, 'His art is that of the short-story writer',[5] and when Professor Stechow compares the fourth movement of Schumann's 'Rhenish' Symphony with certain features of the Cologne Cathedral,[6] we have something of interest and importance. Our attention is refocused on certain works, and we see them in a new light. One of the offices of creative criticism, as of creative aesthetics, is the finding and pointing out of precisely such similarities.

4 *Aesthetic Theories Reconsidered.* Philosophical mistakes are rarely downright howlers; they have a point. What I have said is, I think, correct, but it neglects an important facet of the quest for essences, a by-product of that search, so to speak, which we should not ignore. An aesthetic theory, by which I mean a systematic answer to such questions as 'What is Art?' 'What is Beauty?' and the like, frequently does something quite other than what it sets out to do. The assumption underlying traditional aesthetics, as Parker states it in the passage quoted above, is wrong, and I hope I have shown why it is wrong. It does not follow from this, however, that aesthetic theories are wholly without point, that they are merely mistaken, that formulae like 'Art is Significant Form' are worthless, useless, or meaningless. They do serve a purpose, but their purpose is not that which Parker assigns them. Considered in context, in the historical or personal context, for example, they are frequently seen to have a point which has nothing to do with the philosophical excuses that are made for them.

Take Bell's famous dictum that 'Art is Significant Form'. It does not help us to understand what art is at all, and to that extent it is a failure; its shortcomings in this direction have been exposed on numerous occasions. It is easy to beat Bell down; he is so vulnerable. But when we stop to consider that he was an Englishman and when he wrote his book on art (1913) and what the taste of the English was like then and of his association with Roger Fry, the statement that 'Art is Significant Form' loses some of its mystifying sound. It has a *point*. Not the point that Bell thinks it has, for Bell was also looking for the common denominator; another point. We might put it this way. The taste of Edwardian Englishmen in art was restricted to what we pejoratively call the 'academic'. Subject-matter was of prime importance to them – portraits of eminent persons, landscapes with or without cows, genre scenes, pictures of fox hunts, and the rest. Bell had seen the paintings of Cezanne, Matisse, and Picasso, and he was quick to see that subject-matter was not of prime importance in them, that the value of the paintings did not rest on realism or sentimental associations. It rested on what? Well, 'significant form'; lines and colours and patterns and harmonies that stir apart from associations evoked by subject-matter. He found also that he could look at other paintings, older paintings, paintings by the Venetian and Dutch masters, for example, and at vases and carpets and sculptures in the same way he looked at Cezanne. He found such looking rewarding, exciting. But when he turned to the pictures of the academicians, the thrill disappeared; they could not be looked at profitably in this way. What was more natural, then, than that he should announce his discovery by saying 'Art *is* Significant Form'? He *had* discovered something for himself. Not the essence of Art, as the philosophers would have it, although he thought that this is what he found, but *a new way of looking at pictures.* He wanted to share his discovery with others and to reform English taste. *Here* is the point of his dictum; 'Art is Significant Form' is a slogan, the epitome of a platform of aesthetic reform. It has work to do. Not the work which the philosophers assign it, but a work of teaching people a new way of looking at pictures.

When we blow the dust of philosophic cant away from aesthetic theories and look at them in this way, they take on an importance which otherwise they seem to lack. Read Aristotle's *Poetics*, not as a philosophical exercise in definition, but as instruction in one way to read tragic poetry, and it takes on a new life. Many of the other dicta of the aestheticians can also be examined in this light. We know that as definitions they will not do; but as instruments of instruction or reform they will do. Perhaps that is why they have had more real weight with practising critics than they have had with philosophers. The critics have caught the point, where the philosophers, misguided from the start by a foolish preoccupation with definition, have missed it.

5   *Aesthetics and Criticism; the Second Mistake.* One of the prime reasons for the aesthetician's search for definitions of Art, Beauty, and the rest, is his supposition that unless we know what Art or

Beauty is, we cannot say what good art or beautiful art is. Put it in the form of an assumption: Criticism presupposes Aesthetic Theory. This assumption contains the second mistake on which traditional aesthetics rests, namely, the view that responsible criticism is impossible without standards or criteria universally applicable to all works of art. The second mistake is in this way closely related to the first.

To see more clearly how this assumption operates, we can turn to a recent book by Mr. Harold Osborne,[7] *Aesthetics and Criticism.* Osborne believes that 'a theory of the nature of artistic excellence is implicit in every critical assertion which is other than autobiographical record', and he thinks that 'until the theory has been made explicit the criticism is without meaning' (p.3). By a 'theory of the nature of artistic excellence' Osborne means a theory of the nature of Beauty (p.3).

Osborne examines several theories of the nature of Beauty and finds them all wanting. His moves against them are instructive. Take, for example, his move against a version of the Realistic Theory in Chapter V, that theory holding that artistic excellence consists in 'truth to life' – or so Osborne states it. He correctly notes that practising critics have rarely insisted that verisimilitude is a necessary condition of artistic excellence, and we should all agree that it is not. 'But', says Osborne, 'if correspondence with real or possible actuality is not a necessary condition of artistic excellence, then most certainly it is not and cannot be of itself an *artistic* virtue, or an aesthetic merit, in those works of literature where it happens to occur' (p.93). This is a curious argument. It seems to contain a glaring non-sequitur. But what leads Osborne from his protasis to his conclusion is the assumption that the only acceptable reason offerable for a critical judgement of a work of art is one framed in terms of a characteristic which all works of art, *qua* works of art, must possess. Since we admit that not all works of art must possess truth to life or verisimilitude, we cannot use their adventitious possession of this property as a reason for praising, judging, or commending them as works of art.

Now surely this is mistaken. We can agree that correspondence with real or possible actuality, whatever that may mean, is not a *necessary* condition of artistic excellence; that is, it is *not* necessary that it appear among the reasons offerable for the judgement that a given work of art is good or beautiful. But it does not follow that therefore it does not and cannot appear as *a* reason for such a judgement. We can and do praise works of art, *as* works of art, whatever the force of that is, for a variety of reasons, and not always the same variety. Osborne's reply here is that in doing so we are being 'illogical and inconsistent'. Attacking the users of the Hedonistic Criterion, he says, 'In so far as he [the critic] also uses other criteria [than the hedonistic one] for grading and assessing works of art, he is being illogical and inconsistent with himself whenever he does introduce the hedonistic – or emotional – assumption' (p.139). But why? There is nothing whatever illogical or inconsistent about praising, grading, or judging a work of art for more than one reason, unless we assume with Osborne that one and only one reason is offerable on pain of inconsistency, which is clearly not the case in art or anywhere else.

Osborne, true to the assumptions of traditional aesthetics, is looking for that condition which is both necessary and sufficient for artistic excellence or merit. His own candidate for that condition is what he calls 'configurational coherence'. But if anything pointed were needed to convince us of the emptiness of the search, it is the unintelligibility of Osborne's account of 'beauty as configuration'. If what I have said above about the concepts of Art and Beauty is true, we should not be surprised by this. For 'art' and 'beauty' do not name one and only one substance and attribute respectively; no wonder we cannot find the one thing they name or render intelligible the felt discovery that they do name one thing. We can *make* each of them name one thing if we wish. But why should we bother? We get along very well with them as they are.

6 *Ethics and Criticism; the Second Mistake Again.* 'But surely', someone will say,' this cannot be the whole story. We can and do say that this work of art, this picture, for example, is better than that, or that this is a good one and that one is not. Do we not presuppose certain standards or criteria when we make such judgements? And isn't this really all that Osborne and other aestheticians have in mind when they insist that criticism presupposes aesthetic theory? They are looking for the standards of critical judgement and taste in the nature of art, just as many moralists have looked for the standards of right conduct in the nature of man. They may be looking in the wrong place, but clearly they are right in assuming that there must be something to find.'

My reply is this: they are not looking in the wrong place so much as they are looking for the wrong thing. The bases of responsible criticism are indeed to be found *in* the work of art and nowhere else, but this in no way implies that critical judgements presuppose any canons, rules, standards, or criteria applicable to all works of art.

When we say that a certain knife is a good knife, we have in mind certain features of the knife, or of knives in general, which we believe will substantiate or support this claim: the sharpness of the blade, the sturdiness of the handle, the durability of the metal, the way it fits the hand, and so on. There are a number of such considerations, all of which refer to characteristics of the knife and not to our feelings about or attitudes towards it, which may be said to constitute the criteria of a good knife. Special criteria may be adduced for fishing knives as opposed to butcher knives, and so on, but this does not affect the issue in question. Note first that there is no definite or exhaustively specifiable list of criteria in common and universal employment; it does not make sense to ask how many there are or whether we have considered them all. But there are generally accepted criteria with which we are all familiar which we use to support our judgements, though in cases of special instruments or implements, like ophthalmoscopes, only specialists are acquainted with the criteria. Secondly, note how the criteria are related to the purposes or functions of knives, to the uses to which we put them, the demands we make upon them. 'Knife', we might say, is a function-word, a word that names something which is usually defined by its function or functions. The criteria, we can say loosely, are derivable from the definition. This second consideration has led some aestheticians to look for the standards of taste and criticism in the function of art.

Now take apples. They have, of course, no function. We use them, we do things with them – eat them, use them for decoration, feed them to pigs, press cider from them, and so on – but none of these things can be said to constitute the function of an apple. Depending, however, on how we use them or what we use them for, we can frame lists of criteria similar to the lists for knives. The best apples for decoration are not always the best for eating, nor are the best for making pies always the best for making cider. Now take mathematicians. A mathematician, unless he is assigned a particular work to do, again has no function. There are certain things a mathematician does, however, and in terms of these we can again frame criteria for judging, praising, grading, and commending mathematicians. Finally, take men in general. We often praise a man, *as* a man, as opposed to as a plumber or a mathematician, and we call this sort of praise moral praise. Here again, we have criteria for assessing the moral worth of men, although, theological considerations aside, we do not frame them in terms of man's function, purpose, or task, even if some moralists, like Aristotle, have tried to frame them in terms of man's end. But we make demands on men, moral demands on all men, and our criteria reflect these demands.

Let us turn now to art. The question we have to raise is this: Are critical judgements of pictures and poems logically symmetrical to the sorts of judgements we have been considering? I think they are not, or not entirely. Not because they are somehow more subjective or unreliable than other value judgements (this issue is as false as an issue can be!), but because the pattern of justification and support which is appropriate to them is of a different sort. Any criticial judgement, to be justified, must be supported by reasons; this goes without saying, for this is what 'justification' means. But must the reasons offerable and acceptable in cases of critical appraisal be of the same order or type as those offerable and acceptable in cases of instruments, implements, useful objects, professional services, jobs, offices, or moral conduct? In particular, must there be any general rules, standards, criteria, canons, or laws applicable to all works of art by which alone such critical appraisals can be supported? I think not.

In the first place, we should note that only a man corrupted by aesthetics would think of judging a work of art *as* a work of art in general, as opposed to as this poem, that picture, or this symphony. There is some truth in the contention that the notions of Art and Work of Art are special aestheticians' concepts. This follows quite naturally from the absence of any distinguishing feature or features common to all works of art as such, and from the absence of any single demand or set of demands which we make on all works of art as such. Despite the occasional claim that it has, Art has no function or purpose, in the sense in which knives and ophthalmoscopes have functions, and this is an insight to be gained from the 'art for art's sake' position. This does not mean that we cannot use individual works of art for special purposes; we can and do. We can use novels and poems and symphonies to put us to sleep or wake us up; we can use pictures to cover spots on the wall, vases to hold flowers, and sculptures for paper weights or door stops. This is what lends point to the distinction between judging something *as* a work of art and judging it *as* a sedative, stimulant, or paper weight; but we cannot conclude from this that Art has some special function or purpose in addition to the purposes to which it can be put.

Similarly there is no one thing which we *do* with all works of art: some we hang, some we play, some we perform, some we read; some we look at, some we listen to, some we analyse, some we contemplate, and so on. There is no special aesthetic use of works of art, even though it may make sense, and even be true, to say that a person who uses a statue as a door stop is not using it as a work of art; he is not doing one of the things we normally do with works of art; he is not treating it properly, we might say. But the proper treatment of works of art varies from time to time and from place to place. It was quite proper for a cave man to hurl his spear at the drawing of a bison, just as it was quite proper for the Egyptians to seal up paintings and sculptures in a tomb. Such treatment does not render the object thus treated not a work of art. The attempt to define Art in terms of what we do with certain objects is as doomed as any other. From this and the first consideration it follows that there is no way by which we can derive the criteria of taste and criticism from the function of art or from its use.

The remaining parallel is with moral appraisal, and this is the most interesting of them all. It has been, and perhaps still is, a common view among philosophers that Beauty and Goodness are two species of the same genus, namely, Value, and that therefore there are at least two classes of value judgements, namely, moral judgements and aesthetic judgements. For this reason there is a tendency further to suppose that there is a logical symmetry between the two. But the supposition of symmetry is a mistake, and I am led to suspect that it does little but harm to suppose that Beauty and Goodness are two species of the same genus at all. There are clearly certain similarities between the two, that is, between the logic of statements of the form 'This is good' and the logic of statements of the form 'This is beautiful' – they are used in many of the same ways – but this must not blind us to the differences. Criticism suffers from a very natural comparison with ethics.

Moral appraisal is like the other forms of appraisal, in this respect; it expresses a desire for uniformity. It is when we are interested in uniformity of size, milk producing capacity, conduct, and so on, that standards or criteria become so important. We maintain standards in products and in workmanship; we enforce them, hold ourselves up to them, teach them to our children, insist on them, and so on, all for the sake of a certain uniformity. In morals we *are* interested in uniformity, at least in what we expect men not to do; that is one reason why rules and laws are necessary and why they play such an important rôle in moral appraisal. But in art, unless, like Plato, we wish to be legislators and to require something of art, demand that it perform a specified educational and social service, we are not as a rule interested in uniformity. Some critics and aestheticians are, of course, interested in uniformity – uniformity in the works of art themselves or uniformity in our approach to them. For them it is quite natural to demand criteria. For them it is also quite natural to formulate theories of Art and Beauty. Remember what we said about aesthetic theories above: the definitions in which they issue are often slogans of reform. As such they are also often devices for the encouragement of uniformity. But this merely betrays the persuasive character of many aesthetic theories, and the peculiar legislative posture of some critics and aestheticians is no warrant for the assumption that the criteria in question are necessary for responsible criticism. Nor should it blind us to the fact that we do quite well without them. Criticism has in no way been hampered by the absence of generally applicable canons and norms, and where such norms have been proposed they have either, like the notorious Unities in the case of tragedy, been shown to be absurd, or else, like the requirements of balance, harmony, and unity in variety, they have been so general, equivocal, and empty as to be useless in critical practice. Ordinarily we feel no constraint in praising one novel for its verisimilitude, another for its humour, and still another for its plot or characterization. We remark on the richness of Van Gogh's impasto, but we do not find it a fault in a Chinese scroll painting that it is flat and smooth. Botticelli's lyric grace is his glory, but Giotto and Chardin are not to be condemned because their poetry is of another order. The merits of Keats and Shelley are not those of Donne and Herbert. And why should Shakespeare and Aeschylus be measured by the same rod? Different works of art are, or may be, praiseworthy or blameworthy for different reasons, and not always the same reasons. A quality that is praiseworthy in one painting may be blameworthy in another; realism is not always a virtue, but this does not mean that it is not sometimes a virtue.[8]

Mr. Hampshire has put the reason why the criteria sought by the aestheticians are so 'elusive' and why the parallel with ethics is a mistake in this way: 'A work of art', he says, 'is gratuitous. It is not *essentially* the answer to a question or the solution of a presented problem' (*op. cit.* p.162). There is no one problem being solved or question answered by all poems, all pictures, all symphonies, let alone all works of art. If we set a number of people to doing the same thing, we can rate them on how well they do it. We have, or can frame, a criterion. But not all artists are doing the same thing – solving the same problem, answering the same question, playing the same game, running the same race. Some of them may be, we do group artists together by 'schools', and in other ways, to indicate precisely this kind of similarity; but only in so far as they are does it make sense to compare and appraise them on the same points. It is no criticism of Dickens that he did not write like Henry James. Writing a novel or a lyric poem may, in some interesting respects, be like playing a game or solving a problem, we in fact speak of artists as solving problems. But it is also different; so that if we wish to retain the analogy we must call attention to the differences by saying that not all poets or novelists are playing the *same* game, solving the *same* problems. There is indeed a certain gratuitousness in art which destroys the parallelism or symmetry between moral and aesthetic appraisal.

But there is also a gratuitousness in aesthetic criticism. Moral appraisal, like legal judgement, is a practical necessity; aesthetic appraisal is not. That is why the claim that in art it is all a matter of taste is tolerable, even if it is false, when this sounds so shocking in morals. We can live side by side in peace and amity with those whose tastes differ quite radically from our own; similar differences in moral standards are more serious. And yet, of course, aesthetic criticism is not merely a matter of taste, if by taste we mean unreasoned preferences. Taste does play an important part in the differences among critical appraisals, but we are clearly not satisfied when, in answer to our question 'Why is it good?' or 'What's good about it?', we are told 'It's good because I like it.' Mrs. Knight correctly notes that 'my *liking* a picture is never a criterion of its goodness' (*op. cit.* p.154). That is, my liking a picture is no reason for its *being* good, though it may be a reason for my *saying* that it is good.

But if it is not all a matter of liking and disliking, why is it that a certain feature is a virtue in a given work of art? If someone tells me that a certain work of art is good for such and such reasons, how can I tell whether the reasons he offers are good reasons or not, or even if they are relevant? These questions are not easily answered, for in practice we adduce many considerations for saying that a work of art is good or that a certain feature of it is a virtue. I will make no attempt to canvass these considerations but will close with some observations on a logical feature of the problem.

We are confronted, I think, with a problem that is really two problems: there is the problem of saying why a given work of art is good or bad, and there is the problem of saying why our reasons are good or bad, or even relevant. We may praise a picture, say, for its subtle balance, colour contrast, and draughtsmanship; this is saying why the picture is good. We may now go on to raise the more 'philosophical' question of what makes balance, or this sort of colour contrast, or this kind of draughtsmanship an artistic virtue. The first sort of question, the question of why the work of art is good or bad, is decided by appeal to the 'good-making characteristics' or 'criterion-characters' of the work of art in question, that is, by an appeal to certain objectively discriminable characteristics of the work under discussion. These characteristics are many and various; there is a large variety of reasons offerable for a work of art's being a good or bad work of art. The second sort of question, the question of the worth or relevance of the reasons offered in answer to the first question, is settled by appeal either to custom or to decision. In this respect aesthetic criticism is very like moral appraisal. We either simply praise what is customarily praised and condemn what is customarily condemned or we *decide* what the criteria shall be. This does not mean that the criteria, that is, the reasons offerable for a work of art's being good or bad, are arbitrary. There may be plenty of reasons why one feature is a 'criterion-character' and another is not. Part of the reason may be psychological, part sociological, part metaphysical, or even religious and ethical. Only an aesthete ignores, or tries to ignore, the many relations of a poem or picture to life and concentrates on what are called the purely 'formal' values of the work at hand; but in doing so he *determines* what he will accept as a reason for a work of art's being good or bad. That a work of art assists the cause of the proletariat in the class struggle *is* a reason for its being a good work of art to a convinced Marxist, but it is not a reason, let alone a good reason, to the bourgeois aesthete. That a picture contains nude figures is a reason, to the puritan and the prude, for condemning it, though no enlightened man can be brought to accept it. Thus morals and politics and religion do enter into our critical judgements, even when we claim that they should not.

I noted above that there is no one use which we make of all works of art, nor is there any one demand or set of demands which we make on them. This is, I think, important, and serves to explain, at least in part, the actual relativity of aesthetic criteria. What one age looks for in painting or in literature, another age may neglect.

What one group demands, another forbids. We are not always consistent in even our own demands on art, and I can see no reason why we should be. We can be interested in works of art for many reasons, and some of these reasons may be more decisive at one time or in one set of circumstances than they are at another time or in another set of circumstances. This affects the very logic of critical appraisal by determining the relevance and merit of the reasons we offer for our judgements. We are well aware of the fact that the estimate of a given poet or painter changes from period to period. El Greco's or Shakespeare's reputation has not always been what it is, and no one should be surprised if it should change in the future. But if we examine the reasons that have been offered for the different estimates, we find that they too are different. Different reasons are persuasive at different times and in different contexts. The same explanation is operative: the needs and interests that art gratifies are different from time to time and, to a lesser extent perhaps, from person to person. But as the needs and interests vary, so also will the criteria and the weight we place on them. This is a vicious relativism only to those who are morally disposed to insist on the uniformity of taste.

Summary I have tried to show (1) that the search for essences in aesthetics is a mistake, arising from the failure to appreciate the complex but not mysterious logic of such words and phrases as 'art', 'beauty', 'the aesthetic experience', and so on. But (2) although the characteristics common to all works of art are the object of a fool's errand, the search for similarities in sometimes very different works of art can be profitably pursued, and this search is occasionally stimulated by the formulae of the aestheticians. (3) Although the definitions of the aestheticians are useless for the role usually assigned to them, we must not ignore the live purpose they frequently serve as slogans in the effort to change taste and as instruments for opening up new avenues of appreciation. (4) If the search for the common denominator of all works of art is abandoned, abandoned with it must be the attempt to derive the criteria of critical appreciation and appraisal from the nature of art. (5) Traditional aesthetics mistakenly supposes that responsible criticism is impossible without a set of rules, canons, or standards applicable to all works of art. This supposition arises from an uncritical assimilation of the pattern of critical appraisal to that of appraisal in other areas, particularly morals, and from a failure to appreciate the gratuitousness of art and the manner in which reasons are operative in the justification of critical judgements.

Notes

1   De Witt H. Parker, 'The Nature of Art', *Revue Internationale de Philosophie*, July 1939, p.684; reprinted in E. Vivas and M. Krieger, eds., *The Problems of Aesthetics* (New York, 1953), p.90. Italics mine.

2   P. O. Kristeller, 'The Modern System of the Arts: A Study in the History of Aesthetics', *Journal of the History of Ideas*, xii (1951), 496–527: xiii (1952), 17–46.

3   See F. Waismann, 'Analytic-Synthetic II', *Analysis*, 11 (1950), p.27.

4   Thomas Munro, *The Arts and Their Interrelations* (New York, 1949), p.108.

5   F. R. Leavis, *Revaluation: Tradition and Development in English Poetry* (London, 1936), p.125.

6   Wolfgang Stechow, 'Problems of Structure in Some Relations Between the Visual Arts and Music', *The Journal of Aesthetics and Art Criticism*, xi (1953), 325.

7   Routledge and Kegal Paul Ltd., London, 1955.

8   I owe much in this section to Helen Knight's 'The Use of "Good" in Aesthetic Judgments', *Aesthetics and Language*, William Elton edn. (Oxford, 1954), pp.147ff., and to Stuart Hampshire's 'Logic and Appreciation', *ibid.*, pp.161ff.

On the generality of critical reasons

Monroe C. Beardsley (1915–80)

Kennick's scepticism regarding the possibility of general principles of criticism is vigorously countered in the following essay by Monroe C. Beardsley, who argues that in the absence of general criteria there can be no critical criteria at all. Whereas the sceptic denies that there can be criteria of aesthetic value, or that reasons can be given for critical judgements, Beardsley insists that criticism is a rational activity and that the critic's judgements can be supported by good reasons. Indeed, for Beardsley, any act of critical judgement implicitly assumes the possibility of support by other propositions. He outlines what he calls a 'General Criterion Theory', based on the premise that some form of generality is an essential element of reason-giving.

If giving reasons for an assertion consists in making other assertions and also asserting that they support it, then critics evidently give reasons for their judgments of art. To doubt this is to urge a stricter concept of reason-giving, according to which not every proposition that is alleged to be a reason actually is one. But then, using the narrower definition, we can still say that critics wish to give reasons, and think they are doing so, whether or not they succeed. Whichever way we put it, the critic implicitly makes the same essential claim: namely, that his judgments can be supported in some way by other propositions.

This claim is challenged by the Critical Skeptic. The form of his challenge depends on the latitude given to the term 'reason', but its substance is the same. A few years ago, a colleague of mine and I engaged in correspondence with an English gentleman, author of a monograph entitled *Shakespeare's Hyphens*,[1] who pointed out to us that Shakespeare used a great many hyphenated words and that this practice was also followed by Walt Whitman and Dylan Thomas. Our correspondent argued at one point: the more hyphens, the greater the poet. Now, suppose a critic were to propose the following: This poem is poor, because it is deficient in hyphens. We may choose to say that this is not a reason at all, because it is so wildly irrelevant; in this sense of 'reason,' the skeptic's position is that no reasons can be given for critical judgments. On the other hand, we may take a more charitable view, and call this a reason simply because it is offered as one; in this broad sense, the skeptic's position is that no good, or cogent, reasons can be given for critical judgments.

The critical skeptic may remind us of Wordsworth's assurance in his 1800 Preface, that he was not 'principally influenced by the selfish and foolish hope of *reasoning* him [i.e., the reader] into an approbation of these particular Poems.'[2] Now this was a somewhat peculiar remark in the first place. The hope of reasoning someone into an approbation might conceivably be 'selfish' (if Wordsworth were merely aiming to increase his royalties), but it is 'foolish' only if we take 'approbation' in the sheer sense of *liking*. 'How can anyone be *argued* into liking Wordsworth's "We are Seven"?' the skeptic asks. But I should think that the aim of the reasoner – that is, the critic armed with reasons – is not to get people to *like* the poem, but to get them to acknowledge that it is good. And the question is whether his reasons – or alleged reasons – are of service to him in this enterprise.

I don't think that the skeptic's position, Cartesian though it may in some respects appear, can be disposed of by a simple appeal to paradigm cases. We might try this argument against him: Granted that the number of hyphens does not make a poem poor (or good), still that's not the sort of thing critics usually say. Consider a principle enunciated by Cleanth Brooks:

> A poem, then, to sum up, is to be judged, not by the truth or falsity as such, of the idea which it incorporates, but rather by its character as drama – by its coherence, sensitivity, depth, richness, and tough-mindedness.[3]

Now, suppose the critic says, 'This poem is poor because it is incoherent.' If that is not a good reason for condemning a poem, what *could* be a good reason? Doesn't critical skepticism imply that the expression 'good reason' has no application at all in critical discourse? But surely this term must have some application, or we would never have learned how to use it.

If this sort of argument is ever persuasive, I'm afraid that aesthetics is the last place in which to employ it. Probably a fair number of philosophers would be quite ready to label the whole body of critical reasoning a misuse of language. Let us assume that there must be *some* examples of good reasons, if we can speak intelligibly of good reasons; but it might well be that all of the examples are to be found in other fields than criticism, and that none of the arguments in, say, *The Well Wrought Urn*, come near to meeting the high standards that are exemplified in legal reasoning, in ethics, or the game-theory of nuclear deterrence. No – if we are going to be able to make sense of what the critic does when he gives reasons, and back him up with a philosophical account of how those reasons really work, we must grapple more closely with the skeptic's arguments.

I

The general problem of justifying the critic's appeal to reasons is, of course, large and complex. I propose to deal with only one of its parts – but one that has received some attention in the past few years.

To pass over a number of preliminary matters, let me first say that I hold that the critic does make value judgments and does sometimes inadequately support them by good reasons. A reason is some descriptive or interpretive proposition about the work under consideration – 'The poem is incoherent,' for example. Thus a reason always cites some property of the work, and we may say that this property is then employed as a *criterion of value* by the critic who presents that reason. Criteria cited in reasons supporting favorable judgments are merits; criteria cited on behalf of unfavorable judgments are defects. If the critic says, 'This poem is poor because (among other things) it is incoherent,' then he is treating incoherence as a poetic defect. A critical criterion is thus a feature that helps to make the work good or bad, better or worse; it adds to or detracts from its aesthetic goodness.

This is the position that the skeptic rejects. He holds that, in the sense proposed, there are no criteria of aesthetic value, that is, of goodness or badness in poems, paintings, plays, music, etc. Some skeptics like to invoke John Wisdom's distinction, in another context, between what he called 'dull' and 'interesting' ways of talking about art. A book about art, says Wisdom, 'is dull when it tries to set out in general terms what makes a good picture good' by giving 'rules' or 'canons.'[4] This, by itself, is something of an obiter dictum, but it can be given plausible and perhaps rather convincing support.

If one proposition is a reason for another, in the sense of actually supporting it, then there must be a logical connection of some sort between them. And, being a logical connection, it must relate general concepts in an abstract way. Thus, for example, if a certain degree of sharpness is a merit in knives (we can think of a particular sort of knife, such as the butcher's), then to say that a knife has that degree of sharpness must *always* be a reason to support the conclusion that it is good, and it must apply to *all* knives of the relevant sort. This reason may not be enough to *prove* that the knife is good, since the merit may be outweighed by serious defects, but sharpness to that degree will always make its contribution to the goodness of the knife. It will, at least, never be a fault in a knife: that is, we cannot say, 'That knife is poor, just because it is exactly that sharp.' And, of two knives similar in all other respects, if one is sharp and the other is not, the former will be a better knife than the other. Thus sharpness is a *general* merit in knives.

Generality of this sort appears to be essential to reasons in the logical sense, and if critical criteria are defined as features citable in reasons, then there must be an important sense in which such criteria are general, too. Thus the view that there *are* reasons that support the critic's judgment entails the view that there are general criteria of evaluation. Let us call this view the General Criterion Theory. It is a main target of the critical skeptic's attack.

As my main text for examination, I shall select the very forthright statement by Mr. William E. Kennick, in his article, 'Does Traditional Aesthetics Rest on a Mistake?'[5] In this article, Mr. Kennick holds that there are no 'general rules, standards, criteria, canons, or laws applicable to all works of art by which alone such critical appraisals can be supported' (329). And he goes on to say this:

> Ordinarily we feel no constraint in praising one novel for its verisimilitude, another for its humour, and still another for its plot of characterization.... Botticelli's lyric grace is his glory, but Giotto and Chardin are not to be condemned because their poetry is of a different order.... Different works of art are, or may be, praiseworthy or blameworthy for different reasons, and not always for the same reasons. A quality that is praiseworthy in one painting may be blameworthy in another; realism is not always a virtue, but this does not mean that it is not sometimes a virtue (331).[6]

The problem, then, is this: Do critical reasons have a kind of generality of application, so that it makes sense to try to formulate principles of criticism? I believe they do. Mr. Kennick, like a number of other recent writers, believes they do not. Now, if they do not, there are two possibilities. Some philosophers, including Mr. Kennick, hold that we can still talk of giving reasons in particular cases (that is, supporting the judgment that this or that poem is good or poor), without committing ourselves to any general principles at all. Others, however, hold (and I think with more reason) that some form of generality is essential to reason-giving and, therefore, that if there are no general criteria, there can be no critical criteria at all. My aim is to examine the arguments against the General Criterion Theory.

Before coming to them, however, it may be helpful to remind ourselves that the issue has two close analogues in other fields of philosophy, no less troublesome elsewhere than this is here. First, there is the problem of the universalizability of ethical judgments. Some writers have contended that it is precisely the difference between ethical judgment and critical judgment that one is general and the other is not,[7] but there does seem to be a similar problem in ethics. When we blame a man for not keeping an appointment, are we committed to the universalization of an implicit principle? Most moral philosophers would say we are; and the principle is something like: Anyone else in circumstances that do not differ in relevant ways from this one would be equally to blame. The problem is to provide an adequate criterion of relevance, without circularity. We want to say, for example, that having a different color skin is not relevant, while having been knocked down by a truck *is* relevant. Is there an analogous kind of implicit commitment involved in criticism? (And I don't mean when we blame the painter, but when we set a low estimate on his work.)

Second, there is the problem of the relation between singular causal statements and general laws. According to the traditional view, singular causal statements (such as, 'Dropping caused that pitcher to break') are, and must be, applications of universal lawlike statements, even if we cannot formulate the latter completely ('Whenever a pitcher of this sort is dropped in this way, it will break'). But in recent years some philosophers have suggested that we may be able to know singular causal statements, without relying on *any* general laws. Historical explanations are sometimes alleged to be of this sort. I would be happy to avoid this broad and complicated issue, but there is more than an analogy between my aesthetic problem and the causal problem: the former is in fact a special case of the latter. For, speaking very sketchily, I conceive the peculiar aesthetic goodness of a work of art to consist of its capacity to provide experiences with certain desirable qualities; and the criteria of critical evaluation are simply features that tend to contribute to or detract from this capacity. Hence, according to my theory, there is a causal relationship involved in the notion of critical criteria. And since I side with those who think that some generalized lawful relationships are essential to individual causal actions, by the same token I must suppose that a criterion can be relevant to the value of a particular work of art only if some generality of bearing lurks (so to speak) in the background.

II

A fundamental point alleged against the General Criterion Theory is that works of art are unique. Frequent repetition has not worn off the oddness of this statement. It can be construed in several ways – of which the most sensible are the most pointless. Mary Mothersill and Ruby Meager have analyzed and criticized it very effectively, and I need not review what they have said.[8] No doubt works of art – if we confine our attention to the good ones – tend to have a comparatively high degree of individuality, at least as compared with knives and typewriters. Because there are many human acts that may be called acts of promise-keeping, we can speak of general moral rules. But perhaps there are no genuine classes of aesthetic objects, such as poems and paintings (this seems to be the extreme neo-Crocean view) – or perhaps the members of each class differ so much from one another that no features can be found that are desirable in all or most of them.

But there *are* genuine classes of aesthetic objects, and their members share important properties. I don't see why we cannot admit that visual designs vary enormously in many ways, without denying that certain fundamental laws of perception may be at work in all of them. I should think that people and their moral predicaments are at least as different as poems, yet we can say that courage is a virtue in anyone in whom it may be found.

There is an interesting phrase that turns up here and there. For example: 'A good critic is one who can discern the *peculiar* excellence of a particular work.'[9] Now what is meant by 'the peculiar excellence' of a work? If it means (as I should think it must) an excellence that no other existing work happens to have – then of course many works do have peculiar excellences. (Many also have excellences that are not peculiar to them.) But the existence of such excellences does not in any way contradict the General Criterion

Theory. On the other hand, if it means instead a quality that is an excellence in this work, but that, if it appeared in any other work, could *not* be an excellence – then I have seen no convincing proof that there are 'peculiar excellences' in this sense.

Let us now turn back to Mr. Kennick's propositions and examples. I think his paper contains at least four distinguishable arguments against the General Criterion Theory, each going a little beyond the previous one.

The first argument is this: the General Criterion Theory can't be true because there are no single features of poetry, for example, that are either necessary or sufficient conditions of goodness.[10] That no single feature is sufficient I am prepared to grant at once. That there is no necessary feature I am not prepared to grant without qualification: for example, I have argued that some degree of coherence is a necessary condition of being a poem at all, and a fortiori of being a good poem.[11] I suppose, however, that it could be replied, by way of putting this qualification in its place, that no *special* degree of coherence is necessary to make a poem a good poem. In any case, I shall waive my objection and concede for the sake of argument that there are no necessary or sufficient single conditions of poetic goodness. Does it follow that the General Criterion Theory is wrong?

The answer seems sufficiently obvious. Though a given feature may be present in some poor poems and absent from some good ones, so that it neither guarantees poetic goodness nor is indispensable to it, nevertheless may contribute to the goodness of any poem that contains it and, thus, may be citable as a merit wherever it can be found. A man may be good without being magnanimous, and he may be magnanimous without being good; but that doesn't show that magnanimity is not a virtue in anyone who has it, and to the degree in which he has it. So, too, not every good poem has 'depth,' to recall one of the terms quoted from Cleanth Brooks above, and not every deep poem is good – yet depth may always be a good thing, as far as it goes.

The second argument given by Mr. Kennick involves a shift of ground: What if different features are merits in different contexts? – humor in one case, he suggests, tragic intensity in another. Or lyric grace in one painting, heroic strength in another. Does this refute the possibility of general criteria? I think not. Lyric grace may nevertheless always be a good thing when it can be had, and heroic strength likewise – only it may turn out that they cannot both be had in the same painting, or not without being watered down or confused. The General Criterion Theory certainly need not deny that there are qualitatively different merits that cannot always be combined. We admire one person's physical courage and another person's sensitivity to others, but we find few, if any, who combine both of these virtues to a high degree. So with two of Brooks's criteria – 'sensitivity' and 'tough-mindedness': poems that excel in one of these are perhaps not likely to excel in the other.

The third argument is also Mr. Kennick's – and this time he belongs to a larger company.[12] What if there are features that are merits in some works, but not merits at all in other works? Take realism, Mr. Kennick suggests: sometimes it is a merit, sometimes not. But this does not tell against the General Criterion Theory if we complicate the theory in an easy and convenient way. There are features of poems, and there are pairs and clusters of features. And some contribute value, so to speak, on their own, while others do so only in combination. This principle has an application in many walks of life, as G. E. Moore pointed out some time ago. It's like saying that you don't want butter without bread, or bread without butter, but only the two together. We can say that bread is not desirable, and butter is not desirable, but bread-and-butter is desirable; or we can say that butter is sometimes desirable (namely, when there's bread) and sometimes not (namely, when there isn't).

Thus we should not be surprised to find specific features that may be good in one poem but neutral in another: their goodness depends upon association with other cooperative features. Mr. Kennick's example, realism, is a broad notion, so it's not clear exactly what sort of judgment he has in mind when he says that 'Realism is not always a virtue.' In some of its senses, I'm not sure that realism is *ever* a strictly literary virtue (or, as I would prefer to say, merit – Mr. Kennick's moralistic terms 'virtue' and 'blameworthy' do not seem to me appropriate to the critical context). But a critic might justifiably cite an author's discriminating ear for four-letter words as a merit in, say, *Tropic of Cancer*, where certain types of situation and character are present, though he would not, of course, wish to say that their introduction would improve *The Wings of the Dove* or *The Mill on the Floss*.

III

The fourth argument against the General Criterion Theory takes us a little beyond the third – though, in fact, the examples I have just given would serve for it as well. Suppose there are features that are merits in one work and actually *defects* in another. The touch of humor that is just right in one play is just exactly wrong in another – and so with the four-letter words. How then can there be any general criteria, or true propositions of the form: 'Humor is always a good-enhancing feature'? The General Criterion Theory can meet this objection by one more complication that is natural and sensible. Some criteria are subordinate to others, as constituting their perceptual conditions. For example, suppose the touch of humor (the grave-digger's gags, the drunken porter at the gate) is a merit in one context because it heightens the dramatic tension, but a defect in another context, where it lets the tension down. Then we may admit that the touch of humor is not a general merit, but only because we also admit that something else *is* a general merit (in a play, that is) – namely, high dramatic tension. Remember that this does not mean that dramatic tension is either a necessary or sufficient condition of being a good play, nor does it mean that this desirable feature can be combined with all other desirable features, nor does it mean that all plays that lack a high degree of it would necessarily become better by increasing it, for some plays might thereby lose some other quality that especially adorns them. The point is that the General Criterion Theory can easily take account of such variations as the skeptic points out – providing it is allowed to fall back upon more general and, so to speak, more fundamental criteria.

We may distinguish two ranks of critical criteria, then, in the following way: Let us say that the properties *A*, *B*, *C* are the *primary (positive) criteria* of aesthetic value if the addition of any one of them or an increase in it, without a decrease in any of the others, will always make the work a better one. And let us say that a given property *X* is a *secondary (positive) criterion* of aesthetic value if there is a certain set of other properties such that, whenever they are present, the addition of *X* or an increase in it will always produce an increase in one or more of the primary criteria.

Notice that each of these definitions is formulated in such a way that it contains the word 'always' in an important position and, therefore, that they both define *general* criteria in an important sense. But the secondary criteria are subordinate and conditional: it is only in certain contexts that, for example, elegant variation is a fault of style. (However, some of these secondary criteria are quite broad in their relevance.) The primary criteria, on the other hand, always contribute positively to the value of a work, in so far as they are present. And their absence is always a deficiency, however it may be made up in other ways. Thus I think that Paul Ziff is precisely correct when he says:

> Some good paintings are somewhat disorganized; they are good
> in spite of the fact that they are somewhat disorganized. But no
> painting is good because it is disorganized, and many are bad
> primarily because they are disorganized.[13]

Disorganization, by this exact description, is a primary (negative)
critical criterion.

There is a danger that such a discussion as this may unintentionally confirm John Wisdom's remark that talk about 'canons' and
'rules' is 'dull.' I don't insist that it is interesting – only that it is
possible and reasonable. The act of judging – in the sense of
appraising – works of art is certainly not a purely intellectual act,
and many elements of talent and training are required to perform
it well. But it is, in part, a rational act, for it involves reasoning.

Notes

1 L. C. Thompson, *Shakespeare's Hyphens* (London: Amalgamated Authors).

2 Preface to the *Lyrical Ballads* (1800), in *Complete Poetical Works* (Boston:
Houghton Mifflin, 1911), vol. X, p.5.

3 *The Well Wrought Urn* (New York: Reynal and Hitchock, 1947), p.229.

4 See his paper in the symposium on 'Things and Persons,' *Proceedings of the
Aristotelian Society*, Supplement, 22 (1948): 207.

5 *Mind*, 67 (1958): 317–334.

6 Cf. Mary Mothersill, 'Critical Reasons,' *Philosophical Quarterly*, 11 (1961): 74–
79; this is a reply to Dorothy Walsh, 'Critical Reasons,' *Philosophical Review*, 69
(1960): 386–393: 'There is *no* characteristic which is amenable to independent
explanation and which by its presence enhances the aesthetic value of paintings
or of any sub-class of paintings' (77).

7 The writer most often quoted is Stuart Hampshire, 'Logic and Appreciation,'
in William Elton, ed., *Asthetics and Language* (Oxford: Blackwell, 1954).

8 See Ruby Meager, 'The Uniqueness of a Work of Art,' *Proceedings of the
Aristotelian Society*, 59 (1959): 49–70, and Mary Mothersill, '"Unique" as an
Aesthetic Predicate,' [*Journal of Philosophy*], 58 (1961): 421–437. Cf. Albert
Tsugawa, 'The Objectivity of Aesthetic Judgments,' *Philosophical Review*, 70
(1961), 3–22, esp. 11–12.

9 See Mary Mothersill, *op. cit.*, 428; this sentence appears in her formulation of
the argument for the less radical form of the Autonomy Theory.

10 This seems to be the main point of A. G. Pleydell-Pearce, 'On the Limits
and Use of "Aesthetic Criteria",' *Philosophical Quarterly*, 9 (1959): 29–45.

11 See 'The Definitions of the Arts,' *Journal of Aesthetics and Art Criticism*, 20
(Winter, 1961): 175–187.

12   For example, Helen Knight, 'The Use of "Good" in Aesthetic Judgments,' in William Elton, ed., *op. cit.*, pp.155–156; J. A. Passmore, 'The Dreariness of Aesthetics,' *ibid.*, 49, 51–52; J. Kemp, 'Generalization in the Philosophy of Art,' *Philosophy*, 33 (1958): 152.

13   'Reasons in Criticism.' in Israel Scheffler, ed., *Philosophy and Education* (Boston: Allyn and Bacon, 1958), p.220.

The intentional fallacy

William K. Wimsatt (b.1907) and Monroe C. Beardsley (1915–80)

One of the most influential papers in modern literary aesthetics has been 'The intentional fallacy' (1954) by W. K. Wimsatt and M. C. Beardsley, which is reprinted here. Much twentieth-century criticism has been concerned with identifying the author's intention in a literary work, and then with judging the work in terms of its success in realizing that intention. Wimsatt and Beardsley take issue with this approach, arguing that authorial intention is irrelevant to the act of critical interpretation: 'the design or intention of the author is neither available nor desirable as a standard for judging the success of a work of literary art'. They make a sharp distinction between internal and external evidence for the meaning of a literary work. Internal evidence is drawn from the actual language of the poem and the way it is organized, external from the author's life and times. Only the former is held to have relevance for the critic, who must treat the literary text as a self-contained artefact. Critics and theorists who take either a sociological or psychological approach to literature (Marxists and feminists on the one hand, Freudians on the other) dissent strongly from this view, seeing external evidence as a crucial part of literary analysis.

The claim of the author's 'intention' upon the critic's judgment has been challenged in a number of recent discussions, notably in the debate entitled *The Personal Heresy*, between Professors Lewis and Tillyard. But it seems doubtful if this claim and most of its romantic corollaries are as yet subject to any widespread questioning. The present writers, in a short article entitled 'Intention' for a *Dictionary*[1] of literary criticism, raised the issue but were unable to pursue its implications at any length. We argued that the design or intention of the author is neither available nor desirable as a standard for judging the success of a work of literary art, and it seems to us that this is a principle which goes deep into some differences in the history of critical attitudes. It is a principle which accepted or rejected points to the polar opposites of classical 'imitation' and romantic expression. It entails many specific truths about inspiration, authenticity, biography, literary history and scholarship, and about some trends of contemporary poetry, especially its allusiveness. There is hardly a problem of literary criticism in which the critic's approach will not be qualified by his view of 'intention.'

'Intention,' as we shall use the term, corresponds to *what he intended* in a formula which more or less explicitly has had wide acceptance. 'In order to judge the poet's performance, we must know *what he intended*.' Intention is design or plan in the author's mind. Intention has obvious affinities for the author's attitude toward his work, the way he felt, what made him write.

We begin our discussion with a series of propositions summarized and abstracted to a degree where they seem to us axiomatic.
1   A poem does not come into existence by accident. The words of a poem, as Professor Stoll has remarked, come out of a head, not out of a hat. Yet to insist on the designing intellect as a *cause* of a poem is not to grant the design or intention as a *standard* by which the critic is to judge the worth of the poet's performance.
2   One must ask how a critic expects to get an answer to the question about intention. How is he to find out what the poet tried to do? If the poet succeeded in doing it, then the poem itself shows what he was trying to do. And if the poet did not succeed, then the poem is not adequate evidence, and the critic must go outside the poem – for evidence of an intention that did not become effective in the poem. 'Only one *caveat* must be borne in mind,' says an eminent intentionalist[2] in a moment when his theory repudiates itself; 'the poet's aim must be judged at the moment of the creative act, that is to say, by the art of the poem itself.'
3   Judging a poem is like judging a pudding or a machine. One demands that it work. It is only because an artifact works that we infer the intention of an artificer. 'A poem should not mean but be.' A poem can *be* only through its *meaning* – since its medium is words – yet it *is*, simply *is*, in the sense that we have no excuse for inquiring what part is intended or meant. Poetry is a feat of style by which a complex of meaning is handled all at once. Poetry succeeds because all or most of what is said or implied is relevant; what is irrelevant has been excluded, like lumps from pudding and 'bugs' from machinery. In this respect poetry differs from practical messages, which are successful if and only if we correctly infer the intention. They are more abstract than poetry.

4   The meaning of a poem may certainly be a personal one, in the sense that a poem expresses a personality or state of soul rather than a physical object like an apple. But even a short lyric poem is dramatic, the response of a speaker (no matter how abstractly conceived) to a situation (no matter how universalized). We ought to impute the thoughts and attitudes of the poem immediately to the dramatic *speaker*, and if to the author at all, only by an act of biographical inference.

5   There is a sense in which an author, by revision, may better achieve his original intention. But it is a very abstract sense. He intended to write a better work, or a better work of a certain kind, and now has done it. But it follows that his former concrete intention was not his intention. 'He's the man we were in search of, that's true,' says Hardy's rustic constable, 'and yet he's not the man we were in search of. For the man we were in search of was not the man we wanted.'

'Is not a critic,' asks Professor Stoll, 'a judge, who does not explore his own consciousness, but determines the author's meaning or intention, as if the poem were a will, a contract, or the constitution? The poem is not the critic's own.' He has accurately diagnosed two forms of irresponsibility, one of which he prefers. Our view is yet different. The poem is not the critic's own and not the author's (it is detached from the author at birth and goes about the world beyond his power to intend about it or control it). The poem belongs to the public. It is embodied in language, the peculiar possession of the public, and it is about the human being, an object of public knowledge. What is said about the poem is subject to the same scrutiny as any statement in linguistics or in the general science of psychology.

A critic of our *Dictionary* article, Ananda K. Coomaraswamy, has argued[3] that there are two kinds of inquiry about a work of art: (1) whether the artist achieved his intentions; (2) whether the work of art 'ought never to have been undertaken at all' and so 'whether it is worth preserving.' Number (2), Coomaraswamy maintains, is not 'criticism of any work of art *qua* work of art,' but is rather moral criticism; number (1) is artistic criticism. But we maintain that (2) need not be moral criticism: that there is another way of deciding whether works of art are worth preserving and whether, in a sense, they 'ought' to have been undertaken, and this is the way of objective criticism of works of art as such, the way which enables us to distinguish between a skillful murder and a skillful poem. A skillful murder is an example which Coomaraswamy uses, and in his system the difference between the murder and the poem is simply a 'moral' one, not an 'artistic' one, since each if carried out according to plan is 'artistically' successful. We maintain that (2) is an inquiry of more worth than (1), and since (2) and not (1) is capable of distinguishing poetry from murder, the name 'artistic criticism' is properly given to (2).

II

It is not so much a historical statement as a definition to say that the intentional fallacy is a romantic one. When a rhetorician of the first century A.D. writes: 'Sublimity is the echo of a great soul,' or when he tells us that 'Homer enters into the sublime actions of his heroes' and 'shares the full inspiration of the combat,' we shall not be surprised to find this rhetorician considered as a distant harbinger of romanticism and greeted in the warmest terms by Saintsbury. One may wish to argue whether Longinus should be called romantic, but there can hardly be a doubt that in one important way he is.

Goethe's three questions for 'constructive criticism' are 'What did the author set out to do? Was his plan reasonable and sensible, and how far did he succeed in carrying it out?' If one leaves out the middle question, one has in effect the system of Croce – the culmination and crowning philosophic expression of romanticism. The beautiful is the successful intuition-expression, and the ugly is the unsuccessful; the intuition or private part of art is *the* aesthetic fact, and the medium or public part is not the subject of aesthetic at all.

The Madonna of Cimabue is still in the Church of Santa Maria Novella; but does she speak to the visitor of to-day as to the Florentines of the thirteenth century?

> *Historical interpretation* labours ... to reintegrate in us the psychological conditions which have changed in the course of history. It ... enables us to see a work of art (a physical object) as its *author saw it* in the moment of production.[4]

The first italics are Croce's, the second ours. The upshot of Croce's system is an ambiguous emphasis on history. With such passsages as a point of departure a critic may write a nice analysis of the meaning or 'spirit' of a play by Shakespeare or Corneille – a process that involves close historical study but remains aesthetic criticism – or he may, with equal plausibility, produce an essay in sociology, biography, or other kinds of non-aesthetic history.

III

> I went to the poets; tragic, dithyrambic, and all sorts.... I took
> them some of the most elaborate passages in their own writings,
> and asked what was the meaning of them.... Will you believe
> me?... there is hardly a person present who would not have
> talked better about their poetry than they did themselves. Then
> I knew that not by wisdom do poets write poetry, but by a sort
> of genius and inspiration.

That reiterated mistrust of the poets which we hear from Socrates
may have been part of a rigorously ascetic view in which we hardly
wish to participate, yet Plato's Socrates saw a truth about the
poetic mind which the world no longer commonly sees – so much
criticism, and that the most inspirational and most affectionately
remembered, has proceeded from the poets themselves.

Certainly the poets have had something to say that the critic
and professor could not say; their message has been more exciting:
that poetry should come as naturally as leaves to a tree, that poetry
is the lava of the imagination, or that it is emotion recollected in
tranquillity. But it is necessary that we realize the character and
authority of such testimony. There is only a fine shade of difference
between such expressions and a kind of earnest advice that authors
often give. Thus Edward Young, Carlyle, Walter Pater:

> I know two golden rules from *ethics*, which are no less golden in
> *Composition* than in life. 1. *Know thyself*; 2dly, *Reverence thyself*.

> This is the grand secret for finding readers and retaining them:
> let him who would move and convince others, be first moved and
> convinced himself. Horace's rule, *Si vis me flere*, is applicable in
> a wider sense than the literal one. To every poet, to every writer,
> we might say: Be true, if you would be believed.

> Truth! there can be no merit, no craft at all, without that. And
> further, all beauty is in the long run only *fineness* of truth or what
> we call expression, the finer accommodation of speech to that
> vision within.

And Housman's little handbook to the poetic mind yields this
illustration:

> Having drunk a pint of beer at luncheon – beer is a sedative to

the brain, and my afternoons are the least intellectual portion of my life – I would go out for a walk of two or three hours. As I went along, thinking of nothing in particular, only looking at things around me and following the progress of the seasons, there would flow into my mind, with sudden and unaccountable emotion, sometimes a line or two of verse, sometimes a whole stanza at once.

This is the logical terminus of the series already quoted. Here is a confession of how poems were written which would do as a definition of poetry just as well as 'emotion recollected in tranquillity' – and which the young poet might equally well take to heart as a practical rule. Drink a pint of beer, relax, go walking, think on nothing in particular, look at things, surrender yourself to yourself, search for the truth in your own soul, listen to the sound of your own inside voice, discover and express the *vraie vérité*.

It is probably true that all this is excellent advice for poets. The young imagination fired by Wordsworth and Carlyle is probably closer to the verge of producing a poem than the mind of the student who has been sobered by Aristotle or Richards. The art of inspiring poets, or at least of inciting something like poetry in young persons, has probably gone further in our day than ever before. Books of creative writing such as those issued from the Lincoln School are interesting evidence of what a child can do.[5] All this, however, would appear to belong to an art separate from criticism – to a psychological discipline, a system of self-development, a yoga, which the young poet perhaps does well to notice, but which is something different from the public art of evaluating poems.

Coleridge and Arnold were better critics than most poets have been, and if the critical tendency dried up the poetry in Arnold and perhaps in Coleridge, it is not inconsistent with our argument, which is that judgment of poems is different from the art of producing them. Coleridge has given us the classic 'anodyne' story, and tells what he can about the genesis of a poem which he calls a 'psychological curiosity,' but his definitions of poetry and of the poetic quality 'imagination' are to be found elsewhere and in quite other terms.

It would be convenient if the passwords of the intentional school, 'sincerity,' 'fidelity,' 'spontaneity,' 'authenticity', 'genuineness,' 'originality,' could be equated with terms such as 'integrity,' 'relevance,' 'unity,' 'function,' 'maturity,' 'subtlety,' 'adequacy,' and other more precise terms of evaluation – in short, if 'expression' always meant aesthetic achievement. But this is not so.

'Aesthetic' art, says Professor Curt Ducasse, an ingenious theorist of expression, is the conscious objectification of feelings, in which an intrinsic part is the critical moment. The artist corrects the objectification when it is not adequate. But this may mean that the earlier attempt was not successful in objectifying the self, or 'it may also mean that it was a successful objectification of a self which, when it confronted us clearly, we disowned and repudiated in favor of another.'[6] What is the standard by which we disown or accept the self? Professor Ducasse does not say. Whatever it may be, however, this standard is an element in the definition of art which will not reduce to terms of objectification. The evaluation of the work of art remains public; the work is measured against something outside the author.

IV

There is criticism of poetry and there is author psychology, which when applied to the present or future takes the form of inspirational promotion; but author psychology can be historical too, and then we have literary biography, a legitimate and attractive study in itself, one approach, as Professor Tillyard would argue, to personality, the poem being only a parallel approach. Certainly it need not be with a derogatory purpose that one points out personal studies, as distinct from poetic studies, in the realm of literary scholarship. Yet there is danger of confusing personal and poetic studies; and there is the fault of writing the personal as if it were poetic.

There is a difference between internal and external evidence for the meaning of a poem. And the paradox is only verbal and superficial that what is (1) internal is also public: it is discovered through the semantics and syntax of a poem, through our habitual knowledge of the language, through grammars, dictionaries, and all the literature which is the source of dictionaries, in general through all that makes a language and culture; while what is (2) external is private or idiosyncratic; not a part of the work as a linguistic fact: it consists of revelations (in journals, for example, or letters or reported conversations) about how or why the poet wrote the poem – to what lady, while sitting on what lawn, or at the death of what friend or brother. There is (3) an intermediate kind of evidence about the character of the author or about private or semiprivate meanings attached to words or topics by an author or by a coterie of which he is a member. The meaning of words is the history of words, and the biography of an author, his use of a word, and the associations which the word had for *him*, are part of the word's history and meaning.[7] But the three types of evidence, especially (2) and (3), shade into one another so subtly that it is not always easy to draw a line between examples, and hence arises the difficulty for criticism. The use of biographical evidence need not involve intentionalism, because while it may be evidence of what the author intended, it may also be evidence of the meaning of his words and the dramatic character of his utterance. On the other hand, it may not be all this. And a critic who is concerned with evidence of type (1) and moderately with that of type (3) will in the long run produce a different sort of comment from that of the critic who is concerned with (2) and with (3) where it shades into (2).

The whole glittering parade of Professor Lowes' *Road to Xanadu*, for instance, runs along the border between types (2) and (3) or boldly traverses the romantic region of (2). ' "Kubla Khan," ' says Professor Lowes, 'is the fabric of a vision, but every image that rose up in its weaving had passed that way before. And it would seem that there is nothing haphazard or fortuitous in their return.' This is not quite clear – not even when Professor Lowes explains that there were clusters of associations, like hooked atoms, which were drawn into complex relation with other clusters in the deep well of Coleridge's memory, and which then coalesced and issued forth as poems. If there was nothing 'haphazard or fortuitous' in the way the images returned to the surface, that may mean (1) that Coleridge could not produce what he did not have, that he was limited in his creation by what he had read or otherwise experienced, or (2) that having received certain clusters of associations, he was bound to return them in just the way he did, and that the value of the poem may be described in terms of the experiences on which he had to draw. The latter pair of propositions (a sort of Hartleyan associationism which Coleridge himself repudiated in the *Biographia*) may not be assented to. There were certainly other combinations, other poems, worse or better, that might have been written by men who had read Bartram and Purchas and Bruce and Milton. And this will be true no matter how many times we are able to add to the brilliant complex of Coleridge's reading. In certain flourishes (such as the sentence we have quoted) and in chapter headings like 'The Shaping Spirit,' 'The Magical Synthesis,' 'Imagination Creatrix,' it may be that Professor Lowes pretends to say more about the actual poems than he does. There is a certain deceptive variation in these fancy chapter titles; one expects to pass on to a new stage in the argument, and one finds – more and more sources, more and more about 'the streamy nature of association.'[8]

'Wohin der Weg?' quotes Professor Lowes for the motto of his book. 'Kein Weg! Ins Unbetretene.' Precisely because the way is *unbetreten* [untrod], we should say, it leads away from the poem. Bartram's *Travels* contains a good deal of the history of certain words and of certain romantic Floridian conceptions that appear in 'Kubla Khan.' And a good deal of that history has passed and was then passing into the very stuff of our language. Perhaps a person who has read Bartram appreciates the poem more than one who has not. Or, by looking up the vocabulary of 'Kubla Khan' in the *Oxford English Dictionary*, or by reading some of the other books there quoted, a person may know the poem better. But it would seem to pertain little to the poem to know that *Coleridge* had read Bartram. There is a gross body of life, of sensory and mental experience, which lies behind and in some senses causes every poem, but can never be and need not be known in the verbal and hence intellectual composition which is the poem. For all the objects of our manifold experience, for every unity, there is an action of the mind which cuts off roots, melts away context – or indeed we should never have objects or ideas or anything to talk about.

It is probable that there is nothing in Professor Lowes' vast book which could detract from anyone's appreciation of either *The Ancient Mariner* or 'Kubla Khan.' We next present a case where preoccupation with evidence of type (3) has gone so far as to distort a critic's view of a poem (yet a case not so obvious as those that abound in our critical journals).

In a well known poem by John Donne appears this quatrain:

> Moving of th' earth brings harmes and feares,
>> Men reckon what it did and meant,
> But trepidation of the spheares,
>> Though greater farre, is innocent.

A recent critic in an elaborate treatment of Donne's learning has written of this quatrain as follows:

> He touches the emotional pulse of the situation by a skillful allusion to the new and the old astronomy.... Of the new astronomy, the 'moving of the earth' is the most radical principle; of the old, the 'trepidation of the spheres' is the motion of the greatest complexity.... The poet must exhort his love to quietness and calm upon his departure; and for this purpose the figure

based upon the latter motion (trepidation), long absorbed into the traditional astronomy, fittingly suggests the tension of the moment without arousing the 'harmes and feares' implicit in the figure of the moving earth.[9]

The argument is plausible and rests on a well substantiated thesis that Donne was deeply interested in the new astronomy and its repercussions in the theological realm. In various works Donne shows his familiarity with Kepler's *De Stella Nova*, with Galileo's *Siderius Nuncius*, with William Gilbert's *De Magnete*, and with Clavius' commentary on the *De Sphaera* of Sacrobosco. He refers to the new science in his Sermon at Paul's Cross and in a letter to Sir Henry Goodyer. In *The First Anniversary* he says 'the new philosophy calls all in doubt.' In the *Elegy on Prince Henry* he says that the 'least moving of the center' makes 'the world to shake.'

It is difficult to answer argument like this, and impossible to answer it with evidence of like nature. There is no reason why Donne might not have written a stanza in which the two kinds of celestial motion stood for two sorts of emotion at parting. And if we become full of astronomical ideas and see Donne only against the background of the new science, we may believe that he did. But the text itself remains to be dealt with, the analyzable vehicle of a complicated metaphor. And one may observe: (1) that the movement of the earth according to the Copernican theory is a celestial motion, smooth and regular, and while it might cause religious or philosophic fears, it could not be associated with the crudity and earthiness of the kind of commotion which the speaker in the poem wishes to discourage; (2) that there is another moving of the earth, an earthquake, which has just these qualities and is to be associated with the tear-floods and sigh-tempests of the second stanza of the poem; (3) that 'trepidation' is an appropriate opposite of earthquake, because each is a shaking or vibratory motion; and 'trepidation of the spheres' is 'greater far' than an earthquake, but not much greater (if two such motions can be compared as to greatness) than the annual motion of the earth; (4) that reckoning what it 'did and meant' shows that the event has passed, like an earthquake, not like the incessant celestial movement of the earth. Perhaps a knowledge of Donne's interest in the new science may add another shade of meaning, an overtone to the stanza in question, though to say even this runs against the words. To make the geocentric and heliocentric antithesis the core of the metaphor is to disregard the English language, to prefer private evidence to public, external to internal.

V

If the distinction between kinds of evidence has implications for the historical critic, it has them no less for the contemporary poet and his critic. Or, since every rule for a poet is but another side of a judgment by a critic, and since the past is the realm of the scholar and critic, and the future and present that of the poet and the critical leaders of taste, we may say that the problems arising in literary scholarship from the intentional fallacy are matched by others which arise in the world of progressive experiment.

The question of 'allusiveness,' for example, as acutely posed by the poetry of Eliot, is certainly one where a false judgment is likely to involve the intentional fallacy. The frequency and depth of literary allusion in the poetry of Eliot and others has driven so many in pursuit of full meanings to the *Golden Bough* and the Elizabethan drama that it has become a kind of commonplace to suppose that we do not know what a poet means unless we have traced him in his reading – a supposition redolent with intentional implications. The stand taken by F. O. Matthiessen is a sound one and partially forestalls the difficulty.

> If one reads these lines with an attentive ear and is sensitive to their sudden shifts in movement, the contrast between the actual Thames and the idealized vision of it during an age before it flowed through a megalopolis is sharply conveyed by that movement itself, whether or not one recognizes the refrain to be from Spenser.

Eliot's allusions work when we know them – and to a great extent even when we do not know them, through their suggestive power.

But sometimes we find allusions supported by notes, and it is a nice question whether the notes function more as guides to send us where we may be educated, or more as indications in themselves about the character of the allusions. 'Nearly everything of importance...that is apposite to an appreciation of 'The Waste Land,' writes Matthiessen of Miss Weston's book; 'has been incorporated into the structure of the poem itself, or into Eliot's Notes.' And with such an admission it may begin to appear that it would not much matter if Eliot invented his sources (as Sir Walter Scott invented chapter epigraphs from 'old plays' and 'anonymous' authors, or as Coleridge wrote marginal glosses for *The Ancient Mariner*). Allusions to Dante, Webster, Marvell, or Baudelaire doubtless gain something because these writers existed, but it is doubtful whether the same can be said for an allusion to an obscure Elizabethan:

> The sound of horns and motors, which shall bring
> Sweeney to Mrs. Porter in the spring.

'Cf. Day, *Parliament of Bees*:', says Eliot,

> When of a sudden, listening, you shall hear,
> A noise of horns and hunting, which shall bring
> Actaeon to Diana in the spring,
> Where all shall see her naked skin.

The irony is completed by the quotation itself; had Eliot, as is quite conceivable, composed these lines to furnish his own background, there would be no loss of validity. The conviction may grow as one reads Eliot's next note: 'I do not know the origin of the ballad from which these lines are taken: it was reported to me from Sydney, Australia.' The important word in this note – on Mrs. Porter and her daughter who washed their feet in soda water – is 'ballad.' And if one should feel from the lines themselves their 'ballad' quality, there would be little need for the note. Ultimately, the inquiry must focus on the integrity of such notes as parts of the poem, for where they constitute special information about the meaning of phrases in the poem, they ought to be subject to the same scrutiny as any of the other words in which it is written. Matthiessen believes the notes were the price Eliot 'had to pay in order to avoid what he would have considered muffling the energy of his poem by extended connecting links in the text itself.' But it may be questioned whether the notes and the need for them are not equally muffling. F. W. Bateson has plausibly argued that Tennyson's 'The Sailor Boy' would be better if half the stanzas were omitted, and the best versions of ballads like 'Sir Patrick Spens' owe their power to the very audacity with which the minstrel has taken for granted the story upon which he comments. What then if a poet finds he cannot take so much for granted in a more recondite context and rather than write informatively, supplies notes? It can be said in favor of this plan that at least the notes do not pretend to be dramatic, as they would if written in verse. On the other hand, the notes may look like unassimilated material lying loose beside the poem, necessary for the meaning of the verbal symbol, but not integrated, so that the symbol stands incomplete.

We mean to suggest by the above analysis that whereas notes tend to seem to justify themselves as external indexes to the author's *intention*, yet they ought to be judged like any other parts of a composition (verbal arrangement special to a particular context), and when so judged their reality as parts of the poem, or their imaginative integration with the rest of the poem, may come into question. Mathiessen, for instance, sees that Eliot's titles for poems and his epigraphs are informative apparatus, like the notes. But while he is worried by some of the notes and thinks that Eliot 'appears to be mocking himself for writing the note at the same time that he wants to convey something by it,' Matthiessen believes that the 'device' of epigraphs 'is not at all open to the objection of not being sufficiently structural.' 'The *intention*,' he says, 'is to enable the poet to secure a condensed expression in the poem itself.' 'In each case the epigraph is *designed* to form an integral part of the effect of the poem.' And Eliot himself, in his notes, has justified his poetic practice in terms of intention.

> The Hanged Man, a member of the traditional pack, fits my purpose in two ways: because he is associated in my mind with the Hanged God of Frazer, and because I associate him with the hooded figure in the passage of the disciples to Emmaus in Part V.... The man with Three Staves (an authentic member of the Tarot pack) I associate, quite arbitrarily, with the Fisher King himself.

And perhaps he is to be taken more seriously here, when off guard in a note, than when in his Norton Lectures he comments on the difficulty of saying what a poem means and adds playfully that he thinks of prefixing to a second edition of *Ash Wednesday* some lines from *Don Juan*:

> I don't pretend that I quite understand
> My own meaning when I would be *very* fine;
> But the fact is that I have nothing planned
> Unless it were to be a moment merry.

If Eliot and other contemporary poets have any characteristic fault, it may be in *planning* too much.

Allusiveness in poetry is one of several critical issues by which we have illustrated the more abstract issue of intentionalism, but it may be for today the most important illustration. As a poetic practice allusiveness would appear to be in some recent poems an extreme corollary of the romantic intentionalist assumption, and as a critical issue it challenges and brings to light in a special way the basic premise of intentionalism. The following instance from the poetry of Eliot may serve to epitomize the practical implications of what we have been saying. In Eliot's 'Love Song of J. Alfred Prufrock,' toward the end, occurs the line: 'I have heard the mermaids singing, each to each,' and this bears a certain resemblance to a line in a Song by John Donne, 'Teach me to heare Mermaides singing,' so that for the reader acquainted to a certain degree with Donne's poetry, the critical question arises: Is Eliot's line an allusion to Donne's? Is Prufrock thinking about Donne? Is Eliot thinking about Donne? We suggest that there are two radically different ways of looking for an answer to this question. There is (1) the way of poetic analysis and exegesis, which inquires whether it makes any sense if Eliot-Prufrock *is* thinking about Donne. In an earlier part of the poem, when Prufrock asks, 'Would it have been worth while,... To have squeezed the universe into a ball,' his words take half their sadness and irony from certain energetic and passionate lines of Marvel 'To His Coy Mistress.' But the exegetical inquirer may wonder whether mermaids considered as 'strange sights' (to hear them is in Donne's poem analogous to getting with child a mandrake root) have much to do with Prufrock's mermaids, which seem to be symbols of romance and dynamism, and which incidentally have literary authentication, if they need it, in a line of a sonnet by Gérard de Nerval. This method of inquiry may lead to the conclusion that the given resemblance between Eliot and Donne is without significance and is better not thought of, or the method may have the disadvantage of providing no certain conclusion. Nevertheless, we submit that this is the true and objective way of criticism, as contrasted to what the very uncertainty of exegesis might tempt a second kind of critic to undertake: (2) the way of biographical or genetic inquiry, in which, taking advantage of the fact that Eliot is still alive, and in the spirit of a man who would settle a bet, the critic writes to Eliot and asks what he meant, or if he had Donne in mind. We shall not here weigh the probabilities – whether Eliot would answer that he meant nothing at all, had nothing at all in mind – a sufficiently good answer to such a question – or in an unguarded moment might furnish a clear and, within its limit, irrefutable answer. Our point is that such an answer to such an inquiry would have nothing to do with the poem 'Prufrock'; it would not be a critical inquiry.

Critical inquiries, unlike bets, are not settled in this way. Critical inquiries are not settled by consulting the oracle.

Notes

1 *Dictionary of World Literature*, Joseph T. Shipley, ed. (New York, 1942), 326–29.

2 J. E. Spingarn, 'The New Criticism,' in *Criticism in America* (New York, 1924), 24–25.

3 Ananada K. Coomaraswamy, 'Intention,' in *American Bookman*, I (1944), 41–48.

4 It is true that Croce himself in his *Ariosto, Shakespeare and Corneille* (London, 1920), chap. VI, 'The Practical Personality and the Poetical Personality,' and in his *Defence of Poetry* (Oxford, 1933), 24, and elsewhere, early and late, has delivered telling attacks on emotive geneticism, but the main drive of the *Aesthetic* is surely toward a kind of cognitive intentionalism.

5 See Hughes Mearns, *Creative Youth* (Garden City, 1925), esp. 10, 27–29. The technique of inspiring poems has apparently been outdone more recently by the study of inspiration in successful poets and other artists. See, for instance, Rosamond E. M. Harding, *An Anatomy of Inspiration* (Cambridge, 1940); Julius Portnoy, *A Psychology of Art Creation* (Philadelphia, 1942); Rudolf Arnheim and others, *Poets at Work* (New York, 1947); Phyllis Bartlett, *Poems in Process* (New York, 1951); Brewster Ghiselin (ed.), *The Creative Process: A Symposium* (Berkeley and Los Angeles, 1952).

6 Curt Ducasse, *The Philosophy of Art* (New York, 1929), 116.

7 And the history of words *after* a poem is written may contribute meanings which if relevant to the original pattern should not be ruled out by a scruple about intention.

8 Chaps. VIII, 'The Pattern,' and XVI, 'The Known and Familiar Landscape,' will be found of most help to the student of the poem.

9 Charles M. Coffin, *John Donne and the New Philosophy* (New York, 1927), 97–98.

The possibility of criticism

Monroe C. Beardsley (1915–80)

Beardsley continues his attack on the 'intentionalist fallacy' in the following extract, The Possibility of Criticism *(1970). This possibility is held to depend on two main principles: the 'Principle of Independence' (works exist as individual entities), and the 'Principle of Autonomy' (works are self-sufficient entities). Directing his argument largely against the literary theorist E. D. Hirsch, a staunch defender of intentionalism, whose work will appear in a later reading (27), Beardsley goes on to argue that textual meaning is not identical to authorial meaning: a text can come to take on meanings that its author neither intended nor could have envisaged.*

The authority of the text

The first thing required to make criticism possible is an object to be criticized – something for the critic to interpret and to judge, with its own properties against which interpretations and judgments can be checked. The Principle of Independence, as it might be called, is that literary works exist as individuals and can be distinguished from other things, though it is another question whether they enjoy some special mode of existence, as has been held. I think everyone must agree on this first postulate – here rather roughly stated. But there is another postulate that is logically complementary to the first: that literary works are self-sufficient entities, whose properties are decisive in checking interpretations and judgments. This is sometimes called the Principle of Autonomy, and it is of course the subject of much dispute.

Much of the dispute has raged around that special critical maneuver which William Wimsatt and I once named 'The Intentional Fallacy.' Is it really a fallacy? Or is it sound procedure (when properly understood, of course)? After some initial discussions, there was a period when our doctrine seemed secure, though needing corrections and precisions; however, I have the impression that in recent years there has been an Intentionalist Backlash. I do not propose to meet it head-on in these lectures. But the whole issue is so central to criticism and critical theory that it can hardly be avoided or ignored.

What does the literary interpreter do? He tells us what a literary work means. And whatever else it is, a literary work is first of all a text, a piece of language. So what the interpreter reveals is the meaning of a text. But what is that?

This question will lead us into some fairly fundamental discussion when we later pursue it further. But as a start, let us dispose once and for all, if we can, of a theory that is consciously accepted by many critics and unconsciously followed by many others. It is clearly stated at the very beginning of a recent and significant work on the theory of interpretation – or 'hermeneutics' – by E. D. Hirsch, whose views I shall have more to say about shortly. He writes:

> It is a task for the historian of culture to explain why there has been in the past four decades a heavy and largely victorious assault on the sensible belief that a text means what its author meant.[1]

I think there is no need to consult the historian of culture when the logician can give us the explanation so much more quickly and simply. For unfortunately the belief that a text means what its author meant is not sensible.

Let us call the Hirsch thesis – a common and familiar one – the Identity Thesis: that what a literary work means is identical to what its author meant in composing it.

The question is not whether textual meaning and authorial meaning can coincide – i.e., be very similar. Certainly they can. The question is not whether textual meaning is often adequate evidence of authorial meaning. Certainly it often is. The question is whether they are one and the same thing. If they are, it follows, as Hirsch argues, that when the literary interpreter interprets a text, he is really discovering what the author meant in composing it. And from that proposition follow various consequences about the kinds of evidence that are relevant to interpretation and decisive in validating (i.e., confirming) an interpretation.

I

The Identity Thesis can be conclusively refuted by the following three arguments.

1   Some texts that have been formed without the agency of an author, and hence without authorial meaning, nevertheless have a meaning and can be interpreted, for example, certain kinds of verbal mistake. The following comes from *The Portland Oregonian*, by way of *The New Yorker*:

> 'It showed that there is at least one officer on the Portland police force who had not seen Officer Olsen drunk,' Apley quietly observed.
>   In contrast to Apley, Jensen argued like a man filled with righteous indigestion.

The final phrase is inadvertent, yet it is very intelligible. When Hart Crane wrote 'Thy Nazarene and tender eyes,' a printer's error transformed it into 'Thy Nazarene and tinder eyes'; but Crane let the accidental version stand. Then there are poems composed by computers:

> While life reached evilly through empty faces
> While space flowed slowly o'er idle bodies
> And stars flowed evilly on vast men
> No passion smiled.[2]

Here one might claim that there is something like a hovering 'authorial will,' expressed in the instructions of the programmer; but the instructions were general, and the poem is a particular new composition of words. It has meaning, but nothing was meant by anyone.

There are textual meanings without authorial meanings. Therefore textual meaning is not identical to authorial meaning.

2   The meaning of a text can change after its author has died. But the author cannot change his meaning after he has died. Therefore, the textual meaning is not identical to the authorial meaning.

The *OED* furnishes abundant evidence that individual words and idioms acquire new meanings and lose old meanings as time passes; these changes can in turn produce changes of meaning in sentences in which the words appear. I cite these lines from Mark Akenside, *The Pleasures of Imagination* (II, 311–13), referring to 'the Sovereign Spirit of the world':

> Yet, by immense benignity inclin'd
> To spread about him that primeval joy
> Which fill'd himself, he rais'd his plastic arm

'Plastic arm' has acquired a new meaning in the twentieth century, and this is now its dominant one (though the older one has not disappeared). Consequently the line in which it occurs has also acquired a new meaning.

We are forced, then, to distinguish between what this line meant in 1744 and what it means in 1968. Of course we can inquire into both meanings, if we will; but these are two distinct inquiries. And if today's textual meaning of the line cannot be identified with any authorial meaning, it follows that textual meanings are not the same thing as authorial meanings.

3 A text can have meanings that its author is not aware of. Therefore, it can have meanings that its author did not intend. Therefore, textual meaning is not identical to authorial meaning.

It is not necessary to give examples to support my first premise, since Hirsch concedes that it is true. He himself gives the example[3] of a critic pointing out to an author that in his work he had suggested a similarity by parallel syntax. 'What this example illustrates,' he says, 'is that there are usually components of an author's intended meaning that he is not conscious of.' Thus it is my second proposition that he denies:

> It is not possible to mean what one does not mean, though it is very possible to mean what one is not conscious of meaning. That is the entire issue in the argument based on authorial ignorance. That a man may not be conscious of all that he means is no more remarkable than that he may not be conscious of all that he does.[4]

This analogy gives the case away. If the psychological act of 'meaning' something (supposing that there is such a psychological act) were like the overt physical act of *doing* something, then it *would* be possible to mean unconsciously. But the only way one can mean something unconsciously is to say something that (textually) means something one is not aware of.

Consider Hirsch's discussion of the 'implications' of texts. What can he do about the suggestions and intimations that a text may have, quite independently of what its author has (in Hirsch's words) 'willed to convey' by it? Consider Senator Dodd's remark to the senators investigating the tax-free personal funds he obtained from four 'testimonial dinners' that were advertised as political fund-raising events. He said: 'If there is anything more common to Connecticut than nutmeg it is testimonial affairs, and they go on there every week.' He certainly did not *will* to suggest that his testimonial dinners were as phony as the celebrated wooden nutmegs sold by the old Yankee peddlers, who thus gave Connecticut its nickname. But that is what he did suggest. Hirsch's solution of the problem is not the sensible one of admitting that textual meaning can go beyond authorial meaning; instead, he tries to stretch the concept of will far enough so that whatever the text does mean can be said to be 'willed' by the author – however unwittingly.

'It is possible,' says Hirsch, 'to will an et cetera without in the least being aware of all the individual members that belong to it.'[5] True enough. But what does it prove? I can ask someone to bring me all the books on the top shelf, without knowing the names of any of the books. But then I have not asked for any particular book. Suppose *Huckleberry Finn* is on the top shelf and is brought to me – it does not follow that I asked for *Huckleberry Finn*. Similarly, a poet can agree to stand behind all of the implications of his poem, without knowing what the implications are. But if the poem turns out to have a particular implication that he was not aware of, it does not follow that he willed that particular implication. Whatever is unwitting is unwilled...

The fundamental error, as I see it, in Hirsch's account of verbal meaning is summed up in his statement, quoted above: 'A determinate verbal meaning requires a determining will.' My position is, rather, that texts acquire determinate meaning through the interactions of their words without the intervention of an authorial will. When possible meanings are transformed into an actual meaning, this transformation is generated by the possibilities (the Leibnizian *com*possibilities) themselves.

If this were not the case, I do not believe we could give a really determinate sense to Hirsch's 'indeterminacy.' For what does it mean to say that the noun 'line' is 'indeterminate'? Only, so far as I can see, that it is capable of acquiring different *determinate* meanings when placed in varied contexts: 'dropping someone a line,' 'a line of type,' 'throwing the drowning man a line,' 'the manufacturer's current line,' etc. If the meanings in these contexts were not fairly determinate, it would not make sense to call the single word 'indeterminate,' because we would not have a clear concept of what it is that the word lacks, by itself. It would be beside the point to reply that 'line' in 'a line of type' is also indeterminate, because it does not specify how long the line is. The limitation is *indefiniteness*, which is a quite different thing from 'indeterminacy,' and is removed (when it is removed) in a quite different way – not by enlarging the controlling verbal context but by supplying further information.

Notes

1 E. D. Hirsch, *Validity in Interpretation* (Yale University Press, 1967), p.1. Hirsch has replied to some of his critics in *Genre* 2 (March, 1969): 57–62.

2 Wilbur Cross, 'Machine Miltons,' *New York Times Magazine*, December 4, 1966, p.59.

3 Hirsch, p.21.

4 Ibid., p.22.

5 Ibid., p.49.

Aesthetics

Monroe C. Beardsley (1915–80)

Beardsley's concern in this final extract drawn from his work is to insist on the necessity of distinguishing between an aesthetic object and its creator's intention. Evidence for the interpretation of the one will not always count as evidence for the interpretation of the other. Drawing on a dispute between A. E. Housman and Frank Harris as to the meaning of one of Housman's poems, Beardsley argues that authorial intention can never be the final court of appeal in matters of interpretation. Authors have neither the right nor the power to impose meaning on their work. There are many similarities to be noted here with Barthes' 'death of the author' notion (Reading 5).

The artist's intention

The things that naturally come to mind when we think of works of art are the products of deliberate human activity, sometimes long and arduous – think of the Ceiling of the Sistine Chapel, *Elegy in a Country Churchyard*, *Wozzeck*, and the Cathedral at Chartres. To put it another way, these things were *intended* by someone, and no doubt they are largely what they were intended to be by those who made them.

The artist's intention is a series of psychological states or events in his mind: what he wanted to do, how he imagined or projected the work before he began to make it and while he was in the process of making it. Something was going on in Chaucer's mind when he was planning *The Canterbury Tales* and in Beethoven's mind when he was considering various possible melodies for the choral finale of his *D Minor Symphony (No. 9)*. And these happenings were no doubt among the factors that caused those works to come into being. One of the questions we can ask about any work, but probably not with much hope of a conclusive answer, is: What was its *cause*? And of course a good deal of writing about works of art consists in describing the historical situation, the social, economic and political conditions, under which they were produced –

including the domestic affairs and physical health of the artist – in an attempt to explain, if possible, why they were created, and why they turned out the way they did...

Two sets of problems appear when we consider the connection between the aesthetic object and the artist's intention. One set of problems concerns the role of intention in *evaluating* the object... The other concerns the role of intention in *describing* and *interpreting* the object: these we shall consider here. It is the simple thesis of this section that we must distinguish between the aesthetic object and the intention in the mind of its creator.[1]

When you state the distinction that way, it seems harmless enough, and perfectly acceptable. Yet there are some rather serious and interesting difficulties about it, and we shall have to look into them. First, however, it is worth noting that even critics who would perhaps grant the distinction verbally are quite often not able to see the implications of it, both in their critical theory and in their critical practice. Here is part of a paragraph, for example, from a literary critic who generally blurs the distinction in his writing. He is discussing André Malraux' novel *La Condition Humaine*:

> The handling of this huge and complicated subject must have given the author a good deal of trouble. He evidently sat down like an engineer to the problem of designing a structure that would meet a new set of conditions; and *an occasional clumsiness of mechanics appears. The device of presenting in dramatic scenes the exposition of political events*, to which we owe Garin in *Les Conquérants* and his eternal dispatches, *here appears as a series of conversations so exhaustive and so perfectly to the point in their function of political analysis as* – in spite of the author's efforts to particularize the characters – *occasionally to lack plausibility.*[2]

The clauses in italics are about the novel, the rest are about the novelist; and the paragraph passes from one to the other as though there were no change of subject. But, not to be invidious, we must add that equally good examples of the shift back and forth could be found in numerous critics of all the arts.

The consequences that follow from making a distinction between aesthetic objects and artists' intentions are very important, but they are not all obvious, because they depend upon a general principle of philosophy that is often not kept steadily in mind. If two things are distinct, that is, if they are indeed two, and not one thing under two names (like the Vice President of the United States and the Presiding Officer of the Senate), then the evidence for the existence and nature of one cannot be exactly the same as the evidence for the existence and nature of the other. Any evidence, for example, that the Vice President is tall will automatically be evidence that the Presiding Officer of the Senate is tall, and vice versa. But evidence that the Vice President is tall will have no bearing on the height of the President.

This point is obscured where the two things, though distinct, are causally connected, as are presumably the intention and the aesthetic object. For if Jones, Sr., is the father of Jones, Jr., then any evidence about the height of either of them will be *indirect* evidence about the height of the other, in virtue of certain laws of genetics, according to which the tallness of the father at least affects the probability that the son will be tall, though it does not, of course, render it certain.

Thus, in each case of aesthetic object and intention, we have direct evidence of each: we discover the nature of the object by looking, listening, reading, etc., and we discover the intention by biographical inquiry, through letters, diaries, workbooks – or, if the artist is alive, by asking him. But also what we learn about the nature of the object itself is indirect evidence of what the artist intended it to be, and what we learn about the artist's intention is indirect evidence of what the object became. Thus, when we are concerned with the object itself, we should distinguish between internal and external evidence of its nature. Internal evidence is evidence from direct inspection of the object; external evidence is evidence from the psychological and social background of the object, from which we may infer something about the object itself.

Where internal and external evidence go hand in hand – for example, the painter writes in an exhibition catalogue that his painting is balanced in a precise and complicated way, and we go to the painting and see that it *is* so balanced – there is no problem. But where internal and external evidence conflict, as when a painter tells us one thing and our eyes tell us another, there *is* a problem, for we must decide between them. The problem is how to make this decision. If we consider the 'real' painting to be that which the painter projected in his mind, we shall go at it one way; if we consider the 'real' painting to be the one that is before us, open to public observation, we shall go at it another way.

We generally do not hesitate between these alternatives. As

long as we stick to the simplest descriptive level, we are in no doubt; if a sculptor tells us that his statue was intended to be smooth and blue but our senses tell us it is rough and pink, we go by our senses. We might, however, be puzzled by more subtle qualities of the statue. Suppose the sculptor tells us his statue was intended to be graceful and airy. We might look at it carefully and long, and not find it so. If the sculptor insists, we will give it a second look. But if we still cannot see those qualities, we conclude that they are not there; it would not occur to us to say they must be there, merely because the sculptor is convinced that he has put them there. Yet it is well known that our perceptions can be influenced by what we expect or hope to see, and especially by what we may be socially stigmatized for not seeing. Though no doubt the sculptor cannot talk us into perceiving red as blue, if his words have prestige – if we are already disposed to regard his intention as a final court of appeal – his words may be able to make us see grace where we would otherwise not see it, or a greater airiness than we would otherwise see. If this works on everyone, then everyone will see these qualities in the statue, and for all practical purposes they will be in the statue. Thus the intention, or the announcement of it, actually brings something to pass; what the statue is cannot be distinguished from what it is intended to be. So the argument might go.

But it is precisely this argument that presents a strong reason for not making intention the final court of appeal. Suppose there is an experimental physicist who becomes so emotionally involved in any hypothesis that he cannot help seeing the outcome of his experiments as confirming the hypotheses: he even sees red litmus paper as blue if that is predicted from his hypothesis. No doubt his prospects for a scientific future are dim, but if he is handy around a laboratory, we can still find a way to use him. Let him test other people's hypotheses by performing the experiments called for, but don't tell him until afterward what the hypothesis is. The scientist is wholly imaginary, but the principle is sound. And we shall adopt an analogous rule: If a quality can be seen in a statue *only* by someone who already believes that it was intended by the sculptor to be there, then that quality is not in the statue at all. For what can be seen only by one who expects and hopes to see it is what we would call illusory by ordinary standards – like the strange woman in the crowd who momentarily looks like your wife.

When it comes to *interpreting* the statue, the situation is more complicated. Suppose the sculptor says his status symbolizes Human Destiny. It is a large, twisted, cruller-shaped object of polished teak, mounted at an oblique angle to the floor. We look at it, and see in it no such symbolic meaning, even after we have the hint. Should we say that we have simply missed the symbolism, but that it must be there, since what a status symbolizes is precisely what its maker makes it symbolize? Or should we say, in the spirit of Alice confronting the extreme semantical conventionalism of Humpty Dumpty, that the question is whether that object can be made to mean Human Destiny? If we take the former course, we are in effect saying that the nature of the object, as far as its meaning goes, cannot be distinguished from the artist's intention; if we take the latter course, we are saying it can. But the former course leads in the end to the wildest absurdity: anyone can make anything symbolize anything just by saying it does, for another sculptor could copy the same object and label it 'Spirit of Palm Beach, 1938.' . . .

Suppose someone utters a sentence. We can ask two questions: (1) What does the *speaker* mean? (2) What does the *sentence* mean? Now, if the speaker is awake and competent, no doubt the answers to these two questions will turn out to be the same. And for practical purposes, on occasions when we are not interested in the sentence except as a clue to what is going on in the mind of the speaker, we do not bother to distinguish the two questions. But suppose someone utters a particularly confused sentence that we can't puzzle out at all – he is trying to explain income tax exemptions, or the theory of games and economic behavior, and is doing a bad job. We ask him what he meant, and after a while he tells us in different words. Now we can reply, 'Maybe that's what you meant but it's not what you said,' that is, it's not what the sentence meant. And here we clearly make the distinction.

For what the sentence means depends not on the whim of the individual, and his mental vagaries, but upon public conventions of usage that are tied up with habit patterns in the whole speaking community. It is perhaps easy to see this in the case of an ambiguous sentence. A man says, 'I like my secretary better than my wife'; we raise our eyebrows, and inquire: 'Do you mean that you like her better than you like your wife?' And he replies, 'No, you misunderstand me; I mean I like her better than my wife does.' Now, in one sense he has cleared up the misunderstanding, he has told us what he meant. Since what he meant is still not what the first sentence succeeded in meaning, he hasn't made the original sentence any less ambiguous than it was; he has merely substituted for it a better, because unambiguous, one.

Now let us apply this distinction to a specific problem in literary criticism. On the occasion of Queen Victoria's Golden Jubilee, A. E. Housman published his poem '1887.' The poem refers to celebrations going on all over England. 'From Clee to Heaven the beacon burns,' because 'God has saved the Queen.' It recalls that there were many lads who went off to fight for the Empire, who 'shared the work with God,' but 'themselves they could not save,' and ends with the words,

> Get you the sons your fathers got,
> And God will save the Queen.[3]

Frank Harris quoted the last stanza to Housman, in a bitterly sarcastic tone, and praised the poem highly: 'You have poked fun at the whole thing and made splendid mockery of it.' But this reading of the poem, especially coming from a radical like Harris, made Housman angry:

> I never intended to poke fun, as you call it, at patriotism, and I can find nothing in the sentiment to make mockery of: I meant it sincerely; if Englishmen breed as good men as their fathers, then God will save the Queen. I can only reject and resent your – your truculent praise.[4]

We may put the question, then, in this form: 'Is Housman's poem, and particularly its last stanza, ironic? The issue can be made fairly sharp. There are two choices: (1) We can say that the meaning of the poem, including its irony or lack of it, is precisely what the author intended it to be. Then any evidence of the intention will automatically be evidence of what the poem is: the poem is ironic if Housman says so. He is the last court of appeal, for it is his poem. (2) Or we can distinguish between the meaning of the poem and the author's intention. Of course, we must admit that in many cases an author may be a good reader of his own poem, and he may help us to see things in it that we have overlooked. But at the same time, he is not necessarily the best reader of his poem, and indeed he misconstrues it when, as perhaps in Housman's case, his unconscious guides his pen more than his consciousness can admit. And if his report of what the poem is intended to mean conflicts with the evidence of the poem itself, we cannot allow him to *make* the poem mean what he wants it to mean, just by fiat. So in this case we would have the poem read by competent critics, and if they found irony in it, we should conclude that it is ironical, no matter what Housman says.

Notes

1 As far as I know, the importance of this distinction was first clearly pointed out by W. K. Wimsatt, Jr. ...

2 Edmund Wilson, *The Shores of Light*, New York: Farrar, Straus and Young, 1952, p.570. My italics.

3 From '1887,' from *The Collected Poems of A. E. Housman.* Copyright, 1940, by Henry Holt and Company, Inc. Copyright, 1936, by Barclays Bank Ltd. By permission of the publishers. Canadian clearance by permission of The Society of Authors as the Literary Representative of the Trustees of the Estate of the late A. E. Housman, and messrs. Jonathan Cape Ltd., publishers of A. E. Housman's *Collected Poems.*

4 Frank Harris, *Latest Contemporary Portraits*, New York: Macaulay, 1927, p.280.

The validity of interpretation

E. D. Hirsch (b.1904)

In this extract, E. D. Hirsch puts forward an intentionalist account of meaning of the kind that Beardsley and Wimsatt are opposing in Readings 24–26. Hirsch claims that a determinate meaning requires a determining will: in other words, behind the meaning of a text lies an authorial intention. Intention can be well or badly realized, and where there is ambiguity as regards meaning it is likely to be because an intention has not been fully conveyed. One of the major tasks of the critical interpreter is to examine the context of any such ambiguity very closely, and by process of elimination of possibilities isolate what the intention is (Hirsch's critical method is known as 'hermeneutics'). Hirsch admits that 'an author almost always means more than he is aware of meaning', but argues that there are restrictions as to the interpretation that can be put on any 'submeanings' that occur. In effect, utterances imply a field of meaning (meaning stands under a 'type', in Hirsch's wording), and interpretation has to remain within the boundaries of that field. Derrida and the poststructuralist movement (see Reading 31) will go on to reject such a conception of meaning as determinate.

A determinate verbal meaning requires a determining will. Meaning is not made determinate simply by virtue of its being represented by a determinate sequence of words. Obviously, any brief word sequence could represent quite different complexes of verbal meaning, and the same is true of long word sequences, though it is less obvious. If that were not so, competent and intelligent speakers of a language would not disagree as they do about the meaning of texts. But if a determinate word sequence does not in itself necessarily represent one, particular, self-identical, unchanging complex of meaning, then the determinacy of its verbal meaning must be accounted for by some other discriminating force which causes the meaning to be *this* instead of *that* or *that* or *that*, all of which it could be. That discriminating force must involve an act of will, since unless one particular complex of meaning is *willed* (no matter how 'rich' and 'various' it might be), there would be no distinction between what an author does mean by a word sequence and what he could mean by it. Determinacy of verbal meaning requires an act of will.

It is sometimes said that 'meaning is determined by context,' but this is a very loose way of speaking. It is true that the surrounding text or the situation in which a problematical word sequence is found tends to narrow the meaning probabilities for that particular word sequence; otherwise, interpretation would be hopeless. And it is a measure of stylistic excellence in an author that he should have managed to formulate a decisive context for any particular word sequence within his text. But this is certainly not to say that context determines verbal meaning. At best a context determines the guess of an interpreter (though his construction of the context may be wrong, and his guess correspondingly so). To speak of context as a determinant is to confuse an exigency of interpretation with an author's determining acts. An author's verbal meaning is limited by linguistic possibilities but is determined by his actualizing and specifying some of those possibilities. Correspondingly, the verbal meaning that an interpreter construes is determined by *his* act of will, limited by those same possibilities. The fact that a particular context has led the interpreter to a particular choice does not change the fact that the determination is a choice, even when it is unthinking and automatic. Furthermore, a context is something that has itself been determined – first by an author and then, through a construction, by an interpreter. It is not something that is simply there without anybody having to make any determinations.

While the author's will is a formal requirement for any determinate verbal meaning, it is quite evident that will is not the same as meaning. On the other hand, it is equally evident that verbal meaning is not the same as the 'content' of which an author is conscious... An author almost always means more than he is aware of meaning, since he cannot explicitly pay attention to all the aspects of his meaning. Yet I have insisted that meaning is an affair of consciousness. In what sense is a meaning an object of consciousness even when one is not aware of it? Consider the example given in the earlier passage just referred to, in which a speaker admits he meant something he was not aware of meaning. Such an admission is possible because he conceived his meaning as a whole, and on reflection later perceived that the unattended meaning properly falls within that whole. That is, in fact, the only way the speaker's admission could be true.

What kind of whole is it that could contain a meaning even though the meaning was not explicitly there? And how can such a generous sort of entity still have very stern barriers which exclude other meanings that the author might actually have been attending to, as well as countless others that he was not? Clearly this remarkable characteristic of verbal meaning is the crucial one to examine.

Suppose I say, in a casual talk with a friend, 'Nothing pleases me so much as the Third Symphony of Beethoven.' And my friend asks me, 'Does it please you more than a swim in the sea on a hot day?' And I reply, 'You take me too literally. I meant that no *work of art* pleases me more than Beethoven's Third.' How was my answer possible? How did I know that 'a swim in the sea' did not fall under what I meant by 'things that please me'? (The hyperbolic use of 'nothing' to stand for 'no work of art' is a common sort of linguistic extension and can constitute verbal meaning in any context where it is communicable. My friend could have understood me. He misunderstands for the sake of the example.) Since I was not thinking either of 'a swim in the sea' or 'Brueghel's *Hay Gathering*,' some principle in my meaning must cause it to exclude the first and include the second. This is possible because I meant a certain *type* of 'thing that pleases me' and willed all possible members belonging to that type, even though very few of those possible members could have been attended to by me. Thus, it is possible to will an et cetera without in the least being aware of all the individual members that belong to it. The acceptability of any given candidate applying for membership in the et cetera depends entirely on the type of whole meaning that I willed. That is to say, the acceptability of a submeaning depends upon the *author*'s notion of the subsuming type whenever this notion is sharable in the particular linguistic circumstances.

The definition of verbal meaning given earlier in this chapter [not reproduced here] can now be expanded and made more descriptive. I said before that verbal meaning is whatever an author wills to convey by his use of linguistic symbols and which can be so conveyed. Now verbal meaning can be defined more particularly as a *willed type* which an author expresses by linguistic symbols and which can be understood by another through those symbols. It is essential to emphasize the concept of type since it is only through this concept that verbal meaning can be (as it is) a determinate object of consciousness and yet transcend (as it does) the actual contents of consciousness.

A type is an entity with two decisive characteristics. First, it is an entity that has a boundary by virtue of which something belongs to it or does not. In this respect it is like a class, though it has the advantage of being a more unitary concept: a type can be entirely represented in a single instance, while a class is usually thought of as an array of instances. The second decisive characteristic of a type is that it can always be represented by more than one instance. When we say that two instances are of the same type, we perceive common (identical) traits in the instances and allot these common traits to the type. Thus a type is an entity that has a boundary by virtue of which something belongs to it or does not, and it is also an entity which can be represented by different instances or different contents of consciousness. It follows that a verbal meaning is always a type since otherwise it could not be sharable: If it lacked a boundary, there would be nothing in particular to share; and if a given instance could not be accepted or rejected as an instance of the meaning (the representational character of a type), the interpreter would have no way of knowing what the boundary was. In order that a meaning be determinate for another it must be a type. For this reason, verbal meanings, i.e. shared meanings, are always types and can never relinquish their type character.

Thus verbal meaning can never be limited to a unique, concrete content. It can, of course, refer to unique entities, but only by means that transcend unique entities, and this transcendence always has the character of a typification. This is so even when a verbal meaning has reference to something that is obviously unique, like 'the death of Buonaparte.' 'Death,' the,' and 'of' all retain their type character even though their combination might effect a particular new type. The same is true of 'Buonaparte,' for a name is a type, and the particular name 'Buonaparte' could not relinquish its type character without thereby ceasing to be a name, in which case it would be incomprehensible and unsharable. No doubt this particular name in a particular use would not have a meaning identical to 'Buonaparte' in another usage. But that would simply mean that they are different types as well as, on another level, instances of the same type. However, they could never be merely concrete instances. The determinacy and sharability of verbal meaning resides in its being a type. The particular type that it is resides in the author's determining will. *A verbal meaning is a willed type.*

Course in general linguistics

Ferdinand de Saussure (1857–1913)

The Swiss linguist Ferdinand de Saussure is one of the major sources of structuralist theory, and the Course in General Linguistics *(1916) has been one of the most avidly studied books in continental aesthetic circles this century. Saussure regards language as being a self-contained system with its own self-regulating rules, rather on the analogy of games such as chess. Structuralists have applied this 'linguistic model' to other phenomena, including the arts. Thus literature can be viewed as a self-contained system with its own internal 'grammar' governing the relationship between its elements (say the parts of a narrative). Saussure is also responsible for encouraging the development of 'semiotics', the idea that systems are made up of signs, or signals, which generate predictable responses in human beings (traffic lights are an example of a rudimentary sign-system). In the following extract from the* Course in General Linguistics, *Saussure outlines his theory of the linguistic sign as consisting of the union of a mental concept and a spoken or written word. He then goes on to posit two key distinctions which have since become staple elements of structural analysis: synchronic/diachronic and syntagmatic/associative. The first deals with the effect of time on systems; thus a system can either be viewed as a totality with certain constant features (the synchronic perspective), or as a system evolving over time (the diachronic perspective). In the second case the distinction refers to Saussure's theory of relations. Words are seen to be connected either in linear sequence, as in a grammatically constructed sentence (syntagmatic relation), or by association of ideas in the mind (associative relation).*

Nature of the linguistic sign

1   SIGN, SIGNIFIED, SIGNIFIER

Some people regard language, when reduced to its elements, as a naming-process only – a list of words, each corresponding to the thing that it names. For example:

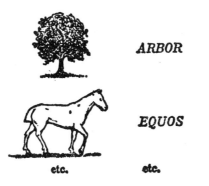

This conception is open to criticism at several points. It assumes that ready-made ideas exist before words...it does not tell us whether a name is vocal or psychological in nature (*arbor*, for instance, can be considered from either viewpoint); finally, it lets us assume that the linking of a name and a thing is a very simple operation – an assumption that is anything but true. But this rather naive approach can bring us near the truth by showing us that the linguistic unit is a double entity, one formed by the associating of two terms.

We have seen in considering the speaking-circuit...that both terms involved in the linguistic sign are psychological and are united in the brain by an associative bond. This point must be emphasized.

The linguistic sign unites, not a thing and a name, but a concept and a sound-image. The latter is not the material sound, a purely physical thing, but the psychological imprint of the sound, the impression that it makes on our senses. The sound-image is sensory, and if I happen to call it 'material,' it is only in that sense, and by way of opposing it to the other term of the association, the concept, which is generally more abstract...

The linguistic sign is then a two-sided psychological entity that can be represented by the drawing:

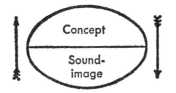

The two elements are intimately united, and each recalls the other. Whether we try to find the meaning of the Latin word *arbor* or the word that Latin uses to designate the concept 'tree,' it is clear that only the associations sanctioned by that language appear to us to conform to reality, and we disregard whatever others might be imagined.

Our definition of the linguistic sign poses an important question of terminology. I call the combination of a concept and a sound-image a *sign*, but in current usage the term generally designates only a sound-image, a word, for example (*arbor*, etc.). One tends to forget that *arbor* is called a sign only because it carries the concept 'tree,' with the result that the idea of the sensory part implies the idea of the whole.

Ambiguity would disappear if the three notions involved here were designated by three names, each suggesting and opposing the others. I propose to retain the word *sign* [*signe*] to designate the whole and to replace *concept* and *sound-image* respectively by *signified* [*signifié*] and *signifier* [*signifiant*]; the last two terms have the advantage of indicating the opposition that separates them from each other and from the whole of which they are parts. As regards *sign*, if I am satisfied with it, this is simply because I do not know of any word to replace it, the ordinary language suggesting no other.

The linguistic sign, as defined, has two primordial characteristics. In enunciating them I am also positing the basic principles of any study of this type.

2   PRINCIPLE I: THE ARBITRARY NATURE OF THE SIGN

The bond between the signifier and the signified is arbitrary. Since I mean by sign the whole that results from the associating of the signifier with the signified, I can simply say: *the linguistic sign is arbitrary*.

The idea of 'sister' is not linked by any inner relationship to the succession of sounds *s-ö-r* which serves as its signifier in French; that it could be represented equally by just any other sequence is proved by differences among languages and by the very existence of different languages: the signified 'ox' has as its signifier *b-ö-f* on one side of the border and *o-k-s* (*Ochs*) on the other.

No one disputes the principle of the arbitrary nature of the sign, but it is often easier to discover a truth than to assign to it its proper place. Principle I dominates all the linguistics of language; its consequences are numberless. It is true that not all of them are equally obvious at first glance; only after many detours does one discover them, and with them the primordial importance of the principle...

The word *arbitrary* also calls for comment. The term should not imply that the choice of the signifier is left entirely to the speaker (we shall see below that the individual does not have the power to change a sign in any way once it has become established in the linguistic community); I mean that it is unmotivated, i.e. arbitrary in that it actually has no natural connection with the signified...

3 PRINCIPLE II: THE LINEAR NATURE OF THE SIGNIFIER

The signifier, being auditory, is unfolded solely in time from which it gets the following characteristics: (a) it represents a span, and (b) the span is measurable in a single dimension; it is a line.

While Principle II is obvious, apparently linguists have always neglected to state it, doubtless because they found it too simple; nevertheless, it is fundamental, and its consequences are incalculable. Its importance equals that of Principle I; the whole mechanism of language depends upon it... In contrast to visual signifiers (nautical signals, etc.) which can offer simultaneous groupings in several dimensions, auditory signifiers have at their command only the dimension of time. Their elements are presented in succession; they form a chain. This feature becomes readily apparent when they are represented in writing and the spatial line of graphic marks is substituted for succession in time...

Immutability and mutability of the sign

1 IMMUTABILITY

The signifier, though to all appearances freely chosen with respect to the idea that it represents, is fixed, not free, with respect to the linguistic community that uses it. The masses have no voice in the matter, and the signifier chosen by language could be replaced by no other. This fact, which seems to embody a contradiction, might be called colloquially 'the stacked deck.' We say to language: 'Choose!' but we add: 'It must be this sign and no other.' No individual, even if he willed it, could modify in any way at all the choice that has been made; and what is more, the community itself cannot control so much as a single word; it is bound to the existing language.

No longer can language be identified with a contract pure and simple, and it is precisely from this viewpoint that the linguistic sign is a particularly interesting object of study; for language furnishes the best proof that a law accepted by a community is a thing that is tolerated and not a rule to which all freely consent.

Let us first see why we cannot control the linguistic sign and then draw together the important consequences that issue from the phenomenon.

No matter what period we choose or how far we go, language always appears as a heritage of the preceding period. We might conceive of an act by which, at a given moment, names were assigned to things and a contract was formed between concepts and sound-images; but such an act has never been recorded. The notion that things might have happened like that was prompted by our acute awareness of the arbitrary nature of the sign.

No society, in fact, knows or has ever known language other than as a product inherited from preceding generations, and one to be accepted as such. That is why the question of the origin of speech is not so important as it is generally assumed to be. The question is not even worth asking; the only real object of linguistics is the normal, regular life of an existing idiom. A particular language-state is always the product of historical forces, and these forces explain why the sign is unchangeable, i.e. why it resists any arbitrary substitution.

Nothing is explained by saying that language is something inherited and leaving it at that. Can not existing and inherited laws be modified from one moment to the next?

To meet that objection, we must put language into its social setting and frame the question just as we would for any other social institution. How are other social institutions transmitted? This more general question includes the question of immutability. We must first determine the greater or lesser amounts of freedom that the other institutions enjoy; in each instance it will be seen that a different proportion exists between fixed tradition and the free action of society. The next step is to discover why in a given category, the forces of the first type carry more weight or less weight than those of the second. Finally, coming back to language, we must ask why the historical factor of transmission dominates it entirely and prohibits any sudden widespread change.

There are many possible answers to the question. For example, one might point to the fact that succeeding generations are not superimposed on one another like the drawers of a piece of furniture, but fuse and interpenetrate, each generation embracing individuals of all ages – with the result that modifications of language are not tied to the succession of generations. One might also recall the sum of the efforts required for learning the mother language and conclude that a general change would be impossible. Again, it might be added that reflection does not enter into the active use of an idiom – speakers are largely unconscious of the laws of language; and if they are unaware of them, how could they modify them? Even if they were aware of these laws, we may be sure that their awareness would seldom lead to criticism, for people are generally satisfied with the language they have received.

The foregoing considerations are important but not topical. The following are more basic and direct, and all the others depend on them.

(1) *The arbitrary nature of the sign.* Above, we had to accept the theoretical possibility of change; further reflection suggests that the arbitrary nature of the sign is really what protects language from any attempt to modify it. Even if people were more conscious of language than they are, they would still not know how to discuss it. The reason is simply that any subject in order to be discussed must have a reasonable basis. It is possible, for instance, to discuss whether the monogamous form of marriage is more reasonable than the polygamous form and to advance arguments to support either side. One could also argue about a system of symbols, for the symbol has a rational relationship with the thing signified... but language is a system of arbitrary signs and lacks the necessary basis, the solid ground for discussion. There is no reason for preferring *soeur* to *sister*, *Ochs* to *boeuf*, etc.

(2) *The multiplicity of signs necessary to form any language.* Another important deterrent to linguistic change is the great number of signs that must go into the making of any language. A system of writing comprising twenty to forty letters can in case of need be replaced by another system. The same would be true of language if it contained a limited number of elements; but linguistic signs are numberless.

(3) *The over-complexity of the system.* A language constitutes a system. In this one respect (as we shall see later) language is not completely arbitrary but is ruled to some extent by logic; it is here also, however, that the inability of the masses to transform it

becomes apparent. The system is a complex mechanism that can be grasped only through reflection; the very ones who use it daily are ignorant of it. We can conceive of a change only through the intervention of specialists, grammarians, logicians, etc.; but experience shows us that all such meddlings have failed.

(4) *Collective inertia toward innovation.* Language – and this consideration surpasses all the others – is at every moment everybody's concern; spread throughout society and manipulated by it, language is something used daily by all. Here we are unable to set up any comparison between it and other institutions. The prescriptions of codes, religious rites, nautical signals, etc., involve only a certain number of individuals simultaneously and then only during a limited period of time; in language, on the contrary, everyone participates at all times, and that is why it is constantly being influenced by all. This capital fact suffices to show the impossibility of revolution. Of all social institutions, language is least amenable to initiative. It blends with the life of society, and the latter, inert by nature, is a prime conservative force.

But to say that language is a product of social forces does not suffice to show clearly that it is unfree; remembering that it is always the heritage of the preceding period, we must add that these social forces are linked with time. Language is checked not only by the weight of the collectivity but also by time. These two are inseparable. At every moment solidarity with the past checks freedom of choice. We say *man* and *dog*. This does not prevent the existence in the total phenomenon of a bond between the two antithetical forces – arbitrary convention by virtue of which choice is free and time which causes choice to be fixed. Because the sign is arbitrary, it follows no law other than that of tradition, and because it is based on tradition, it is arbitrary.

2 MUTABILITY

Time, which insures the continuity of language, wields another influence apparently contradictory to the first: the more or less rapid change of linguistic signs. In a certain sense, therefore, we can speak of both the immutability and the mutability of the sign.

In the last analysis, the two facts are interdependent: the sign is exposed to alteration because it perpetuates itself. What predominates in all change is the persistence of the old substance; disregard for the past is only relative. That is why the principle of change is based on the principle of continuity.

Change in time takes many forms, on any one of which an important chapter in linguistics might be written. Without entering into detail, let us see what things need to be delineated.

First, let there be no mistake about the meaning that we attach to the word change. One might think that it deals especially with phonetic changes undergone by the signifier, or perhaps changes in meaning which affect the signified concept. That view would be inadequate. Regardless of what the forces of change are, whether in isolation or in combination, they always result in a *shift in the relationship between the signified and the signifier...*

Language is radically powerless to defend itself against the forces which from one moment to the next are shifting the relationship between the signified and the signifier. This is one of the consequences of the arbitrary nature of the sign.

Unlike language, other human institutions – customs, laws, etc. – are all based in varying degrees on the natural relations of things; all have of necessity adapted the means employed to the ends pursued. Even fashion in dress is not entirely arbitrary; we can deviate only slightly from the conditions dictated by the human body. Language is limited by nothing in the choice of means, for apparently nothing would prevent the associating of any idea whatsoever with just any sequence of sounds...

Mutability is so inescapable that it even holds true for artificial languages. Whoever creates a language controls it only so long as it is not in circulation; from the moment when it fulfills its mission and becomes the property of everyone, control is lost. Take Esperanto as an example; if it succeeds, will it escape the inexorable law? Once launched, it is quite likely that Esperanto will enter upon a fully semiological life; it will be transmitted according to laws which have nothing in common with those of its logical creation, and there will be no turning backwards. A man proposing a fixed language that posterity would have to accept for what it is would be like a hen hatching a duck's egg: the language created by him would be borne along, willy-nilly, by the current that engulfs all languages.

Signs are governed by a principle of general semiology: continuity in time is coupled to change in time; this is confirmed by orthographic systems, the speech of deaf-mutes, etc....

Static and evolutionary linguistics

1 INNER DUALITY OF ALL SCIENCES CONCERNED WITH VALUES

Very few linguists suspect that the intervention of the fact of time creates difficulties peculiar to linguistics and opens to their science two completely divergent paths.

Most other sciences are unaffected by this radical duality; time produces no special effects in them. Astronomy has found that the stars undergo considerable changes but has not been obliged on this account to split itself into two disciplines. Geology is concerned with successions at almost every instant, but its study of strata does not thereby become a radically distinct discipline. Law has its descriptive science and its historical science; no one opposes one to the other. The political history of states is unfolded solely in time, but a historian depicting a particular period does not work apart from history. Conversely, the science of political institutions is essentially descriptive, but if the need arises it can easily deal with a historical question without disturbing its unity.

On the contrary, that duality is already forcing itself upon the economic sciences. Here, in contrast to the other sciences, political economy and economic history constitute two clearly separated disciplines within a single science; the works that have recently appeared on these subjects point up the distinction. Proceeding as they have, economists are – without being well aware of it – obeying an inner necessity. A similar necessity obliges us to divide linguistics into two parts, each with its own principle. Here as in political economy we are confronted with the notion of *value*; both sciences are concerned with *a system for equating things of different orders* – labor and wages in one and a signified and signifier in the other.

Certainly all sciences would profit by indicating more precisely the co-ordinates along which their subject matter is aligned. Everywhere distinctions should be made, according to the following illustration, between (1) *the axis of simultaneities* (AB), which stands for the relations of coexisting things and from which the intervention of time is excluded; and (2) *the axis of successions* (CD), on which only one thing can be considered at a time but upon which are located all the things on the first axis together with their changes.

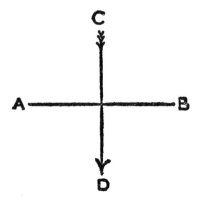

For a science concerned with values the distinction is a practical necessity and sometimes an absolute one. In these fields scholars cannot organize their research rigorously without considering both co-ordinates and making a distinction between the system of values per se and the same values as they relate to time.

This distinction has to be heeded by the linguist above all others, for language is a system of pure values which are determined by nothing except the momentary arrangement of its terms. A value – so long as it is somehow rooted in things and in their natural relations, as happens with economics (the value of a plot of ground, for instance, is related to its productivity) – can to some extent be traced in time if we remember that it depends at each moment upon a system of coexisting values. Its link with things gives it, perforce, a natural basis, and the judgments that we base on such values are therefore never completely arbitrary; their variability is limited. But we have just seen that natural data have no place in linguistics.

Again, the more complex and rigorously organized a system of values is, the more it is necessary, because of its very complexity, to study it according to both co-ordinates. No other system embodies this feature to the same extent as language. Nowhere else do we find such precise values at stake and such a great number and diversity of terms, all so rigidly interdependent. The multiplicity of signs, which we have already used to explain the continuity of language, makes it absolutely impossible to study simultaneously relations in time and relations within the system.

The reasons for distinguishing two sciences of language are clear. How should the sciences be designated? Available terms do not all bring out the distinction with equal sharpness. 'Linguistic history' and 'historical linguistics' are too vague. Since political history includes the description of different periods as well as the narration of events, the student might think that he is studying a language according to the axis of time when he describes its successive states, but this would require a separate study of the phenomena that make language pass from one state to another. *Evolution* and *evolutionary linguistics* are more precise, and I shall use these expressions often; in contrast, we can speak of the science of *language-states* [*états de langue*] or *static linguistics*.

But to indicate more clearly the opposition and crossing of two orders of phenomena that relate to the same object, I prefer to speak of *synchronic* and *diachronic* linguistics. Everything that relates to the static side of our science is synchronic; everything that has to do with evolution is diachronic. Similarly, *synchrony* and *diachrony* designate respectively a language-state and an evolutionary phase...

Syntagmatic and associative relations

1 DEFINITIONS

In a language-state everything is based on relations. How do they function?

Relations and differences between linguistic terms fall into two distinct groups, each of which generates a certain class of values. The opposition between the two classes gives a better understanding of the nature of each class. They correspond to two forms of our mental activity, both indispensable to the life of language.

In discourse, on the one hand, words acquire relations based on the linear nature of language because they are chained together. This rules out the possibility of pronouncing two elements simultaneously... The elements are arranged in sequence on the chain of speaking. Combinations supported by linearity are *syntagms.*[1] The syntagm is always composed of two or more consecutive units (e.g. French *re-lire* 're-read,' *contre tous* 'against everyone,' *la vie humaine* 'human life,' *Dieu est bon* 'God is good,' *s'il fait beau temps, nous sortirons* 'if the weather is nice, we'll go out,' etc.). In the syntagm a term acquires its value only because it stands in opposition to everything that precedes or follows it, or to both.

Outside discourse, on the other hand, words acquire relations of a different kind. Those that have something in common are associated in the memory, resulting in groups marked by diverse relations. For instance, the French word *enseignement* 'teaching' will unconsciously call to mind a host of other words (*enseigner* 'teach,' *renseigner* 'acquaint,' etc.; or *armement* 'armament,' *change-ment* 'amendment,' etc.; or *éducation* 'education,' *apprentissage* 'apprenticeship,' etc.). All those words are related in some way.

We see that the co-ordinations formed outside discourse differ strikingly from those formed inside discourse. Those formed outside discourse are not supported by linearity. Their seat is in the brain; they are a part of the inner storehouse that makes up the language of each speaker. They are *associative relations*.

The syntagmatic relation is *in praesentia*. It is based on two or more terms that occur in an effective series. Against this, the associative relation unites terms *in absentia* in a potential mnemonic series.

From the associative and syntagmatic viewpoint a linguistic

unit is like a fixed part of a building, e.g. a column. On the one hand, the column has a certain relation to the architrave that it supports; the arrangement of the two units in space suggests the syntagmatic relation. On the other hand, if the column is Doric, it suggests a mental comparison of this style with others (Ionic, Corinthian, etc.) although none of these elements is present in space: the relation is associative.

Note

1 It is scarcely necessary to point out that the study of *syntagms* is not to be confused with syntax. Syntax is only one part of the study of syntagms...[Ed.]

The raw and the cooked

Claude Lévi-Strauss (b.1908)

*The influence of the structural anthropologist Claude Lévi-Strauss
on the development of structuralist aesthetics has been considerable.
His work on primitive myth, with its concentration on comparative
formal analysis and its insistence on there being an underlying unity
to all myths, is in many ways a paradigm for the art of structuralist
analysis. Lévi-Strauss's analysis of a group of South American Indian
myths, in the extract from* The Raw and the Cooked *(1970) that
follows, assumes a basic narrative model which is then varied in the
case of each myth. The key point that Lévi-Strauss is making is that
'in all these instances we are dealing with the same myth... the
apparent divergences between the versions are to be treated as the
result of transformations occurring within a set'. Rather as in a game
of chess, various moves are possible within the context of the basic
narrative model (whose formal constants are displayed on page 382)
without in any way altering its overall structural unity. The myths
dealt with here form a self-contained system with its own self-
regulating grammar concerning the disposition of its narrative elements (the 'linguistic model' inherited from Saussure), and interpretation becomes a matter of examining, and then comparing, how the
grammar has been applied in each case.*

Bororo Song

A   THE BIRD-NESTER'S ARIA

The following is one of many myths told by the Bororo Indians of
central Brazil, whose territory used to extend from the upper
reaches of the Paraguay River to beyond the valley of the Araguaya:

M_1 (key myth). *Bororo: o xibae e iari. 'The macaws and their nest'*

In olden times the women used to go into the forest to gather
the palms used in the making of *ba*. These were penis sheaths
which were presented to adolescents at their initiation ceremony.

$\mathcal{T}$able of Symbols

$\left\{\begin{array}{l}\triangle \\ \bigcirc\end{array}\right.$	man woman

$\triangle = \bigcirc$ marriage (disjunction of marriage : #)

$\underset{\triangle \qquad \bigcirc}{\overline{\quad\quad\quad}}$ brother and sister (their disjunction : $|{-}{-}|$)

$\begin{array}{cc}\triangle & \bigcirc \\ | & | \\ \triangle & , \bigcirc\end{array}$ father and son, mother and daughter, etc.

T   transformation

$\longrightarrow$ is transformed into

$\left\{\begin{array}{l}: \\ ::\end{array}\right.$ is to . . .
as . . .

/   contrast

$\left\{\begin{array}{l}\equiv \\ \not\equiv\end{array}\right.$ congruence, homology, correspondence
noncongruence, nonhomology, noncorrespondence

$\left\{\begin{array}{l}= \\ \neq\end{array}\right.$ identity
difference

$\approx$ isomorphism

$\left\{\begin{array}{l}\cup \\ //\end{array}\right.$ union, reunion, conjunction
disunion, disjunction

$\left\{\begin{array}{l}\longrightarrow \\ \#\!\!\longrightarrow\end{array}\right.$ conjoins with . . .
is in a state of disjunction with . . .

f function

$x^{(-1)}$ inverted x

+ , −   these signs are used with various connotations depending on the context:
plus, minus; presence, absence; first or second term of a pair of opposites

One youth secretly followed his mother, caught her unawares, and raped her.

When the woman returned from the forest, her husband noticed feathers caught in her bark-cloth belt, which were similar to those worn by youths as adornment. Suspecting that something untoward had occurred, he decreed that a dance should take place in order to find out which youth was wearing a similar adornment. But to his amazement he discovered that his son was the only one. The man ordered another dance, with the same result.

Convinced now of his misfortune and anxious to avenge himself, he sent his son to the 'nest' of souls, with instructions to bring back the great dance rattle (bapo), which he coveted. The young man consulted his grandmother who revealed to him the mortal danger that such an undertaking involved; she advised him to obtain the help of the hummingbird.

When the hero, accompanied by the hummingbird, reached the aquatic region of souls, he waited on the shore, while the hummingbird deftly stole the rattle by cutting the short cord from which it was hanging. The instrument fell into the water, making a loud noise – jo. Alerted by this noise, the souls fired arrows from their bows. But the hummingbird flew so fast that he reached the shore safe and sound with the stolen rattle.

The father then ordered his son to fetch the small rattle belonging to the souls; and the same episode was repeated, with the same details, only this time the helpful animal was the quick flying juriti (Leptoptila species, a kind of dove). During a third expedition, the young man stole some buttore; these are jingling bells made from the hoofs of the caititu (Dicotyles torquatus, a type of wild pig), which are strung on a piece of rope and worn as anklets. He was helped by the large grasshopper (Acridium cristatum...), which flew more slowly than the birds so that the arrows pierced it several times but did not kill it.

Furious at the foiling of his plans, his father invited his son to come with him to capture the macaws, which were nesting in the face of a cliff. The grandmother did not know how to ward off this fresh danger, but gave her grandson a magic wand to which he could cling if he happened to fall.

The two men arrived at the foot of the rock; the father erected a long pole and ordered his son to climb it. The latter had hardly reached the nests when the father knocked the pole down; the boy only just had time to thrust the wand into a crevice. He remained suspended in the void, crying for help, while the father went off.

Our hero noticed a creeper within reach of his hand; he grasped hold of it and with difficulty dragged himself to the top of the rock. After a rest he set out to look for food, made a bow and arrows out of branches, and hunted the lizards which abounded on the plateau. He killed a lot of them and hooked the surplus ones to his belt and to the strips of cotton wound round his legs and ankles. But the dead lizards went bad and gave off such a vile smell that the hero fainted. The vultures (*Cathartes urubu*, *Coragyps atratus foetens*) fell upon him, devoured first of all the lizards, and then attacked the body of the unfortunate youth, beginning with his buttocks. Pain restored him to consciousness, and the hero drove off his attackers which, however, had completely gnawed away his hindquarters. Having eaten their fill, the birds were prepared to save his life; taking hold of his belt and the strips of cotton round his arms and legs with their beaks, they lifted him into the air and deposited him gently at the foot of the mountain.

The hero regained consciousness 'as if he were awaking from a dream.' He was hungry and ate wild fruits but noticed that since he had no rectum, he was unable to retain the food, which passed through his body without even being digested. The youth was at first nonplussed and then remembered a tale told him by his grandmother, in which the hero solved the same problem by molding for himself an artificial behind out of dough made from pounded tubers.

After making his body whole again by this means and eating his fill, he returned to his village, only to find that it had been abandoned. He wandered around for a long time looking for his family. One day he spotted foot and stick marks, which he recognized as being those of his grandmother. He followed the tracks but, being anxious not to reveal his presence, he took on the appearance of a lizard, whose antics fascinated the old woman and her grandson, the hero's younger brother. Finally, after a long interval, he decided to reveal himself to them. (In order to re-establish contact with his grandmother, the hero went through a series of transformations, turning himself into four birds and a butterfly, all unidentified...)

On that particular night there was a violent wind accompanied by a thunder storm which put out all the fires in the village except the grandmother's. Next morning everybody came and asked her for hot embers, in particular the second wife of the father who had tried to kill his son. She recognized her stepson, who was supposed to be dead, and ran to warn her husband. As if there were nothing wrong, the latter picked up his ceremonial rattle and welcomed his son with the songs of greeting for returned travelers.

However, the hero was full of thoughts of revenge. One day while he was walking in the forest with his little brother, he broke off a branch of the api tree, which was shaped like a deer's antler. The child, acting on his elder brother's instructions, then managed to make the father promise to order a collective hunt; in the guise of a mea, a small rodent, he secretly kept watch to discover where their father was lying in wait for the game. The hero then donned the false antlers, changed into a deer, and rushed at his father with such ferocity that he impaled him on the horns. Without stopping, he galloped toward a lake, into which he dropped his victim, who was immediately devoured by the Buiogoe spirits who are carnivorous fish. All that remained after the gruesome feast were the bare bones which lay on the bottom of the lake, and the lungs which floated on the surface in the form of aquatic plants, whose leaves, it is said, resemble lungs.

When he returned to the village, the hero took his revenge on his father's wives (one of whom was his own mother).

This myth provides the theme of a song, called *xobogeu*, belonging to the Paiwe clan of which the hero was a member...

An older version ends as follows. The hero declared: 'I no longer want to live with the Orarimugu who have ill-treated me, and in order to have my revenge on them and my father, I shall send them wind, cold, and rain.' Then he took his grandmother into a beautiful and distant land, and returned to punish the Indians as he said he would...

Ge Variations

The story of the bird-nester, which forms the central part of the key myth, occurs in an initial position in the case of the Ge, in the myth about the origin of fire, which is found in all the central and eastern Ge tribes that have been studied up to the present.

I shall begin with the versions peculiar to the northern group, the Kayapo...

A. FIRST VARIATION

M7. Kayapo-Gorotire. 'The origin of fire'

Noticing that a pair of macaws had built their nest on top of a steep rock, an Indian took his young brother-in-law, Botoque, with him to help him to capture the nestlings. He made Botoque climb up an improvised ladder; but when the boy got up to the nest, he said that he could find only two eggs. (It is not clear whether he was lying or telling the truth.) His brother-in-law insisted that he should take them; but as the eggs fell down, they changed into stones which hurt the older man's hand. This made him furious, with the result that he dismantled the ladder and went away, not realizing that the birds were enchanted (*oaianga*) ...

Botoque remained caught on top of the rock for several days. He grew thin: hunger and thirst obliged him to eat his own excrement. Eventually he noticed a spotted jaguar carrying a bow and arrow and all kinds of game. He would have liked to call out to it for help, but fear kept him silent.

The jaguar saw the hero's shadow on the ground and, after trying in vain to catch it, looked up, asked what had happened, repaired the ladder, and invited Botoque to come down. The latter was afraid and hesitated a long time; in the end he made up his mind, and the jaguar, in friendly fashion, suggested that if he would sit astride its back, it would take him to its home to have a meal of grilled meat. But the young man did not understand the meaning of the word 'grilled' because in those days, the Indians were unacquainted with fire and ate their meat raw.

At the jaguar's home the hero saw a big jatoba trunk burning; beside it was a pile of stones such as the Indians now use to build their earth ovens (*ki*). He ate his first meal of cooked meat.

But the jaguar's wife, who was an Indian, disliked the young man and referred to him as *me-on-kra-tum* 'foreign, or abandoned, son'; in spite of this, the jaguar, being childless, decided to adopt him.

Each day the jaguar went off to hunt, leaving the adopted son with the wife whose aversion for him steadily increased; she gave him only old wizened pieces of meat to eat, and leaves. When the boy complained, she scratched his face, and the poor child had to take refuge in the forest.

The jaguar scolded the wife, but in vain. One day it gave Botoque a brand new bow and some arrows, taught him how to use them, and advised him to use them against the woman, should the need arise. Botoque killed her by shooting an arrow into her breast. He fled in terror, taking with him the weapons and a piece of grilled meat.

He reached his village in the middle of the night, groped his way to his mother's bed, and had some difficulty in making his identity known (because he was thought to be dead); he told his tale and shared the meat. The Indians decided to get possession of the fire.

When they arrived at the jaguar's home, there was no one there; and since the wife was dead, the game caught the day before had not been cooked. The Indians roasted it and took away the fire. For the very first time it was possible to have light in the village at night, to eat cooked meat, and to warm oneself at a hearth.

But the jaguar, incensed by the ingratitude of his adopted

son, who had stolen 'fire and the secret of the bow and arrow,' was to remain full of hatred for all living creatures, especially human beings. Now only the reflection of fire could be seen in its eyes. It used its fangs for hunting and ate its meat raw, having solemnly renounced grilled meat...

B. SECOND VARIATION

M_8. *Kayapo-Kubenkranken.* '*The origin of fire*'

Formerly, men did not know how to make fire. When they killed game, they cut the flesh into thin strips, which they laid out on stones to dry in the sun. They also ate rotten wood.

One day a man noticed two macaws coming out of a hole in a cliff. To get at their nest, he made his young brother-in-law (his wife's brother) climb a tree trunk in which he had cut foot holds. But there were nothing but round stones in the nest. An argument ensued, degenerating into a quarrel, which ended as in the previous version. In this case, however, it seems that the lad, annoyed by his brother-in-law's taunts, threw the stones deliberately and wounded him.

In response to his wife's anxious inquiries, the man said the boy must have got lost, and to allay suspicion, he pretended to go and look for him. Meanwhile, suffering extreme hunger and thirst, the hero was reduced to eating his excrement and drinking his urine. He was nothing but skin and bone when a jaguar came along carrying a caititu pig on his shoulders; the animal noticed the boy's shadow and tried to catch it. On each occasion the hero moved back and the shadow disappeared. 'The jaguar looked all round, then covering its mouth, looked up and saw the lad on the rock.' They entered into conversation.

Explanations and discussions took place as in the preceding version. The hero was too frightened to sit directly on the jaguar but agreed to bestride the caititu, which the latter was carrying on his back. They reached the jaguar's home, where his wife was busy spinning. She reproached her husband, saying 'you have brought home another's son.' Unperturbed, the jaguar announced that he was going to adopt the boy as his companion, and intended to feed him and fatten him up.

But the jaguar's wife refused to give the lad any tapir meat and allowed him only venison and threatened to scratch him at the slightest opportunity. Acting on the jaguar's advice, the boy killed the woman with the bow and arrow given him by his protector.

He went off with the jaguar's belongings: the spun cotton, the meat, and the burning ash. When he reached his village, he made himself known first to his sister, then to his mother.

He was summoned to the *ngobe* 'men's house,' where he

related his adventures. The Indians decided to change themselves into animals to take possession of the fire: the tapir would carry the trunk, the yao bird would put out the burning ash that might be dropped on the way, while the deer would take charge of the meat, and the peccary of the spun cotton. The expedition was a success, and the men shared the fire between them...

C. THIRD VARIATION

M_9. Apinaye. 'The origin of fire'

A man found a macaw's nest with two young birds in a high and vertical cliff. He took his little brother-in-law along, chopped down a tree, leaned it against the wall of rock, and bade the boy climb. The boy went up, but the parent birds rushed at him with fierce screams; so he got frightened. Then the man got angry, knocked the tree aside, and left.

The boy, unable to descend, remained sitting by the nest for five days. He nearly died of thirst and hunger. He was completely covered by the droppings of the macaws and swallows that flew above him. Then a jaguar came past, saw the boy's shadow, and tried in vain to catch it. Then the boy spat down, and now the jaguar raised his head and saw him. They entered into conversation. The jaguar demanded to have the two young macaws, which the hero flung down to him one after the other, and which he immediately devoured. Then the jaguar brought up the tree and asked the boy to step down, promising him that he would not eat him, and that he would give him water to quench his thirst. Somewhat hesitantly, the hero complied. The jaguar took him on his back and carried him to a creek. The boy drank his fill and fell asleep. At last the jaguar pinched his arm and awakened him. He washed the dirt off him and said that, having no children, he would take him home as his son.

In the jaguar's home a huge jatoba trunk was lying on the floor and burning at one end. In those days the Indians were unacquainted with fire and ate only flesh dried in the sun. 'What is smoking there?' asked the boy. 'That is fire,' answered the jaguar. 'You will find out at night when it warms you.' Then he gave the roast meat to the boy, who ate till he fell asleep. At midnight he woke up, ate again, and then again fell asleep.

Before daybreak the jaguar went hunting. The boy climbed a tree to await his return. But toward noon he got hungry, returned to the jaguar's house, and begged his wife for food. 'What!' she shouted, baring her teeth. 'Look here!' The hero cried out from fear and ran to meet the jaguar and told him of the occurrence. The jaguar scolded his wife, who excused herself, saying that she was merely jesting. But the same scene occurred again the next day.

Following the advice of the jaguar (who had made him a bow and arrow and told him to shoot at a termite's nest), the boy killed the aggressive wife. His adopted father said, 'That does not matter,' gave him a lot of roast meat, and explained to him how to return to his village by following along the creek. But he was to be on guard: if a rock or the aroeira tree called him, he should answer; but was to keep still if he heard 'the gentle call of a rotten tree.'

The hero moved along the brook, replied to the first two calls and, forgetting the jaguar's warnings, to the third as well. That is why men are short-lived: if the boy had answered only the first two, they would enjoy as long life as the rock and the aroeira tree.

After a while the boy again heard a call and replied to it. It was Magalon kamduré, an ogre, who tried unsuccessfully to pass himself off as the hero's father by means of various disguises (long hair, ear ornaments). When the hero finally discovered the ogre's identity, the latter wrestled with him until he was quite worn out, whereupon he put the boy in his big carrying basket.

On his way home the ogre stopped to hunt coatis. Speaking from inside the basket, the hero called to him to make a trail through the woods first, so he could carry the load better. While the ogre was doing this, the hero escaped, after weighting the basket with a heavy stone.

When the ogre reached home, he promised his children a choice morsel, even better than the coatis. But all he found in the bottom of the basket was a stone.

Meanwhile the boy had found his way back to his village, where he related his adventures. All the Indians set off to look for the fire. Various animals offered their help: the jaó was to extinguish the fallen embers; the jacu was spurned, but the tapir was considered strong enough to carry the tree. The jaguar gave them the fire. 'I have adopted your son,' he said to the boy's father...

Another version (M_{9a}) differs in several respects from this one. The two men are a father-in-law and his son-in-law. The jaguar's wife, who is an expert spinner (cf. M_8), welcomes the boy first of all; and when she starts to threaten him, he kills her on his own initiative. His action is disapproved of by the jaguar, who does not believe in his wife's wickedness. The three calls that are then mentioned in the story are uttered, the first by the jaguar himself who from afar guides the hero back to his village; the others by stone and rotten wood; but we are not told how the hero reacts to the last two calls. When the Indians arrive in search of the fire, the jaguar is even more friendly than in the previous version, since it is he who engages the services of the helpful animals. He objects to the caititus and the queixadas but agrees that the tapirs should transport the log, while the birds pick up the fallen embers...

As can be seen, the version above maintains the bond of affinity and age difference between the two men; and these, as will subsequently appear, are the invariant features of the set. But at first glance we have here such an unexpected inversion of the functions of the 'wife-giver' and the 'taker' that we are tempted to suppose that there must be some linguistic error. As a matter of fact, the narrative was given directly in Portuguese by an Apinaye Indian who, together with three companions, had come to Belem to see the authorities. In every case where it is possible to make a comparison with texts that Nimuendaju collected in the field about the same time, it is noticeable that the versions by the Belem Apinaye, although more long-winded, contain less information... It is significant, however, that the jaguar's wife appears less hostile in M_{9a} than in all the other versions, and that the jaguar is even more friendly than in M_9, where he was already extremely friendly: although he does not believe his wife to be guilty, he bears the hero no grudge for having killed her; he shows great eagerness to give the Indians fire and organizes its transport himself.

Once this has been noted, the anomaly pointed out in the preceding paragraph becomes clearer. Among the Apinaye, as among other matrilineal and matrilocal communities, the wife's father is not, properly speaking, a 'giver.' This role falls rather to the young girl's brothers, who furthermore do not so much 'give' their sister to her future husband as 'take' the latter and compel him to accept, simultaneously, marriage and matrilocal residence... In these conditions the father-in-law/son-in-law relation in M_{9a} appears less like an inverted form of affinity than as a distended form, since it occurs, as it were, at two removes. This aspect of the situation clearly emerges from a comparison between M_{9a} and the key myth, in which the matrilineal line of descent and matrilocal residence are also relevant factors:

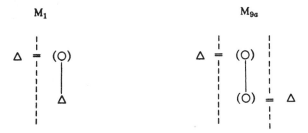

In M_{9a} we have, therefore, a variant in which all family relations, as well as the corresponding moral attitudes, are equally relaxed. In all respects this version is probably the weakest known to us.

D. FOURTH VARIATION

M_{10}. Eastern Timbira. 'The origin of fire'

Formerly men were unacquainted with fire and dried their meat by laying it out in the sun on a flat stone, so that it was not completely raw.

In those days a man once took his young brother-in-law on an expedition to rob macaws' nests in a cleft of a vertical cliff. But the fledglings made such an outcry that the boy did not dare take hold of them. The man grew angry, knocked down the ladder, and went off. The hero remained sitting by the nest, suffering from thirst, his head covered with birds' droppings, 'so that maggots grew there; and the young birds soon lost all fear of him.'

What follows is identical with the Apinaye version. It is explained, however, that the jaguar's wife was *pregnant* and could not bear the slightest noise; she therefore flew into a rage whenever the hero made a noise as he chewed the grilled meat his adopted father had given him. But try as he might, he could not eat silently, since the meat was too crisp. With the weapons given him by the jaguar, he wounded the wife in the paw and fled. The wife, hampered by her pregnancy, was unable to follow him.

The hero recounted his adventure to his father, who summoned all his companions. They placed runners at intervals all the way to the jaguar's house and organized a relay system: the burning log was passed from hand to hand and finally reached the village. The jaguar's wife begged them in vain to leave her a burning ember; the toad spat on all those that remained, and put them out...

E. FIFTH VARIATION

M_{11}. Eastern Timbira (Kraho group). 'The origin of fire'

The two civilizing heroes, Pud and Pudlere, formerly lived with men and put fire at their disposal. But when the heroes went away, they took the fire with them, and men were reduced to eating their meat raw, sun-dried, and accompanied by *pau puba*.

It was during this period that the brothers-in-law undertook their expedition. The younger of the two men was abandoned on the cliff face, where he wept among the angry birds: 'After two days the birds became used to him. The macaw deposited its droppings on his head, which swarmed with vermin. He was hungry.'

The end is similar to the other versions. The jaguar's wife was pregnant and liked to frighten the boy by threatening to eat him. The jaguar showed the boy the secret of the bow and arrows; and, following his advice, the boy wounded the wife in the paw and ran away. The Indians, after being informed of what had happened, organized a system of runners to get possession of the fire. 'But for the jaguar, they would still be eating their meat raw.'…

In a different context, a Kraho myth, which deals with a visit by a human hero to the jaguar's home, contains the following remark which forms a direct link between the fire theme and the pregnancy theme: 'The jaguar's wife was very pregnant [sic] and on the point of giving birth. Everything was ready for the confinement, and in particular a good fire was burning, because the jaguar is master of fire.'…

F. SIXTH VARIATION

M_{12}. Sherente. 'The origin of fire'

One day a man went into the woods with his little brother-in-law in order to take young macaws out of a nest in the hollow of a tree. The man made his brother-in-law climb a pole; but when he got up there, the young man declared that there were only eggs there. When the man said he knew there were young in the nest, the hero took a white stone in his mouth and threw it down. The stone turned into an egg that was smashed against the ground. The man was angry, pulled away the ladder, and went home, leaving the hero in the tree where he was forced to remain for five days.

Then a jaguar passed by and asked what he was doing up there, made him first throw down the two young macaws (which were in fact in the nest), told him to jump after them, and, growling, caught the boy between his front paws. Then the boy was very much afraid, but nothing happened to him.

The jaguar carried the hero on his shoulders until they came to a creek. Although the boy was suffering greatly from thirst, he was not allowed to drink, because, as the jaguar explained, the water belonged to the camon vulture (urubu). The same thing happened at the second creek, because the water there belonged to 'the little birds.' Finally, at the third creek, the hero drank so much as to drain the whole creek, in spite of the entreaties of the alligator, the owner of the creek.

The hero was given a chilly welcome by the jaguar's wife, who reproached her husband for having brought back 'a lean and ugly boy.' She called the boy to delouse her, but when she had him between her paws, she frightened him with her growls. He complained to the jaguar, who made him a bow and arrows and ornaments, gave him two basketfuls of roast meat, and helped him back to his village, after advising him to aim for the wife's carotid, should she try to pursue him. Everything happened as had been foreseen, and the wife was killed.

Shortly afterward the young man heard people coming. It was his two brothers, to whom he revealed his identity, and who ran home to tell their mother. 'You lie,' said their mother. 'He's been dead long since.' But the boy concealed himself again. He came out of hiding on the occasion of the Aikman funeral festival.

Everybody was amazed when they saw the roast meat he had brought back. 'Why, how is it roasted?' 'In the sunshine,' the boy kept repeating, although he finally revealed the truth to his uncle.

An expedition was organized to capture fire from the jaguar. The mutum and the water fowl, both good runners, seized the trunk, but the jacu, following them, picked up the scattered embers...

B. SECOND MOVEMENT: BORORO

Let us now return to the myths assembled in Part One. What has the key myth (M_1) in common with the Ge set about the origin of fire (M_7–M_{12})? At first sight, only the episode of the bird-nester. Otherwise, the Bororo myth begins with the story of incest which does not occur explicitly in the Ge myths. The latter are constructed around the visit to the jaguar, who is master of fire; and this visit is taken as explaining the origin of the practice of cooking food; there is nothing comparable in the Bororo myth. Hasty analysis would lead one to suppose that the bird-nester episode had been borrowed either by the Bororo or the Ge and introduced by either group into an entirely different context from the original one. If so, the myths are made up of odds and ends.

I propose to establish, on the contrary, that in all these instances we are dealing with the same myth, and that the apparent divergences between the versions are to be treated as the result of transformations occurring within a set.

In the first place, all versions (Bororo: M_1; and Ge: M_7–M_{12}) refer to the use of a bow and arrows made out of branches. Some imply that this explains the origin of hunting weapons which, like fire, were unknown to men, and the secret of which was also in the jaguar's possession. The Bororo myth does not contain the jaguar episode, but the lost and famished hero at the top of the cliff face makes a bow and arrows with the material to hand; and this creation or re-creation of hunting weapons is a theme common to the whole series of myths under consideration. It will be noted, however, that the invention of the bow and arrows in the jaguar's absence (he is absent from the myth) is perfectly congruous with the invention of fire by the monkey in the (momentary) absence of the jaguar in M_{55}; whereas, according to the Ge myths, the hero receives the bow and arrows directly from the jaguar (instead of inventing them), and the fire is already kindled.

We now come to the most serious disparity. All the Ge myths (M_7-M_{12}) are patently myths about the origin of fire, a theme that seems to be completely absent from the Bororo myth. But is this certain?

The authors of *Os Bororos orientais* make an important comment on this myth, in two different places. According to them, it deals with 'the origin of wind and rain'... and they go into such geological questions as erosion by rain, laterization of soil, and the formation of steep rock faces with potholes at their base, through the dripping of water. During the rainy season these potholes, which are normally full of earth, fill up with water and look like receptacles. This remark, which has no reference to any incident in the myth (although it occurs as a preliminary statement), is particularly significant if, by any chance, it comes direct from the informant, as is often the case in the work in question. The Ge myths, which I am trying to link with the key myth, refer expressly to the origin of cooking.

But the Bororo myth refers to only one storm and nothing in the text indicates that it was the first. It will be remembered that the hero returns to his village, and that a violent storm occurs during his first night there and puts out all the fires except one. However, the conclusion of the first published version of M_1 plainly suggests its etiological character... and although the sentence has disappeared from the second version, the commentary confirms that the natives interpret the myth in this way. It follows that the Bororo myth, too, is about origins: the origin not of fire but of rain and wind which (as the text clearly states) are the opposite of fire, since they put it out. They are, as it were, 'anti-fire.'

The analysis can be carried further. Since the storm has put out all the fires in the village, apart from the one in the hut where the hero has taken refuge, the latter finds himself temporarily in the position of the jaguar: he is master of fire, and all the inhabitants of the village must apply to him to obtain firebrands with which to rekindle the lost fire. In this sense the Bororo myth also relates to the origin of fire, but by a procedure of omission. The difference between it and the Ge myths therefore lies in the weaker treatment of the common theme. The occurrence is situated within the known history of village life, instead of in mythical times to mark the introduction of the arts of civilization. In the first case the fire is lost by a limited community which had previously been in possession of it; in the second it is bestowed on humanity as a whole, after being totally unknown. However, the Kraho version (M_{11}) provides an intermediary formula, since in it mankind (as a whole) is deprived of fire by the culture heroes, who carry it away with them.

The preceding demonstration would be still further strengthened if it were possible to interpret the name of the hero in the key myth, Geriguiguiatugo, as a compound of *gerigigi* 'firewood' and *atugo* 'jaguar.' This would give 'the firewood jaguar,' with whom we are acquainted as a Ge hero, and who is obviously absent from the Bororo myths, but whose existence would be indicated by the etymology of the name attributed to this character who, as we have seen, performs his precise function. However, it would be dangerous to pursue this idea, since the available transcriptions are doubtful from the phonological point of view. On the other hand, the accuracy of the etymology put forward by Colbacchini and Albisetti will be confirmed below, without its being necessary for us to exclude *a priori* the possibility that the same name may admit of several interpretations.

Be that as it may, we do not need any further proof in order to accept the fact that the Bororo myth belongs to the same set as the Ge myths and constitutes a transformation of the same themes. The transformation appears in the following points: (1) a weakening of the polar opposites, in regard to the origin of fire; (2) an inversion of the explicit etiological content, which in this instance is the origin of wind and rain: anti-fire; (3) the mutation of the hero who occupies the position attributed to the jaguar in the Ge myths: master of fire; (4) a correlative inversion of the relations of kinship: the Ge jaguar is the (adopted) father of the hero, whereas the Bororo hero, who is congruous with the jaguar, is a (real) son of a human father; (5) a mutation of family attitudes (equivalent to an inversion): in the Bororo myth the mother is 'close' (incestuous), the father 'remote' (murderous); in the Ge versions, on the contrary, it is the adopted father who is 'close': he protects the child *like* a mother – he carries it, cleans it, satisfies its thirst, feeds it – and *against* the mother – whom he encourages his son to wound or kill – whereas the adopted mother is 'remote' since her intentions are murderous.

Lastly, the Bororo hero is not a jaguar (although he discreetly performs the jaguar's function), but we are told that, to kill his father, he turns himself into a deer. The problems raised by the semantic position of the Cervidae in South American mythology will be discussed elsewhere; here I shall restrict myself to formulating the rule that allows us to transform this episode into a corresponding episode of the Ge set. The latter presents us with a real jaguar, who does not kill his 'false' (adopted) son, although such an act would have been in keeping both with the nature of the jaguar (a flesh-eater) and with that of the hero (who is in the position of the jaguar's prey). The Bororo myth reverses the situation: a false deer (the hero in disguise) kills his real father, although this act is contrary to the nature of the deer (a herbivorous animal) and to that of the victim (a hunter stalking his prey). It will be remembered that the killing takes place during a hunt directed by the father.

Introduction to the structural analysis of narratives

Roland Barthes (1915–80)

In the next extract Roland Barthes outlines a comprehensive grammar of the narrative by means of which structuralist analysis can be conducted. The objective is to construct a theory capable of describing and classifying the infinite amount of narratives to be found in the world. There is clear evidence of Saussurean linguistics to be noted, with Barthes seeking to discover the common formal elements underlying narrative viewed as a semiotic system. Narrative is to be broken down into its smallest constituent units, or 'functions' as Barthes calls them, in order to facilitate comparative analysis – one of the primary concerns of the structuralist, as we saw in Reading 29 (Lévi-Strauss). It is worth noting how wide a concept narrative is in Barthes, seeming to embrace almost any sequence of human events. Structuralism's concern with form enables it to range well beyond the aesthetic realm.

The narratives of the world are numberless. Narrative is first and foremost a prodigious variety of genres, themselves distributed amongst different substances as though any material were fit to receive man's stories. Able to be carried by articulated language, spoken or written, fixed or moving images, gestures, and the ordered mixture of all these substances; narrative is present in myth, legend, fable, tale, novella, epic, history, tragedy, drama, comedy, mime, painting (think of Carpaccio's *Saint Ursula*), stained glass windows, cinema, comics, news items, conversation. Moreover, under this almost infinite diversity of forms, narrative is present in every age, in every place, in every society; it begins with the very history of mankind and there nowhere is nor has been a people without narrative. All classes, all human groups, have their narratives, enjoyment of which is very often shared by men with different, even opposing,[1] cultural backgrounds. Caring nothing for the division between good and bad literature, narrative is international, transhistorical, transcultural: it is simply there, like life itself.

Must we conclude from this universality that narrative is insignificant? Is it so general that we can have nothing to say about it except for the modest description of a few highly individualized varieties, something literary history occasionally undertakes? But then how are we to master even these varieties, how are we to justify our right to differentiate and identify them? How is novel to be set against novella, tale against myth, drama against tragedy (as has been done a thousand times) without reference to a common model? Such a model is implied by every proposition relating to the most individual, the most historical, of narrative forms. It is thus legitimate that, far from the abandoning of any idea of dealing with narrative on the grounds of its universality, there should have been (from Aristotle on) a periodic interest in narrative form and it is normal that the newly developing structuralism should make this form one of its first concerns – is not structuralism's constant aim to master the infinity of utterances [*paroles*] by describing the 'language' ['*langue*'] of which they are the products and from which they can be generated. Faced with the infinity of narratives, the multiplicity of standpoints – historical, psychological, sociological, ethnological, aesthetic, etc. – from which they can be studied, the analyst finds himself in more or less the same situation as Saussure confronted by the heterogeneity of language [*langage*] and seeking to extract a principle of classification and a central focus for description from the apparent confusion of the individual messages. Keeping simply to modern times, the Russian Formalists, Propp and Lévi-Strauss have taught us to recognize the following dilemma: either a narrative is merely a rambling collection of events, in which case nothing can be said about it other than by referring back to the storyteller's (the author's) art, talent or genius – all mythical forms of chance – or else it shares with other narratives a common structure which is open to analysis, no matter how much patience its formulation requires. There is a world of difference between the most complex randomness and the most elementary combinatory scheme, and it is impossible to combine (to produce) a narrative without reference to an implicit system of units and rules.

Where then are we to look for the structures of narrative? Doubtless, in narratives themselves. *Each and every* narrative? Many commentators who accept the idea of a narrative structure are nevertheless unable to resign themselves to dissociating literary analysis from the example of the experimental sciences; nothing daunted, they ask that a purely inductive method be applied to narrative and that one start by studying all the narratives within a genre, a period, a society. This commonsense view is utopian. Linguistics itself, with only some three thousand languages to embrace, cannot manage such a programme and has wisely turned deductive, a step which in fact marked its veritable constitution as a science and the beginning of its spectacular progress, it even succeeding in anticipating facts prior to their discovery. So what of narrative analysis, faced as it is with millions of narratives? Of necessity, it is condemned to a deductive procedure, obliged first to devise a hypothetical model of description (what American linguists call a 'theory') and then gradually to work down from this model towards the different narrative species which at once conform to and depart from the model. It is only at the level of these conformities and departures that analysis will be able to come back to, but now equipped with a single descriptive tool, the plurality of narratives, to their historical, geographical and cultural diversity.

Thus, in order to describe and classify the infinite number of narratives, a 'theory' (in this pragmatic sense) is needed and the immediate task is that of finding it, of starting to define it. Its development can be greatly facilitated if one begins from a model able to provide it with its initial terms and principles. In the current state of research, it seems reasonable that the structural analysis of narrative be given linguistics itself as founding model...

LEVELS OF MEANING

From the outset, linguistics furnishes the structural analysis of narrative with a concept which is decisive in that, making explicit immediately what is essential in every system of meaning, namely its organization, it allows us both to show how a narrative is not a simple sum of propositions and to classify the enormous mass of elements which go to make up a narrative. This concept is that of *level of description*...

Discourse analysis, however, is as yet only able to work on rudimentary levels. In its own way, rhetoric had assigned at least two planes of description to discourse: *dispositio* and *elocutio*. Today, in his analysis of the structure of myth, Lévi-Strauss has already indicated that the constituent units of mythical discourse (mythemes) acquire meaning only because they are grouped in bundles and because these bundles themselves combine together. As too, Tzvetan Todorov, reviving the distinction made by the Russian Formalists, proposes working on two major levels, themselves subdivided: *story* (the argument), comprising a logic of actions and a 'syntax' of characters, and *discourse*, comprising the tenses, aspects and modes of the narrative. But however many levels are proposed and whatever definition they are given, there can be no doubt that narrative is a hierarchy of instances. To understand a narrative is not merely to follow the unfolding of the story, it is also to recognize its construction in 'storeys', to project the horizontal concatenations of the narrative 'thread' on to an implicitly vertical axis; to read (to listen to) a narrative is not merely to move from word to the next, it is also to move from one level to the next...

It is proposed to distinguish three levels of description in the narrative work: the level of *'functions'* (in the sense this word has in Propp and Bremond), the level of *'actions'* (in the sense this word has in Greimas when he talks of characters as actants) and the level of *'narration'* (which is roughly the level of 'discourse' in Todorov). These three levels are bound together according to a mode of progressive integration: a function only has meaning insofar as it occupies a place in the general action of an actant, and this action in turn receives its final meaning from the fact that it is narrated, entrusted to a discourse which possesses its own code.

Functions

1 THE DETERMINATION OF THE UNITS

Any system being the combination of units of known classes, the first task is to divide up narrative and determine the segments of narrative discourse that can be distributed into a limited number of classes. In a word, we have to define the smallest narrative units.

Given the integrational perspective described above, the analysis cannot rest satisfied with a purely distributional definition of the units. From the start, meaning must be the criterion of the unit: it is the functional nature of certain segments of the story that makes them units – hence the name 'functions' immediately attributed to these first units. Since the Russian Formalists, a unit has been taken as any segment of the story which can be seen as the term of a correlation. The essence of a function is, so to speak, the seed that it sows in the narrative, planting an element that will come to fruition later – either on the same level or elsewhere, on another level. If in *Un Coeur simple* Flaubert at one point tells the reader, seemingly without emphasis, that the daughters of the Sous-Préfet of Pont-l'Evêque owned a parrot, it is because this parrot is subsequently to have a great importance in Félicité's life; the statement of this detail (whatever its linguistic form) thus constitutes a function, or narrative unit.

Is everything in a narrative functional? Does everything, down to the slightest detail, have a meaning? Can narrative be divided up entirely into functional units? We shall see in a moment that there are several kinds of functions, there being several kinds of correlations, but this does not alter the fact that a narrative is never made up of anything other than functions: in differing degrees, everything in it signifies. This is not a matter of art (on the part of the narrator), but of structure; in the realm of discourse, what is noted is by definition notable. Even were a detail to appear irretrievably insignificant, resistant to all functionality, it would nonetheless end up with precisely the meaning of absurdity or uselessness: everything has a meaning, or nothing has. To put it another way, one could say that art is without noise (as that term is employed in information theory): art is a system which is pure, no unit ever goes wasted, however long, however loose, however tenuous may be the thread connecting it to one of the levels of the story...

2 CLASSES OF UNITS

The functional units must be distributed into a small number of classes. If these classes are to be determined without recourse to the substance of content (psychological substance for example), it is again necessary to consider the different levels of meaning: some units have as correlates units on the same level, while the saturation of others requires a change of levels; hence, straightaway, two major classes of functions, distributional and integrational. The former correspond to what Propp and subsequently Bremond (in particular) take as functions but they will be treated here in a much more detailed way than is the case in their work. The term *'functions'* will be reserved for these units (though the other units are also functional)...the purchase of a revolver has for correlate the moment when it will be used (and if not used, the notation is reversed into a sign of indecision, etc.); picking up the telephone has for correlate the moment when it will be put down; the intrusion of the parrot into Félicité's home has for correlate the episode of the stuffing, the worshipping of the parrot, etc. As for the latter, the integrational units, these comprise all the *'indices'* (in the very broad sense of the word), the unit now referring not to a complementary and consequential act but to a more or less diffuse concept which is nevertheless necessary to the meaning of the story: psychological indices concerning the characters, data regarding their identity, notations of 'atmosphere', and so on. The relation between the unit and its correlate is now no longer distributional (often several indices refer to the same signified and the order of their occurrence in the discourse is not necessarily pertinent) but integrational...

These two main classes of units, functions and indices, should already allow a certain classification of narratives. Some narratives are heavily functional (such as folktales), while others on the contrary are heavily indicial (such as 'psychological' novels); between these two poles lies a whole series of intermediary forms, dependent on history, society, genre. But we can go further. Within each of the two main classes it is immediately possible to determine two sub-classes of narrative units. Returning to the class of functions, its units are not all of the same 'importance': some constitute real hinge-points of the narrative (or of a fragment of the narrative); others merely 'fill in' the narrative space separating the hinge functions. Let us call the former *cardinal functions* (or *nuclei*) and the latter, having regard to their complementary nature, *catalysers*. For a function to be cardinal, it is enough that the action to which it refers open (or continue, or close) an alternative that is of direct consequence for the subsequent development of the story, in short that it inaugurate or conclude an uncertainty...

3 FUNCTIONAL SYNTAX

How, according to what 'grammar', are the different units strung together along the narrative syntagm? What are the rules of the functional combinatory system? Informants [units of information serving to locate scenes in time and space: 'pure data with immediate signification' as Barthes puts it] and indices can combine freely together: as for example in the portrait which readily juxtaposes data concerning civil status and traits of character. Catalysers and nuclei are linked by a simple relation of implication: a catalyser necessarily implies the existence of a cardinal function to which it can connect, but not vice-versa. As for cardinal functions, they are bound together by a relation of solidarity: a function of this type calls for another function of the same type and reciprocally...

What then is the logic which regulates the principle narrative functions? It is this that current work is actively trying to establish and that has so far been the major focus of debate. Three main directions of research can be seen. The first (Bremond) is more properly logical in approach: it aims to reconstitute the syntax of human behaviour utilized in narrative, to retrace the course of the 'choices' which inevitably face the individual character at every point in the story and so to bring out what could be called an energetic logic, since it grasps the characters at the moment when they choose to act. The second (Lévi-Strauss, Jakobson) is linguistic: its essential concern is to demonstrate paradigmatic oppositions in the functions, oppositions which, in accordance with the Jakobsonian definition of the 'poetic', are 'extended' along the line of the narrative (new developments in Greimas's work correct or complete the conception of the paradigmatic nature of functions). The third (Todorov) is somewhat different in that it sets the analysis at the level of the 'actions' (that is to say, of the characters), attempting to determine the rules by which narrative combines, varies and transforms a certain number of basic predicates.

There is no question of choosing between these working hypotheses; they are not competitive but concurrent, and at present moreover are in the throes of elaboration. The only complement we will attempt to give them here concerns the dimensions of the analysis. Even leaving aside the indices, informants and catalysers, there still remains in a narrative (especially if it is a novel and no longer a tale) a very large number of cardinal functions and many of these cannot be mastered by the analyses just mentioned, which until now have worked on the major articulations of narrative. Provision needs to be made, however, for a description sufficiently close as to account for *all* the narrative units, for the smallest narrative segments. We must remember that cardinal functions cannot be determined by their 'importance', only by the (doubly implicative) nature of their relations. A 'telephone call', no matter how futile it may seem, on the one hand itself comprises some few cardinal functions (telephone ringing, picking up the receiver, speaking, putting down the receiver), while on the other, taken as a whole it must be linkable – at the very least proceeding step by step – to the major articulations of the anecdote. The functional covering of the narrative necessitates an organization of relays the basic unit of which can only be a small group of functions, hereafter referred to (following Bremond) as a *sequence*.

A sequence is a logical succession of nuclei bound together by a relation of solidarity: the sequence opens when one of its terms has no solidary antecedent and closes when another of its terms has no consequent. To take a deliberately trivial example, the different functions order a drink, obtain it, drink it, pay for it, constitute an obviously closed sequence, it being impossible to put anything before the order or after the payment without moving out of the homogeneous group '*Having a drink*'. The sequence indeed is always nameable. Determining the major functions of the folktale, Propp and subsequently Bremond have been led to name them (*Fraud, Betrayal, Struggle, Contract, Seduction*, etc.); the naming operation is equally inevitable in the case of trivial sequences, the 'micro-sequences' which often form the finest grain of the narrative tissue. Are these namings solely the province of the analyst? In other words, are they purely metalinguistic? No doubt they are, dealing as they do with the code of narrative. Yet at the same time they can be imagined as forming part of an inner meta-language in the reader (or listener) him who grasps every logical succession of actions as a nominal whole: to read is to name; to listen is not only to perceive a language, it is also to construct it. Sequence titles are similar enough to the *cover-words* of translation machines which acceptably cover a wide variety of meanings and shades of meaning. The narrative language [*la langue du récit*] within us comprises from the start these essential headings: the closing logic which structures a sequence is inextricably linked to its name; any function which initiates a *seduction* prescribes from the moment it appears, in the name to which it gives rise, the entire process of seduction such as we have learned it from all the narratives which have fashioned in us the language of narrative.

Note

1   It must be remembered that this is not the case with either poetry or the essay, both of which are dependent on the cultural level of their consumers.

Structure, sign and play in the discourse of the human sciences

Jacques Derrida (b.1930)

Jacques Derrida has been one of the most controversial figures in late twentieth-century continental aesthetic thought. The creator of 'deconstruction', a method of textual analysis that aims at demonstrating the inherent instability of meaning in texts, Derrida has often been accused of encouraging critical anarchy. Deconstruction relies heavily on the use of word-play, punning, and association of ideas – techniques rarely used by traditional criticism – to make the point that the meaning of words cannot be pinned down. Any given word can suggest (by its sound quality, for example) other words, thus setting up associations of ideas that render meaning indeterminate and unstable. Derrida has been a consistent critic of structuralism, holding that it assumes words and texts do have stable meanings that the critic can isolate for his audience's inspection. In the extract that follows, he attacks Lévi-Strauss (see Reading 29) for his claim that myths can be reduced to a common structure describable in detail by the critic. Such universal structures do not exist, in Derrida's opinion, since meaning can never be grasped in its entirety, being a constantly evolving phenomenon. The idea that meaning *can be grasped in its entirety is what Derrida calls the 'metaphysics of presence', and he feels that structuralism, indeed most of Western philosophy, is crucially dependent on this notion. If the metaphysics of presence can be undermined then structuralism's credibility will collapse; hence the energy that Derrida devotes to the exploration of what presence involves in this extract. The inability of meaning to achieve full presence is known as* différance. *Derrida argues that it is the role of the critic to play with texts – that is, to subject texts to word-play, punning, and association of ideas – in order to show just how shaky the notion of presence actually is.*

Perhaps something has occurred in the history of the concept of structure that could be called an 'event,' if this loaded word did

not entail a meaning which it is precisely the function of structural –
or structuralist – thought to reduce or to suspect. Let us speak of
an 'event,' nevertheless, and let us use quotation marks to serve as
a precaution. What would this event be then? Its exterior form
would be that of a *rupture* and a redoubling.

It would be easy enough to show that the concept of structure
and even the word 'structure' itself are as old as the *epistēmē*
['discourse'] ... – as old as Western science and Western philosophy –
and that their roots thrust deep into the soil of ordinary language, into
whose deepest recesses the *epistēmē* plunges in order to gather them
up and to make them part of itself in a metaphorical displacement.
Nevertheless, up to the event which I wish to mark out and define,
structure – or rather the structurality of structure – although it has
always been at work, has always been neutralized or reduced, and
this by a process of giving it a center or of referring it to a point
of presence, a fixed origin. The function of this center was not only
to orient, balance, and organize the structure – one cannot in fact
conceive of an unorganized structure – but above all to make sure
that the organizing principle of the structure would limit what we
might call the *play* of the structure. By orienting and organizing
the coherence of the system, the center of a structure permits the
play of its elements inside the total form. And even today the notion
of a structure lacking any center represents the unthinkable itself.

Nevertheless, the center also closes off the play which it opens
up and makes possible. As center, it is the point at which the
substitution of contents, elements, or terms is no longer possible.
At the center, the permutation or the transformation of elements
(which may of course be structures enclosed within a structure) is
forbidden. At least this permutation has always remained *interdicted*
(and I am using this word deliberately). Thus it has always been
thought that the center, which is by definition unique, constituted
that very thing within a structure which while governing the
structure, escapes structurality. This is why classical thought
concerning structure could say that the center is, paradoxically,
within the structure and *outside* it. The center is at the center of the
totality, and yet, since the center does not belong to the totality (is
not part of the totality), the totality *has its center elsewhere*. The
center is not the center. The concept of centered structure – although
it represents coherence itself, the condition of the *epistēmē* as
philosophy or science – is contradictorily coherent. And as always,
coherence in contradiction expresses the force of a desire. The
concept of centered structure is in fact the concept of a play based

on a fundamental ground, a play constituted on the basis of a fundamental immobility and a reassuring certitude, which itself is beyond the reach of play. And on the basis of this certitude anxiety can be mastered, for anxiety is invariably the result of a certain mode of being implicated in the game, of being caught by the game, of being as it were at stake in the game from the outset. And again on the basis of what we call the center (and which, because it can be either inside or outside, can also indifferently be called the origin or end, *archē* or *telos*), repetitions, substitutions, transformations, and permutations are always *taken* from a history of meaning [*sens*] – that is, in a word, a history – whose origin may always be reawakened or whose end may always be anticipated in the form of presence. This is why one perhaps could say that the movement of any archaeology, like that of any eschatology, is an accomplice of this reduction of the structurality of structure and always attempts to conceive of structure on the basis of a full presence which is beyond play.

If this is so, the entire history of the concept of structure, before the rupture of which we are speaking, must be thought of as a series of substitutions of center for center, as a linked chain of determinations of the center. Successively, and in a regulated fashion, the center receives different forms or names. The history of metaphysics, like the history of the West, is the history of these metaphors and metonymies. Its matrix – if you will pardon me for demonstrating so little and for being so elliptical in order to come more quickly to my principal theme – is the determination of Being as *presence* in all senses of this word. It could be shown that all the names related to fundamentals, to principles, or to the center have always designated an invariable presence – *eidos, archē, telos, energeia, ousia* (essence, existence, substance, subject) *alētheia*, transcendentality, consciousness, God, man, and so forth.

The event I called a rupture, the disruption I alluded to at the beginning of this paper, presumably would have come about when the structurality of structure had to begin to be thought, that is to say, repeated, and this is why I said that this disruption was repetition in every sense of the word. Henceforth, it became necessary to think both the law which somehow governed the desire for a center in the constitution of structure, and the process of signification which orders the displacements and substitutions for this law of central presence – but a central presence which has never been itself, has always already been exiled from itself into its own substitute. The substitute does not substitute itself for anything which has somehow existed before it. Henceforth, it was necessary to begin thinking that there was no center, that the center could not be thought in the form of a present-being, that the center had no natural site, that it was not a fixed locus but a function, a sort of nonlocus in which an infinite number of sign-substitutions came into play. This was the moment when language invaded the universal problematic, the moment when, in the absence of a center or origin, everything became discourse – provided we can agree on this word – that is to say, a system in which the central signified, the original or transcendental signified, is never absolutely present outside a system of differences. The absence of the transcendental signified extends the domain and the play of signification infinitely.

Where and how does this decentering, this thinking the structurality of structure, occur? It would be somewhat naïve to refer to an event, a doctrine, or an author in order to designate this occurrence. It is no doubt part of the totality of an era, our own, but still it has always already begun to proclaim itself and begun to *work*. Nevertheless, if we wished to choose several 'names,' as indications only, and to recall those authors in whose discourse this occurrence has kept most closely to its most radical formulation, we doubtless would have to cite the Nietzschean critique of metaphysics, the critique of the concepts of Being and truth, for which were substituted the concepts of play, interpretation, and sign (sign without present truth); the Freudian critique of self-presence, that is, the critique of consciousness, of the subject, of self-identity and of self-proximity or self-possession; and, more radically, the Heideggerean destruction of metaphysics, of onto-theology, of the determination of Being as presence. But all these destructive discourses and all their analogues are trapped in a kind of circle. This circle is unique. It describes the form of the relation between the history of metaphysics and the destruction of the history of metaphysics. There is no sense in doing without the concepts of metaphysics in order to shake metaphysics. We have no language – no syntax and no lexicon – which is foreign to this history; we can pronounce not a single destructive proposition which has not already had to slip into the form, the logic, and the implicit postulations of precisely what it seeks to contest. To take one example from many: the metaphysics of presence is shaken with the help of the concept of *sign*. But, as I suggested a moment ago, as soon as one seeks to demonstrate in this way that there is no transcendental or privileged signified and that the domain or play of signification henceforth has no limit, one must reject even the concept and word 'sign' itself – which is precisely what cannot be done. For the signification 'sign' has always been understood and determined, in its meaning, as sign-of, a signifier referring to a signified, a signifier different from its signified. If one erases the radical difference between signifier and signified, it is the word 'signifier' itself which must be abandoned as a metaphysical concept. When Lévi-Strauss says in the preface to *The Raw and the Cooked* that he has 'sought to transcend the opposition between the sensible and the intelligible by operating from the outset at the level of signs,' the necessity, force, and legitimacy of his act cannot make us forget that the concept of the sign cannot in itself surpass this opposition between the sensible and the intelligible. The concept of the sign, in each of its aspects, has been determined by this opposition throughout the totality of its history. It has lived only on this opposition and its system. But we cannot do without the concept of the sign, for we cannot give up this metaphysical complicity without also giving up the critique we are directing against this complicity, or without the risk of erasing difference in the self-identity of a signified reducing its signifier into itself or, amounting to the same thing, simply expelling its signifier outside itself. For there are two heterogeneous ways of erasing the difference between the signifier and the signified: one, the classic way, consists in reducing or deriving the signifier, that is to say, ultimately in *submitting* the sign to thought; the other, the one we are using here against the first one, consists in putting into question the system in which the preceding reduction functioned: first and foremost, the opposition between the sensible and the intelligible. For the *paradox* is that the metaphysical reduction of the sign needed the opposition it was reducing. The opposition is systematic with the reduction. And what we are saying here about the sign can be extended to all the concepts and all the sentences of metaphysics, in particular to the discourse on 'structure.' But there are several ways of being caught in this circle. They are all more or less naïve, more or less empirical, more or less systematic, more or less close to the formulation – that is, to the formalization – of this circle. It is these differences which explain the multiplicity of destructive discourses and the disagreement between those who elaborate them. Nietzsche, Freud, and Heidegger, for example, worked within the inherited concepts of metaphysics. Since these concepts are not elements or atoms, and since they are taken from a syntax and a system, every particular borrowing brings along with it the whole of metaphysics. This is what allows these destroyers to destroy each other reciprocally – for example, Heidegger regarding Nietzsche, with as much lucidity and rigor as bad faith and misconstruction, as the last metaphysician, the last 'Platonist.' One could do the same for Heidegger himself, for Freud, or for a number of others. And today no exercise is more widespread.

What is the relevance of this formal schema when we turn to what are called the 'human sciences?' One of them perhaps occupies a privileged place – ethnology. In fact one can assume that ethnology could have been born as a science only at the moment when a decentering had come about: at the moment when European culture – and, in consequence, the history of metaphysics and of its concepts – had been *dislocated*, driven from its locus, and forced to stop considering itself as the culture of reference. This moment is not first and foremost a moment of philosophical or scientific discourse. It is also a moment which is political, economic, technical, and so forth. One can say with total security that there is nothing fortuitous about the fact that the critique of ethnocentrism – the very condition for ethnology – should be systematically and historically contemporaneous with the destruction of the history of metaphysics. Both belong to one and the same era. Now, ethnology – like any science – comes about within the element of discourse. And it is primarily a European science employing traditional concepts, however much it may struggle against them. Consequently, whether he wants to or not – and this does not depend on a decision on his part – the ethnologist accepts into his discourse the premises of ethnocentrism at the very moment when he denounces them. This necessity is irreducible; it is not a historical contingency...

If we consider, as an example, the texts of Claude Lévi-Strauss, it is not only because of the privilege accorded to ethnology among the social sciences, nor even because the thought of Lévi-Strauss weighs heavily on the contemporary theoretical situation. It is above all because a certain choice has been declared in the work of Lévi-Strauss and because a certain doctrine has been elaborated there, and precisely, in a *more or less explicit manner*, as concerns both this critique of language and this critical language in the social sciences.

In order to follow this movement in the text of Lévi-Strauss, let us choose as one guiding thread among others the opposition between nature and culture. Despite all its rejuvenations and disguises, this opposition is congenital to philosophy. It is even older than Plato. It is at least as old as the Sophists. Since the statement of the opposition *physis/nomos, physis/technē*, it has been relayed to us by means of a whole historical chain which opposes 'nature' to law, to education, to art, to technics – but also to liberty, to the arbitrary, to history, to society, to the mind, and so on. Now, from the outset of his researches, and from his first book (*The Elementary Structures of Kinship*) on, Lévi-Strauss simultaneously has experienced the necessity of utilizing this opposition and the impossibility of accepting it. In the *Elementary Structures*, he begins from this axiom or definition: that which is *universal* and spontaneous, and not dependent on any particular culture or on any determinate norm, belongs to nature. Inversely, that which depends upon a system of *norms* regulating society and therefore is capable of *varying* from one social structure to another, belongs to culture. These two definitions are of the traditional type. But in the very first pages of the *Elementary Structures* Lévi-Strauss, who has begun by giving credence to these concepts, encounters what he calls a *scandal*, that is to say, something which no longer tolerates the nature/culture opposition he has accepted, something which *simultaneously* seems to require the predicates of nature and of culture. This scandal is the *incest prohibition*. The incest prohibition is universal; in this sense one could call it natural. But it is also a prohibition, a system of norms and interdicts; in this sense one could call it cultural:

> Let us suppose then that everything universal in man relates to the natural order, and is characterized by spontaneity, and that everything subject to a norm is cultural and is both relative and particular. We are then confronted with a fact, or rather, a group of facts, which, in the light of previous definitions, are not far removed from a scandal: we refer to that complex group of beliefs, customs, conditions and institutions described succinctly as the prohibition of incest, which presents, without the slightest ambiguity, and inseparably combines, the two characteristics in which we recognize the conflicting features of two mutually exclusive orders. It constitutes a rule, but a rule which, alone among all the social rules, possesses at the same time a universal character.

Obviously there is no scandal except within a system of concepts which accredits the difference between nature and culture. By commencing his work with the *factum* of the incest prohibition, Lévi-Strauss thus places himself at the point at which this difference, which has always been assumed to be self-evident, finds itself erased or questioned. For from the moment when the incest prohibition can no longer be conceived within the nature/culture opposition, it can no longer be said to be a scandalous fact, a nucleus of opacity within a network of transparent significations. The incest prohibition is no longer a scandal one meets with or comes up against in the domain of traditional concepts; it is something which escapes these concepts and certainly precedes them – probably as the condition of their possibility. It could perhaps be said that the whole of philosophical conceptualization, which is systematic with the nature/culture opposition, is designed to leave in the domain of the unthinkable the very thing that makes this conceptualization possible: the origin of the prohibition of incest.

This example, too cursorily examined, is only one among many others, but nevertheless it already shows that language bears within itself the necessity of its own critique. Now this critique may be undertaken along two paths, in two 'manners.' Once the limit of the nature/culture opposition makes itself felt, one might want to question systematically and rigorously the history of these concepts. This is a first action. Such a systematic and historic questioning would be neither a philological nor a philosophical action in the classic sense of these words. To concern oneself with the founding concepts of the entire history of philosophy, to deconstitute them, is not to undertake the work of the philologist or of the classic historian of philosophy. Despite appearances, it is probably the most daring way of making the beginnings of a step outside of philosophy. The step 'outside philosophy' is much more difficult to conceive than is generally imagined by those who think they made it long ago with cavalier ease, and who in general are swallowed up in metaphysics in the entire body of discourse which they claim to have disengaged from it.

The other choice (which I believe corresponds more closely to Lévi-Strauss's manner), in order to avoid the possibly sterilizing effects of the first one, consists in conserving all these old concepts within the domain of empirical discovery while here and there denouncing their limits, treating them as tools which can still be used. No longer is any truth value attributed to them; there is a readiness to abandon them, if necessary, should other instruments appear more useful. In the meantime, their relative efficacy is exploited, and they are employed to destroy the old machinery to which they belong and of which they themselves are pieces. This is how the language of the social sciences criticizes *itself*. Lévi-Strauss thinks that in this way he can separate *method* from *truth*, the instruments of the method and the objective significations envisaged by it. One could almost say that this is the primary affirmation of Lévi-Strauss; in any event, the first words of the *Elementary Structures* are: 'Above all, it is beginning to emerge that this distinction between nature and society ('nature' and 'culture' seem preferable to us today), while of no acceptable historical significance, does contain a logic, fully justifying its use by modern sociology as a methodological tool.'

Lévi-Strauss will always remain faithful to this double intention: to preserve as an instrument something whose truth value he criticizes.

On the one hand, he will continue, in effect, to contest the value of the nature/culture opposition. More than thirteen years after the *Elementary Structures*, *The Savage Mind* faithfully echoes the text I have just quoted: 'The opposition between nature and culture to which I attached much importance at one time ... now seems to be of primarily methodological importance.' And this methodological value is not affected by its 'ontological' nonvalue (as might be said, if this notion were not suspect here): 'However, it would not be enough to reabsorb particular humanities into a general one. This first enterprise opens the way for others which ... are incumbent on the exact natural sciences: the reintegration of culture in nature and finally of life within the whole of its physico-chemical conditions.'

On the other hand, still in *The Savage Mind*, he presents as what he calls *bricolage* what might be called the discourse of this method. The *bricoleur*, says Lévi-Strauss, is someone who uses 'the means at hand,' that is, the instruments he finds at his disposition around him, those which are already there, which had not been especially conceived with an eye to the operation for which they are to be used and to which one tries by trial and error to adapt them, not hesitating to change them whenever it appears necessary, or to try several of them at once, even if their form and their origin are heterogeneous – and so forth. There is therefore a critique of language in the form of *bricolage*, and it has even been said that *bricolage* is critical language itself. I am thinking in particular of the article of G. Genette, 'Structuralisme et critique littéraire,' published in homage to Lévi-Strauss in a special issue of *L'Arc* (no. 26, 1965), where it is stated that the analysis of *bricolage* could 'be applied almost word for word' to criticism, and especially to 'literary criticism.'

If one calls *bricolage* the necessity of borrowing one's concepts from the text of a heritage which is more or less coherent or ruined, it must be said that every discourse is *bricoleur*. The engineer, whom Lévi-Strauss opposes to the *bricoleur*, should be the one to construct the totality of his language, syntax, and lexicon. In this sense the engineer is a myth. A subject who supposedly would be the absolute origin of his own discourse and supposedly would construct it 'out of nothing,' 'out of whole cloth,' would be the creator of the verb, the verb itself. The notion of the engineer who supposedly breaks with all forms of *bricolage* is therefore a theological idea; and since Lévi-Strauss tells us elsewhere that *bricolage* is mythopoetic, the odds are that the engineer is a myth produced by the *bricoleur*. As soon as we cease to believe in such an engineer and in a discourse which breaks with the received historical discourse, and as soon as we admit that every finite discourse is bound by a certain *bricolage* and that the engineer and the scientist are also species of *bricoleurs*, then the very idea of *bricolage* is menaced and the difference in which it took on its meaning breaks down.

This brings us to the second thread which might guide us in what is being contrived here.

Lévi-Strauss describes *bricolage* not only as an intellectual activity but also as a mythopoetical activity. One reads in *The Savage Mind*, 'Like *bricolage* on the technical plane, mythical reflection can reach brilliant unforeseen results on the intellectual plane. Conversely, attention has often been drawn to the mythopoetical nature of *bricolage*.'

But Lévi-Strauss's remarkable endeavor does not simply consist in proposing, notably in his most recent investigations, a structural science of myths and of mythological activity. His endeavor also appears – I would say almost from the outset – to have the status which he accords to his own discourse on myths, to what he calls his 'mythologicals.' It is here that his discourse on the myth reflects on itself and criticizes itself. And this moment, this critical period, is evidently of concern to all the languages which share the field of the human sciences. What does Lévi-Strauss say of his 'mythologicals'? It is here that we rediscover the mythopoetical virtue of *bricolage*. In effect, what appears most fascinating in this critical search for a new status of discourse is the stated abandonment of all reference to a *center*, to a *subject*, to a privileged *reference*, to an origin, or to an absolute *archia*. The theme of this decentering could be followed throughout the 'Overture' to his last book, *The Raw and the Cooked*. I shall simply remark on a few key points.

1   From the very start, Lévi-Strauss recognizes that the Bororo

myth which he employs in the book as the 'reference myth' does not merit this name and this treatment. The name is specious and the use of the myth improper. This myth deserves no more than any other its referential privilege: 'In fact, the Bororo myth, which I shall refer to from now on as the key myth, is, as I shall try to show, simply a transformation, to a greater or lesser extent, of other myths originating either in the same society or in neighboring or remote societies. I could, therefore, have legitimately taken as my starting point any one representative myth of the group. From this point of view, the key myth is interesting not because it is typical, but rather because of its irregular position within the group.'

2   There is no unity or absolute source of the myth. The focus or the source of the myth are always shadows and virtualities which are elusive, unactualizable, and nonexistent in the first place. Everything begins with structure, configuration, or relationship. The discourse on the acentric structure that myth itself is, cannot itself have an absolute subject or an absolute center. It must avoid the violence that consists in centering a language which describes an acentric structure if it is not to shortchange the form and movement of myth. Therefore it is necessary to forego scientific or philosophical discourse, to renounce the *epistēmē* which absolutely requires, which is the absolute requirement that we go back to the source, to the center, to the founding basis, to the principle, and so on. In opposition to *epistemic* discourse, structural discourse on myths – *mythological* discourse – must itself be *mythomorphic*. It must have the form of that of which it speaks...

Nevertheless, even if one yields to the necessity of what Lévi-Strauss has done, one cannot ignore its risks. If the mythological is mythomorphic, are all discourses on myths equivalent? Shall we have to abandon any epistemological requirement which permits us to distinguish between several qualities of discourse on the myth? A classic, but inevitable question. It cannot be answered – and I believe that Lévi-Strauss does not answer it – for as long as the problem of the relations between the philosopheme or the theorem, on the one hand, and the mytheme or the mythopoem, on the other, has not been posed explicitly, which is no small problem. For lack of explicitly posing this problem, we condemn ourselves to transforming the alleged transgression of philosophy into an unnoticed fault within the philosophical realm. Empiricism would be the genus of which these faults would always be the species. Transphilosophical concepts would be transformed into philosophical naïvetés. Many examples could be given to demonstrate this risk: the concepts of sign, history, truth, and so forth. What I want to emphasize is simply that the passage beyond philosophy does not consist in turning the page of philosophy (which usually amounts to philosophizing badly), but in continuing to read philosophers *in a certain way*. The risk I am speaking of is always assumed by Lévi-Strauss, and it is the very price of this endeavor. I have said that empiricism is the matrix of all faults menacing a discourse which continues, as with Lévi-Strauss in particular, to consider itself scientific. If we wanted to pose the problem of empiricism and *bricolage* in depth, we would probably end up very quickly with a number of absolutely contradictory propositions concerning the status of discourse in structural ethnology. On the one hand, structuralism justifiably claims to be the critique of empiricism. But at the same time there is not a single book or study by Lévi-Strauss which is not proposed as an empirical essay which can always be completed or invalidated by new information. The structural schemata are always proposed as hypotheses resulting from a finite quantity of information and which are subjected to the proof of experience. Numerous texts could be used to demonstrate this double postulation. Let us turn once again to the 'Overture' of *The Raw and the Cooked*, where it seems clear that if this postulation is double, it is because it is a question here of a language on language:

If critics reproach me with not having carried out an exhaustive inventory of South American myths before analyzing them, they are making a grave mistake about the nature and function of these documents. The total body of myth belonging to a given community is comparable to its speech. Unless the population dies out physically or morally, this totality is never complete. You might as well criticize a linguist for compiling the grammar of a language without having complete records of the words pronounced since the language came into being, and without knowing what will be said in it during the future part of its existence. Experience proves that a linguist can work out the grammar of a given language from a remarkably small number of sentences... And even a partial grammar or an outline grammar is a precious acquisition when we are dealing with unknown languages. Syntax does not become evident only after a (theoretically limitless) series of events has been recorded and examined, because it is itself the body of rules governing their production. What I have tried to give is an outline of the syntax of South American mythology. Should fresh data come to hand, they will be used to check or modify the formulation of certain grammatical laws, so that some are abandoned and replaced by new ones. But in no instance would I feel constrained to accept the arbitrary demand for a total mythological pattern, since, as has been shown, such a requirement has no meaning.

Totalization, therefore, is sometimes defined as *useless*, and sometimes as *impossible*. This is no doubt due to the fact that there are two ways of conceiving the limit of totalization. And I assert once more that these two determinations coexist implicitly in Lévi-Strauss's discourse. Totalization can be judged impossible in the classical style: one then refers to the empirical endeavor of either a subject or a finite richness which it can never master. There is too much, more than one can say. But nontotalization can also be determined in another way: no longer from the standpoint of a concept of finitude as relegation to the empirical, but from the standpoint of the concept of *play*. If totalization no longer has any meaning, it is not because the infiniteness of a field cannot be covered by a finite glance or a finite discourse, but because the nature of the field – that is, language and a finite language – excludes totalization. This field is in effect that of *play*, that is to say, a field of infinite substitutions only because it is finite, that is to say, because instead of being an inexhaustible field, as in the classical hypothesis, instead of being too large, there is something missing from it: a center which arrests and grounds the play of substitutions. One could say – rigorously using that word whose scandalous signification is always obliterated in French – that this movement of play, permitted by the lack or absence of a center or origin, is the movement of *supplementarity*. One cannot determine the center and exhaust totalization because the sign which replaces the center, which supplements it, taking the center's place in its absence – this sign is added, occurs as a surplus, as a *supplement*. The movement of signification adds something, which results in the fact that there is always more, but this addition is a floating one because it comes to perform a vicarious function, to supplement a lack on the part of the signified...

The *overabundance* of the signifier, its *supplementary* character, is thus the result of a finitude, that is to say, the result of a lack which must be *supplemented*.

It can now be understood why the concept of play is important in Lévi-Strauss. His references to all sorts of games, notably to roulette, are very frequent, especially in his *Conversations*, in *Race and History*, and in *The Savage Mind*. Further, the reference to play is always caught up in tension.

Tension with history, first of all. This is a classical problem, objections to which are now well worn. I shall simply indicate what seems to me the formality of the problem: by reducing history, Lévi-Strauss has treated as it deserves a concept which has always been in complicity with a teleological and eschatological metaphysics, in other words, paradoxically, in complicity with that philosophy of presence to which it was believed history could be opposed. The thematic of historicity, although it seems to be a somewhat late arrival in philosophy, has always been required by the determination of Being as presence. With or without etymology, and despite the classic antagonism which opposes these significations throughout all of classical thought, it could be shown that the concept of *epistēmē* has always called forth that of *historia*, if history is always the unity of a becoming, as the tradition of truth or the development of science or knowledge oriented toward the appropriation of truth in presence and self-presence, toward knowledge in consciousness-of-self. History has always been conceived as the movement of a resumption of history, as a detour between two presences. But if it is legitimate to suspect this concept of history, there is a risk, if it is reduced without an explicit statement of the problem I am indicating here, of falling back into an ahistoricism of a classical type, that is to say, into a determined moment of the history of metaphysics. Such is the algebraic formality of the problem as I see it. More concretely, in the work of Lévi-Strauss it must be recognized that the respect for structurality, for the internal originality of the structure, compels a neutralization of time and history. For example, the appearance of a new structure, of an original system, always comes about – and this is the very condition of its structural specificity – by a rupture with its past, its origin, and its cause. Therefore one can describe what is peculiar to the structural organization only by not taking into account, in the very moment of this description, its past conditions: by omitting to posit the problem of the transition from one structure to another, by putting history between brackets. In this 'structuralist' movement, the concepts of chance and discontinuity are indispensable. And Lévi-Strauss does in fact often appeal to them, for example, as concerns that structure of structures, language, of which he says in the 'Introduction to the Work of Marcel Mauss' that it 'could only have been born in one fell swoop':

Whatever may have been the moment and the circumstances of its appearance on the scale of animal life, language could only have been born in one fell swoop. Things could not have set about acquiring signification progressively. Following a transformation the study of which is not the concern of the social sciences, but rather of biology and psychology, a transition came about from a stage where nothing had a meaning to another where everything possessed it.

This standpoint does not prevent Lévi-Strauss from recognizing the slowness, the process of maturing, the continuous toil of factual transformations, history (for example, *Race and History*). But, in accordance with a gesture which was also Rousseau's and Husserl's, he must 'set aside all the facts' at the moment when he wishes to recapture the specificity of a structure. Like Rousseau, he must always conceive of the origin of a new structure on the model of catastrophe – an overturning of nature in nature, a natural interruption of the natural sequence, a setting aside *of* nature.

Besides the tension between play and history, there is also the tension between play and presence. Play is the disruption of presence. The presence of an element is always a signifying and substitutive reference inscribed in a system of differences and the movement of a chain. Play is always play of absence and presence, but if it is to be thought radically, play must be conceived of before the alternative of presence and absence. Being must be conceived as presence or absence on the basis of the possibility of play and not the other way around. If Lévi-Strauss, better than any other, has brought to light the play of repetition and the repetition of play, one no less perceives in his work a sort of ethic of presence, an ethic of nostalgia for origins, an ethic of archaic and natural innocence, of a purity of presence and self-presence in speech – an ethic, nostalgia, and even remorse, which he often presents as the motivation of the ethnological project when he moves toward the archaic societies which are exemplary societies in his eyes. These texts are well known.

Turned towards the lost or impossible presence of the absent origin, this structuralist thematic of broken immediacy is therefore the saddened, *negative*, nostalgic, guilty, Rousseauistic side of the thinking of play whose other side would be the Nietzschean *affirmation*, that is the joyous affirmation of the play of the world and of the innocence of becoming, the affirmation of a world of signs without fault, without truth, and without origin which is offered to an active interpretation. *This affirmation then determines the noncenter otherwise than as loss of the center.* And it plays without security. For there is a *sure* play: that which is limited to the *substitution* of *given* and *existing, present,* pieces. In absolute chance, affirmation also surrenders itself to *genetic* indetermination, to the *seminal* adventure of the trace.

There are thus two interpretations of interpretation, of structure, of sign, of play. The one seeks to decipher, dreams of deciphering a truth or an origin which escapes play and the order of the sign, and which lives the necessity of interpretation as an exile. The other, which is no longer turned toward the origin, affirms play and tries to pass beyond man and humanism, the name of man being the name of that being who, throughout the history of metaphysics or of ontotheology – in other words, throughout his entire history – has dreamed of full presence, the reassuring foundation, the origin and the end of play. The second interpretation of interpretation, to which Nietzsche pointed the way, does not seek in ethnography, as Lévi-Strauss does, the 'inspiration of a new humanism' (again citing the 'Introduction to the Work of Marcel Mauss').

There are more than enough indications today to suggest we might perceive that these two interpretations of interpretation – which are absolutely irreconcilable even if we live them simultaneously and reconcile them in an obscure economy – together share the field which we call, in such a problematic fashion, the social sciences.

For my part, although these two interpretations must acknowledge and accentuate their difference and define their irreducibility, I do not believe that today there is any question of *choosing* – in the first place because here we are in a region (let us say, provisionally, a region of historicity) where the category of choice seems particularly trivial; and in the second, because we must first try to conceive of the common ground, and the *différance* of this irreducible difference. Here there is a kind of question, let us still call it historical, whose *conception, formation, gestation,* and *labor* we are only catching a glimpse of today. I employ these words, I admit, with a glance toward the operations of childbearing – but also with a glance toward those who, in a society from which I do not exclude myself, turn their eyes away when faced by the as yet unnamable which is proclaiming itself and which can do so, as is necessary whenever a birth is in the offing, only under the species of the nonspecies, in the formless, mute, infant, and terrifying form of monstrosity.